MUSIC, CRITICISM, AND THE CHALLENGE OF HISTORY

AMS Studies in Music

Mary Hunter, *General Editor*

Conceptualizing Music:
Cognitive Structure, Theory, and Analysis
Lawrence Zbikowski

Inventing the Business of Opera:
The Impresario and His World in
    Seventeenth-Century Venice
Beth L. Glixon and Jonathan Glixon

Lateness and Brahms:
Music and Culture in the Twilight
    of Viennese Liberalism
Margaret Notley

The Critical Nexus:
Tone-System, Mode, and Notation
    in Early Medieval Music
Charles M. Atkinson

Music, Criticism, and the Challenge of History:
Shaping Modern Musical Thought in
    Late Nineteenth-Century Vienna
Kevin C. Karnes

MUSIC, CRITICISM, AND THE CHALLENGE OF HISTORY

Shaping Modern Musical Thought in
Late Nineteenth-Century Vienna

Kevin C. Karnes

OXFORD
UNIVERSITY PRESS

OXFORD

UNIVERSITY PRESS

Oxford University Press is a department of the University of Oxford.
It furthers the University's objective of excellence in research, scholarship,
and education by publishing worldwide.

Oxford   New York

Auckland   Cape Town   Dar es Salaam   Hong Kong   Karachi
Kuala Lumpur   Madrid   Melbourne   Mexico City   Nairobi
New Delhi   Shanghai   Taipei   Toronto

With offices in

Argentina   Austria   Brazil   Chile   Czech Republic   France   Greece
Guatemala   Hungary   Italy   Japan   Poland   Portugal   Singapore
South Korea   Switzerland   Thailand   Turkey   Ukraine   Vietnam

Oxford is a registered trade mark of Oxford University Press
in the UK and certain other countries.

Published in the United States of America by
Oxford University Press
198 Madison Avenue, New York, NY 10016

© Oxford University Press 2008

First issued as an Oxford University Press paperback, 2016

Library of Congress Cataloging-in-Publication Data
Karnes, Kevin, 1972–
Music, criticism, and the challenge of history : shaping modern musical
thought in late nineteenth-century Vienna / Kevin C. Karnes.
p. cm. — (AMS studies in music)
Includes bibliographical references (p.   ) and index.
ISBN 978-0-19-536866-6 (hardcover); 978-0-19-062843-7 (paperback)
1. Musicology—Austria—Vienna—History—19th century.   2. Music theory—Austria—
Vienna—History—19th century.   3. Musical criticism—Austria—Vienna—History—
19th century.   4. Hanslick, Eduard, 1825–1904—Criticism and interpretation.
5. Adler, Guido, 1855–1941—Criticism and interpretation.   6. Schenker,
Heinrich, 1868–1935—Criticism and interpretation. I. Title.
ML3797.K36   2008
780.72'0436—dc22   2007043091

skaistai varavīksnei, mākonim

ACKNOWLEDGMENTS

My work on this project began with a dissertation on the early writings of Heinrich Schenker (Brandeis University, 2001), a study that benefited immeasurably from the guidance and readings of Allan Keiler, Jessie Ann Owens, and Ian D. Bent. Since then, it has been shaped just as profoundly through innumerable conversations with Walter Frisch, for whose insights, encouragement, unfailing generosity, and impeccably good sense I am deeply grateful. I also wish to express my gratitude to Silvio dos Santos for reading and commenting on several chapters—sometimes in several versions—in preparation, and for his constant friendship during a long season of change.

Over the course of years spent writing this book, I have been fortunate to receive invaluable advice, suggestions, and help from many others as well. Some kindly shared their thoughts and impressions regarding a related article or a chapter- or proposal-in-progress: Styra Avins, Daniel Beller-McKenna, Conny Chen, Stephen Crist, John Daverio, Yayoi Uno Everett, James Hepokoski, William Horne, Mary Hunter, Kevin Korsyn, Margaret Notley, and William Pastille. Others provided other sorts of help, support, or materials: Ian Bent, Lynn Wood Bertrand, David Brodbeck, Eric Chafe, Mary DuPree, Bonnie Gordon, Ellen T. Harris, Allan Keiler, Lowell Lindgren, Sandra McColl, Jessie Ann Owens, and Harry Zohn. I gratefully acknowledge the keen editorial work of Mary Hunter, editor of AMS Studies in Music, and the suggestions and probing questions offered by three anonymous readers of the manuscript or portions thereof. Suzanne Ryan, Norman Hirschy, Lora Dunn, and Katharine Boone at Oxford University Press have been great to work with on the production end, and Chris Wilson did a nice job with the musical examples. It goes without saying that I am wholly responsible for all errors, omissions, and shortcomings that remain in the present study.

For access to collections and permission to cite from unpublished and archival materials, I wish to thank the Special Collections Library of the University of California, Riverside; the Hargrett Rare Book and Manuscript Library of the University of Georgia; and both the Österreichische Nationalbibliothek and the Wienbibliothek im Rathaus (formerly the Wiener Stadt- und Landesbibliothek) in Vienna. I also wish to thank Georg Olms Verlag for allowing me to cite extensively, in the notes to chapters 3 and 4, from Heinrich Schenker, *Heinrich Schenker als Essayist und Kritiker. Gesammelte Aufsätze, Rezensionen und kleinere Berichte aus den Jahren 1891–1901*, ed. Hellmut Federhofer, Studien und Materialien zur Musikwissenschaft, no. 5 (Hildesheim: Georg Olms, 1990). Finally, I wish to acknowledge the staff of Emory University's Heilbrun Music and Media Library and the Interlibrary Loan Office of Emory's Woodruff Library, who have proven exceptionally helpful in every way.

Financial support for this project was provided, at its beginnings, by a Sachar Grant from Brandeis University and a Karl Geiringer Scholarship from the American Brahms Society; during its middle stages by a Summer Stipend from the National Endowment for the Humanities; and at its end by a grant from the Emory University Research Committee. I am grateful to Ian Bent, Ellen Harris, Allan Keiler, and Jessie Ann Owens for graciously supplying the letters of recommendation that assured this project's continued funding throughout the course of its development. Emory College and Department of Music provided additional support for travel and research.

Some of the material examined in this book I first considered in articles. I first explored, in an abbreviated way, the thesis set forth in chapter 2 in "Eduard Hanslick's History: A Forgotten Narrative of Brahms's Vienna," *American Brahms Society Newsletter* 22, no. 2 (2004), 1–5. The middle section of chapter 3 revisits material previously published in "Another Look at Critical Partisanship in the Viennese *fin de siècle*: Schenker's Reviews of Brahms's Vocal Music, 1891–1892," *19th-Century Music* 26, no. 1 (2002), 73–93. And I have based chapter 4 upon "Schenker's Brahms: Composer, Critic, and the Problem of Creativity in Late Nineteenth-Century Vienna," *Journal of Musicological Research* 24, no. 2 (2005), 145–176, though I provide a different interpretation of the evidence in the present book.

CONTENTS

A NOTE ON TRANSLATIONS

Whenever possible, I have consulted previously published English translations of all German texts cited in this book. In most cases, however, I have found it necessary either to provide new translations from the German or to modify the previously published translations in some way. Wherever this has been done, I have provided references to both the German original and the published translation in an endnote, along with the complete German text of the passage cited. Unless otherwise noted, all translations are my own.

In order to make the discussion as accessible as possible to those who do not read German, I have provided English translations of key terms and institutional names when they first appear in a chapter. For books and essays that are widely known by English titles (Wagner's *Opera and Drama* and Nietzsche's *The Birth of Tragedy*, for instance), I have given their titles only in English. In other cases, I have used English translations of their titles in the text and given the original in either parentheses or an endnote.

ABBREVIATIONS USED
IN THE NOTES

Hanslick/Payzant	Eduard Hanslick, *On the Musically Beautiful: A Contribution towards the Revision of the Aesthetics of Music*, trans. Geoffrey Payzant (Indianapolis: Hackett, 1986).
Hanslick/Strauß	Eduard Hanslick, *Vom Musikalisch-Schönen. Ein Beitrag zur Revision der Ästhetik in der Tonkunst*, ed. Dietmar Strauß, 2 vols. (Mainz and London: Schott, 1990).
Schenker	Heinrich Schenker, *Heinrich Schenker als Essayist und Kritiker. Gesammelte Aufsätze, Rezensionen und kleinere Berichte aus den Jahren 1891–1901*, ed. Hellmut Federhofer, Studien und Materialien zur Musikwissenschaft, no. 5 (Hildesheim: Georg Olms, 1990).
Wagner	Richard Wagner, *Sämtliche Schriften und Dichtungen*, 6th ed., 16 vols. (Leipzig: Breitkopf und Härtel and C. F. W. Siegel, 1911).
Wagner/Ellis	*Richard Wagner's Prose Works*, trans. William Ashton Ellis, 8 vols. (London: Kegan Paul, Trench, Trübner, 1895–99).

MUSIC, CRITICISM, AND THE CHALLENGE OF HISTORY

THE SPIRIT OF POSITIVISM AND
THE SEARCH FOR ALTERNATIVES

Musicology and Criticism at the End
of the Nineteenth Century

More than a hundred years after Guido Adler's appointment to the first chair in musicology at the University of Vienna, the ambivalence, uncertainties, and ideological dilemmas that characterized the discipline at the time of its institutionalization remain largely unacknowledged and little understood. While musicology in Adler's day is widely identified with a positivist endeavor to transform the discipline into a science, this book argues that the field consisted of a contested array of diverse and often highly personal visions of music study, its value, and its future. Exploring for the first time the encounters of three of the period's leading writers on the art—Adler, Eduard Hanslick, and Heinrich Schenker—with the work of each other and their contemporaries, it elaborates a portrait of the nascent discipline that is far more complex than has previously been suspected.[1] It suggests that these figures' pioneering work owed as much to such skeptical and irrationalist currents in the fin de siècle cultural discourse as Nietzsche's philosophy of science, Richard Wagner's theories of nation and identity, and Julius Langbehn's "idealism of anti-modernity" as it did to the positivist movement itself.[2] And it argues that some of the most pressing questions to figure in

---

1. For representative views of music study and positivist scholarship, see Joseph Kerman, *Contemplating Music: Challenges to Musicology* (Cambridge, MA: Harvard University Press, 1985); Bojan Bujić, ed., *Music in European Thought, 1851–1912*, Cambridge Readings in the Literature of Music (Cambridge: Cambridge University Press, 1988); Kurt Blaukopf, *Pioniere empiristischer Musikforschung. Österreich und Böhmen als Wiege der modernen Kunstsoziologie*, Wissenschaftliche Weltauffassung und Kunst, no. 1 (Vienna: Hölder-Pichler-Tempsky, 1995); and Alastair Williams, *Constructing Musicology* (Aldershot: Ashgate, 2001).

2. Classic studies of such skeptical ideologies and the movements to which they gave rise include Fritz Stern, *The Politics of Cultural Despair: A Study in the Rise of the Germanic Ideology* (New York:

present-day discussions of musicology's disciplinary identities—about the relationship between musicology and criticism, the role of the subject in analysis and the narration of history, and the responsibilities of the music scholar to the extra-academic community—have points of origin in the discipline's conflicted and largely forgotten beginnings.[3]

In six chapters, this book engages in close readings of studies and essays by its three central figures alongside contemporary statements on science, history, art, and modernity; documentary sources related to their teaching, cultural activism, and other activities; and archival materials illuminating the institutional contexts in which their work found support. It casts light on a forgotten side of Hanslick, who, once tenured by the University of Vienna, refused the challenge of positivist scholarship and devoted himself to penning a self-consciously subjective history of Viennese musical life whose narrative continuity would be assured only by the experience of a single listener. It suggests that Schenker's analytical work originated in a Wagner-inspired search for a critical alternative to Adler's style-obsessed scholarship. And it reveals that Adler, once appointed to the university's faculty in 1898, dedicated himself to a search for means by which to respond to Nietzsche's warnings about the vitality of artistic and spiritual life in an increasingly scientific age. In short, it explores an array of forgotten yet seminal episodes in the history of modern musical thought in light of the competing ideological demands that shaped them.

Before embarking upon this investigation, it is necessary to define our terms—or at least to reflect upon those historical and ideological circumstances that hamper easy definitions. First, we must try to find out what late-century critics and scholars meant when they invoked the term "science" (*Wissenschaft*) and its derivatives: "natural science" (*Naturwissenschaft*), the "science" or study of art (*Kunstwissenschaft*), and the "science of music" or musicology (*Musikwissenschaft*). Then, we may consider some of the skeptical and ambivalent strains of scholarship and criticism that responded to such notions.

"WHAT IS SCIENCE?"

"The longing for knowledge that is as objective as possible, which is, in our time, felt in all areas of inquiry, must necessarily make itself felt in the investigation of

---

Anchor Books, 1961) (cited from chapter 2, "The Idealism of Antimodernity"); George L. Mosse, *The Crisis of German Ideology: Intellectual Origins of the Third Reich* (New York: Gossett and Dunlap, 1964); and William J. McGrath, *Dionysian Art and Populist Politics in Austria* (New Haven: Yale University Press, 1974).

3. I am thinking here of such recent and well-known disciplinary critiques as Williams, *Constructing Musicology*; Kevin Korsyn, *Decentering Music: A Critique of Contemporary Musical Research* (Oxford: Oxford University Press, 2003); Rose Rosengard Subotnik, "Musicology and Criticism," in *Developing Variations: Style and Ideology in Western Music* (Minneapolis: University of Minnesota Press, 1991); Kerman, *Contemplating Music*; and Kerman, "How We Got Into Analysis, and How to Get Out," *Critical Inquiry* 7, no. 2 (1980), 311–31, repr. in *Write All These Down: Essays on Music* (Berkeley and Los Angeles: University of California Press, 1994), 12–32.

beauty as well." Thus Eduard Hanslick declared his intention, in the second edition of his *On the Musically Beautiful* (*Vom Musikalisch-Schönen*, 1858), to pioneer a new and revolutionary approach to music study. Admonishing his readers to set aside their traditional concerns with speculative metaphysics and Romantic poetics, Hanslick challenged them to embrace instead the spirit of a dawning, scientific age. If the search for musical understanding "is not to be wholly illusory," he argued, "it will need to approach the methods of the natural sciences" (*naturwissenschaftliche Methoden*).[4] Twenty-seven years later, in a document recently described as "signaling the establishment of musicology" as an institutionalized field of inquiry, the young Guido Adler announced his intention to answer the call of his former teacher.[5] In an essay entitled "Umfang, Methode und Ziel der Musikwissenschaft" (1885), he endeavored to define, as his title proclaimed, the "Scope, Method, and Goal of Musicology" for a new generation of scholars. "The most important point" for the musicologist to remember as he carries out his work, Adler explained, is "the analogy between the methods of art study and those of the natural sciences."[6]

With these programmatic statements, both Hanslick and Adler sought to carve out a place for music scholarship—and for themselves—within an academic community in the throes of intellectual upheaval. Throughout much of Central and Western Europe, the middle decades of the nineteenth century saw the displacement of idealist traditions of philosophical inquiry from the center of university curricula by the physical and biological sciences.[7] The esteem once accorded to philosophers was rapidly fading before the recent and stunning achievements of chemists, physicists, physicians, and biologists. In Berlin, Vienna, and other centers of learning, this rise to prominence of the natural sciences was accompanied by an unprecedented wave of government investment in faculty and resources, and whoever wished to benefit from this trend—or to avoid being left out entirely—was compelled to align himself with one or the other of the newly favored fields. For scholars of music, as for those working in almost every other discipline, "the proper model of explanatory theory," as Terry Pinkard has observed, was quickly becoming "whatever it was that the natural

---

4. Hanslick/Strauß, 1:22: "Der Drang nach einer möglichst objectiven Erkenntniß der Dinge, wie er in unserer Zeit alle Gebiete des Wissens bewegt, muß nothwendig auch an die Erforschung des *Schönen* rühren. ... Sie wird, will sie nicht ganz illusorisch werden, sich der naturwissenschaftlichen Methode wenigstens nähern müssen." For an alternate translation, see Hanslick/Payzant, 1.

5. Bruno Nettl, "The Institutionalization of Musicology: Perspectives of a North American Ethnomusicologist," in *Rethinking Music*, ed. Nicholas Cook (Oxford: Oxford University Press, 1999), 288.

6. Guido Adler, "Umfang, Methode und Ziel der Musikwissenschaft," in *Vierteljahrsschrift für Musikwissenschaft* 1 (1885), 15: "...das Schwergewicht der Betrachtung liegt in der Analogie der kunstwissenschaftlichen Methode mit der naturwissenschaftlichen Methode." An alternative translation of this passage is provided in Bujić, *Music in European Thought*, 351.

7. The classic study of the rise of the natural sciences in nineteenth-century academe is David Knight, *The Age of Science: The Scientific World-view in the Nineteenth Century* (Oxford: Basil Blackwell, 1986). See also Timothy Lenoir, *Instituting Science: The Cultural Production of Scientific Disciplines*, Writing Science (Stanford, California: Stanford University Press, 1997).

sciences were doing."[8] Of course, such a reorientation of the humanistic disciplines was easier described than accomplished. Just how the study of music, for instance, could be made to approximate the "methods of the natural sciences" was, for many, anything but clear.

Drawing upon the latest research on the physics of sound and the workings of the inner ear, Hermann von Helmholtz in Heidelberg and Gustav Fechner in Leipzig made significant inroads along these lines in the fields of acoustics, psychoacoustics, and even, to some extent, music theory.[9] But as Helmholtz himself admitted, their work did little to clarify, with "scientific" precision, questions regarding the aesthetic experience of music—questions that had, since Kant, typically been regarded as the domain of metaphysical philosophy. While wholly satisfied that he had described definitively "the physiological properties of the sensation of hearing," Helmholtz concluded his epoch-making *On the Sensations of Tone* (1863) by acknowledging his persistent inability "to explain the wonders of great works of art."[10] A different yet no less vexing set of difficulties confronted those who wished to engage in research on music's structure, style, and history, the primary fields of interest for both Adler and his onetime mentor. How, many wondered, could the study of music, in *all* of its aspects, be transformed into a "science" as methodologically rigorous as physics or chemistry? And if, as I will suggest, such a transformation was widely acknowledged to be impracticable, then what did Hanslick and Adler really mean when they spoke of an approach to music study that approximated as closely as possible "the methods of the natural sciences"?

To begin, it is important to note, as many have previously, that the German term *Wissenschaft* often connotes something much broader than the English word *science*. Indeed, commentators as diverse as William Ashton Ellis, writing in the 1890s of Wagner's statements on *Wissenschaft* from a half-century earlier, and Babette E. Babich, writing recently of Nietzsche's statements on the same, have argued that their subjects did not, in fact, invoke the term in order to refer specifically to either the natural sciences or methodologies of research peculiar to them. As Babich writes, "*Wissenschaft*," for the young Nietzsche, was simply "an ordered, systematic and coherent disciplinary arena of knowledge."[11] In a similar vein, Charles E. McClelland, in his classic study of the structure of the university in nineteenth-century Germany, writes of "the revolution in

8. Terry Pinkard, *German Philosophy, 1760–1860: The Legacy of Idealism* (Cambridge: Cambridge University Press, 2002), 357.

9. On Helmholtz and Fechner, see Bujić, *Music in European Thought*, 275–77 and 280–92. On Helmholtz, see also Burdette Green and David Butler, "From Acoustics to *Tonpsychologie*," in *The Cambridge History of Western Music Theory*, ed. Thomas Christensen (Cambridge: Cambridge University Press, 2002), 246–71.

10. Hermann von Helmholtz, *On the Sensations of Tone as a Physiological Basis for the Theory of Music*, trans. Alexander J. Ellis (New York: Dover, 1954), 371.

11. Babbette E. Babich, "Nietzsche's Critique of Scientific Reason and Scientific Culture: On 'Science as a Problem' and Nature as Chaos," in *Nietzsche and Science*, ed. Gregory Moore and Thomas H. Brobjer (Aldershot and Burlington, VT: Ashgate, 2004), 133–53 (cited at 137). For Ellis's remarks, see Wagner/Ellis, 1:71 n.

Wissenschaft" as nothing more specific than a new seriousness with which scholarship of all sorts was pursued.[12] Yet in Bojan Bujić's *Music in European Thought, 1851–1912*, which remains our most comprehensive source in English for contemporary statements on the art, the term is taken to mean something different. Bujić acknowledges that "in German it does not denote only the exact, natural or technical sciences, but is also applied to the humanistic disciplines, including the philosophical ones." But "of course," he continues, "anybody stressing the word *Wissenschaft* in the second half of the nineteenth century wishes to underline the link between the humanities and the exact sciences and to draw attention to the application of scientific method, however loosely defined, to the fields of philosophy and history."[13] As we will see, Wagner, in *The Artwork of the Future* (1849), and Nietzsche, in *The Birth of Tragedy* (1872), certainly stressed (to use Bujić's term) the word *Wissenschaft* in their critiques of contemporary society and its fascination with rationalistic inquiry. Given the competing assertions of Babich, Bujić, Ellis, and McClelland, how, then, should we read the work of these nineteenth-century writers?

I would argue that the ambiguity and diversity of opinion that characterize present-day attempts to render in English what Wagner, Nietzsche, or Hanslick intended do not derive only from problems of translation, historical distance, and cultural difference, though these all certainly play a role. Rather, the idea of *Wissenschaft*, particularly in its application to the study of music and the arts, was a source of confusion, befuddlement, and significant contention among nineteenth-century writers themselves. To be sure, as Babich observes, *Wissenschaft* had long been understood by German speakers to refer quite generally to "learning, scholarship, erudition, and knowledge." But over the course of the eighteenth century, and particularly during the middle decades of the nineteenth, it *also*, and simultaneously, came to assume a distinctly "non-arts connotation," in Babich's terms—to refer more specifically, in some contexts and for some writers and readers, to the biological and physical sciences.[14] For this reason, as not just *Wissenschaft* but the explicitly "non-arts" *Naturwissenschaft* came to be touted as models to which the study of art itself must aspire during this same period, it was only natural that confusion, anxiety, and disagreement would arise among those who sought to engage in it.

To illustrate this point, we may consider briefly a discussion that Adler claimed to have had with Wagner in the summer of 1876 at a reception held in the composer's Bayreuth villa:

[Wagner:] Adler, I've heard that you're dedicating yourself to science
           [*Wissenschaft*]. What is science? My doctor told me once that
           I should open the upper half of my window at night, but another
           time he said I should open the lower half, and a third time he told
           me to open the whole thing...

---

12. Charles E. McClelland, *State, Society, and University in Germany, 1700–1914* (Cambridge: Cambridge University Press, 1980), Part III ("The German Universities and the Revolution in Wissenschaft, 1819–1866").

13. Bujić, *Music in European Thought*, 342.

14. Babich, "Nietzsche's Critique of Scientific Reason," 137.

[Adler:]   Most revered master, allow me to say, with the greatest of respect,
that that is not at all what science is about. Since I don't possess the
talent required to become a composer capable of meeting my own
standards and I don't find performance either enjoyable or fulfilling,
I have latched onto the science of music [*Wissenschaft der Musik*]. I am
especially concerned with the uncovering of history and with making
accessible to the public the immortal works of the past. This can be of
use to the artist as well. Indeed, you have found your own materials
in products of research into the history of literature.[15]

To be sure, there is much that one might doubt in this exchange: its authen-
ticity for one (recounted as it was nearly sixty years after the supposed event),
and the sincerity of Wagner's good-natured questioning for another. But the
terms invoked in this dialogue and the associations they carry are nonetheless
illustrative, if not of Wagner's understanding of them, then certainly of Adler's
impressions of a pervasive attitude toward his chosen discipline within the intellectual world of the 1870s. Following Wagner's question (*What is science?*), the
composer's ramblings about his doctor and his fussy prescriptions suggest the
existence of a clear, popular association between the general term *Wissenschaft*
and the natural sciences in particular. Adler's recollection of Wagner's jesting
also makes clear that some of the period's most prominent artists and intellectuals considered the imposition of the "methods of the natural sciences" upon the
study of music to be implausible, even laughable. Such an exchange would surely
not have transpired, even in Adler's imagination, if *Wissenschaft* were widely
understood to connote simply "scholarship" or "erudition."

In Adler's response to Wagner's musings (*that is not at all what science is about*),
we find what was, to his mind, at the heart of the matter. Namely, his response
suggests that the *Wissenschaft* of which he wrote and spoke was not concerned
with the literal emulation of the working methods of physicists, biologists, or
physicians. Indeed, aside from narrow inquiries into acoustical or optical phenomena, it was widely acknowledged among Adler's like-minded colleagues that
the emulation, to say nothing of the assimilation, of such methods was impossible. As one among them, the art historian Moriz Thausing, observed in a seminal
essay of 1873, "artistic phenomena are not as easily grasped as natural objects...
for us, there are no experiments, much less a *corpus vile*"—a body or object sus-

---

15. Adler, *Wollen und Wirken. Aus dem Leben eines Musikhistorikers* (Vienna: Universal Edition,
1935), 15–16 (ellipses in original): "Später sagte er zu mir: 'Adler, ich hab' gehört, Sie widmen
sich der Wissenschaft; was ist Wissenschaft? Der Arzt sagt mir einmal, ich soll in der Nacht die
obern Flügel der Fenster offen lassen, ein anderes Mal die unteren Flügel, ein drittes Mal das ganze
Fenster...' 'Verehrtester Meister gestatten mir in Ehrerbietung die Bemerkung, daß das wohl mit
Wissenschaft nichts zu tun hat. Da ich nicht die nach meinen Ansprüchen notwendige Begabung
für produktive Kunst habe und die reproduzierende mich nicht befriedigt und ausfüllt, so greife ich
zur Wissenschaft der Musik, besonders mit Hinblick auf die Aufdeckung der Geschichte und der
Zugänglichmachung unvergänglicher Werke der Vergangenheit. Auch diese können dem Künstler
nützen, geradeso wie Sie Ihre Stoffe den Ergebnissen der literarhistorischen Forschung entnommen
haben.'"

ceptible to literal dissection.[16] When Adler invoked the "methods of the natural sciences" in his "Scope, Method, and Goal of Musicology," he, like Thausing, did so rhetorically and for distinctly political ends. He sought to justify—and to solidify—the position of his nascent discipline within an academic culture increasingly enamored with the natural sciences.

But though Adler recognized the impossibility of bridging the methodological divide between research in his own discipline and in such fields as chemistry or physics, he did not simply throw up his hands in the face of Hanslick's challenge. Significantly, he did not embrace a vision of his field like the one advanced by his contemporary Wilhelm Dilthey, who argued that the arts called for their own, distinct modes of inquiry, and who lobbied for a hermeneutic approach to their study under the rubric of *Geisteswissenschaft*, a science of the mind or spirit.[17] And he did not argue, like Wilhelm Windelband (another famous historian contemporary), that historical study and research in the natural sciences constituted two fundamentally different varieties of inquiry with respect to their intellectual aims (*Erkenntnisziele*)—the former being "idiographic" or "picture-making" and the latter "nomothetic" or "law-contriving."[18] Rather, Adler proposed an approach to music study that embodied what seemed to him the *spirit* of the natural sciences, or what Bujić has called the "spirit of positivism."[19] To be sure, Adler's "positivist" musicology had only general similarities with, and no real connection to, the original meaning of its oft-applied descriptor, coined by the founder of philosophical positivism, the Frenchman Auguste Comte. But it did share a great deal with what R. G. Collingwood and others have characterized as the positivist historiography of such influential nineteenth-century political and social historians as Barthold Niebuhr and Leopold von Ranke.[20]

16. Moriz Thausing, "Die Stellung der Kunstgeschichte als Wissenschaft" (1873), in *Wiener Kunstbriefe* (Leipzig: E. A. Seemann, 1884), 11: "...die Kunstgegenstände nicht so leicht erreichbar sind wie Naturobjecte...für uns absolut kein Experiment, und am wenigsten ein *corpus vile* gibt."

17. On Dilthey and his notion of *Geisteswissenschaft* as it relates to the nineteenth-century discourse on music, see Ian D. Bent, ed., *Music Analysis in the Nineteenth Century*, 2 vols., Cambridge Readings in the Literature of Music (Cambridge: Cambridge University Press, 1994), 2:9–21.

18. Wilhelm Windelband, "Geschichte und Naturwissenschaft" (1894), in *Präludien. Aufsätze und Reden zur Philosophie und ihrer Geschichte*, 6th ed., 2 vols. (Tübingen: J. C. B. Mohr, 1919), 2:144–46. I borrow the terms "picture-making" and "law-contriving" from Hayden White, who provides a useful discussion of Windelband's ideas and a comparison of Windelband's theory of historical knowledge with Dilthey's *Geisteswissenschaft* in *Metahistory: The Historical Imagination in Nineteenth-Century Europe* (Baltimore: Johns Hopkins University Press, 1973), 381–82 (cited at 381).

19. Bujić, *Music in European Thought*, 305. On this issue, see also Barbara Boisits, "Ästhetik versus Historie? Eduard Hanslicks und Guido Adlers Auffassung von Musikwissenschaft im Lichte zeitgenössischer Theorienbildung," in *Das Ende der Eindeutigkeit. Zur Frage des Pluralismus in Moderne und Postmoderne*, ed. Barbara Boisits and Peter Stachel, Studien zur Moderne, no. 13 (Vienna: Passagen, 2000), esp. 91–94.

20. R. G. Collingwood, *The Idea of History* (Oxford: Clarendon Press, 1946), esp. 126–33. See also Helge Kragh, *An Introduction to the Historiography of Science* (Cambridge: Cambridge University Press, 1987), 41–42. On the positivism of Comte and his followers, see W. M. Simon, *European Positivism in the Nineteenth Century: An Essay in Intellectual History* (Ithaca, NY: Cornell University Press, 1963).

Like the scholarship of his "positivist" colleagues publishing on a variety of historical topics, Adler's *Musikwissenschaft* or "science of music" rejected, as the cornerstone of its scientific credentials, metaphysical speculation as the foundation for the historian's work. Instead, Adler advocated "acquiring knowledge about human affairs…through the perception of the particular" rather than "through abstraction," as Ranke had written in the 1830s.[21] Furthermore, Adler conceived of his discipline, like the natural sciences themselves, as systematically divisible into sub- and ancillary branches, as evinced in his famous tabular survey of *Musikwissenschaft* published in his "Scope, Method, and Goal of Musicology." (Adler's tabular survey is reproduced as Figure 1.1.)[22] Finally, and most important, Adler called for an approach to music study that valorized empirical observation and inductive reasoning. The musicologist, he argued, must begin his work by describing, to the best of his ability, the historical—or structural, in the case of music analysis—*facts* as revealed by a careful examination of documentary sources: scores, sketches, treatises, and the like. "From a number of examples" thus described, Adler explained, the musicologist must then attempt to "distinguish what each has in common with the others from that which is unique."[23] This latter, second stage in the investigation typically entailed extensive philological criticism, of a sort made famous through Niebuhr's pioneering work on ancient Roman history.[24] Finally, proceeding inductively from this set of empirical observations thus gathered, the musicologist must attempt to identify the "laws" that govern music's formal and stylistic evolution (*Kunstgesetze*) over the course of historical time. In Windelband's view, it was precisely this kind of "law-contriving" that lay at the heart of a "nomothetic" undertaking, the prototypical example of which being *Naturwissenschaft* itself.[25]

With respect to all of these points, Adler's *Musikwissenschaft* indeed had affinities with the working methods of chemists and biologists, but only of the most general kind. As Bujić's term suggests, Adler's musicologist was to carry out his work in the *spirit*, not on the model, of his naturalist colleagues. And as we will see, if one were to look for models upon which Adler appears to have drawn as he laid out his disciplinary vision, one would find them not in such seminal contributions to the natural sciences as Ernst Mach's essays on acoustics, Helmholtz's theories of sound and color, or Theodor Meynert's studies of the brain. Rather, they would be found in the work of a figure like Thausing, the art historian, who sought to outline, in a scientifically inspired polemic of his own entitled

21. Leopold von Ranke, "Weltgeschichte" (posth., 1888), trans. in Fritz Stern, ed., *The Varieties of History: From Voltaire to the Present* (New York: Meridian, 1957), 58.

22. Adler's tabular survey is published in "Umfang, Methode und Ziel," 16–17; reprinted and translated in Bujić, *Music in European Thought*, 354–55.

23. All citations from Adler in this paragraph are from "Umfang, Methode und Ziel," 15; trans. in Bujić, *Music in European Thought*, 351.

24. On Niebuhr, see Collingwood, *The Idea of History*, 129–30.

25. Windelband himself acknowledged that a nomothetic perspective could, technically, be adopted in historical study, but he himself did not advocate such an approach. See Windelband, "Geschichte und Naturwissenschaft," 145–46. The significance of Windelband's theory of historical knowledge for late-century music historiography will be considered in greater detail in chapter 2.

"The Status of Art History as a Science" ("Die Stellung der Kunstgeschichte als Wissenschaft," 1873), the "scope, method, and problems" (*Umfang, Methode und Probleme*) of art-historical research.[26]

Finally, we must not overlook the fact that Adler's "Scope, Method, and Goal of Musicology" also draws in important yet widely unacknowledged ways upon the model of Hanslick's *On the Musically Beautiful*. This indebtedness is evident not only in Adler's call to his readers to follow the example of the natural sciences but also in his clarification of the latter to mean empirical and inductive modes of inquiry. This fact is of considerable significance for our present examination, as it brings us face to face with the diversity of opinions, skepticism, and pervasive ambivalence that greeted the positivist movement in music study throughout the second half of the century. For as we will see, it was from out of Hanslick's troubled relationship with this movement and its goals that some of the most vexing problems facing modern musical inquiry first arose.

SKEPTICISM, RESISTANCE, AND THE SEARCH FOR ALTERNATIVES

The first section of this book, "Eduard Hanslick and the Challenge of *Musikwissenschaft*," provides a substantial reevaluation of Hanslick's work by situating it at the center of late-century debates about the future of the discipline he helped to found. Through the medium of his writings, chapter 1, "Forgotten Histories and Uncertain Legacies," illuminates the complex ideological and institutional contexts in which musicology first found a place in Austrian academe. Amid a wave of postrevolutionary reforms, Hanslick was hired by the University of Vienna in 1856 to advance an empiricist movement in art-historical study fostered by the Imperial Ministry of Education in an attempt to distinguish Austrian letters from the traditions of metaphysical inquiry that still prevailed in many German institutions. To his employers, Hanslick's formalist *On the Musically Beautiful* seemed an ideal complement to the work of the art historian Rudolf Eitelberger, the philosopher Robert Zimmermann, and others recently hired. Yet soon after Hanslick embarked upon the project of revising his polemical treatise into a systematic study in the 1860s, he had a change of heart. He became convinced that musical beauty cannot be assessed via empirical observation but must be regarded as something historically, culturally, and even personally relative. In response, he resolved to dedicate himself to the study of cultural history in the Hegelian tradition and, ultimately, to exploring the boundaries between one's subjective impressions of musical works and the historical narratives one constructs. Significantly, it was in terms of just such a distinction between historical study and critical engagement that a number of Hanslick's prominent historian colleagues, including Thausing and the musicologist Philipp Spitta, were simultaneously working to define and delimit the "scientific" study of art. From their perspective, Hanslick's attempt to dissolve this distinction threatened to undermine their own efforts to transform art-historical research into a science

---

26. Thausing, "Die Stellung," 1.

as rigorous as physics or chemistry. Alarmed by Hanslick's abandonment of the empiricist path, the university's faculty, at the time of his retirement in 1895, vowed to reorient the study of music along the scientific lines that Spitta had prescribed. In Adler, who called for an approach to music research that followed as closely as possible "the methods of the natural sciences," they placed their hopes for the future of the discipline and of the institution that Adler's *Musikwissenschaft* would represent.

Chapter 2, "Music Criticism as Living History," takes a close look at the self-consciously subjective—and all but forgotten—historiography of music to which Hanslick devoted the final decades of his career. After abandoning his work on speculative aesthetics in favor of the writing of cultural history, Hanslick published his second book, *History of Concert Life in Vienna*, in 1869. There, he elaborated a portrait of 150 years of Viennese concert life whose Hegelian underpinnings flew in the face of the empiricist ideals he had earlier espoused. Then, taking another, more radical turn, he proceeded to publish a dozen books over the next thirty years that he insisted were historical studies, despite the fact that they consisted of little more than his own, previously published, critical reviews. In those volumes, which he collectively called a "living history" (*lebendige Geschichte*) of Viennese musical life, Hanslick flouted the calls of Spitta and Thausing for an empirical approach to historical research by declaring the critic's pen his historical "camera" and the critical essay his historical "photograph." Aligning himself with an eclectic host of contemporaries, from Nietzsche to the statistician Ludwig Schlözer and the historian Jacob Burckhardt, he declared his intention to pioneer a new approach to the writing of history whose narrative continuity would be assured only by the experience of a single listening subject. In this massive, day-by-day account of the unfolding of musical life during the second half of the century, Hanslick placed his own impressions at the center of the historical record and produced a model example of what might be called, after Leo Treitler, a "particularist" historiography of music. And in doing that, he strove to undermine the criticism-versus-history dichotomy by which his colleagues sought to delimit the musicological field. While Spitta and others sought to banish subjective impression from the products of art-historical research, Hanslick maintained that criticism and scholarship were not mutually exclusive but deeply inscribed within each other. Most disturbingly, from the perspective of his detractors, he espoused such views from within the halls of the University of Vienna itself.

The early work of Heinrich Schenker, considered in the second part of this book, exhibits different varieties of ambivalence with respect to the positivist challenge. Though Schenker later became notorious for his disparaging of Wagner and his work, chapter 3, "Music Analysis as Critical Method," argues that his early critical apologies for Brahms's music invoke theories of musical structure and meaning that are conspicuously Wagnerian. In a pair of analytical reviews published in 1891 and 1892, Schenker elucidated the sense and coherence of Brahms's songs and choral works by drawing upon Wagnerian arguments regarding the relationship between poetic form and musical structure and the motivic process known as the *leitmotive* technique. This unexpected pairing of critical agenda and analytical strategy complicates a widely held image of Schenker's work as a precursor to an array of later structuralist experiments and confounds the persistent assumption that late-century critics were sharply divided by their aesthetic allegiances to one or the other of these artists. Significantly, however, Schenker adopted this analytical approach in an attempt to counter what he considered the deleterious influence of Adlerian scholarship upon his fellow music critics, who had failed to appreciate Brahms's genius in their rush to chart the stylistic evolution of the composer's output over time. Seeking an alternative approach to Brahms's work, Schenker invoked key tenets of Wagnerian aesthetics, which had kept alive a Romantic fascination with creative genius well into the final years of the century. Passing hermeneutically from descriptions of musical structure to investigations of the artistic mind, Schenker embraced an interpretive strategy that was deeply rooted in a century of Romantic poetics. And he aligned himself with a critical tradition that had been singled out for methodological ridicule by none other Thausing, one of the founding fathers of the positivist movement in art-historical research.

But the lure of empiricism was felt even by Schenker and even in his studies of the creative act. This is the subject of chapter 4, which examines Schenker's encounters with the working methods of some of the leading artists of the age and illuminates his first substantive break from the critical mainstream of his time. As an aspiring composer as well as a critic, Schenker was fascinated by the compositional process, and he toyed, in the early 1890s, with an array of speculative theories of artistic creativity indebted to Wagner, E. T. A. Hoffmann, and many other Romantic writers. Shortly after mid-decade, however, he made a radical turn. Disavowing all speculative approaches to the study of the subject, he lobbied his readers to assume a self-consciously realistic and empirical perspective by considering only those insights into the compositional act provided by the sketches and reminiscences of practicing composers. This new emphasis in Schenker's writings made clear his newly found sympathies with the positivist spirit famously exemplified in Gustav Nottebohm's pioneering studies of Beethoven's sketchbooks. But in a dramatic twist, Schenker went on to reject the tenets of positivist scholarship once again in his first book-length study, *Harmony* (1906). And a quarter-century after that, he went so far as to suggest that his early, fleeting brush with empiricism was prompted not by his own experiences with reasoned, empirical modes of inquiry but by meetings with Brahms held in the composer's home. To be sure, we have reason to doubt the accuracy of Schenker's recollections of his conversations with the artist. But whether or not his early brush with empiricism was truly inspired by Brahms, his elderly hints of revelatory rather than rational causes for his turn of the 1890s testifies to the depth and persistence of the ideological dilemmas posed by the positivist challenge for writers of his generation.

Indeed, as we will see in the final part of this book, dilemmas such as Schenker's were also experienced by at least one founding father of the positivist movement itself. Chapter 5, "A Science of Music for an Ambivalent Age," elaborates a portrait of Guido Adler as figure deeply troubled by the implications of an increasingly scientific culture for the vitality of his nation's artistic life. Although he spent his early years penning positivist polemics in an attempt to win for music study the academic respect widely granted to the natural sciences, Adler turned his attention, once his employment was secure, in a very different direction. Following his appointment to the University of Vienna in 1898, he revisited the discussions of science and art in which he had engaged during his student years with the likes of the political activist Victor Adler (no relation to Guido) and the poet Siegfried Lipiner. And he endeavored to respond as a newly tenured historian to an array of Wagner- and Nietzsche-inspired critiques of science and historical study. In an important yet largely forgotten corrective to his earlier positivist polemics, he outlined a new and provocative program for his discipline. Rejecting assertions made by Spitta and Thausing, Adler argued that musicologists must work to advance historical understanding not as an end in itself but in the service of composers, who would work in turn to transform historical styles and idioms into the "living" music of the present.[27] Modeling this vision of the scholar's charge in his subsequent publications and tireless advocacy of Mahler, Schoenberg, and other contemporary artists, Adler strove to answer Nietzsche's call to "struggle on behalf of culture" by fostering "the production of the genius."[28]

The final chapter considers a question that has vexed critical discussions of Western musicology's ideological heritage for decades: its nationalist underpinnings. Chapter 6, "German Music in an Age of Positivism," explores the complex of diverse and even contradictory cultural associations that Adler forged through the medium of his scholarly work. Immediately after his "Scope, Method, and Goal of Musicology" appeared in 1885, Adler penned essays on Mozart, Bach, Handel that are remarkable for their cultural chauvinism and that draw extensively upon the literature on German identity, from Fichte and Wagner to Johann Abraham Peter Schulz.[29] Each of these essays was commissioned for an event that called for such rhetorical bluster, and Adler evidently approached these assignments with enthusiasm. But the positions Adler staked out in these essays contrast strikingly with those that he assumed in his studies of the history of music theory, published during these same years. Seeking to understand the historical origins of harmony, a field in which such prominent historians as Hugo Riemann and Richard Batka held that harmonic singing was a specifically Germanic innovation, Adler took pains to distance himself from his colleagues' attempts to claim national origins for polyphonic phenomena. As the years progressed, such studied neutrality became a hallmark of Adler's scholarship, as evidenced in his work on the *Monuments of Music in Austria* (*Denkmäler der Tonkunst in Österreich*) series of critical editions, which celebrated the supranational image of Austrian identity promoted by Habsburg officialdom. However, as Adler's first book-length

27. Adler, "Musik und Musikwissenschaft. Akademische Antrittsrede, gehalten am 26. Oktober 1898 an der Universität Wien," *Jahrbuch der Musikbibliothek Peters* 5 (1898), 27–39.

28. Friedrich Nietzsche, "Schopenhauer as Educator," in *Untimely Meditations*, ed. Daniel Breazeale, trans. R. J. Hollingdale, Cambridge Texts in the History of Philosophy (Cambridge: Cambridge University Press, 1997), 163.

29. Adler, "Johann Sebastian Bach und Georg Friedrich Händel. Ihre Bedeutung und Stellung in der Geschichte der Musik," *Monatsblätter des Wissenschaftlichen Club* 12 (1885) (offprint, Vienna: Adolf Holzhausen, 1885); Adler, "W. A. Mozart," *Deutsche Arbeit* 5 (1906; orig. 1887): 300–304.

study, *Richard Wagner* (1904), makes clear, the historian's later negotiations of the national question were anything but unproblematic. In that book, Adler invoked, at times, the cover of scientific objectivity in order to avoid confronting the significant ethical questions posed by Wagner's inflammatory prose. And it is here, I suggest, that the contradictions inherent in his musicological program become most readily apparent. Through his scholarship, Adler sought, as Nietzsche had counseled, to provide a catalyst for new creative work undertaken by contemporary artists—a project entailing, as Nietzsche understood, both value judgments and significant ethical responsibilities. But in failing to engage critically with the substance of Wagner's prose, Adler favored empirical description over a critical engagement with German cultural history. And in doing that, he turned his back upon the Nietzschean tradition that he ostensibly sought to uphold.

Looking beyond the fin de siècle, the epilogue, "Into the Twentieth Century," considers the legacy of work such as Adler's over the course of the next half-century and examines the politicization of late-century debates under the pressures of new ideological realities. Though Schenker abandoned his empiricist position on the study of creativity sometime around 1900, his statements were soon picked up and amplified in essays by his younger acquaintance, Arnold Schoenberg. Schoenberg's most elaborate exposition of Schenker's early position appeared later still, in the published version of his famous essay "Brahms the Progressive" (1947). There, Schoenberg echoed Schenker's valorization of the rational artist in a manner that had the effect of removing from the academic discourse on Brahms the ideological tint of the Wagnerian cult of irrational genius celebrated by many German musicologists during the 1930s and 1940s. In this way, as Daniel Beller-McKenna points out, Schoenberg's essay had the effect of cleansing or "de-Germanizing" Brahms in the immediate postwar years.[30] In contrast to Schoenberg, the theorist Ernst Kurth, once one of Adler's favorite students, drew different conclusions from the late-century discourse on music and suffered a markedly different fate in later years. Shortly after 1900, Kurth, like Hanslick a quarter-century earlier, rejected the positivist movement in its entirety and sought to connect his analytical investigations to those very strains of irrationalist cultural criticism rooted in the work of Nietzsche and Wagner. Shortly after the Second World War, however, Kurth's work, though voluminous and initially influential, fell into neglect in a German-dominated academic culture that sought to distance itself from every sort of pre-war irrationalist discourse and that attempted to do so by embracing a positivist ideology far more radical than anything broached in Adler's time. It has only been in recent decades, with the questioning of this peculiarly postwar variety of positivism, that Kurth's work has been rediscovered.

Revisiting the work of Fritz Stern, George L. Mosse, and other pioneering historians of late nineteenth-century German society, a number of scholars have

---

30. Daniel Beller-McKenna, *Brahms and the German Spirit* (Cambridge, MA: Harvard University Press, 2004), 182–93.

recently suggested that the organized, radical, and antimodern movements whose activities Mosse and Stern document are widely granted too prominent a place in postwar narratives of German cultural history. Indeed, some argue that late-century German society was shaped just as profoundly by a seemingly limitless diversity of ambivalent and mostly nondogmatic attitudes toward science, rationalism, and modern culture exhibited in the work of countless individual artists and intellectuals. Walter Frisch has addressed this latter phenomenon under the rubric of "ambivalent modernism," which he describes as "admiring and fostering the new" while simultaneously "clinging fervently to the past out of a sense that the past...was an essential part of the German character that could not be abandoned."[31] In a similar vein, Allan Janik has called attention to what he describes as the "critical modernism" evident in the work of many late-century Viennese. Critical modernists, Janik explains, were those artists, writers, philosophers, and critics who exhibited "a peculiarly skeptical healthy reaction against the spellbinding power that modernity exerts upon us." They engaged in "a critique of modernity that...was not a rejection of modernity pure and simple, but an immanent critique of its limits."[32] And in a recent study of diverse strains of Wilhelmine cultural criticism, Kevin Repp has argued that many turn-of-the-century German intellectuals "felt just as at home with the discourse of cultural despair"—referring to the subject of Stern's research—"as they did with the discourse of progressive optimism." Indeed, Repp suggests, the popular discussion of German modernity in the decades surrounding 1900 was characterized, above all else, by a wide-ranging "search for alternatives."[33]

What I want to suggest in the present book is that the learned discourse on music, as part and parcel of broader discussions of society, art, culture, and modernity, was likewise, and also immanently, ambivalent and searching. I would suggest that Adler, Schenker, Hanslick, and their peers were not the "crusading positivists" or unblinking formalists that we have tended to assume and that there never was a single, unambiguous positivist program upon which the discipline of musicology was founded.[34] Rather, all of these figures were ambivalent and conflicted with regard to contemporary calls to transform the study of music into a science. They were all, in various and highly personal ways, critical modernists engaged in a lively search for alternative futures for their discipline. To be sure, the present study attempts to illuminate only one small corner of a complex and broad-based discussion, confined to the half-century separating Hanslick's *On*

31. Walter Frisch, *German Modernism: Music and the Arts*, California Studies in 20th-Century Music, no. 3 (Berkeley and Los Angeles: University of California Press, 2005), 8.

32. Allan Janik, "Vienna 1900 Revisited: Paradigms and Problems," in *Rethinking Vienna 1900*, ed. Steven Beller, Austrian History, Culture, and Society, no. 3 (New York and Oxford: Berghahn, 2001), 40. Janik's idea of critical modernism is elaborated more fully in his *Wittgenstein's Vienna Revisited* (New Brunswick, NJ: Transaction, 2001).

33. Kevin Repp, *Reformers, Critics, and the Paths of German Modernity: Anti-Politics and the Search for Alternatives, 1890–1914* (Cambridge, MA: Harvard University Press, 2000), 14.

34. I borrow the quoted term from Joseph Kerman, who describes Philipp Spitta as a "crusading positivist" in *Contemplating Music*, 50.

the Musically Beautiful from Adler's *Richard Wagner* and focused primarily upon Austria's Germans. But if we find, even within these confines, that the anxieties and ambivalence evident in these writers' work remind us of some of our own, then I would suggest that we take heart in the situation. For it would suggest that some of the "crises" of disciplinary identity that have recently concerned so many music scholars—as one among us has characterized the situation[35]—are not so recent after all but perennial and as old as the discipline itself.

---

35. Korsyn, *Decentering Music*, chapter 1 ("Musical Research in Crisis: The Tower of Babel and the Ministry of Truth").

PART I

EDUARD HANSLICK AND THE CHALLENGE OF *MUSIKWISSENSCHAFT*

Eduard Hanslick in His Sixty-Eighth Year (1893 or 1894). From his *Aus meinem Leben* (Berlin: Allgemeiner Verein für Deutsche Litteratur, 1894).

CHAPTER ONE

FORGOTTEN HISTORIES
AND UNCERTAIN LEGACIES

If we wish to understand the radical transformations in musical thought that accompanied the institutionalization of musicology in the second half of the nineteenth century, we must begin at the start of that period, with a book that sparked a revolution in the learned discourse on the art. "Epoch-making," was the term used by the philosopher Robert Zimmermann in 1885 to describe Hanslick's *On the Musically Beautiful* (1854), the first polemical tract on music aesthetics to reach far beyond the walls of academe, and the first such book to suggest that neither the language of feeling nor the arguments of metaphysics can account for music's meaning and beauty.[1] In the century and a half that has followed its publication, the arguments advanced in Hanslick's book have been widely regarded as constituting the writer's definitive contribution to the discipline. They have been subjected to extensive critique and dissection, with the verdicts of most commentators corroborating Joseph Kerman's evaluation of nearly thirty years ago. Hanslick, it is generally held, was a formalist, who boldly prepared the philosophical ground for a century of structuralist analysis and positivist historical inquiries to come.[2] As we will see in the first part of this book, however, such a picture of Hanslick's legacy does not correspond to the views of his work held by many of his late-century peers. Indeed, from the perspective of his colleagues at the University of Vienna, where he taught from 1856 until 1895, Hanslick's contributions to his nascent discipline were, as a whole, disappointing.

---

1. Robert Zimmermann, "Ed. Hanslick: Vom Musikalisch-Schönen," *Vierteljahrsschrift für Musikwissenschaft* 1 (1885), 251.

2. See Joseph Kerman, "How We Got into Analysis, and How to Get Out," *Critical Inquiry* 7, no. 2 (1980), 311–31, repr. in *Write All These Down: Essays on Music* (Berkeley and Los Angeles: University of California Press, 1994), 12–32. Kerman's arguments are echoed and elaborated in, for instance, Richard Taruskin, *The Oxford History of Western Music*, 6 vols. (Oxford: Oxford University Press, 2005), 3:441–42; Daniel K. L. Chua, *Absolute Music and the Construction of Meaning*, New Perspectives in Music History and Criticism (Cambridge: Cambridge University Press, 1999), 224–34; and Fred Everett Maus, "Hanslick's Animism," *Journal of Musicology* 10, no. 3 (1992), 273–92.

To be sure, many of the arguments advanced in *On the Musically Beautiful* were both formalist and revolutionary. But we must not forget that this was only the first of more than a dozen books that Hanslick published over the course of his career. And though this fact has been all but forgotten in the century that has passed since his death, the pioneering formalist publicly rejected the tenets of his epoch-making treatise little more than a decade after its publication. In the 1860s, shortly after he had been tenured by the university on the strength of the empiricist positions elaborated in his 1854 volume, Hanslick abandoned his attempts to write the systematic aesthetics for which he had called at the start of his career. Instead, he turned attention in a new and very different direction: toward the study of cultural history and, eventually, toward an ambitious attempt to pioneer a new approach to historical writing that placed the subjective impressions characteristic of journalistic criticism at the center of the historical narrative.[3]

But although Hanslick spent his final decades searching for alternatives to positivist scholarship, there was, in the end, a significant dose of irony in his efforts. For in turning his back on the empiricist movement in Austrian academe, he sparked a chain of responses that did more to solidify the place of positivist scholarship in the academy than his formalist treatise ever did. Among those responses must be counted that most famous of positivist disciplinary manifestos, "The Scope, Method, and Goal of Musicology," penned in 1885 by the young Guido Adler, a onetime student of Hanslick himself. Those responses culminated a decade later, when the university named Adler to Hanslick's newly vacated post and opened a scientifically oriented Institute for Music History (Musikhistorisches Institut) under Adler's direction. Before taking a close look at Hanslick's forgotten, critical historiography of music, we must examine the institutional structures and ideological currents that fostered his empiricist beginnings and rejected his subjectivist conclusions. To this end, there is perhaps no better place to start than at the end of Hanslick's story, with his retirement from the university in 1895 and with the discussions that ensued among his colleagues about his ambivalent, uncertain legacy.

THE END OF AN ERA

When Hanslick retired from the University of Vienna after occupying, for nearly forty years, the institution's first and only professorship in the history and aesthetics of music (*Geschichte und Aesthetik der Tonkunst*), he unwittingly granted his colleagues a historic opportunity to reconsider the question of how the study of music should be undertaken at the institution. To be sure, the esteem accorded to Hanslick's *feuilletons* published in Vienna's *Neue freie Presse* and other dailies was beyond the doubt of even his most committed detractors. And *On the Musically*

---

3. On the practice and character of journalistic criticism in Hanslick's Vienna, see especially Sandra McColl, *Music Criticism in Vienna, 1896–1897: Critically Moving Forms*, Oxford Monographs on Music (Oxford: Clarendon Press, 1996); and Leon Botstein, "Music and Its Public: Habits of Listening and the Crisis of Musical Modernism in Vienna, 1870–1914" (Ph.D. diss., Harvard University, 1985), esp. 863–926. This topic will be considered in detail in chapter 2.

Beautiful was among the most widely read aesthetic treatises ever published in German-speaking Europe. But notes taken by the philosopher Friedrich Jodl during meetings held by the committee charged with naming his successor reveal that the bulk of Hanslick's academic work had left many of his colleagues deeply unsatisfied. As Jodl remarked in a note of October 27, 1896, Hanslick "is not," in spite of his academic title, "simultaneously a writer on aesthetics [*Aesthetiker*] and a scholar [*Gelehrter*], but rather the former only."⁴ In the minutes of a committee meeting held four days later, Jodl elaborated upon this point:

> Inherent in the lectureship granted to Hanslick "on the History and Aesthetics of Music," there seems to be a combination of demands that, considering the present state of knowledge, is not entirely impossible to satisfy, but is satisfied only rarely and with difficulty. This is not a reproach against any particular individual. But we must take note of the fact that, as a result of the changed scientific climate, just as with Prof. Hanslick the critic and writer on aesthetic subjects overshadowed the historian, with most younger talents the historian overshadows the writer on aesthetics. Without question, the university, as an abode of learned research, has above all the right and the need to assure that the study of music history is under-taken by the faculty according to the same methods as those used in every other historical discipline—that is, that the researcher will have the capacity to penetrate the sources on his own and to interpret the monuments of earlier musical epochs. This assumes not only a great deal of paleographical knowledge, since our present-day system of notation is only a very recent invention, but also, since the music of every century is constructed according to more strict laws than any other art form, a comprehensive and penetrating familiarity with those laws—i.e., with music theory and its transformations through the centuries.⁵

4. Cited in Theophil Antonicek, "Musikwissenschaft in Wien zur Zeit Guido Adlers," in *Studien zur Musikwissenschaft* 37 (1986), 176. Further accounts of the committee's deliberations are provided in Gabriele Johanna Eder, "Eduard Hanslick und Guido Adler. Aspekte einer menschlichen und wissenschaftlichen Beziehung," in *Kunst, Kunsttheorie und Kunstforschung im wissenschaftlichen Diskurs. In memoriam Kurt Blaukopf (1914–1999)*, ed. Martin Seiler and Friedrich Stadler, Wissenschaftliche Weltauffassung und Kunst, no. 5 (Vienna: ÖBV/HPT, 2000), 118–21; and Eder, *Alexius Meinong und Guido Adler. Eine Fruendschaft in Briefen*, Studien zur österreichischen Philosophie, no. 24 (Amsterdam and Atlanta: Rodopi, 1995), 16–21.

5. Cited in Antonicek, "Musikwissenschaft in Wien," 176–77: "...daß in dem s. Z. an Prof. Hanslick erteilten Lehrauftrage 'für Geschichte und Aesthetik der Tonkunst' Forderungen verknüpft erscheinen, welche in dieser Vereinigung durch die heutige Entwicklung der Wissenschaft nicht gerade unmöglich, aber wenigstens überaus selten und schwierig geworden sind. Nicht als ein Vorwurf gegen Personen, sondern als ein Ergebnis veränderter wissenschaftler Strömungen soll es ausgesprochen werden, daß ebenso, wie in Prof. Hanslick der Aesthetiker und Kritiker den Historiker, umgekehrt bei den meisten jüngeren Kräften der Historiker den Aesthetiker überwiegt. Unzweifelhaft hat die Universität, als eine Stätte gelehrter Forschung, ein erster Linie das Recht und das Bedürfnis, die Geschichte der Musik in der Weise u. mit den Methoden im Lehrkörper vertreten zu sehen, wie jede andere historische Disciplin, dh. daß der Studierende in die Stande gesetzt werde, selbständig in die Quellen einzudringen u. die Monumente älterer Musikperioden zu interpretiren. Dies setzt nicht nur eine Summe von paläographischen Kenntnissen voraus, da ja unsere heutige Notenschrift einer sehr jungen Vergangenheit angehort, sondern zugleich, da die Musik aller Jahrhunderte auf einer strengeren Gesetzmäßigkeit aufgebaut ist, als irgendeine andere Kunst, eine vollkommene und eindringende Vertrautheit mit dieser Gesetzmäßigkeit dh. mit der musikalischen Theorie und ihren Wandlungen durch die Jahrhunderte."

Immediately striking in Jodl's statements is an overlapping pair of opposed terms: *scholar* versus *writer on aesthetics*, and *writer on aesthetics* versus *historian*. To take the latter opposition first, Hanslick was, obviously enough, an accomplished writer on aesthetics. But to say that he was not also a historian seems odd. After all, *On the Musically Beautiful* was his only original statement on aesthetic topics, and he had gone on to publish over a dozen volumes that were, to his mind at least, historical studies: the two volumes of his *History of Concert Life in Vienna* (1869–70), the nine volumes of his *Modern Opera* (1875–1900), and a handful of other books.[6] However, Jodl's *other* pair of opposed terms, of *writer on aesthetics* (*Aesthetiker*) versus *scholar* (*Gelehrter*), clarifies his meaning. For as Carl Dahlhaus has observed, this latter opposition was of central concern to many historians working in a variety of fields throughout much of the nineteenth century.[7] While Hanslick's studies from the 1860s onward indeed considered historical topics, Jodl charged, the *approach* that Hanslick took to those topics was more like a writer on aesthetic questions than a true "scholar" of music's history. In framing his conception of Hanslick's legacy in these polemical terms, Jodl made clear that he saw more at stake in his committee's work than the evaluation of individual candidates vying for Hanslick's post. Indeed, Jodl and his colleagues faced nothing less than a choice between two vastly different paradigms of music research that had coalesced during the preceding decades.

With respect to work in the emergent field of musicology, the opposition of *Aesthetiker* versus *Gelehrter* received a seminal treatment in a lecture of 1883 by one of the leading music historians of the age, Philipp Spitta. And significantly, the relevance of Spitta's work to the committee's deliberations did not go unnoticed by contemporary observers. One such observer, Eusebius Mandyczewski—librarian and archivist at Vienna's Society of Friends of Music (Gesellschaft der Musikfreunde), an aspirant to Hanslick's recently vacated post, and a careful follower of the committee's progress—noted as much in a letter penned to Brahms in the summer of 1895. "Since work in the field of music history has, under Spitta's magnificent influence, seen an upswing and an expansion that was almost unimaginable twenty-five years ago," Mandyczewski noted, "today one expects a completely different kind of knowledge from someone who occupies a pulpit like the one on which Hanslick stood."[8] Spitta's lecture on the issue weighed by Jodl and his colleagues, entitled

6. Eduard Hanslick, *Geschichte des Concertwesens in Wien*, 2 vols. (Vienna: Wilhelm Braumüller, 1869–70); *Die moderne Oper*, 9 vols. (Berlin: A. Hofmann & Co. and Allgemeiner Verein für Deutsche Litteratur, 1875–1900); *Suite. Aufsätze über Musik und Musiker* (Vienna and Teschen: Karl Prochaska, 1884); and *Concerte, Componisten und Virtuosen der letzten fünfzehn Jahre. 1870–1885* (Berlin: Allgemeiner Verein für Deutsche Litteratur, 1886). A complete list of Hanslick's book-length publications is provided in Table 2.1.

7. The history and historiographical implications of this opposition are a central concern of Dahlhaus's *Foundations of Music History*, trans. J. Bradford Robinson (Cambridge: Cambridge University Press, 1983). See also Dahlhaus, *Esthetics of Music*, trans. William W. Austin (Cambridge: Cambridge University Press, 1982), 69–73; and Rudolf Heinz, *Geschichtsbegriff und Wissenschaftscharakter der Musikwissenschaft in der zweiten Hälfte des 19. Jahrhunderts. Philosophische Aspekte einer Wissenschaftsentwicklung*, Studien zur Musikgeschichte des 19. Jahrhunderts, no. 11 (Regensburg: Gustav Bosse, 1968), 14–42.

8. Cited in Antonicek, "Musikwissenschaft in Wien," 173.

"Art and the Study of Art" ("Kunstwissenschaft und Kunst"), was published three years prior to the beginning of the committee's deliberations.[9]

Having completed the first volume of his monumental biography of J. S. Bach in 1873 and cofounded the Leipzig Bach Society shortly thereafter, Spitta was recruited two years later to assume the first-ever professorship of music history and musicology (*Musikgeschichte und Musikwissenschaft*) at the University of Berlin. Spitta detested the prospect of life in that city. But he was attracted to the institution by its promise of support for the advancement of his emergent discipline within an academic environment that had already shown great enthusiasm for the application of philological and scientifically inspired modes of research to the study of history, literature, and the visual arts.[10] It was this concern, how best to secure for the study of music a permanent and respected place within the academic community, that motivated Spitta's writing of "Art and the Study of Art." If his goals for his field were ever to be realized, Spitta argued in his lecture, one would first need to learn to distinguish between two distinct and ultimately incompatible approaches to the study of the arts. The first, which he called the historical (*geschichtliche*) and the scientific (*wissenschaftliche*), was that which characterized the work of the scholar, the *Gelehrter*. The second, in Spitta's view, was an approach rightly embraced only by practicing artists themselves: the aesthetic.

To judge a work of art from the aesthetic standpoint, Spitta argued, is to consider solely "the finished, self-contained work itself." For one inclined to such an orientation, "the degree to which the creation of a work was shaped by the individuality of its creator, by his age, by his nation, or by any other kind of external circumstances might be of interest to a certain extent." However, "such considerations will never be of decisive importance to him." Instead, the attention of such an observer "is always directed toward . . . the most beautiful and the highest, toward that which lifts life upward beyond the stars." Grounding his judgments in metaphysical, presumably Hegelian assumptions about the nature of art and its significance, the aesthetically inclined individual regards the artwork as a manifestation of "the idea" (*das Idee*). He assesses its effectiveness and worth accordingly, by striving to ascertain whether it embodies the idea "wholly or in part." "That," for Spitta, "is what determines the worth of an artwork" for the *Aesthetiker*.[11]

To consider a work of art from the historical or scientific perspective, on the other hand, is to endeavor to describe the objects of one's studies in as objective a

9. Philipp Spitta, "Kunstwissenschaft und Kunst," in *Zur Musik. Sechzehn Aufsätze* (Berlin: Gebrüder Paetel, 1892), 3–14.

10. Spitta's colleague, Heinrich Bellermann, and his predecessor, Adolf Bernhard Marx, had been professors of, simply, *Musik*. For a detailed account of Spitta's life and work during this period, see Wolfgang Sandberger, *Das Bach-Bild Philipp Spittas. Ein Beitrag zur Geschichte der Bach-Rezeption im 19. Jahrhundert*, Beihefte zum Archiv für Musikwissenschaft, no. 39 (Stuttgart: Franz Steiner Verlag, 1997), 27–56.

11. Spitta, "Kunstwissenschaft und Kunst," 4–5: "Das Urtheil, welches ein Künstler über ein Kunstwerk hat, wird entscheidend bedingt nur durch die fertige, in sich abgeschlossene Ereshcinung. Er kennt nur absolute Maßstäbe. Inwieweit der Schöpfer eines Werkes durch seine Individualität, seine Zeit, seine Nation, durch allerhand äußere Umstände gebunden war, das mag ihn gelegentlich mehr oder weniger interessiren. Durchschlagende Bedeutung mißt er solchen Erwägungen niemals bei. . . . Sein Augenmerk richtet sich auf jene 'bildende Kraft, die,' wie es in Mignons Requiem

manner as possible and to eschew all attempts at aesthetic judgment in favor of the simple pleasures of empirical discovery. Spitta left no doubt as to where his own sympathies lay. "The man of science" (*der Mann der Wissenschaft*), he proclaimed, "recognizes no absolute and final goal toward which his work advances. Our knowledge is incomplete, and will always remain so." For Spitta, "the essence of the life of a scholar is simply the search for truth. He is fascinated by the part, not the whole—by that which is certain rather than that which is uncertain. For this reason he longs to know not *what* the artwork and its creator (the artistic personality) *are*, but *how they came to be*."[12]

To Spitta's mind, it was of the utmost importance that the scholar or *Gelehrter* take care to approach his work without lapsing, consciously or otherwise, into the mindset of the *Aesthetiker*. The scholar must endeavor to practice his craft by employing exclusively the "established methods" of the discipline, "acquired through extensive practice founded upon solid, positive knowledge" (*bestimmten positiven Wissens*). Above all else, the scholar must strive never to allow his emotional or sensual experience of an artwork to cloud his perception of it. "An energetic personality"—an artist or anyone else invested in questions of aesthetic worth—"will always be in danger of unconsciously introducing itself, a foreign element, into the artwork under consideration."[13] In order to avoid this situation, Spitta argued, scholars "must ignore beauty in all its abundance, as it can find no place in their system."[14] In Spitta's view, a person who seeks to understand and record the history of art must do everything within his power to bar his subjective impressions from intruding upon his investigations. He must strive to erase all traces of his personality from his writing, and he must overcome his inclinations to cast judgments that cannot be verified via empirical observations. In short, Spitta argued, the historian of art must endeavor to present its history, in Leopold von Ranke's famous yet perplexing words, "as it actually was" (*wie es eigentlich gewesen*).[15]

---

heißt, 'das Schönste, das Höchste, hinauf über die Sterne das Leben trägt.' Die Idee, welche in der Phantasie des Schaffenden aufgegangen ist, soll von ihm zur sinnlichen Erscheinung gebracht werden. Ob dies ganz, oder bis zu welchem Grade es gelungen ist, darnach richtet sich für ihn der Werth des Kunstwerks."

12. Spitta, "Kunstwissenschaft und Kunst," 5 (emphasis added): "Der Mann der Wissenschaft kennt kein absolutes Endziel seiner Arbeit. Unser Wissen ist Stückwerk und wird es immerdar bleiben. ... Der Inhalt des Lebens eines Gelehrten ist nur das Suchen nach Wahrheit. Ihn fesselt der Theil, nicht das Ganze, das Bedingte und nicht das Unbedingte. So will er auch gegenüber dem Kunstwerke und seinem Schöpfer, der Künstlerpersönlichkeit, nicht sowohl wissen, was sie sind, als wie sie geworden sind." As Dahlhaus's work suggests, Spitta's essay was, with respect to these arguments, representative of a broader trend. "In the latter part of the nineteenth century," Dahlhaus writes, "following the collapse of Hegelianism, the 'being' of a work was regularly consigned to aesthetics and its 'becoming' to history" (Dahlhaus, *Foundations*, 127).

13. Spitta, "Kunstwissenschaft und Kunst," 7: "Ein energisch ausgeprägte Individualität wird stets in Gefahr sein, sich selbst unbewußt einen fremden Zug in das vorhandene Kunstwerk hineinzutragen."

14. Spitta, "Kunstwissenschaft und Kunst," 9: "Gelehrte...müssen eine Fülle von Schönheit ignoriren, weil sie in ihr System sich nicht einfügen läßt."

15. Cited in R. G. Collingwood, *The Idea of History* (Oxford: Clarendon Press, 1946), 130.

While the dozen volumes that Hanslick published from 1870 through the end of the century did indeed consider historical subjects, they were decidedly *not*, in Jodl's view, the work of a *Gelehrter* as Spitta had described it. In those volumes, Hanslick had not striven to separate himself from the objects of his research. In the manner of Spitta's derided *Aesthetiker*, Hanslick made no attempt to disguise the fact that his historical narratives were peppered throughout with subjective impressions of the value and meaning of individual artworks. With this situation in mind, it is important to recall that Spitta's arguments, no less than Jodl's, were disciplinary, even political in nature. In raising them, the pioneering historian responded to a question broached two decades earlier by his fellow historian of music, Friedrich Chrysander: how to bestow academic respectability upon the study of an art that was widely deemed "too vague to be subjected to the strictest demands of science" (*Wissenschaft*).[16] In Spitta's view, the doubts expressed by late-century academics about the merits of music study were not prompted by music's "vagueness" but by the lack of methodological rigor with which writers on the art had typically approached their work. Historians and scholars of music, Spitta held, had simply failed to behave like their colleagues working in other disciplines. Rather than adopting an empirical, objective stance toward the objects of their studies, they had approached their material like artists, or like writers still in thrall to the idealist philosophies and speculative modes of inquiry that had long ago ceded their once-central place in German academe to the natural sciences and scientifically inspired modes of research. While students of the visual arts had made great strides explaining problems of style, transmission, and perception by way of empirical observation and inductive modes of investigation, scholars of music still occupied themselves with such unscientific pursuits as speculative aesthetics and hermeneutic analysis. What his colleagues needed to do, Spitta felt, was to focus upon the description rather than the evaluation of artworks and events. They needed to approach their work in a methodical fashion, to engage in painstaking study, and to strive to separate themselves, as observing subjects, from the objects of their research. Picking up on Spitta's arguments in his "Scope, Method, and Goal of Musicology" of 1885, the young Guido Adler went one step further in his own attempt to delimit the boundaries of acceptable music scholarship. In his now-famous tabular representation of the musicological field, Adler exiled aesthetic theorizing (*Aesthetik der Tonkunst*) to the discipline's "systematic" (*Systematisch*) branch (Figure 1.1). In doing so, he signaled its genetic separation from what he considered the other, more essential side of music research, the "historical" (*Historisch*).[17]

16. Friedrich Chrysander, "Vorwort und Einleitung," *Jahrbücher für musikalische Wissenschaft* 1 (1863), 10; trans. in Bojan Bujić, ed., *Music in European Thought, 1851–1912*, Cambridge Readings in the Literature of Music (Cambridge: Cambridge University Press, 1988), 345–46.

17. Guido Adler, "Umfang, Methode und Ziel der Musikwissenschaft," *Vierteljahrsschrift für Musikwissenschaft* 1 (1885), 16–17. The outline is reprinted, with translation, in Bujić, *Music in European Thought*, 354–55. Adler cites Spitta's "Kunstwissenschaft und Kunst" as inspiration for his work on pages 19–20 of his essay (353 in Bujić's volume). The secondary status of the systematic branch is made clear in Adler's prose description of his outline, where he observes that the

16   Guido Adler.   Umfang, Methode und Ziel der Musikwissenschaft.   17

In tabellarischer Übersicht ergiebt sich das Gesammtgebäude¹ also:

Musikwissenschaft.

I. Historisch.

(Geschichte der Musik nach Epochen, Völkern, Reichen, Ländern, Gauen, Städten, Kunstschulen, Künstlern).

A. musikalische Paläographie (Notationen).	B. Historische Grundclassen (Gruppirung der musikalischen Formen).	C. Historische Aufeinanderfolge der Gesetze, 1. wie sie in den Kunstwerken je einer Epoche vorliegen, 2. wie sie von den Theoretikern der betreffenden Zeit gelehrt werden. 3. Arten der Kunstausübung.	D. Geschichte der musikalischen Instrumente.

Hülfswissenschaften: Allgemeine Geschichte mit Paläographie, Chronologie, Diplomatik, Bibliographie, Bibliotheks- und Archivkunde. Literaturgeschichte und Sprachenkunde. Geschichte der Liturgien. Geschichte der musikalischen Künste und des Tanzes. Biographik der Tonkünstler, Statistik der musikalischen Associationen, Institute und Aufführungen.

II. Systematisch.

Aufstellung der in den einzelnen Zweigen der Tonkunst zuhöchst stehenden Gesetze.

A. Erforschung und Begründung derselben in der 1. Harmonik (tonal od. tonlich). 2. Rhythmik (tonal und temporär). 3. Melik (Cohärenz von tonal- und temporär).	B. Aesthetik der Tonkunst. 1. Vergleichung und Werthschätzung der Gesetze und deren Relation mit den apperzipirenden Subjecten behufs Feststellung der *Kriterien des musikalisch Schönen.* 2. Complex, unmittelbar und mittelbar damit zusammenhängender Fragen.	C. Musikalische Pädagogik und Didaktik [Zusammenstellung der Gesetze mit Rücksicht auf den Lehrzweck]: 1. Tonlehre, 2. Harmonielehre, 3. Kontrapunkt, 4. Compositionslehre, 5. Instrumentationslehre, 6. Methoden des Unterrichtes im Gesang und Instrumentalspiel.	D. Musikologie (Untersuchung und Vergleichung zu ethnographischen Zwecken).

Hülfswissenschaften: Akustik und Mathematik. Physiologie (Tonempfindungen). Psychologie (Tonvorstellungen). Logik (das musikalische Denken). Grammatik, Metrik und Poetik. Pädagogik. Aesthetik etc.

¹ Zum Vergleiche diene die synoptische Tafel nach Aristides Quintilianus, welche die vollständigste Übersicht über das musikalische Unterrichtsystem der Griechen enthält; die Übersetzung giebt die griechischen termini möglichst getreu, manchmal umschreibend, wenn der vollkommen deckende Ausdruck im Deutschen fehlt.

Systema der Musik.

I. ΘΕΩΡΗΤΙΚΟΝ (Theoretischer oder speculativer Theil.)

A. φυσικόν (Physikalisch-wissenschaftlich)		B. τεχνικόν (Special-technisch)		
a. ἀριθμητικόν (Arithmetik)	b. φυσικόν (Physik)	c. ἁρμονικόν (Harmonik)	d. ῥυθμικόν (Rhythmik)	e. μετρικόν (Metrik)

II. ΠΡΑΚΤΙΚΟΝ (Unterricht oder praktischer Theil.)

C. χρηστικόν (Compositionslehre)			D. ἐξαγγελτικόν (Ausübung oder Execution)		
f. μελοποιΐα (melodische Composition)	g. ῥυθμοποιΐα (rhythmische Composition oder angewandte Rhythmik)	h. ποίησις (Poetik)	i. ὀργανικόν (Instrumental-Spiel)	k. ᾠδικόν (Gesang)	l. ὑποκριτική (dramatische Aktion).

1885.

2

FIGURE 1.1   Guido Adler's tabular survey of *Musikwissenschaft*, from his "Scope, Method, and Goal of Musicology," 1885 (Adler, "Umfang, Methode und Ziel der Musikwissenschaft," 16–17).

To Jodl and his colleagues at the University of Vienna, pondering the future of music study at the turn of the twentieth century, Hanslick's work, however he had defined it, epitomized the working methods of the hopelessly unscientific *Aesthetiker*. Adler, in contrast, seemed to them a *Gelehrter* through and through. In the spring of 1898, after a protracted search by Jodl's committee, Adler was named Hanslick's successor. And with this, Jodl and his colleagues believed, an era had come to a close. No longer would the university provide a forum for debate about such vague aesthetic categories as the "the musically beautiful." With the establishment of the university's Institute for Music History under Adler's supervision in the fall of that year, the institution seemed newly poised to become a major center for empirical, scientifically oriented music research. Finally, Jodl and his colleagues hoped, the University of Vienna would play a leading role in directing the course of music study in a modern, scientific age.

But as we will see, the story behind the institutional revolution signaled by Adler's appointment was not as simple as one might suppose. For Hanslick, roundly dismissed as insufficiently scholarly at the time of his retirement in 1895, had begun his career as Austria's leading advocate for a scientifically inspired approach to music study. Having considered the reception of Hanslick's work at the end of his long career, we may now return to its beginning—to revisit the promise of his early work as regarded by his imperial employers and to pinpoint the ways in which they felt that that promise was unfulfilled.

HANSLICK'S AMBIVALENT LEGACY

When Hanslick declared, in the second edition of *On the Musically Beautiful* (1858), that if the search for musical understanding "is not to be wholly illusory, it will need to approach the methods of the natural sciences," he had a disciplinary point to prove.[18] Two years earlier, he had been appointed unpaid lecturer or *Privatdozent* at the University of Vienna, where he was charged with offering the institution's first-ever courses in music appreciation. Before he was awarded that post, he had earned his living as a clerk at the Imperial Ministries of Finance and Education and by writing reviews for *Die Presse*, one of Vienna's leading daily papers. Reflecting upon his life before academe in his autobiography of 1894, he recalled spending his nights at the Imperial Library, poring over volume after volume on music aesthetics. Over the course of his self-directed studies, he became aware that nearly all who had previously written on the subject had "posited the nature of music to consist in the 'feelings' aroused by it." Finding such positions curious at first and then increasingly troubling, he became deeply agitated by the

---

systematic branch "depends" or "is founded upon" the historical branch: "Der zweite Haupttheil der Musikwissenschaft ist der *systematische*: er stützt sich auf den historischen Theil" (11). Gabriele Eder has plausibly suggested that Adler's division of his field into historical and systematic branches might have been influenced by discussions with his friend, the philosopher Alexius Meinong; see Eder, *Alexius Meinong und Guido Adler*, 37–41.

18. Hanslick/Strauß, 1:22. For an alternate translation, see Hanslick/Payzant, 1. Historical and ideological contexts for Hanslick's statement are considered in the introduction to the present volume.

popular enthusiasm for Wagner's music and aesthetic theorizing that exploded shortly after mid-century. Finally, he took up his pen. "At that time," Hanslick wrote, "there arose noisily the first enthusiastic voices trumpeting Wagner's operas and Liszt's program symphonies. I allowed my own ideas about the subject to develop and mature within me until they took shape in the well-known pamphlet, *On the Musically Beautiful*."[19] Thus, simply, he recounted the writing of his soon-to-be-famous book, whose first edition appeared in 1854.

In *On the Musically Beautiful*, Hanslick laid out a program for listening to and discussing music that stood in deliberate contradistinction to the idealist modes of musical inquiry that reigned throughout most of mid-century German-speaking Europe. Taking aim at a broad array of writers—from Hegel to Wagner—whom he posited to represent prevailing attitudes toward his subject in his society, Hanslick urged his readers to focus their critical attention not upon any feelings aroused by hearing a work or upon any extra-musical ideas that it might conjure in the imagination but upon what he called, in a notoriously enigmatic turn of phrase, its "sounding form in motion." The latter, he argued, typically understood to denote the formal parameters of a composition, constituted music's "sole and exclusive content and object."[20] Hanslick pleaded for a reasoned, dispassionate discourse on the art that focused upon the empirical description of musical structures rather than abstract philosophizing about music's supposedly inherent qualities. And he implored his contemporaries to avoid confusing their subjective responses to the musics they heard for universally valid critical judgments.[21]

At the time he was drafting *On the Musically Beautiful*, filled with frustration over Wagner-inspired developments, Hanslick's work at the Ministry of Education afforded him a unique perspective on another aspect of Austrian culture in the midst of rapid change. In the wake of the uprisings of students, workers, and intellectuals that had swept through the Empire in 1848, the government

19. Hanslick, *Aus meinem Leben*, 2 vols. (Berlin: Allgemeiner Verein für Deutsche Litteratur, 1894), 1:236–37.

20. Hanslick/Strauß, 1:75; Hanslick/Payzant, 29: *"Tönend bewegte Formen* sind einzig und allein Inhalt und Gegenstand der Musik." The translation I have adopted here is from Mark Evan Bonds, *Music as Thought: Listening to the Symphony in the Age of Beethoven* (Princeton: Princeton University Press, 2006), 107. For helpful discussions of Hanslick's complicated statements on music's form and content, see also Dahlhaus, *The Idea of Absolute Music*, trans. Roger Lustig (Chicago: University of Chicago Press, 1989), 108–13; and Dahlhaus, "Eduard Hanslick und der musikalische Formbegriff," *Die Musikforschung* 20, no. 2 (1967), 145–53.

21. Hanslick's arguments remain deeply controversial with respect to both their author's intentions and their implications for music study, and the literature on his treatise is vast. For critiques of Hanslick's essential argument, see those studies cited in footnote 2 above. For more sympathetic readings of Hanslick's assertions, see, for instance, Geoffrey Payzant, *Hanslick on the Musically Beautiful: Sixteen Lectures on the Musical Aesthetics of Eduard Hanslick* (Christchurch, New Zealand: Cybereditions, 2002); Robert W. Hall, "Hanslick and Musical Expressiveness," *Journal of Aesthetic Education* 29, no. 3 (1995), 85–92; Christoph Khittl, "Eduard Hanslicks Verhältnis zur Ästhetik," in *Biographische Beiträge zum Musikleben Wiens im 19. und frühen 20. Jahrhundert*, ed. Friedrich C. Heller, Studien zur Musikgeschichte Österreichs, no. 1 (Vienna: Verband der wissenschaftlichen Gesellschaften Österreichs, 1992), 81–109; Peter Kivy, "What Was Hanslick Denying?" *Journal of Musicology* 8, no. 1 (1990), 3–18; and Payzant, "Hanslick on Music as Product of Feeling," *Journal of Musicological Research* 9, nos. 2–3 (1989), 133–45.

of the newly enthroned Emperor Franz Joseph had embarked upon a program of radical reform in the Habsburg Empire's leading institution of learning.[22] Beginning in 1849, the Ministry of Education, under the direction of the philosopher Franz Exner and the Count Leo Thun-Hohenstein, undertook to wean the university's philosophical faculty from centuries of control by the Catholic Church. Enlisting the help of one of Hanslick's childhood friends, the philosopher Robert Zimmermann, Exner and Thun-Hohenstein endeavored to refashion the faculty's curriculum, encompassing both the liberal arts and the natural sciences, in such a way as to rival the great universities of Berlin, Heidelberg, and Leipzig. They sought, however, to revise this curriculum along distinctly Austrian lines. Significantly, all three of these figures were devoted followers of the Bohemian philosopher Bernard Bolzano (1781–1848), who espoused a peculiar, Leibniz-inspired brand of anti-idealist metaphysics that devalued the experience of the perceiving subject and defined as the central goal of philosophical inquiry the search for permanent, objective truths. Long before the revolutionary year, Bolzano had become engulfed in political scandal, and as a result his work could be admired only from afar. But Exner, Zimmermann, and Thun-Hohenstein found a surrogate in the Saxon philosopher Johann Friedrich Herbart (1776–1841). Herbart shared Bolzano's dedication to the quest for absolute objectivity, and he preached a vision of static social harmony that readily found official support in a society where Hegelian idealism was widely associated with the political ideologies that had fueled the revolutions of 1848 and 1789.

From his post at the Ministry of Education, Hanslick could sense that the climate at the university might be amenable to an unprecedented addition to its curriculum: a course in music appreciation. Moreover, he felt that he himself would be the ideal person to teach it. After all, he already wrote about music for *Die Presse*. And the university had, in 1852, made its first-ever hire of an art historian, Rudolf Eitelberger.[23] But Hanslick also knew that his proposal would not be approved if it did not appear to be a natural fit with the broader plans of

22. The historical and philosophical contexts of these reforms are elaborated in Kurt Blaukopf, *Pioniere empiristischer Musikforschung. Österreich und Böhmen als Wiege der modernen Kunstsoziologie*, Wissenschaftliche Weltauffassung und Kunst, no. 1 (Vienna: Hölder-Pichler-Tempsky, 1995); and William M. Johnston, *The Austrian Mind: An Intellectual and Social History 1848–1938* (Berkeley and Los Angeles: University of California Press, 1972), esp. 274–96. A recent examination of the political background is provided in Karl Vocelka, *Geschichte Österreichs. Kultur – Gesellschaft – Politik* (Munich: Wilhelm Hayne, 2000), 198–220. My discussion in this paragraph is based upon these sources. For further consideration of Hanslick's relationship to this reform movement, see Christoph Landerer, "Ästhetik von oben? Ästhetik von unten? Objektivität und 'naturwissenschaftliche' Methode in Eduard Hanslicks Musikästhetik," *Archiv für Musikwissenschaft* 61, no. 1 (2004): 38–53; Landerer, "Eduard Hanslicks Ästhetikprogramm und die Österreichische Philosophie der Jahrhundertmitte," *Österreichische Musikzeitschrift* 54, no. 9 (1999), 6–20; and Payzant, "Eduard Hanslick and Robert Zimmermann," in *Hanslick on the Musically Beautiful*, 129–42. A valuable consideration of this movement in relation to Austrian art-historical study is provided in Michael Gubser, *Time's Visible Surface: Alois Riegl and the Discourse on History and Temporality in Fin-de-Siècle Vienna*, Kritik: German Literary Theory and Cultural Studies (Detroit: Wayne State University Press, 2006).

23. On Eitelberger's appointment, see Blaukopf, *Pioniere*, 105–8; Gubser, *Time's Visible Surface*, 106–7; and Martin Seiler, "Empiristische Motive im Denken und Forschen der Wiener Schule der Kunstgeschichte," in *Kunst, Kunsttheorie und Kunstforschung*, ed. Seiler and Stadler, 53–58.

Exner and Thun-Hohenstein. Eitelberger, at the time of his appointment, had professed himself a Herbartian.[24] And Thun-Hohenstein's petition to Emperor Franz Joseph on behalf of Eitelberger's candidacy had made clear the Count's belief that Eitelberger would contribute to the "Herbartization" of a field still in thrall to speculative traditions of aesthetic inquiry. "It is a matter of urgent necessity," Thun-Hohenstein wrote, "that the study of aesthetics be set upon a new foundation—namely, the rules of theory—and that this be developed from out of a penetrating study of the monuments of art themselves. The evaluation of these monuments must not follow, as has previously been the case, from the application of a theory arrived at by following an abstract path."[25] What Thun-Hohenstein called for, in Gustav Fechner's terms of two decades later, was an *ästhetik von unten*, an aesthetics "from below." No longer, the count argued, should scholars of art allow themselves to be guided in their work by a preconceived theory of artistic meaning and beauty—by an *ästhetik von oben*, one imposed "from above." Henceforth, and with Eitelberger's guidance, they must begin their studies by examining, in an empirical manner, the objectively verifiable characteristics inherent and unique to individual works of art.[26]

In Thun-Hohenstein's view, and in Eitelberger's as well, such an approach to the study of art had the potential to distinguish the work of Austrian scholars from the idealist traditions of art-historical inquiry that still reigned under the Hegelian Friedrich Vischer and his colleagues in the North.[27] When Hanslick drafted his own letter of application for a university post in 1856, he took pains to align himself with Thun-Hohenstein's program.[28] He argued that the establishment of a lectureship in music history and aesthetics was a logical next step after the recent founding of such a chair in the visual arts. And he assured the ministry that, in his own scholarship, "I keep my distance from discussions of a purely metaphysical sort. I stand closest to the philosophical system of *Herbart*."[29]

24. Seiler, "Empiristische Motive," 55.

25. Cited in Seiler, "Empiristische Motive," 54: "Dringend erforderlich sei daher, das Studium der Ästhetik 'auf neue Grundlagen zu stellen, nämlich die Regeln der Theorie und einer eindringlichen Betrachtung der Denkmale der Künste selbst zu entwickeln, und nicht wie bisher eine auf abstraktem Wege gewonnene Theorie zur Würdigung der Kunstdenkmale anzuwenden.'"

26. Fechner coined these terms in his *Vorschule der Aesthetik* (1876), after which they quickly found their way into discussions of aesthetic texts extending back to Hanslick's work of the 1850s. See, for instance, Arthur Seidl, "Zur Aesthetik der Tonkunst," *Musikalisches Wochenblatt* 17 (1886), 273–75, 287–88, 303–4, 318–21. For a recent consideration of Hanslick's ideas in light of such discussions, see Christoph Landerer, "Ästhetik von oben." On Fechner's use of these terms, see Bujić, *Music in European Thought*, 275–76.

27. For more on Vischer's work, and for a selection from his *Aesthetik oder Wissenschaft des Schönen* (1857), see Bujić, *Music in European Thought*, 82–89. For Eitelberger's views on Vischer, see Blaukopf, *Pioniere*, 105–6.

28. The text of Hanslick's letter is transcribed in Hanslick/Strauß, 2:143–45. Further discussion of this document is provided in Blaukopf, *Pioniere*, 94–95; Payzant, "Eduard Hanslick and Robert Zimmermann," 136–37; and Khittl, "Eduard Hanslicks Verhältnis zur Ästhetik," 90.

29. Hanslick/Strauß, 2:145 (italics in the original): "Mein Prinzip, die aesthetischen Grundsätze einer Kunst aus deren eigenster, spezifischer Natur zu gewinnen, hält mich von rein metaphysischen Erörterungen fast gänzlich fern. Am nächsten stehe ich jedoch dem philosophischen System Herbarts."

In the first edition of *On the Musically Beautiful*, and without any reference to Herbart himself, Hanslick had staked out a position clearly in line with Thun-Hohenstein's Herbartianism. In his letter of application to the university, in an obvious reference to the *Habilitationsschrift* or book that would qualify him for the position he sought, he made clear that a revision of that book, the "imperfection" of which he readily acknowledged, was already well under way. His appointment was quickly approved.

Once he had embarked upon an academic career in the autumn of 1856, Hanslick immediately undertook a modest revision of his 1854 treatise. As Dahlhaus has observed (he has recently been joined by others), the bulk of Hanslick's revisions consisted of altering or removing those statements that had, in the first edition of his volume, most clearly revealed the idealist underpinnings of many of its central arguments.[30] He deleted his earlier reflections about music as the "sounding image of the great motions of the universe," about musical works revealing to the listener "the infinite in works of human talent," and about art as a "reflection of the great laws of the world."[31] He also revised his statements about the need to model the study of music after the empirical and inductive "methods of the natural sciences," already present in the first edition of his treatise, into a virtual credo.[32] But as Christoph Landerer has recently suggested, we have good reason to doubt the sincerity of many of Hanslick's gestures. First, in spite of its author's assertions to the contrary, *On the Musically Beautiful* was, at its heart, a deeply idealist work. Second, Hanslick's reference to Herbart in his letter of application was his first mention of the philosopher's name in any of his surviving writings. And third, statements like Hanslick's about "the methods of the natural sciences" were ubiquitous in Austrian texts of the period. In addition to making clear one's

---

30. Dahlhaus, *The Idea of Absolute Music*, esp. 27–30 and 108–13; Dahlhaus, "Eduard Hanslick und der musikalische Formbegriff," 145–53; and Dahlhaus, *Esthetics*, esp. 52–57. Other studies that examine the idealist underpinnings of *On the Musically Beautiful* include Landerer, "Ästhetik von oben"; Mark Evan Bonds, *Music as Thought*, 108–11; Mark Burford, "Hanslick's Idealist Meterialism," *19th-Century Music* 30, no. 2 (2006), 166–81; Yoshida Hiroshi, "Zur Idee der musikalischen Öffentlichkeit: Eine erneuerte Interpretation der Musikästhetik Eduard Hanslicks," *Aesthetics* [Japan] 10 (2002), 87–94; and Bonds, "Idealism and the Aesthetics of Instrumental Music at the Turn of the Nineteenth Century," *Journal of the American Musicological Society* 50, nos. 2–3 (1997), 387–420.

31. These passages are found in Hanslick/Strauß, 1:75 and 171. They are translated in Bonds, *Music as Thought*, 109–10; and Bonds, "Idealism," 414–15.

32. The change in Hanslick's tone is evident, for instance, in his prefatory statements about "the methods of the natural sciences." In the first edition of his treatise (1854), Hanslick implored his readers "to make way for an upswing of science [*Wissenschaft*] in the treatment of aesthetic questions as well," and he predicted that, "in time," one would see, in music research, both "a powerful influence and the upper hand granted to an orientation directed toward the inductive method of the natural sciences rather than metaphysical principles." In the second edition (1858), he asserted bluntly that "the longing for knowledge that is as objective as possible, which is, in our time, felt in all areas of inquiry, must necessarily make itself felt in the investigation of *beauty* as well." And he insisted that if the significance of such inquiry is not be "wholly illusory, it will need to approach the methods of the natural sciences." For the original texts, see Hanslick/Strauß, 1:21, 22.

ostensible allegiance to the Herbartian movement in art-historical scholarship, they also—and no less importantly—signaled one's employability in the culture of post-1848 Austrian academe.[33]

After Hanslick was promoted to the salaried, tenured rank of associate (*außerordentlicher*) professor in 1861, he set to work upon the project at which he had hinted in his letter of application: to expand the arguments advanced in *On the Musically Beautiful* into a systematic, Herbartian aesthetics of music. Soon after he embarked upon that task, however, he grew disillusioned in his work. As we will see in chapter 2, he quickly became frustrated in his efforts to identify objective criteria by which musical beauty can be judged. In the mid-1860s, feeling worn out by the exercise, he veered sharply from his original path, disavowing the Herbartian movement and turning instead to the study of cultural history. In 1869, Hanslick completed his second book-length study, *History of Concert Life in Vienna*, in a strongly Hegelian vein. And almost immediately after that, he made another, more radical turn. In his third book, *From the Concert Hall* (1870), he elaborated a novel and self-consciously subjective history of Viennese musical life whose documentary sources consisted entirely of his own previously published critical essays. Thus he arrived at the project that would occupy him until the end of his career.[34]

With Hanslick's abandonment of the Herbartian path, Thun-Hohenstein's hope that the university's new chair in music would become a bastion of scientifically inspired research faded. Indeed, the center of gravity with regard to the empirical study of musical phenomena seemed to shift outside the faculty of music altogether when the physicist Ernst Mach took up the cause of Hermann von Helmholtz's psychoacoustic theories of music perception in 1863. Declaring his intention to elucidate for the public "Helmholtz's theory of music, which grounds the laws of music in the simple laws of physics and psychology and ties together acoustics, music theory, and aesthetics," Mach all but announced his intention to seize from Hanslick's grasp the vanguard of the Herbartian movement.[35] Soon, the pioneering work of Mach and Helmholtz would be complemented by the psychoacoustic research of Gustav Fechner in Leipzig and Carl Stumpf in Prague. Given Hanslick's continuing failure to produce a "scientific" study of his own, these developments could only have made matters worse in Thun-Hohenstein's view.

33. Landerer, "Ästhetik von oben." As Payzant has observed with respect to this issue, "if one sought a teaching position in Austria, philosophical or otherwise, one had to be, or profess to be, a Herbartian" (Payzant, "Eduard Hanslick and Robert Zimmermann," 131).

34. It should be noted that although Hanslick published ten editions of *Vom Musikalisch-Schönen* during his lifetime, he made few substantial changes to the text after the publication of the second in 1858. The text of all ten editions is provided in Hanslick/Strauß, vol. 1.

35. Ernst Mach, *Einleitung in die Helmholtz'sche Musiktheorie. Populär für Musiker dargestellt* (1866); cited in Blaukopf, *Pioniere*, 112. A photographic reproduction of an advertisement for Mach's University of Vienna lectures on Helmholtz's work from the 1863–64 academic year can be seen in John T. Blackmore, *Ernst Mach: His Work, Life, and Influence* (Berkeley and Los Angeles: University of California Press, 1972), first photographic plate after page 202.

To be sure, Hanslick's failure to complete his promised Herbartian aesthetics was seen by some as a sign of more spectacular failings: of the University of Vienna and the Ministry of Education to foster a revolution in music study comparable to that already well underway in other fields of humanistic inquiry. But Hanslick's work as a philosopher, limited though it was, was wildly successful in other ways. For as Rudolf Schäfke was first to observe almost a century ago, the simple language and lively style of *On the Musically Beautiful* succeeded in drawing legions of readers from diverse backgrounds into aesthetic debate.[36] Inspired by the frequent reprinting of Hanslick's text, generations of writers, from August Wilhelm Ambros in the 1850s to Heinrich Schenker in the 1890s, sought to make their mark upon the musical world by challenging Hanslick's formalist assertions in aesthetic tracts of their own.[37] Moreover, despite—or, in many cases, because of—the fact that Hanslick had implored his readers to proceed empirically and "from below" in their investigations, many of his detractors framed their rebuttals in avowedly speculative, even subjective terms. This too, ironically, became an enduring part of Hanslick's intellectual legacy.

One such response to Hanslick's volume, particularly revealing of the disciplinary conundrums posed by this polemical trend, came from Friedrich von Hausegger, a philosopher and music critic who taught aesthetics at the University of Graz. In a volume entitled *Music as Expression* (*Die Musik als Ausdruck*, 1885), Hausegger confronted one of the cardinal concerns of contemporary aesthetic inquiry: the source and nature of the listener's sense of musical coherence. Like many writers of his generation, Hausegger was inspired in his work by his doubts about Hanslick's formalist arguments.[38] Significantly, two decades before Hausegger published his book, Helmholtz, in his *On the Sensations of Tone* (1863), had identified by way of empirical observation and described with mathematical precision the "tonal relationship" that provides an essential, psychoacoustical basis for our sense of musical coherence.[39] Hausegger, however, was as unconcerned with harmony as he was with empirical investigations generally. Writing in the second edition of his book, published in 1887, he argued that the coherence of a work owes its origins to a phenomenon he called the *impulse*: a

36. Rudolf Schäfke, *Eduard Hanslick und die Musikästhetik* (Leipzig: Breitkopf und Härtel, 1922), 3–4.

37. The most thorough consideration of contemporary responses to Hanslick's work remains Schäfke, *Eduard Hanslick*, esp. 32–47.

38. Friedrich von Hausegger, *Die Musik als Ausdruck*, 2d ed. (Vienna: Carl Konegen, 1887). On Hausegger's life and work, see Joachim Danz, *Die objektlose Kunst. Untersuchungen zur Musikästhetik Friedrich von Hauseggers*, Kölner Beitrag zur Musikforschung, no. 118 (Regensburg: Gustav Bosse, 1981). On Hausegger's book as a response to Hanslick, see also Schäfke, *Eduard Hanslick*, 40–42. Further consideration of the relationship between the aesthetic positions of these figures is provided in Stephen McClatchie, *Analyzing Wagner's Operas: Alfred Lorenz and German Nationalist Ideology*, Eastman Studies in Music (Rochester: University of Rochester Press, 1998), 34–41.

39. Hermann von Helmholtz, *On the Sensations of Tone as a Physiological Basis for the Theory of Music*, trans. Alexander J. Ellis (New York: Dover, 1954). A summary of Helmholtz's arguments regarding the "tonal relationship" is provided on pages 246–49. Its aesthetic implications are considered on pages 362–71; the term itself appears on page 364.

psychological stimulus that provides the impetus for artistic creativity. "Unity of form," Hausegger explained, "is perceived as an organizational scheme that can be traced back to a single, indivisible, dynamic impulse. That is, a pattern is apparent in the collection of tones that we can recognize as the product of a *single* stimulus."[40] As listeners, he argued, we recognize this property of a composition when it arouses in our own minds and bodies the physiological symptoms of its composer's emotional state at the moment of its genesis. This sense of unity, Hausegger explained, was something intuitively felt but ultimately impervious to empirical description or analysis. He wrote:

> It does not suffice that the parts of the form appear to the examining eye as a symmetrical construction. Just as we place higher demands on the perfectly correct melody, if it should appear to us as an artistic product, we also demand from musical form that it satisfy more than our sense for symmetry and harmonic ordering. We want to *feel* the unity and beauty of form. In the sympathetic vibrations of our body it becomes clear to us that the form has sprung from similar bodily vibrations, which have arisen as the necessary result of an arousing impulse, and thus as an inclination toward expressive motion.[41]

In contrast to Helmholtz, Hausegger made no attempt to support his assertions with objectively verifiable data. Indeed, he provides no indication that his theory is founded upon empirical research of even the most informal kind. At its foundations, Hausegger's theory is literally subjective; it is, in the words of Andrew Bowie, "grounded in ourselves."[42]

Hausegger was not, however, interested in the problem of coherence merely for the sake of philosophical exercise. Rather, he published *Music as Expression* in order to elaborate, in general and abstract terms, theories about music's structure and meaning that might be relevant to the study of real-world musical problems. When confronted with the lapses of coherence that he detected in Bruckner's symphonies, for instance, he invoked his theory of the impulse in order to account for his impressions and to defend the value of the composer's work in spite of such occasional problems. Writing in the *Grazer Tagblatt* in 1895, he observed:

> If [Bruckner] appears, in the midst of his massive themes, suddenly overcome by their power—as it were, abandoning himself to their flow—so the master gains control over them—contrary to his genius—in contrapuntal or developmental

---

40. Hausegger, *Die Musik als Ausdruck*, 197: "Die Einheitlichkeit der Form bekundet sich in einer Eintheilung, welche sich auf einen einheitlichen Bewegungsimpuls zurückführen läßt, so daß sich in der Gruppirung der Tonmassen eine Gliederung erkennbar macht, welche sich als Ausfluß *eines* Anstoßes kennzeichnet."

41. Hausegger, *Die Musik als Ausdruck*, 197–98: "Es genügt nicht, daß die Theile der Form dem prüfenden Auge als ein symmetrischer Aufbau erscheinen. Genau so, wie wir an die vollkommen correcte Melodie noch eine höhere Anforderung stellen, wenn sie als künstlerisches Product wirken soll, verlangen wir auch von der musikalischen Form, daß sie mehr vermöge, als unsere Sinne für Symmetrie und harmonische Anordnung zu befriedigen. Die einheit und Schönheit der Form wollen wir *empfinden*. In den Mitschwingungen unseres Körpers wird es unserer Empfindung klar, daß die Form ähnlichen Körperschwingungen entsprungen ist, welche sich als die nothwendige Folge eines erregenden Impulses, demnach als eine Inclination zu Ausdrucksbewegungen ergeben haben."

42. Andrew Bowie, *Aesthetics and Subjectivity from Kant to Nietzsche*, 2d ed. (Manchester: Manchester University Press, 2003), 2.

passages. Then, at times, the unity of form is lost beneath the artful folding of the gown. It is not as if his artistic skill overpowers the impulse entirely. Indeed, the impulse is always felt. That is what makes Bruckner a great symphonist. But his artistic skill does get the upper hand at times.[43]

With Bruckner, Hausegger argued, the unconscious functioning of the creative impulse assures the coherence of most of his work. Only when the composer attempts, consciously and unwisely, to direct the spontaneous outpourings of his imagination does the unity of his music suffer.

Significantly, Hausegger's statements on Bruckner and his symphonies touched upon a number of issues that also figured prominently in the scholarly investigations of Adler, Spitta, and their scientifically inspired colleagues: questions about musical form, the compositional process, and a host of biographical issues. And it was in this fact, from the perspective of the latter group, that the danger of work such as Hausegger's resided. In an age that had seen the dominant methodologies of research in almost every other academic discipline shift from the philosophical to the scientific, they wondered, could the study of music continue to be dominated by subjective investigations and metaphysical philosophizing? Would music study ever be taken seriously within the academic community if it remained invested in speculative aesthetics and subjective criticism, those very modes of musical inquiry that Hanslick's work had, ironically, encouraged? The answer, Adler reasoned, was no.

As Spitta and Adler were well aware, neither Hausegger's work nor that of his critic-cum-aesthetic-philosopher peers had engendered much respect for music scholarship among the physicists, chemists, and other natural scientists who had risen to the top of German academe over the course of the preceding half-century. Surely, Adler felt, there must be a way to approach the study of music's history, structure, style, and meaning that would approximate the methodological rigor foreseen by the Herbartians and that had been exemplified in Helmholtz's investigations of harmony.[44] If the study of music, in all of its aspects, was ever to attain a respected place in the universities of German-speaking Europe, its practitioners would have to take seriously the challenge that Hanslick set forth in 1858 but had abandoned shortly thereafter. The field as a whole, Adler reasoned, would have to become a science.

43. Hausegger, "Anton Bruckner," *Grazer Tagblatt* (February 8, 1895); repr. in *Gedanken eines Schauenden. Gesammelte Aufsätze*, ed. Siegmund von Hausegger (Munich: F. Bruckmann, 1903), 243: "Erscheint er aber in seinen wuchtigen Themen unmittelbar erfasst von ihrer Gewalt, sich gleichsam willenlos hingebend ihrem Flusse, so gewinnt in den kontrapunktischen Durchführungen nicht selten an Stelle des Genius der Meister Herrschaft über sie. Die Einheit der Gestalt verliert sich dann zuweilen hinter der kunstreichen Faltung des Gewandes. Nicht als ob die Kunstfertigkeit den Impuls dann ersetzen würde; der Impuls ist stets zu spüren, und dieser ist es ja, welcher Bruckner zum grossen Symphoniker macht. Die Kunstfertigkeit übermeistert ihn aber zuweilen."

44. Adler made this point explicitly in a pair of unpublished drafts of his "Scope, Method, and Goal of Musicology," possibly delivered as lectures. See his "Das Studium der Musikwissenschaft" (undated manuscript), 7; and "Das Studium der Musikwissenschaft auf der Universitaet" (dated, apparently in Adler's hand, "?1881 1885"), 9. Both are preserved in the Guido Adler Papers (MS 769; hereafter cited GAP) of the Hargrett Rare Book and Manuscript Library/University of Georgia Libraries, box 1, folder 16. Later in life, Adler recorded his disparaging views of Hausegger's work in letters to his friend Alexius Meinong; see Eder, *Alexius Meinong und Guido Adler*, 31–32 and 157.

RESPONSES AND REPERCUSSIONS: ADLER'S "SCOPE, METHOD, AND GOAL OF MUSICOLOGY"

Although Hanslick's break from the Herbartian movement was complete by 1870, the reforms underway at the University of Vienna that had led to his appointment continued unabated in their course. In 1874, the university's philosophical faculty was joined by Franz Brentano, a bold, even audacious anti-idealist who preached to his students—Adler among them—that "the true method of philosophy is nothing other than that of the natural sciences."[45] One year earlier, another empiricist had been appointed to the faculty of art history: Moriz (also Moritz) Thausing, an Eitelberger student who sought to codify in lectures and writings what his mentor had been teaching for years.[46] In the seminal lecture Thausing delivered to inaugurate his appointment, he strove to cast off, once and for all, all associations that art-historical study might still seem to have with speculative aesthetics. "It is with great injustice that one heaps these two fields of study [*Wissenschaften*] together," he argued, "since they are completely different with respect to their methods and the problems they consider." In the published version of his lecture, entitled "The Status of Art History as a Science" ("Die Stellung der Kunstgeschichte als Wissenschaft"), Thausing explained:

> Art history has nothing in common with aesthetics as a philosophical discipline, or at least nothing more than political history has with moral philosophy, physiology has with psychology, or natural history [*Naturkunde*] has with metaphysics. That is, it supplies aesthetics with the materials required [by the latter] for philosophizing. But whatever comes of this has no bearing whatsoever upon the study of art history. In turn, art history is absolutely forbidden from reaching over into the territory of philosophy and appropriating from it any kind of system, and also from making use of such a system in its presentations. Art history has nothing whatsoever to do with deduction, with speculation. Its charge is to trade not in aesthetic judgments but in historical facts, which can serve as material for inductive research. ... The question, for instance, about whether a painting is beautiful is, for art history, unjustified. And a question about such an issue as whether Raphael or Michelangelo, Rembrandt or Rubens achieved greater perfection in their work is an art-historical absurdity. For me, the best history of art is one in which the word *beautiful* never appears.[47]

In Thausing's lecture, there is a great deal that resonates with Spitta's "Art and the Study of Art" considered at the beginning of this chapter. Most importantly, both authors sought to draw an unbridgeable line of separation between "his-

---

45. Blaukopf, *Pioniere*, 119: "...die wahre Methode der Philosophie keine andere als die der Naturwissenschaften sei." On Brentano's work and influence at the university, see pages 118–21 and 140–42 of Blaukopf's study; and Johnston, *The Austrian Mind*, 290–307.

46. For a valuable consideration of Thausing, a neglected figure, see Gubser, *Time's Visible Surface*, chapter 6.

47. Moriz Thausing, "Die Stellung der Kunstgeschichte als Wissenschaft," in *Wiener Kunstbriefe* (Leipzig: E. A. Seemann, 1884), 5; also cited in Seiler, "Empiristische Motive," 62: "Sehr mit Unrecht wirft man diese beiden Wissenschaften zusammen, denn dieselben sind in Methode und

torical" and "aesthetic" approaches to art-historical research. And there is also much in Thausing's essay that anticipates Adler's "Scope, Method, and Goal of Musicology." For the art historian as for the musicologist, the question of his discipline's academic legitimacy hinged upon his colleagues' embrace of the spirit of "the most real [*realsten*] of our sciences, the natural sciences."[48] And this, as both writers repeatedly emphasized, meant adopting empirical and inductive approaches to the study of one's material. Indeed, it is possible that Adler drew more than a little inspiration from Thausing's polemic as he sat down to record his own scientifically inspired vision of the future of his discipline. In the opening paragraph of the published version of Thausing's inaugural lecture, which appeared two years before Adler's essay, Thausing declared his intention to outline the "scope, method, and problems of art-historical research" (*Umfang, Methode und Probleme der kunstgeschichtlichen Forschung*). Toward his lecture's end, he, like Adler, turned to a consideration of his discipline's "goals" (*Ziele*).[49]

By the time he began drafting his manifesto in the early 1880s, Adler had become painfully aware that although Thausing's notion of a scientific approach to the study of the visual arts had been widely embraced by contemporary academics, the idea of an analogous "science of music" was still widely regarded as laughable. We have already considered Wagner's joking response to such a proposition in the mid-1870s, as recorded in Adler's memoirs.[50] A decade later, when Adler moved to Prague to assume a professorship in music history at that city's German University, he found that the very idea of a science of music was mocked by none other than his dean. In his autobiography, Adler recalled that

---

Problem von einander völlig verschieden. Mit der Aesthetik als philosophischer Disciplin hat die Kunstgeschichte nichts gemein, oder doch nicht mehr, als etwa die politische Geschichte mit der Moralphilosophie, die Physiologie mit der Psychologie, die Naturkunde mit der Metaphysik, d. h. sie liefert der Aesthetik wohl einen Theil ihres Stoffes zur weiteren philosophischen Verarbeitung, ob aber diese davon Gebrauch macht oder nicht, das tangirt die kunstgeschichtliche Forschung keineswegs. Die Kunstgeschichte ist jedenfalls nicht berechtigt, auch ihrerseits in das philosophische Gebiet hinüber oder hinauf zu greifen und ästhetische Formeln oder Ausdrücke irgend eines Systemes zu ihren Zwecken und in ihrer Darstellung zu verwerthen. Sie hat nichts zu thun mit Deduction, mit Speculation überhaupt; was sie zu Tage fördern will, sind nicht ästhetische Urtheile, sondern historische Thatsachen, welche dann etwa einer inductiven Forschung als Materiale dienen können. ... Die Frage z. B., ob ein Gemälde schön sei, ist in der Kunstgeschichte eigentlich gar nicht gerechtfertigt; und eine Frage wie: ob z. B. Raphael oder Michelangelo, Rembrandt oder Rubens das Vollkommenere geleistet haben, ist eine kunsthistorische Absurdität. Ich kann mir die beste Kunstgeschichte denken, in der das Wort 'schön' gar nicht vorkommt."

48. Thausing, "Die Stellung," 11: "Vielmehr ist es nur ein Weg genauer Prüfung und fortwährender Vergleichung, ähnlich demjenigen, den die realsten unserer Wissenschaften, die Naturwissenschaften einzuschlagen pflegen."

49. Thausing, "Die Stellung," 1; also cited in Seiler, "Empiristische Motive," 61. Thausing discusses the goals of art-historical study on pages 13–14. Along these lines, it is interesting to note that two drafts of Adler's "Scope, Method, and Goal of Musicology," one of which may have been written as early as 1881, bear the title "The Study of Musicology ("Das Studium der Musikwissenschaft"). It is possible that Adler devised the final title for this essay only after encountering the published version of Thausing's lecture, which first appeared in the journal *Oesterreichische Rundschau* in 1883. These drafts are preserved in GAP, box 1, folder 16.

50. See Adler, *Wollen und Wirken. Aus dem Leben eines Musikhistorikers* (Vienna: Universal Edition, 1935), 15–16. This exchange is discussed in detail in the introduction to the present study.

the dean, himself an art historian, greeted the young professor with the dismissive quip, "What shall the piano-player do for us?"[51] Adler's appointment in Prague, however, had come not at the urging of the dean but at the behest of Stumpf and Mach, both of whom, as natural scientists, occupied influential positions on the university's faculty and were themselves engaged in empirical research into a variety of musical phenomena.[52] Moreover, by the time he began lecturing at his new university, Adler already felt that he had a good idea about how the sorry state in which the musicological field had languished might, with his help, be improved.

Adler's plan, as he had begun to frame it over the course of the preceding years, was to do for music study precisely what Eitelberger and Thausing had done for the study of the visual arts. He would polemicize tirelessly on behalf of a scientific approach to music research and do whatever he could to galvanize those members of the musicological community who shared his views and concerns. His first step was to found a periodical that would serve as a mouthpiece for his colleagues and himself.[53] In Spitta, whose "Art and the Study of Art" echoed Thausing's inaugural lecture in many of its central points, he found an eager cofounder for his journal. He found his other collaborator in Friedrich Chrysander, an independent scholar from the Hanoverian town of Bergedorf who had attempted, single-handedly and with little success, to launch a similar periodical in the 1860s. Writing in the inaugural issue of his short-lived *Jahrbücher für musikalische Wissenschaft* (*Yearbooks for the Science of Music*) in 1863, Chrysander observed:

> If doubts have been expressed about whether the study of music [*musikalische Wissenschaft*] will ever attain the profundity and thoroughness attained by the study of the visual arts, that view may well be confirmed, even if unconsciously, by the various difficulties it faces. We understand this misjudgment quite well. Nonetheless, we shall permit ourselves to reveal as a misconception the primary reason generally adduced: that music is in essence far too vague to be subjected to the strictest demands of science [*Wissenschaft*].[54]

In answer to skeptics, Chrysander declared: "We use the word SCIENCE in the strictest and fullest sense. We are publishing these yearbooks with the title

---

51. Adler, *Wollen und Wirken*, 35: "Was soll uns der Klavierspieler?"

52. See Adler, *Wollen und Wirken*, 35–36; and Eder, *Alexius Meinong und Guido Adler*, 7–10. The peregrinations of Mach and Stumpf can be confusing and merit reviewing. Mach moved from the University of Vienna to the University of Graz in 1864, and from there to the German University in Prague in 1867, where he served as rector in 1883–84. He returned to the University of Vienna as a full professor (*ordinarius*) in 1895. Stumpf taught at Prague's German University, where he served as dean of the philosophical faculty, until the 1884–85 academic year.

53. For Adler's account of the founding of the journal, see *Wollen und Wirken*, 28–33.

54. Chrysander, "Vorwort und Einleitung," 10: "Hat man bezweifelt, dass die musikalische Wissenschaft an Höhe und innerer Vollendung je an die der bildenden Künste hinan reichen werde, so wird das Urtheil, wenn auch unbewusst, durch derartige Schwierigkeiten mit bestimmt sein. Wir begreifen eine solche Verkennung sehr wohl; nur den gemeinhin angeführten Hauptgrund, die Musik sei geistig viel zu unbestimmt als dass in ihrem Gebiete eine den höchsten Anforderungen entsprechende Wissenschaft entstehen könne, erlauben wir uns für eine Täuschung zu erklären." For an alternative translation, see Bujić, *Music in European Thought*, 345–46.

'for the science of music' [*für musikalische Wissenschaft*] in order to make it clear that it is the territory of science that we are entering, that we submit to the strictest claims of science, and that we intend to serve it, to the best of our powers, on the widest possible scale."[55] When the first issue of Adler's cooperatively edited journal, the *Vierteljahrsschrift für Musikwissenschaft* (*Quarterly Journal of Musicology*), appeared in January 1885, he, Spitta, and Chrysander announced in their prefatory essay that the new periodical would "take up again the experiment first attempted by the *Jahrbücher für musikalische Wissenschaft*." "The single purpose" of the *Vierteljahrsschrift*, they announced, would be "to serve science."[56]

In his lead article for the *Vierteljahrsschrift*, "The Scope, Method, and Goal of Musicology," Adler laid out his vision for the future development of his discipline. And although he did not address directly the question of musicology's institutional legitimacy in the published version of the essay, a manuscript draft reveals that this was indeed among his primary concerns when he wrote it.[57] In the spirit of Thausing's inaugural lecture and Thun-Hohenstein's Herbartian declarations, Adler argued that the scholarly study of music cannot begin with philosophical speculation but must proceed from a careful, objective, and empirical look at documentary sources—at individual musical works preserved in their unique and various ways.[58] To this end, he outlined a four-stage procedure, proceeding "from below," by which such source studies should be undertaken. First, the historian must make sure that he or she understands the notational system in which a work has been preserved.[59] Second, he or she must describe its formal construction: its rhythmic, harmonic, and polyphonic structures; the relationship between music and text; and its orchestration. Third, he or she must make comparative observations about the form, style, and genre of the work in relation

55. Chrysander, "Vorwort und Einleitung," 11; trans. in Bujić, *Music in European Thought*, 346: "WISSENSCHAFT nennen wir dies im ächten und vollen Sinne; und um es anzudeuten, dass wir hier in ihren Kreis eintreten, uns ihren strengsten Anforderungen nicht entziehen und ihr nach Kräften in ihrem ganzen Umfange dienen möchten, lassen wir die Jahrbücher unter dem Titel '*für musikalische Wissenschaft*' ausgehen."

56. Chrysander, Spitta, and Adler, "Vorwort," *Vierteljahrsschrift für Musikwissenschaft* 1 (1885), 3: "Die Vierteljahrsschrift für Musikwissenschaft will einen Versuch wieder aufnehmen, welcher zuerst mit den 'Jahrbüchern für musikalische Wissenschaft' gemacht... Die Unterzeichneten täuschen sich nicht über die Schwierigkeiten des Unternehmens, hoffen jedoch, daß es bei dem immer entschiedener hervortretenden Bedürfnisse und in der nunmehr gewählten Form leichter gelingen wird, dieselben zu überwinden und ein lebenskräftiges Organ zu schaffen, dessen einziger Zweck sein soll, der Wissenschaft zu dienen."

57. Adler, "Das Studium der Musikwissenschaft auf der Universitaet," esp. 11–12; preserved in GAP, box 1, folder 16. In this version of the essay, Adler frames his discussion around the question of whether the emergent discipline can best be fostered in universities or in conservatories. He concludes that it must be fostered in both.

58. For Thausing's remarks on source studies, see "Die Stellung," 8–10.

59. My choice of pronouns is deliberate. In his autobiography, Adler insisted that musicological research should be carried out by women as well as men, and he remarked proudly about the number of women who had attended his lectures and graduated from the University of Vienna's Musikhistorisches Institut under his supervision. Of course, however, academic appointments remained out of reach for women throughout Adler's lifetime. See Adler, *Wollen und Wirken*, 34 and 37–38.

to others that appear to be constructed similarly. Finally, the scholar may attempt to assess the effectiveness of the work according to aesthetic criteria. This latter stage, Adler explained, was that aspect of the scholar's task that had all too often been considered the "the only element, the Alpha and Omega of critical analysis." In his view, however, it was just one of four stages of the musicologist's charge, to be attempted only after an empirical, objective analysis of the musical artifact was complete.[60] Together, Adler argued, these four stages represent, "in general outline, the objectives of musical research. From these, the henceforth firmly established, systematic procedures of this science will be constructed."[61]

Echoing Thausing's remarks about the inductive mode of investigation as the cornerstone of scientific method, Adler elaborated upon the relationship between music study and the methods of the natural sciences. Identifying scholars of music with historians of the visual arts and charging both with uncovering the "laws" that determine the manifest character of their objects of study (the very activity that lay at the heart of Wilhelm Windelband's "nomothetic" understanding of *Naturwissenschaft*),[62] he explained:

> In order to complete his primary task, namely the study of artistic laws of different periods and their organic connection and development, the art historian will make use of the same methods as the natural scientist [*Naturforscher*]: in particular, *inductive* methods. From a number of examples he will separate what each has in common with the others from that which is unique, and he will make use of this abstract, giving preference to some features while leaving others to the side. The making of hypotheses is certainly permitted. To give further reasons for this would require a special essay, but the most important point regarding this issue consists in the analogy between the methods of art study and those of the natural sciences.[63]

In the spirit of Fechner's "aesthetics from below," Adler argued that scholars of music must proceed methodically in their research, from observations of particulars through increasing levels of abstraction, until the "central point" of their

60. Adler, "Umfang, Methode und Ziel," 6–8; trans. in Bujić, *Music in European Thought*, 349–50.

61. Adler, "Umfang, Methode und Ziel," 8 (this passage is not included in Bujić's volume): "Dies sind in allgemeinen Umrissen die Untersuchungsobjecte der musikwissenschaftlichen Forschung. Daraus wird das nunmehr festzustellende System dieser Wissenschaft aufzubauen sein."

62. Wilhelm Windelband, "Geschichte und Naturwissenschaft" (1894), in *Präludien. Aufsätze und Reden zur Philosophie und ihrer Geschichte*, 6th ed., 2 vols. (Tübingen: J. C. B. Mohr, 1919), 2:144–46. Adler's notion of *Kunstgesetze* and its relationship to Windelband's theory of historical knowledge is considered in the introduction to the present study.

63. Adler, "Umfang, Methode und Ziel," 15; trans. in Bujić, *Music in European Thought*, 351: "Zur Erreichung seiner Hauptaufgabe, nämlich zur Erforschung der Kunstgesetze verschiedener Zeiten und ihrer organischen Verbindung und Entwicklung wird sich der Kunsthistoriker der gleichen Methode bedienen wie der Naturforscher: vorzugsweise der *inductiven* Methode. Er wird aus mehreren Beispielen das Gemeinsame abheben, das Verschiedene absondern und sich auch der Abstraction bedienen, indem von concret gegebenen Vorstellungen einzelne Theile vernachlässigt und andere bevorzugt werden. Auch die Aufstellung von Hypothesen ist nicht ausgeschlossen. Die nähere Begründung des Gesagten sei einer speciellen Abhandlung vorbehalten, das Schwergewicht der Betrachtung liegt in der Analogie der kunstwissenschaftlichen Methode mit der naturwissenschaftlichen Methode."

endeavor is reached: "the study of *artistic laws* [*Kunstgesetze*] of different ages."[64] And above all else, he declared, his discipline "must restrict itself to focusing upon the obvious task that lies before it": achieving "mastery" of its methods.[65] In laying out his program for musicological study in his "Scope, Method, and Goal of Musicology," Adler attempted nothing less than to respond to the challenge posed to his discipline by Hanslick a quarter-century earlier. He sought to define a mode of music research that approached, as nearly as possible, the "methods of the natural sciences." In doing so, he hoped to correct the wrong turn that his discipline had taken with Hanslick's abandonment of the Herbartian path, and to redirect the course of music study in the Habsburg Empire and Europe as a whole. And in doing *that*, he sought to position himself to attain a goal he had coveted since his earliest years as a university lecturer: to succeed his former teacher in what seemed to him a university chair held for far too long.[66]

As important as Adler's essay was in making plain his disciplinary ambitions, his position was further clarified, as Kurt Blaukopf has pointed out, by the critique to which the disciplinary status quo—represented in the work and person of Hanslick—was subjected in a number of essays chosen for publication in the first volume of the *Vierteljahrsschrift*.[67] In a review of *On the Musically Beautiful* published in the *Vierteljahrsschrift* in 1885, Robert Zimmermann remarked that "if one were to lodge a single complaint" about the treatise, "it would be that its author has thus far failed to found, in a systematic way, an organic science of aesthetics upon his own principles."[68] And in another *Vierteljahrsschrift* essay from that year, Carl Stumpf, whose support for Adler had been crucial to the latter's appointment in Prague, likewise chided Hanslick for abandoning the challenge that he had posed to his colleagues at midcentury: to relinquish speculative approaches to music study in favor

---

64. Adler, "Umfang, Methode und Ziel," 9 (this passage is not included in Bujić's volume): "Den höchsten Rang nimmt die Erforschung der *Kunstgesetze* verschiedener Zeiten ein; diese ist der eigentliche Kernpunkt aller musikhistorischen Arbeit."

65. Adler, "Umfang, Methode und Ziel," 19; trans. in Bujić, *Music in European Thought*, 352.

66. As Eder has documented, Hanslick confided to his friend Alexius Meinong his desire to inherit Hanslick's post as early as 1883, and also his annoyance at Hanslick's apparent lack of inclination to retire as he approached his sixtieth year. See Eder, *Alexius Meinong und Guido Adler*, 8; and Eder, "Eduard Hanslick und Guido Adler," 116–17.

67. Blaukopf, *Pioniere*, 121–23. Significantly, Adler himself did not partake in open criticism of Hanslick, under whose guidance he had earned his doctorate. As Leon Botstein has observed, Adler remained, throughout his career, a professed admirer of his teacher despite the many differences that existed between the two; see Botstein, "Music and Its Public," 1368–71. In turn, Hanslick remained a firm supporter of Adler and his research in spite of the latter's polemics about the discipline. Hanslick even wrote a letter of recommendation on Adler's behalf when he was preparing to retire from the University of Vienna in 1895. In this letter, Hanslick praised Adler's achievements as a scholar, his facility as a writer, and his inauguration of the *Monuments of Music in Austria* (*Denkmäler der Tonkunst in Österreich*) series of critical editions. He did not, however, mention Adler's attempts to reform the musicological field. A photocopy of this letter, dated February 7, 1895, is preserved in GAP, box 22, folder 29.

68. Zimmermann, "Ed. Hanslick: Vom Musikalisch-Schönen," 252; also cited in Blaukopf, *Pioniere*, 122: "Wenn man eines beklagen darf, so ist es, daß dem Verfasser bisher nicht vergönnt war, seine Prinzipien in systematischer Weise als Ausbau einer organischen Wissenschaft der Ästhetik der Tonkunst zu gestalten."

of scientifically oriented ones. "Unfortunately," Stumpf wrote, "Hanslick himself has not once attempted to complete his task"—to outline a course of research "from below"—"within the boundaries that he himself identified as appropriate."[69]

In the decade that followed the launch of Adler's *Vierteljahrsschrift* in 1885, the University of Vienna emerged as one of Europe's leading centers for empirical, source-based studies of the visual arts. With the hiring of Alois Riegl in 1889, one even began to speak of a "Viennese School" of art-historical research.[70] In sharp contrast, this same decade saw the center of gravity for music research shift decisively outside of the Austrian capital. While Hanslick occupied himself with an ambitious attempt to dissolve the boundaries between historical research and critical reporting, empirical, inductive, and source-based approaches to music study were taking hold throughout much of the rest of the German-speaking world. In Leipzig, members of the Bach Society (Bach-Gesellschaft), dedicated to publishing critical editions of all of J. S. Bach's works, were unwittingly answering Thun-Hohenstein's call to historians to focus upon empirical studies of the "monuments" of art. In Hanover, Chrysander single-handedly launched a similar project dedicated to the work of George Frederic Handel. And the German University in Prague, which boasted Adler and Mach among its faculty, had emerged as the uncontested center of cutting-edge, scientifically oriented music research in the Austro-Hungarian Empire.

In the spring of 1895, however, change was in the air. With Hanslick's retirement at the age of sixty-nine, the University of Vienna was finally freed to change its course. That May, Ernst Mach moved from Prague to Vienna, and by the following year he had made his way onto the committee charged with naming Hanslick's successor. In 1896, the ethicist Friedrich Jodl likewise moved to Vienna from Prague and was immediately appointed the committee's recording secretary.[71] Convinced that they recognized what ailed the faculty of music at their new institution, Jodl and Mach also believed that they knew how the situation might be remedied and who would be the right person to do it. With the hiring of Adler in 1898, the migration of Prague's musicological minds to the Austrian capital was complete, and the transformation of the university's curriculum officially got under way. In the field of *Musikwissenschaft*, it seemed, a new age had finally dawned.

In a pair of pencil sketches made in the Austrian resort town of St. Gilgen during the summer of 1889, the Viennese painter Julius Schmid, on a holiday visit

69. Carl Stumpf, "Musikpsychologie in England. Betrachtungen über Herleitung der Musik aus der Sprache und aus dem thierischen Entwickelungsproceß, über Empirismus und Nativismus in der Musiktheorie," *Vierteljahrsschrift für Musikwissenschaft* 1 (1885), 345; also cited in Blaukopf, *Pioniere*, 122: "Leider hat Hanslick selbst die Aufgabe nicht einmal innerhalb der Grenzen, in denen er sie für ausführbar hält, zu lösen unternommen."

70. On Riegl and the Vienna School of Art History, see Gubser, *Time's Visible Surface*; Seiler, "Empiristische Methode"; and Margaret Iversen, *Alois Riegl: Art History and Theory* (Cambridge, MA: MIT Press, 1993).

71. Antonicek, "Musikwissenschaft in Wien," 174 and 176.

with Adler, recorded an image of the historian and his mentor that would have resonated with many in their day.[72] In the first of these sketches, preserved in Adler's estate (Figure 1.2a), a youthful Adler, head held high, strides forward confidently, as if on a mission of historical import and inevitable, necessary outcome. The only obstacle in his path is a tottering, aged Hanslick, eyes downcast and seemingly oblivious to the train of history about to run him over. In Schmid's second sketch, the moment of overcoming has arrived (Figure 1.2b). Adler literally overtakes his former teacher, leapfrogging Hanslick and, in the process, pushing him to the ground. The caption of this caricature reads "Guido and his predecessor" (*Guido und sein Vorgänger*).[73] Though still nearly a decade away at the time when these sketches were completed, the changing of Vienna's musicological guard already seemed, to the painter and his musicologist friend, a virtual fait accompli.

Recounting the story of the rise of positivism in Austrian academe from the perspective of the present day, it would be easy to dismiss Hanslick and his legacy as Schmid, Jodl, and many others did. But I would argue that to regard

FIGURES 1.2A, 1.2B   Julius Schmid, pencil drawings of Eduard Hanslick and Guido Adler, 1889, captioned "Guido and his predecessor." Courtesy of the Hargrett Rare Book and Manuscript Library/University of Georgia Libraries.

72. These sketches are preserved in GAP, box 71A, folder Familienbilder. The context in which they were apparently drawn is insightfully discussed Eder, "Eduard Hanslick und Guido Adler," 107–13.

73. Eder notes that this caption appears to be in Adler's hand rather than Schmid's, and she remarks as well on Adler's curious misspelling of Schmid's name (as *Schmidt*), given the closeness of their relationship and Schmid's reputation in late-century Vienna. See Eder, "Eduard Hanslick und Guido Adler," 113.

FIGURE I.2B

Hanslick as an old-fashioned, even sentimental foil to Adler and his scientifically inspired contemporaries would be neither fair nor accurate. For as we will
see, Hanslick became, in the final quarter of the century, a powerful, indeed
prescient antagonist of the intellectual movement he had helped to pioneer.
When he distanced himself from Herbartianism and the attempt to transform
musicology into a science, Hanslick did not retire from disciplinary debate, and
he did not put down his pen. He spent the remaining decades of his life publishing volume after volume—a dozen in all—of what he would eventually call a
"living history" (*lebendige Geschichte*) of Viennese musical life. In those volumes,
he strove not only to describe the events that comprised the historical unfolding
of musical life in his contemporary society but also to recount the impressions
made by those events upon the mind of the listener. In doing that, he engaged
in a provocative critique of the positivist movement and issued a prescient diag-
nosis of its risks. And most disturbingly, from the perspective of his detractors,
Hanslick issued this new challenge to his discipline from within the halls of the
university itself.

CHAPTER TWO

MUSIC CRITICISM AS
LIVING HISTORY

When Hanslick abandoned his Herbartian ambitions in the 1860s, his career took an unexpected turn. Rejecting the tenets of *On the Musically Beautiful* within a handful of years of its publication, he dedicated himself, while writing his second book (1869), to the study of Viennese cultural history in the idealist tradition of Hegel and his followers. Then, in his third book (1870), he veered once again, provocatively declaring *criticism*—the recording of subjective impressions, the casting of value judgments, and the indulging of aesthetic speculation—the central object of the *historian's* properly executed work. From that point forward, Hanslick held steadfastly to this latter position, proceeding to publish a dozen volumes in which he strove to transform the learned discourse on music in ways that were no less profound than those attempted by Adler and Spitta, Ernst Mach and Friedrich Chrysander. In those volumes, which he collectively called a "living history" (*lebendige Geschichte*) of Viennese musical life, Hanslick inscribed the critical essay within the historical narrative and insisted upon the history-making import of recording one's subjective impressions. In doing that, he attempted nothing less than to dissolve the opposition of *Aesthetiker* versus *Gelehrter* by which Friedrich Jodl and his university colleagues strove to delimit the musicological field.

To understand how the familiar Hanslick of *On the Musically Beautiful* became the forgotten author of a dozen volumes that brought a distinctly critical sensibility to the writing of music's history, we must retrace the stages by which he redefined himself not once but twice over the course of his career. We must consider those circumstances that led him, in the 1860s, to abandon his quest for aesthetic certainty and to embark upon a new life as a historian. Then we may examine his second turn, completed by 1870, when his transformation was even more remarkable.

FROM AESTHETICS TO HISTORY

At first blush, Hanslick's concern for dissolving the distinction between criticism and history might seem a natural outgrowth of his life's work as a critic.

After all, his career as a reviewer of concerts and newly published music began well before his turn to philosophy with the drafting of *On the Musically Beautiful*. Having made his debut in the critical press in the 1840s while a student in Prague, Hanslick's life as a critic seemed blessed at every turn. By 1855, he had become a regular contributor to *Die Presse*, one of Vienna's leading daily papers. A few years later, he followed his editor to the *Neue freie Presse* and thus became the chief music critic for what would soon become one of the leading periodicals in all of late-century Europe.[1]

By the time he was hired by the University of Vienna in 1856, Hanslick had risen to the top of the critical field. And that made him, *de facto*, one of the most influential music educators in the whole of the Habsburg Empire. For as Leon Botstein has observed, the critical essays of Hanslick and his colleagues served as an indispensable "guiding medium" for legions of late-century readers. Especially for those unable to play the piano and for whom concerts were financially out of reach, Hanslick's reviews provided "prose translations of the musical experience," imparting to their readers knowledge of, and a sense of proximity to, the unfolding of cultural life in their city.[2] Considered in this light, it is easy to understand why Hanslick, the consummate *feuilletonist*, would have been attracted by the opportunity to teach courses in music appreciation when an opportunity arose in the wake of the university's midcentury reforms. Indeed, we might reasonably assume that his critical historiography was born of similar concerns.

Yet to account for Hanslick's "living history" in this way would be to skip over a crucial stage in his intellectual development. For Hanslick's turn to a critical approach to historical writing was engendered not by feelings about the educational promise of music criticism but by his attempts to elaborate the empiricist program of music research outlined in *On the Musically Beautiful* into a systematic aesthetics of the art. Shortly after he was promoted to the salaried rank of associate (*außerordentlicher*) professor, as he recalled in his autobiography, he set to work revising his treatise along the Herbartian lines he had promised the Ministry of Education. Soon after he embarked upon this project, however, he felt his work bog down. Then, at some point toward the middle of the decade, he had a crisis of confidence and an epiphany. He described this series of events as follows:

> When I traded my post in civil service for that of an associate professor in the autumn of 1861, I was finally able to devote more time to my studies. But by then my studies had begun to move in a different direction. Within the span of a couple years, I had studied so many volumes on "aesthetics" and read so many books about

1. For Hanslick's account of his early years as a critic, see his *Aus meinem Leben*, 2 vols. (Berlin: Allgemeiner Verein für Deutsche Litteratur, 1894), 1:101–5 and 230–34.

2. Leon Botstein, "Music and Its Public: Habits of Listening and the Crisis of Musical Modernism in Vienna, 1870–1914" (Ph.D. diss., Harvard University, 1985), 878. See also Botstein, "Listening through Reading: Musical Literacy and the Concert Audience," *19th-Century Music* 16, no. 2 (1992), 129–45. Margaret Notley has examined the lopsided supply and demand for symphony concerts in Hanslick's Vienna in "*Volksconcerte* in Vienna and Late Nineteenth-Century Ideology of the Symphony," *Journal of the American Musicological Society* 50, nos. 2–3 (1997), 421–53; and Notley, *Lateness and Brahms: Music and Culture in the Twilight of Viennese Liberalism*, AMS Studies in Music, no. 3 (Oxford: Oxford University Press, 2007), 150–60.

the nature of music (finally arriving back at my own) that I became satiated with such philosophizing and tired of working with abstract concepts. On the other hand, I found salvation and inexhaustible pleasure in music history. These studies brought me to the conclusion that a truly fruitful aesthetics of music can only be developed if it is founded upon a penetrating historical awareness; at the least, it must proceed hand-in-hand with it. What is beautiful in music? Indeed, this has been answered in differing ways in different times, by different people and within different schools of thought. The more I immersed myself in the study of music's history, the more an aesthetics of music seemed to flutter all the more vaguely and airily before my eyes, almost like a mirage. It began to occur to me than an "Aesthetics of Music" worthy of the name cannot be written at this time.[3]

The more intensely Hanslick struggled to find the source of music's beauty in "the body of the thing itself," as he had written in *On the Musically Beautiful*, the more firmly he became convinced that he was looking in the wrong place if he wished to acquire such an understanding.[4] Indeed, he found himself sensing that the aesthetic criteria by which a work must be judged are not absolute and empirically verifiable but rather products of culture, the latter defined in both historical and geographical terms. He began to suspect that an illuminating understanding of musical phenomena can only be attained if one takes account of their embeddedness within creative and performative contexts that are each constitutive of their meaning. And to acquire that sort of understanding, he sensed, would require that one look beyond the boundaries of either formal analysis or philosophical speculation. Reflecting upon this realization from the perspective of later years, Hanslick described it as having marked a decisive turning point in his thinking and his career. Thereafter, he abandoned his plans to write the aesthetic volume he had promised his ministerial employer and turned his attention instead in a new and unexpected direction: toward the writing of cultural history.[5]

---

3. Hanslick, *Aus meinem Leben*, 1:242–43: "Als ich dann im Herbst 1861 meine Anstellung als Ministerialbeamter mit der eines außerordentlichen Professors vertauschte, da gewann ich allerdings freiere Zeit für meine Studien, aber diese selbst hatten allmählich eine andere Richtung genommen. Ich hatte ein paar Jahre lang so viele 'Ästhetiken' studiert, so viele Abhandlungen über das Wesen der Tonkunst, zuletzt über meine eigene Schrift gelesen, daß ich übersättigt war von diesem Philosophieren über Musik, müde des Arbeitens mit abstrakten Begriffen. Ich fand dagegen eine Rettung und einen unerschöpflichen Genuß in der *Geschichte* der Musik. Dieses Studium brachte mir die Überzeugung, daß eine wirkliche fruchtbare Ästhetik der Tonkunst nur auf Grundlage eindringender geschichtlicher Erkenntnis, oder doch nur Hand in Hand mit dieser möglich sei. Was ist schöne in der Musik? Ja, das haben verschiedene Zeiten, verschiedene Völker, verschiedene Schulen ganz verschieden beantwort. Je mehr ich mich in historisches Musikstudium vertiefte, desto vager, luftiger zerflatterte die abstrakte Musikästhetik, fast wie eine Luftspiegelung, vor meinen Augen. Es wollte mir scheinen, daß eine diesen Namen verdienende 'Ästhetik der Tonkunst' derzeit noch unausführbar sei."

4. Hanslick/Strauß, 1:22: "Sie wird, will sie nicht ganz illusorisch werden, sich der naturwissenschaftlichen Methode wenigstens soweit nähern müssen, daß sie versucht, den Dingen selbst an den Leib zu rücken."

5. The only previous study of which I am aware to consider Hanslick's turn from Herbartianism is Rudolf Schäfke, *Eduard Hanslick und die Musikästhetik* (Leipzig: Breitkopf und Härtel, 1922). With respect to this issue, my analysis of Hanslick's work might be read as a response to Schäfke's, for although we assume the same point of departure, Schäfke reads Hanslick's volumes of "living history" as statements of primarily aesthetic rather than historiographical import.

This is Hanslick's account of his turn. Yet, as the work of Carl Dahlhaus suggests, the roots of Hanslick's crisis of confidence can be found within *On the Musically Beautiful* itself. Although he considers neither Hanslick's memoirs nor his other historical writings, Dahlhaus identifies at the heart of Hanslick's aesthetic treatise a "paradox" that appears to foreshadow his epiphany of the 1860s.[6] In the first chapter of *On the Musically Beautiful*, Hanslick tried to prove that the feelings aroused by a work in the mind of the perceiving subject cannot constitute a proper foundation upon which to found an aesthetic system. He did this by arguing that such feelings are ephemeral and, moreover, conditioned by the personal and cultural experiences of a multitude of individual listeners. "Indeed, we can often barely understand how our grandparents could have considered *this* sequence of tones an adequate expression of precisely *that* affect," he explained in the first edition of his book. "Every age and cultural orientation [*Gesittung*] carries with it a different way of hearing and feeling, but the music remains the same. The only thing that changes is the effect that it has in accordance with changing conventional biases."[7] Any aesthetic judgment capable of standing up to reasoned scrutiny, Hanslick argued, must be founded upon more permanent, universal, and objectively verifiable criteria than these.

But when he turned, in the third chapter of his book, to a consideration of just what such criteria might be, he made a revealing slip: he conceded that the very idea of musical *beauty*—the central object of his own aesthetic inquiry—is likewise both culturally and historically relative. Just like an individual's emotional response, the listener's sense of beauty is also subject to the passing of time and, moreover, contingent upon the irreducible complexities of one's personal history and cultural biases. Musical beauty, in other words, is no more permanent or universal than the feelings that a work might arouse—feelings that, as he had previously argued, cannot provide a foundation for aesthetic judgment precisely on account of their transience. He wrote:

> There is no art that wears out so many forms as quickly as music. Modulations, cadences, melodic figures and harmonic progressions all in this manner go stale in fifty—nay, thirty—years, so that the gifted composer can no longer make use of them and will always be making his way toward the discovery of new, purely musical modes of expression. Without inaccuracy we may say, of many compositions that were outstanding in their day, that they *were*, once upon a time, beautiful.[8]

6. Carl Dahlhaus, *The Idea of Absolute Music*, trans. Roger Lustig (Chicago: University of Chicago Press, 1989; German orig., 1978), 108–13; Dahlhaus, "Eduard Hanslick und der musikalische Formbegriff," *Die Musikforschung* 20, no. 2 (1967), 146–48.

7. Hanslick/Strauß, 1:36: "Ja, wir befreifen oft kaum, wie unsre Großeltern *diese* Tonreihe für einen adäquaten Ausdruck gerade *dieses* Affectes ansehen konnten. Jede Zeit und Gesittung bringt ein verschiedenes Hören, ein verschiedenes Fühlen mit sich. Die Musik bleibt dieselbe, allein es wechselt ihre Wirkung mit dem wechselnden Standpunkt conventioneller Befangenheit." This passage, from the first edition of Hanslick's book, is not found in Hanslick/Payzant, a translation of the eighth edition of 1891. However, an elaboration of this point that Hanslick produced for the sixth edition (1881) is included in Hanslick/Payzant, 6–7.

8. Hanslick/Strauß, 1:86–87; Hanslick/Payzant, 35: "Es gibt keine Kunst, welche so bald und so viele Formen verbraucht, wie die Musik. Modulationen, Cadenzen, Intervallenfortschreitungen, Harmoniefolgen nützen sich in 50, ja 30 Jahren dergestalt ab, daß der geistvolle Componist sich

To be sure, it might have been an incautious slip of the pen that induced Hanslick to use the word *beautiful* (*schön*) in this instance. But it is nonetheless suggestive that he acknowledged, as early as 1854, that the listener's emotional response is not the only aspect of the musical experience contingent upon personal, historical, and cultural circumstance. Rather, he conceded that the very notion of beauty itself is also inherently relative. Perhaps it was the emergence into consciousness of this paradox and its implications that gave rise to Hanslick's epiphany of the 1860s. At any rate, with the experience of that epiphany fresh in his mind, he determined to cast aside his ambitions as an aesthetic philosopher once and for all. If he could not define with empirical certainty what musical beauty *is* (to paraphrase Spitta's "Art and the Study of Art," considered in the previous chapter), he would henceforth endeavor to describe what it *had been* to different people in different times and in different places.[9] The result of this new round of research and writing was a work of cultural history that drew inspiration from some of the great historical scholars of his time, his second original book-length study, *History of Concert Life in Vienna* (*Geschichte des Concertwesens in Wien*, 1869).[10]

As he set to work compiling his *History of Concert Life*, a survey of a century and a half of Viennese musical life, Hanslick came to regard his historical field as elegantly divisible into four chronological periods. Each of these he associated, in a manner reminiscent of the work of the pioneering historian of music Raphael Georg Kiesewetter, with the names of those artists whose music had seemed to define the creative spirit of their time. The period from 1750 to 1800 was, for Hanslick, the epoch of Haydn and Mozart; 1800 to 1830, of Beethoven and Schubert; 1830 to 1848, of Franz Liszt and the pianist Sigismond Thalberg; and 1848 to 1868, of the postrevolutionary "musical Renaissance" led, albeit somewhat anachronistically, by Robert Schumann and Felix Mendelssohn.[11]

But whereas Kiesewetter had attempted, in his widely read *History of Our Present-Day Western European Music* (1834), to account for the historical development of music in terms of its formal characteristics alone, Hanslick approached

---

deren nicht mehr bedienen kann und fortwährend zur Erfindung neuer, rein musikalischer Züge gedrängt wird. Mann kann von einer Menge Compositionen, die hoch über den Alltagsstand ihrer Zeit stehen, ohne Unrichtigkeit sagen, daß sie einmal schön *waren*."

9. See Philipp Spitta, "Kunstwissenschaft und Kunst," in *Zur Musik. Sechzehn Aufsätze* (Berlin: Gebrüder Paetel, 1892), 5. Spitta's argument about the being and becoming of an artwork is considered in chapter 1.

10. Hanslick, *Geschichte des Concertwesens in Wien* (Vienna: Wilhelm Braumüller, 1869). Although Hanslick published ten editions of *Vom Musikalisch-Schönen* during his lifetime, he made few substantial changes to the text after the publication of the second in 1858. The text of all ten editions is provided in Hanslick/Strauß, vol. 1.

11. Hanslick, *Geschichte*, xi–xii. Kiesewetter, who worked in the Austrian War Ministry and was, from 1845 onwards, the first musician member of the Austrian Academy of Sciences, authored several books on music history, including one that is widely considered to epitomize the "Great Man" approach to the subject: *Geschichte der europäisch-abendlandischen oder unsrer heutigen Musik* (*History of Our Present-Day Western European Music*; Leipzig: Breitkopf und Härtel, 1834). For further discussion of Kiesewetter's work, see Warren Dwight Allen, *Philosophies of Music History: A Study of General Histories of Music 1600–1960*, rev. ed. (New York: Dover, 1962), 86–89.

the task at hand with his newfound convictions regarding the cultural-rooted-ness of aesthetic values planted securely at the front of his mind. As he explained in the preface to his *History of Concert Life*, Hanslick intended his volume to be read as more than a study of music—much less of musical form—in itself. Indeed, he aspired to write what amounted to a cultural history of the Austrian capital as reflected in its musical heritage. The study of "public concert life," he observed,

> a product of the previous century that arose partly from the development of the art itself and partly from the broadening of social life, is highly significant in two respects, one *specifically musical* and the other related to *cultural history*. With respect to the latter, the lively connection between concerts and sociability, of various forms and in various times, offers a richly detailed record of customs and traditions. To look at the public and private musical activities of Haydn's time is to glimpse an already-foreign world.[12]

In contrast to Kiesewetter's formalist experiments, Hanslick's statement regarding musical works as windows into "already-foreign worlds" signaled the spiritual kinship of his endeavor with the work of one of the leading cultural historians of the age, his friend (and Kiesewetter's nephew) August Wilhelm Ambros. As Ambros had observed in the preface to the second volume of his own *History of Music (Geschichte der Musik)*, published five years earlier, when confronted with the artistic products of a bygone age, "I looked and I looked again. I could hardly believe my eyes. Here was a previously unknown world, passing before my gaze."[13]

Like Ambros, Hanslick was motivated, in writing his *History of Concert Life*, by a pair of historiographical convictions that carried significant ethical weight. The first was his belief, as we have already seen, in the cultural relativity of aesthetic judgment—a belief for which Ambros himself was notorious.[14] The second, again shared by Ambros, was his faith in the Hegelian maxim that works of art are phenomenal manifestations of the human spirit in its evolution through time. Like all artistic works, the work of music reveals to the listener traces of the "spirit of the age" (*Zeitgeist*) in which it arose, an age whose other products, and

---

12. Hanslick, *Geschichte*, ix: "Das öffentliche Concertwesen—ein Product des vorigen Jahrhunderts, entsprungen theils aus der Entwicklung der Kunst selbst, theils aus den Erweiterungen des geselligen Lebens—hat eine zweifache hohe Bedeutung: eine *specifisch musikalische* und eine *culturhistorische*. In letzterer Hinsicht bietet der rege Zusammenhang der Concerte mit der Geselligkeit in verschiedenen Zeiten und Formen eine reiche Ausbeute von Sittenbildern. Blicken wir doch in das öffentliche und intime Musiktreiben zu Haydn's Zeit bereits wie in eine fremde Welt."

13. August Wilhelm Ambros, *Geschichte der Musik*, 3d ed., 5 vols. (Leipzig: F. E. C. Leuckart, 1891), 2:x: "'Ich sah', erzählt er, 'ich sah wieder; ich traute meinen Augen nicht: eine bisher unbekannte Welt ging hier vor meinen Blicken auf.'" In this passage, Ambros cites from the memoirs of the art historian Joseph von Führich (1800–1876), originally published in the journal *Libussa* in 1844.

14. It should be noted, however, that Hanslick's convictions regarding the cultural relativity of aesthetic judgment did not engender within him, as with Ambros, a respect for the musics of peoples residing outside of Western Europe. Hanslick was, in fact, critical of his friend for including what he considered overly detailed considerations of Chinese, Indian, Egyptian, and other non-Western musics in the first volume of his *Geschichte der Musik*. See Hanslick, *Aus meinem Leben*, 1:334–39.

especially its social structures and political institutions, are likewise time-bound manifestations of that same universal spirit.[15] From the Hegelian perspective of Hanslick and Ambros, the historian's duty is not merely to record the unfolding of historical events. Rather, the writer of history must endeavor to grasp and describe the nature of the spirit that pervades, underlies, and gave rise to the artifacts and phenomena under consideration. Both of these convictions, the one rooted in Hegel's philosophy of history and both providing the foundation for Ambros's pioneering research, strongly informed Hanslick's study of 1869.

As he laid out the four-part schema into which he divided the history of Viennese musical life in the preface to his *History of Concert Life*, Hanslick made clear that the chronological "epochs" he delineated cannot be understood in terms of the artistic contributions of their eponymous musicians alone. Indeed, he argued, these same periods, defined by the same temporal boundaries, also correspond to important phases in the evolution of the city's music-making and concert-supporting organizations. The earliest years, the epoch of Haydn and Mozart, comprised as well the "patriarchal period" of predominantly royal patronage of music and the arts. The year 1800, marking the beginning of the age of Beethoven and Schubert, saw the rise of systems of private patronage and "associations of dilettantes" such as the Society of Friends of Music (Gesellschaft der Musikfreunde). The stunning appearance of Liszt and Thalberg on the musical scene in the 1830s typified concert life during the "time of the virtuosos," and the contemporary, postrevolutionary atmosphere had given rise to philharmonic concerts, choral societies, and other "associations of artists" themselves.[16]

Circling back to survey his field from a loftier perspective still, Hanslick argued that the entire history of Viennese concert life had paralleled the great and inevitable trajectory of Austrian society as a whole: a gradual yet unstoppable evolution from absolute rule by monarchical authorities to the "democratization" of society, politics, and artistic and musical life. The culmination of this historical process had recently arrived, and it had been ushered in by the events of the Revolution of 1848. (For Hegel, who saw the history of the world in a similar light, the culminating moment arrived with the French Revolution of 1789.)[17] Although the Austrian Revolution, which had begun with student

15. The most thorough examination of Ambros's work remains Philipp Otto Naegele, "August Wilhelm Ambros: His Historical and Critical Thought" (Ph.D. diss., Princeton University, 1954). Much of Part II of Naegele's dissertation concerns the Hegelian foundations of Ambros's *Geschichte der Musik*. For a general consideration of Hegel's philosophy of history, and especially his views on the value of art and the concept of *Zeitgeist*, see Terry Pinkard, *German Philosophy 1760–1860: The Legacy of Idealism* (Cambridge: Cambridge University Press, 2002), 296–300. The influence of Hegel's philosophy upon the historiography of music is considered in Richard Taruskin, *The Oxford History of Western Music*, 6 vols. (New York: Oxford University Press, 2005), 3:411–16.

16. Hanslick, *Geschichte*, xii.

17. On Hegel's notion of historical reason as the animating force behind history's unfolding, see R. G. Collingwood, *The Idea of History* (Oxford: Clarendon Press, 1946), 113–22; and Leonard Krieger, *Time's Reasons: Philosophies of History Old and New* (Chicago: University of Chicago Press, 1989), 53–62. A related consideration of Hegel's convictions regarding history's advance toward the attainment of individual freedom and its apogee in the French Revolution is provided in Pinkard, *German Philosophy*, 233–42.

uprisings outside the Hofburg in March 1848, was quashed and widely regarded as a failure by the end of the revolutionary year, it had, by the time Hanslick began work on his *History of Concert Life*, been reconsidered by many as a harbinger of recent, hopeful changes. These changes included the advent of male suffrage, the drafting of a constitution, and the rise of Austrian liberalism as a political force.[18] In Hanslick's view, the crisis of confidence in authoritarian rule that had precipitated the upheavals of 1848 was felt not only in the political sphere but also in what he called, with explicit reference to revolutionary events, the "pre-March" or *vormärzliche* period of musical life in the city. As "the musical correlate of a period of intellectual idleness and the worst kind of political depravity," he observed, concert life in the immediate prerevolutionary period was epitomized by a demoralized population's instinctive turn toward art as "distraction" in an environment where restrictions on the press and public association had succeeded in "sealing off" the common man and woman "from every kind of serious intellectual interest."[19] Seeking pleasant diversion from the intellectual vacuity of prerevolutionary life, the Viennese public had occupied itself with music that promised pleasant escape: Italian operas, waltzes, and virtuosic display pieces by the likes of Thalberg and Liszt.

With the outbreak of revolution in the spring of 1848, Hanslick argued, the musical climate changed dramatically. First came the public's turn away from Italian opera, which now appeared to many as "representative of exclusive artistic luxuries...the music of the court, the aristocracy, and the rich."[20] Then came a similar turning away from the kind of bravura displays of virtuosity that had captivated audiences in previous years. In place of such performances, the public began to seek a new, more thoughtful kind of virtuosity from its performers, one demanded not by the epic transcriptions of Liszt and Thalberg but by the works of Bach, Scarlatti, and Handel, of Beethoven, Chopin, and Schumann. Foremost among this new class of virtuosos, for Hanslick, stood Clara Schumann and a recent, promising arrival to the city, the young Johannes Brahms.[21]

More important, the *Nachmärz* (the period "after March" of 1848) was for Hanslick the age in which functional democracy made an appearance, for the first time in Viennese history, not only in the halls of parliament but also within the city's artistic institutions. The general relaxation of the political discourse that followed the authoritarian crackdown of the immediate postrevolutionary

18. For a recent account of the events of the revolution of 1848 and its aftermath, see Karl Vocelka, *Geschichte Österreichs. Kultur – Gesellschaft – Politik* (Munich: Wilhelm Hayne, 2000), 198–220. Hanslick recorded his impressions of the 1848 uprisings in *Aus meinem Leben*, 1:120–60.

19. Hanslick, *Geschichte*, 364: "Der entsprechende musikalische Aufputz einer Periode geistigen Unthätigkeit und größter politischer Verkommenheit in Oesterreich! Von allen großen geistigen Interessen abgesperrt, warf sich das Wiener Publicum auf den Cultus der kleinlichen, auf das schlectweg Zerstreuende und Unterhaltende in der Kunst."

20. Hanslick, *Geschichte*, 375: "Der gewaltige Sturm der Märzerhebung fand fast augenblicklich sein nachzitterndes Echo in dem Kunstleben Wiens. Das erste Lebenszeichen des neuen politischen Umschwungs, das auf künstlerischem Gebiete sich kundgab, war destructiver Natur: die Verjagung der italienischen Oper. ...die italienische Oper galt nun einmal als Repräsentant des exclusiven Kunstluxus, als die Musik des Hofes, der Aristokratie und der Reichen."

21. Hanslick, *Geschichte*, 412–21.

years was mirrored in the restructuring of the city's leading music-making organizations. Under the leadership of Joseph Hellmesberger and Johann Herbeck, the Society of Friends of Music sponsored the foundation of the Singing Society and the Orchestra Society (Singverein and Orchesterverein), both of which were placed under the control of specialist musicians (*Fachmusiker*) rather than the philistine representatives of "organized dilettantism" who had constituted "the ruling power in *vormärzliche* concert life."[22] Similarly, the Philharmonic had become, under the direction of Otto Dessoff, an *"association of artists* in the strongest sense," with conductors and repertoire chosen not by an all-powerful director but by the orchestra's members themselves.[23]

Looking back over the decades that had elapsed since the revolutionary season of 1848, Hanslick observed that although the number of concerts offered annually in the city had not noticeably increased, the number of concerts of *quality* had increased dramatically. The Viennese public had, in his words, been provided with performances of "richer content" (*reichere Gehalt*) and more "musical substance" (*musikalische Substanz*).[24] Even the belated appearance of the work of Richard Wagner on the musical scene in the 1860s was for Hanslick a good omen of things to come: it was a sign that the customary Viennese "indolence" and intolerance of the new was finally beginning to weaken.[25] Considered as a whole, he observed with satisfaction, the evolution of musical life in the Austrian capital had followed—as it must—a path analogous to that trodden by Habsburg society more generally. Looking ahead, he saw for the future of concert life the same kind of promise that recent transformations in the political sphere seemed to portend for the Empire as a whole. "When one looks in conclusion from the end back to the beginning," he remarked upon this point, "one perceives in the development of concert life a kind of progress from a patriarchal and aristocratic lack of freedom in artistic affairs to a full democratization of the same."[26]

MUSIC CRITICISM AS "LIVING HISTORY"

If Hanslick had continued to work after 1869 in the manner that led to the publication of his *History of Concert Life in Vienna*, Friedrich Jodl and the com-

22. Hanslick, *Geschichte*, 384: "Hingegen gewannen zwei Neuschöpfungen der Gesellschaft der Musikfreunde bleibenden Bestand und blühenden Entfaltung: der 'Singverein' und der 'Orchesterverein'. Beide bilden merkwürdige Wahrzeichen für den neuen Charakter dieser Periode: sie kennzeichnen die gänzlich veränderte Stellung der Fachmusiker gegen die Dilettanten. Das Liebhaberthum, die 'organisirte Dilettantenschaft', war die herrschende Macht in dem vormärzlichen Concertwesen; sie ging als solche zu Grunde an ihrem Unvermögen, den gesteigerten künstlerischen Anforderungen zu genügen."

23. Hanslick, *Geschichte*, 389: "Die 'Philharmonie' ist *Künstler-Association* im allerstrengsten Sinne. ... Die Philharmonischen Concerte habe überdies die Eigenthümlichkeit einer demokratischen Verfassung: die Orchestermitglieder wählen den Dirigenten, und ein Wohlfahrtsausschuß von 12 Köpfen entscheidet über die Aufnahme oder Ablehnung neuer Compositionen."

24. Hanslick, *Geschichte*, 427.

25. Hanslick, *Geschichte*, 430–31.

26. Hanslick, *Geschichte*, xiii: "Blickt man schließlich vom Ende wieder zurück zum Anfang, so gewahrt man in der Entwicklung des Concertwesens das Fortschreiten von patriarchalisch-aristokratischer Unfreiheit der Kunst bis zu deren vollständiger Demokratisirung."

mittee charged with naming his successor at the University of Vienna might not have been so dismissive of his historical contributions. To be sure, Hanslick's Hegelian interpretation of the events he chronicled might not have been to Jodl's—or to Spitta's, Thausing's, or Adler's—liking. But he nevertheless proceeded in his work from a painstaking examination of documentary sources, precisely as Adler and his colleagues advocated. In preparing his concert history, Hanslick spent years combing through the pages of early periodicals, going back to the *Wienerische Diarium*, founded in 1703. He mined the collection of concert flyers and programs maintained by Florian Gaßmann's Society of Musicians, and he delved into the archives of Vienna's Burgtheater.[27] In the opening pages of his *History of Concert Life*, he even took pains to associate his project with the endeavors and good will of some of the leading historians of the age. His efforts were inspired, he explained, by Otto Jahn's explorations of the musical culture encountered by Mozart during the composer's Viennese years. Jahn, as Hanslick surely knew, was an early advocate for approaching one's work as a historian in the manner of a "scientific investigation" (*wissenschaftlicher Untersuchung*), and he was merciless in his condemnation of those who strayed, like Mozart's biographer Aleksandr Ulïbïshev, from impartial analysis of the objects of their studies.[28] Jahn was even ridiculed by the young Friedrich Nietzsche for the "insensitive sobriety" that he purportedly brought to all matters about which he wrote.[29] Hanslick also expressed his thanks for the enthusiasm shown for his project by Ferdinand Pohl, a noted biographer of Haydn, and Gustav Nottebohm, whose groundbreaking thematic catalogue of Beethoven's work appeared the previous year and whose pioneering studies of Beethoven's sketches were already well under way.

Such a situation, however, was not to be. For immediately following the publication of his *History of Concert Life* in the summer of 1869, Hanslick experienced a second epiphany, one every bit as momentous as that which had doomed his plans for a Herbartian aesthetics a half-decade earlier. As was the case with the first such turn in Hanslick's professional life, this second gave rise to a flurry of authorial productivity. He recalled his second turn in the foreword to *From the Concert Hall (Aus dem Concertsaal)*, the resulting book, in 1870:

> What induced me [to write *From the Concert Hall*] was in fact a glance back at a work that appeared earlier from this same publisher: *History of Concert Life in Vienna*. Indeed, the plan and scope of [the latter] "concert history" allowed for a thorough treatment of older and somewhat more recent musical periods, but it compelled the author to limit himself to the requisite general trends when discussing more recent times. Some reproached me for having provided far too meager a portrayal of the last twenty years—precisely that musical epoch that I myself experienced in Vienna, and that I accompanied, critically and affectionately, every

27. Hanslick, *Geschichte*, xiii–xv.

28. Otto Jahn, *W. A. Mozart*, 4 vols. (Leipzig: Breitkopf und Härtel, 1856–59), 1:xix. Jahn's critique of Ulïbïshev (Oulibicheff) and his *Nouvelle biographie de Mozart* (1843) is found on pages xvii–xx.

29. Friedrich Nietzsche, *The Birth of Tragedy Out of the Spirit of Music*, in *The Birth of Tragedy and the Case of Wagner*, trans. Walter Kaufmann (New York: Vintage, 1967), 120.

step of the way. But to account in detail for every meaningful artistic event that occurred within that rich period I would have needed to provide not just another chapter in my "concert history" but rather another whole volume. Then I realized that I had already written and published this "whole volume" in a manner that had not occurred to me previously: namely, as a mountain of old newspaper articles that only needed to be unearthed and cleaned up a bit. I thus embarked courageously upon a survey of twenty-six years of my journalistic activities.[30]

The realization that both inspired and enabled Hanslick to write *From the Concert Hall* was a novel yet fairly straightforward refinement of the methodology of research that underlay his earlier studies at the Hofbibliothek and the Burgtheater archives. In the 1860s, while preparing his *History of Concert Life in Vienna*, Hanslick had found the bulk of his primary source material in critical reviews published in such decades- and even centuries-old periodicals as the *Wienerische Diarium*, the *Wiener Theaterzeitung*, and the *Wiener Zeitschrift für Kunst, Literatur und Mode*. At some point in 1869 (his foreword to *From the Concert Hall* is dated from the Christmas season of that year), he simply realized that he could just as well rely upon his *own* critical essays, published in the *Neue freie Presse* and other contemporary papers, for the primary source materials from which a "history" of more recent musical events could be distilled. The goal of this new approach to historical research and writing, he later explained, was to provide his readers, both contemporary and posthumous, with what he called a "living history of recent Viennese concert life" (*eine lebendige Geschichte des neueren Wiener Konzertwesens*).[31]

Apart from the paragraph just cited, Hanslick did not theorize in *From the Concert Hall* about either the foundations or the implications of the radical new historiography that underlay his recent work. He also made no attempt, as he had in his earlier *History of Concert Life*, to divide his material into chronological periods or to draw comparisons between musical events and those transpiring in the broader realms of culture or politics. What he provided instead was a chronological survey of Viennese musical life between 1848 and 1868 *as he himself had experienced it*. He revisited, in other words, what he had earlier characterized

---

30. Hanslick, *Aus dem Concertsaal* (*Geschichte des Concertwesens in Wien*, vol. 2) (Vienna: Wilhelm Braumüller, 1870), xi: "Was mich jetzt dennoch dazu veranlaßt, ist vorzüglich die Rücksicht auf ein früheres im selben Verlag erschienenes Werk: 'Geschichte des Concertwesens in Wien'. Anlage und Umfang dieser 'Concertgeschichte' gestatteten zwar eine ausführliche Darstellung der älteren und mittleren Musikperiode, zwangen jedoch den Verfasser, sich in der Schilderung der neuesten Zeit auf die nothwendigen, allgemeinen Grundzüge zu beschränken. Es wurde mir ein Vorwurf gemacht aus der allzu knappen Darstellung der letzten 20 Jahre, gerade jener Musik-Epoche, die ich selbst in Wien miterlebt und liebevoll Schritt für Schritt kritisch begleitet hatte. Aber um jede bedeutende Kunsterscheinung dieser reichen Periode eingehend zu würdigen, hätte ich statt eines Kapitels meiner 'Concertgeschichte' einen ganzen Band schreiben müssen. Da wurde ich aufmerksam, daß dieser 'ganze Band' eigentlich schon geschrieben und gedruckt bei mir versteckt liege,—nämlich in einem Berg von alten Zeitungsartikeln, aus dem er blos herauszugraben und von Schlacken zu reinigen war. So ging ich denn muthig an die Durchsicht der 26 Jahrgänge meiner journalistischen Thätigkeit."

31. Hanslick, *Aus meinem Leben*, 1:245.

as the *nachmärzliche* "musical Renaissance" of Schumann and Mendelssohn from the first-person perspective of one who had lived and participated in that history. Proceeding in a year-by-year fashion, Hanslick's third book guides the reader through the day-to-day unfolding of two decades of musical events. Some of the volume's chapters reflect upon individual concerts offered by the Singakademie, the Philharmonic, and other professional organizations. Others treat aspects of contemporary musical life more generally: "The Viennese Concert Season, 1853–1854," "Austrian Military Music," "Johannes Brahms" (documenting his initial impressions of Brahms's music and piano playing), and so forth. Throughout, Hanslick is candid in voicing his impressions of the topics he considers. In his earlier *History of Concert Life*, he had argued, with the even-handedness and broad cultural perspective to which many historians of the period aspired, that the postrevolutionary Viennese embrace of the music of Wagner was a positive development, a symptom of the general liberalization of the Austrian cultural discourse as a whole. In *From the Concert Hall*, he admitted that, such issues aside, he himself did not care for Wagner's work. Writing in the latter volume about the Philharmonic's first performance of the prelude to *Tristan and Isolde*, he observed that "the impression made by this restlessly surging, undifferentiated tone-mass, with its incessant repetition of the same little motive, was anything but pleasant. Nowhere does the ear find a resting place or a cadence; [the work] gives rise to the same painful feeling that must be caused by hearing a long series of antecedents whose consequent is missing."[32]

Throughout *From the Concert Hall*, Hanslick's discussions of the events he describes are unabashedly subjective. They are written in such as way as to provide the reader with an unambiguous statement of their author's impressions of occurrences personally experienced. Yet by framing these discussions within a volume that he labeled, on its title page, *History of Concert Life in Vienna*, Volume 2 (*Zweiter Theil*), he profoundly problematized the criticism-versus-history dichotomy by which Spitta and his colleagues were then attempting to define and delimit the musicological field. The individual chapters of Hanslick's text are nothing other than critical essays, literally so; as he made clear in his foreword to the volume, all had been published previously on the pages of the city's daily and weekly periodicals. Yet here, bound together and published as a book, they were labeled *history*. And not just that: they constituted the second volume of a study whose first installment was a work of historical scholarship in the tradition of Ambros, Jahn, and even Spitta himself. Inscribing the critical essay within the historical work and, by extension, the recording of subjective impressions within the narration of cultural history, *From the Concert Hall* marked the beginning—tacitly at this point—of what would become for its author a thirty-year effort to deconstruct one of the central disciplinary oppositions upon which the

---

32. Hanslick, *Aus dem Concertsaal*, 227: "Günstig war der Eindruck durchaus nicht, welchen diese ruhelos wogende, unterschiedlose Tonmasse mit ihrer unaufhörlichen Wiederholung desselben Motivchens machte. Das Ohr findet nirgends einen Ruhepunkt oder Abschluß, was ungefähr dieselbe peinliche Empfindung erregt, als müßten wir eine lange Reihe von Vordersätzen vorlesen hören, deren Nachsätze wegbleiben."

positivist movement was founded.[33] Five years later, he would make explicit what had earlier been tacit, defending his radical departure from the ideals of Spitta and others in an essay that serves as a preface to the second volume of his "living history" series, *Modern Opera (Die moderne Oper)*.[34]

In the opening pages of *Modern Opera*, Hanslick explained that his critique of his fledgling discipline had been engendered by a need to confront what he perceived as a crisis looming over the scholarly community of his time. Referring to the peculiar circumstances of his own bifurcated career (and apparently noting the inability of even hardened positivists to banish the word *beauty* from their vocabularies), Hanslick observed that "he who is active simultaneously as a music critic and a professor of history stands daily before the ever-widening rift that exists between those works that historians celebrate as beautiful and significant and those that still exercise a lively pull upon the populace."[35] In Hanslick's view, the barrier that some had sought to erect between aesthetic appreciation and historical scholarship had succeeded only in isolating such scholarship from the listening public—the very community to which the historian's work was, in his view, rightly addressed. With few exceptions, those musical works regarded as timeless in the annals of history had lost their hold on the contemporary imagination. And if they had survived at all beyond the pages of historians' studies, they were heard and enjoyed only on the margins of contemporary musical life. For Hanslick, this situation posed a dilemma: whether to persist in delving into the histories of repertoires beloved by scholars but increasingly alien to the concert-going public or to endeavor to observe and understand that which still possesses "an effective, living strength" and answers the "aesthetic needs of the nation."[36] For Hanslick, the choice was clear. Henceforth, he declared, he would dedicate himself to illuminating the attitudes and experiences of inhabitants of his own, "living" musical culture. He determined to devote his life to recording the history of that culture at the countless individual moments of its unfolding.

As he proceeded to elaborate upon the theoretical foundations of his "living history" project, Hanslick found support and precedent in fields that might seem, at first glance, incongruously different from his own: photography and statistics.

---

33. I use the word *deconstruct* loosely, for its utility with regard to explicating my interpretation of Hanslick's work yet without intending to impose a post-structuralist interpretation upon it or to suggest that Hanslick intended such a critique. In doing so, I am indebted to Kevin Korsyn's critical exploration of the idea, formation, and deconstruction of "disciplinary identities." See Korsyn, *Decentering Music: A Critique of Contemporary Musical Research* (Oxford: Oxford University Press, 2003), chapter 3.

34. Hanslick, *Die moderne Oper* (Berlin: A. Hofmann, 1875).

35. Hanslick, *Die moderne Oper*, v: "Wer gleichzeitig als Musikkritiker und als Geschichtsprofessor thätig ist, der steht tagtäglich vor der immer breiteren Kluft zwischen den Werken, welche die Kunstgeschichte als schön und bedeutend feiert und jenen, welche heute noch auf die Gesammtheit lebendige Wirkung üben." Cf. Moriz Thausing, writing in 1873: "The best history of art is one in which the word *beautiful* never appears" (Thausing, "Die Stellung der Kunstgeschichte als Wissenschaft," in *Wiener Kunstbriefe* [Leipzig: E. A. Seemann, 1884], 5).

36. Hanslick, *Die moderne Oper*, v: "Es gewährt einen absonderlichen Reiz, ein so abgegrenztes Kunstgebiet wie die Oper darauf anzusehen, was von seinen aufgehäuften Schätzen noch heute als lebendige Kraft wirkt und zu den ästhetischen Bedürfnissen der Nation gehört."

If one wishes to engage in the sort of research he foresaw, he explained, "one must think of history, which indeed flows by in an unceasing current, as if it were frozen in the moment, and one must, in a sense, take a photograph [*photographiren*] of it—to fix it, as it were, *à l'instant*."[37] The historical "photographs" to which Hanslick referred, of course, were the individual critical essays that comprised the bulk of *From the Concert Hall, Modern Opera*, and the other volumes of his "living history" series. Switching metaphors, he addressed what he regarded as the affinity between his own concerns and those of August Ludwig von Schlözer, an eighteenth-century political observer who sought to illuminate the status of German society by compiling statistical tables of population figures, agricultural productivity, and other demographic information. For Schlözer, the "statistical science" (*statistische Wissenschaft*) was first and foremost a tool for the aid of "statists"—political leaders and their advisors. However, he argued, statistical study is also an invaluable, even inevitable component of historical research and writing. To observe and describe the material circumstances of a culture at a specific point in its history, Schlözer explained, is nothing other than to undertake a wide-ranging statistical study of the same. In turn, to survey the evolution of a culture over a span of historical time is to engage in a comparative examination of a series of statistical studies. "The writer of history," Schlözer observed, "must therefore be a statistician," since "history" is nothing more than "a progression of statistical surveys."[38] Indeed, he argued, "the statistical survey is frozen history [*stillstehende Geschichte*]. It enables one to stand still wherever one wants and for however long one wants. That is, one may select time frames from years or centuries past and compare them to those that came before and afterwards."[39] This, Hanslick explained, was precisely what he himself intended when compiling his own volumes of "living history." "Schlözer," Hanslick wrote,

> the father of statistics, arrived in this way at the idea of his science, which he understood as "frozen history." In a related sense I set out to attempt a kind of aesthetic statistics of opera, a critical account of that which is presently living upon the stage. I conceived of the "single moment" I would attempt to fix as the last

37. Hanslick, *Die moderne Oper*, v: "Zu diesem Endzweck muß man die Geschichte, die ja im unaufhaltsamen Wechsel dahin strömt, sich in Einem Moment stillstehend denken und die also im Geist fixirte gleichsam à l'instant photographiren."

38. August Ludwig von Schlözer, *Theorie der Statistik nebst Ideen über das Studium der Politik überhaupt*, vol. 1, *Einleitung* (Göttingen: Vandenhoek und Ruprecht, 1804), 93, 86: "...der Geschichtschreiber muß sie kraft tragenden Amtes registriren; er muß also Statistiker seyn. Oder mit andern Worten: Geschichte ist das Ganze, *Statistik* ein Teil derselben"; "Geschichte ist eine fortlaufende Statistik." On statistics as an adjunct to the work of the "statist," see Theodore M. Porter, *The Rise of Statistical Thinking, 1820–1900* (Princeton: Princeton University Press, 1986), 23–24. Neither Schlözer's historiography nor his ideas about statistical methods have received much attention from present-day historians. The most thorough account of his historical work is found in Daniel Fulda, *Wissenschaft aus Kunst. Die Entstehung der modernen deutschen Geschichtsschreibung 1760–1860*, European Cultures: Studies in Literature and the Arts, no. 7 (Berlin: Walder de Gruyter, 1996), 174–83. Fulda does not, however, consider Schlözer's *Theorie der Statistik*.

39. Schlözer, *Theorie der Statistik*, 1:86–87: "Statistik ist eine stillstehende Geschichte: nun so lasse man sie stille stehen, wo man will, und so lange man will; d. i. man hebe ZeitRäume vergangner Jare oder JarHunderte aus, die sich von vorhergegangnen und nachfolgenden auszeichnen."

twenty years (art history advances in long strides). The place where the photograph would be taken: Vienna.[40]

Five years earlier, in *From the Concert Hall*, Hanslick had inscribed the critical essay within the historical narrative. In *Modern Opera*, he inverted this relationship. Endeavoring to record the experiences and attitudes of a living participant in the midst of the unfolding of historical events, he identified the critic's pen as the historian's camera, and the critical essay as the historical photograph. To "take a photograph" of the present moment was, for Hanslick, to record one's impressions of it critically. And that, in turn, is to engage in a historical act, to take part in the writing of history.

Elaborating more broadly upon his "living history" project in the remainder of his 1875 essay, Hanslick stressed that the student of contemporary culture must strive for neither exhaustiveness nor an impartial, objective stance in his accounting of history-making events. One should simply attempt to document, to the best of one's ability, one's own responses to what one experiences—responses that are, by virtue of the historian's embeddedness within the culture he studies, themselves a part of that culture's history. Referring to the contents of the volume in hand, Hanslick admitted that "the complete operas of a master are not discussed here, and that which is discussed is by no means considered within the context of a uniformly exhaustive criticism. The discussion is not even restricted to a consideration of the historical or aesthetic standing of these works, but rather considers their real life upon the stage."[41] Above all else, Hanslick argued, one must resist the temptation to extract from one's reactions a prediction about how the phenomena one describes will be understood by subsequent generations of readers and listeners. Like all aesthetic judgments, our impressions of our objects of study are necessarily colored by our broader experiences of the historical cultures we inhabit. Future generations will judge these works and events from perspectives that are their own:

> We must renounce our lovely belief in immortality! Indeed, every period, with the same misplaced confidence, proclaims the timelessness of its best operas. Adam Hiller in Leipzig asserted that the operas of Hasse would cease to delight audiences only if barbarism should befall the world. And Schubart, the writer on music aesthetics from Hohenasperg, expressing his assurances about Jomelli, argued that it was well nigh unthinkable that this composer would ever sink into the ranks of the forgotten. Yet what are Hasse and Jomelli to us today?... History teaches us that operas that were at one time trumpeted as "immortal" have an average life-span

40. Hanslick, *Die moderne Oper*, v–vi: "*Schlözer*, der Vater der Statistik, gelangte auf diesem Wege zu dem Begriff seiner Wissenschaft, die er als 'stillstehende Geschichte' auffaßte. In verwandtem Sinn hatte ich vor, eine Art ästhetischer Statistik der Oper zu versuchen, eine kritische Schilderung dessen, was gegenwärtig auf der Bühne lebendig ist. Als den zu fixirenden Einen Moment—die Kunstgeschichte macht lange Schritte—dachte ich mir die letzten zwanzig Jahre; als den Ort der Aufnahme: Wien."

41. Hanslick, *Die moderne Oper*, vi: "Nicht sämmtliche Opern eines Meisters sind hier besprochen, und die besprochenen keineswegs in gleichmäßig erschöpfender Kritik. Es galt eben nicht lediglich der geschichtlichen oder ästhetischen Stellung dieser Werke, sondern ihrem realen Leben auf der Bühne."

of forty to fifty years—a period that only a few works of genius will outlast, and that the great majority of more light-weight yet beloved operas will almost never attain.[42]

As he emphasized in another volume in his "living history" series, the historical record preserved in his work is "not historically objective but rather subjectively colored in a double sense, since each critical essay gives voice only to the views of a single individual, and moreover since it shimmers here in the still-glistening colors of the first, immediate impression."[43]

In terms of their methodological implications, polemical intentions, and potential to reshape the whole of the field in which their author worked, Hanslick's writings from the 1870s onward appear to be unique in the musicological literature of the period. Yet as Leo Treitler's research suggests, Hanslick was not entirely alone in his endeavors. Indeed, he was one among a small but distinguished handful of historians simultaneously attempting to effect similar transformations within numerous and diverse branches of the historical field. Although Treitler does not write on Hanslick's "living history," the latter project is in fact exemplary of what one might characterize, following his lead, as a *particularist* historiography of music.[44] Typically, Treitler observes, historians working in the post-Hegelian tradition sought to "apprehend the individual event as part of an organic whole and to regard the particular as exemplification of the general."[45] Such was, in terms made famous by the nineteenth-century historian of philosophy Wilhelm Windelband, a "nomothetic" or "law-contriving" approach to historical understanding. It was, as we have seen, precisely what Hanslick attempted in the first volume of his *History of Concert Life in Vienna*, and likewise what Adler called for when he wrote of the search for "artistic laws" (*Kunstgesetze*) in his "Scope, Method, and Goal of Musicology." In contrast to this, the historian who adopts a particularist orientation assumes what

42. Hanslick, *Die moderne Oper*, vii–viii: "Dem schönen Unsterblichkeitsglauben müssen wir entsagen,—hat doch jede Zeit mit demselben getäuschten Vertrauen die Unvergänglichkeit *ihrer* besten Opern proklamirt. Noch Adam Hiller in Leipzig behauptete, daß wenn jemals die Opern *Hasse's* nicht mehr entzücken sollten, die allgemeine Barbarei hereinbrechen müßte. Noch Schubart, der Musikästhetiker vom Hohenasperg, versicherte von *Jomelli*, es sei gar nicht denkbar, daß dieser Tondichter jemals in Vergessenheit gerathen könnte. Und was sind uns heute Hasse und Jomelli?... Die Historie lehrt uns, daß Opern, für deren 'Unsterblichkeit' man sich ehedem todtschlagen ließ, eine durchschnittliche Lebensdauer von 40 bis 50 Jahren haben, eine Frist, die nur von wenigen genialen Schöpfungen überdauert, von der Menge leichterer Lieblingsopern aber fast nie erreicht wird." For an insightful analysis of Hanslick's *Die moderne Oper* essay that considers its suggestiveness with regard to the critical rather than the scholarly culture of the period, see Botstein, "Music and Its Public," 863–69.

43. Hanslick, *Concerte, Componisten und Virtuosen der letzten fünfzehn Jahre. 1870–1885* (Berlin: Allgemeiner Verein für Deutsche Litteratur, 1886), unnumbered dedication page: "Freilich kein historisch-objectives, sondern ein subjectiv gefärbtes in dem doppelten Sinne, daß jede Kritik nur die Ansicht eines Einzelnen ausspricht und daß sie hier obendrein in den noch feuchten Farben des ersten unmittelbaren Eindrucks schillert."

44. Leo Treitler, "History, Criticism, and Beethoven's Ninth Symphony," in *Music and the Historical Imagination* (Cambridge, MA, 1989), 36–45.

45. Treitler, "History," 39.

Windelband called an "idiographic" or "picture-making" approach to his work.[46] He seeks, Treitler explains, "to stop the past in its tracks and hold it still, as if it were a present."[47] In this way, the "generalizing consideration of the human forces in history [is replaced] by an individualizing one." Within one's field of inquiry, however broad, "the focus is always on the particular."[48]

Given the emphasis granted by particularist historians to the individuality of the historical moment (Treitler singles out Windelband, Johann Gustav Droysen, Wilhelm Dilthey, and Jacob Burckhardt especially), it is only natural that those historians should tend toward a critical treatment of the objects of their studies. As Treitler argues, "the correspondence" between particularist historiography and criticism "is not a matter of chance coincidence but a fundamental agreement of aim and outlook." Indeed, he observes, "criticism answers exactly to the description of historical knowledge given by the writers who developed that position." Like criticism, particularist historiography "makes value an issue. It is the conception of history as critical engagement with the object that directs attention to the individual and to the particular."[49]

Treitler's argument has profound implications for our understanding of Hanslick's history, for it suggests that the latter was not, in fact, an isolated phenomenon. It was, rather, part of a broad and at times deliberately subversive trend that had been explored, in fits and starts, throughout the second half of the nineteenth century by some of the leading historians of the period.[50] It may well have been within this context that Adler, Jodl, and others among Hanslick's colleagues perceived the danger of his work. Indeed, Spitta, whose disciplinary polemics would provide a store of ideological ammunition for Hanslick's detractors at the time of his retirement from the university, appears to have taken aim directly at Hanslick's "living history" in his seminal "Art and the Study of Art" of 1883. Although he does not mention Hanslick's name in the published version of his talk, Spitta's colorful references to an unconventional and subversive historiography make the target of his polemic clear. "That which one might presently call a 'daily history of art' [*künstlerische Tagesgeschichte*]," Spitta wrote, "has nothing in common with science [*Wissenschaft*]." He continued,

> To achieve secure, scientific results, it is above all necessary for the object to stand still before the researcher. And only that which is far removed from the interests of the present day can fulfill this requirement. One cannot fathom what right the scholar might claim to place himself between the artist and his public. If he seeks

46. On Windelband's notion of "nomothetic" and "idiographic" modes of historical understanding, see his "Geschichte und Naturwissenschaft" (1894), in *Präludien. Aufsätze und Reden zur Philosophie und ihrer Geschichte*, 6th ed., 2 vols. (Tübingen: J. C. B. Mohr, 1919), 2:144–46 and the introduction to the present volume. Useful discussions of Windelband's ideas are provided in Treitler, "History," 39; and Hayden White, *Metahistory: The Historical Imagination in Nineteenth-Century Europe* (Baltimore: Johns Hopkins University Press, 1973), 381–82 (cited at 381).

47. Treitler, "History," 37.

48. Treitler, "History," 44, 39.

49. Treitler, "History," 39, 44.

50. As R. G. Collingwood observes of Windelband's own "idiographic" brand of historiography, "it represent[ed] a kind of secessionist movement of historians from the general body of a civilization in thrall to natural science" (Collingwood, *The Idea of History*, 167).

to trumpet to [his readers] those images that the development of the art presents before his gaze, he will only bewilder them. And if he seeks to instruct, he will only be instructing from an improper standpoint.[51]

We do not know if Hanslick was aware of Spitta's thinly veiled rebuke. But if he was, he was unmoved. From 1870 until the end of his life, he remained convinced that his "living history" was anything but a misguided affair. Whatever the disciplinary consequences of his late-century work might be, Hanslick believed that adopting a critical approach to studying and writing about music was the only hope for contemporary musicologists if they wished to bring their fledgling discipline back from the brink of cultural and intellectual obscurity.

THE USES OF HISTORY AND THE
TRACES OF CULTURE

Once Hanslick had defended his new historiography in the foreword to *Modern Opera*, he never returned to the kind of work that gave rise to *History of Concert Life in Vienna*, and he never again published a historiographical essay. He spent his remaining thirty-four years producing more books along the lines of those of the 1870s. In these volumes, he avoided the construction of connecting or explanatory narratives such as those that animated his earlier *History of Concert Life*. He eschewed a nomothetic treatment of his material—one shaped by the assumption of historical laws—and avoided those narrative strategies that Hayden White has called "emplotment" and "formal argument," by which the historian attempts to "explicate 'the point of it all' or 'what it all adds up to.' "[52] Hanslick also avoided, in most of his work from these decades, that most basic of the historian's pre-compositional acts: the arranging of one's material in chronological fashion, the construction of what White calls a "chronicle."[53] Of the twelve volumes that would eventually comprise Hanslick's "living history," only two treat their historical subjects in a chronological manner. In the rest, even in those that feature date ranges in their titles, he arranged his discussions topically—according to musical genre or kind of event or even literary type. (The three topics considered in Hanslick's *At the End of the Century [1895–1899]*, for instance, are "Operas," "Concerts," and "Monuments," the latter consisting of essays commemorating

51. Spitta, "Kunstwissenschaft und Kunst," 10: "Mit dem, was man künstlerische Tagesgeschichte nennen könnte, hat die Wissenschaft überhaupt nichts zu thun. Damit sichere wissenschaftliche Ergebnisse erzielt werden, ist es vor allem nothwendig, daß das Object dem Forscher stille hält, und nur was dem Interesse der Gegenwart entrückt ist, erfüllt diese Forderung. Es ist nicht einzusehen, mit welchem Rechte sich der Gelehrte zwischen den Künstler und sein Publicum stellt. Soll er diesem die Anschauung einimpfen, in welcher das Bild der Kunstentwickelung sich dem Blick des Wissenschafters darbietet, so wird er es verwirren. Soll er belehren, so belehrt er am unrechten Orte."

52. White, *Metahistory*, 7–21 (cited at 11).

53. On White's notion of the chronicle as "a primitive element in the historical account," an "unprocessed historical record" that the historian illuminates by way of emplotment, formal argument, and other means, see his *Metahistory*, 5–7.

the achievements of departed artists.)[54] Even the titles of Hanslick's "living history" volumes—*Suite, Sketchbook, Waystations, Diary, Criticisms, Accounts*—emphasize the deeply subjective, even impressionistic nature of their contents. Indeed, Hanslick's overturning of historiographical assumptions regnant in his time was nearly complete. (A list of Hanslick's book-length publications is provided in Table 2.1.)

Given these facts, it is perhaps not surprising that Hanslick's work as a historian was dismissed out of hand by so many of his colleagues. In this respect, he shared his fate with his more famous particularist contemporary, Jacob Burckhardt. In his monumental study *The Civilization of the Renaissance in Italy* (1860), Burckhardt had argued, in defense of his volume's evident subjectivity, that "To each eye, perhaps, the outlines of a given civilization present a different picture. And in treating of a civilization which is the mother of our own, and whose influence is still at work among us, it is unavoidable that individual judgement and feeling should tell every moment both on the writer and on the

TABLE 2.1. Hanslick's book-length publications

On the Musically Beautiful (*Vom Musikalisch-Schönen*, 1854; subsequent eds: 2/1858, 3/1865, 4/1874, 5/1876, 6/1881, 7/1885, 8/1891, 9/1896, 10/1902)

History of Concert Life in Vienna (*Geschichte des Concertwesens in Wien*, 1869)

From the Concert Hall (*Aus dem Concertsaal* [*Geschichte des Concertwesens in Wien*, vol. 2], 1870)

Modern Opera: Criticisms and Studies (*Die moderne Oper. Kritiken und Studien* [*DMO*], 1875)

Musical Waystations (*Musikalische Stationen* [*DMO*, vol. 2], 1880)

From the Operatic Life of the Present: New Criticisms and Studies (*Aus dem Opernleben der Gegenwart. Neue Kritiken und Studien* [*DMO*, vol. 3], 1884)

Suite: Essays on Music and Musicians (*Suite. Aufsätze über Musik und Musiker*, 1884)

Concerts, Composers, and Virtuosos of the Last Fifteen Years: 1870–1885 (*Concerte, Componisten und Virtuosen der letzten fünfzehn Jahre. 1870–1885*, 1886)

Musical Sketchbook: New Criticisms and Accounts (*Musikalisches Skizzenbuch. Neue Kritiken und Schilderungen* [*DMO*, vol. 4], 1888)

Things Musical and Literary: Criticisms and Accounts (*Musikalisches und Litterarisches. Kritiken und Schilderungen* [*DMO*, vol. 5], 1889)

From the Diary of a Musician: Criticisms and Accounts (*Aus dem Tagebuche eines Musikers. Kritiken und Schilderungen* [*DMO*, vol. 6], 1892)

From My Life (*Aus meinem Leben* [autobiography], 1894)

Five Years of Music (1891–1895): Criticisms (*Fünf Jahre Musik (1891–1895). Kritiken* [*DMO*, vol. 7], 1896)

At the End of the Century (1895–1899): Musical Criticisms and Accounts (*Am Ende des Jahrhunderts (1895–1899). Musikalische Kritiken und Schilderungen* [*DMO*, vol. 8], 1899)

From Recent and the Most Recent Times: Musical Criticisms and Accounts (*Aus neuer und neuester Zeit. Musikalische Kritiken und Schilderungen* [*DMO*, vol. 9], 1900)

---

54. The two volumes whose contents Hanslick arranged chronologically are *Aus dem Concertsaal* (1870) and *Concerte, Componisten und Virtuosen* (1886).

reader."[55] This, of course, is very much like what Hanslick would argue a decade or so later as he worked to lay the theoretical foundations for his "living history" project. Yet as White observes, however "unavoidable" Burckhardt felt his own subjective stance to be, most historians in late-century Germany simply felt "that he was too irresponsible, too subjective, to merit their attention."[56]

As was the case with Burckhardt, few if any of Hanslick's academic peers took to heart the methodological reforms he proposed. But as we saw in chapter 1, the heated deliberations about Hanslick's legacy that occupied the committee charged with appointing his successor at the university make clear that Jodl, Ernst Mach, and others among his colleagues took the threat posed by Hanslick's work seriously indeed. After all, Hanslick's "living history" was not merely a provocative critique of the positivist movement and its disciplinary goals. It was such a critique issued by a writer who had earlier played a leading role in the coalescence of the Austrian empiricist movement and whose essays and lectures continued to exert a powerful influence upon the opinions and attitudes of a vast swath of the reading and listening public. We have only to revisit a handful of responses to Hanslick's work to gain a sense of the magnitude of the conundrum it posed for his colleagues. One such response, particularly revealing of the historiographical complexities and broad cultural significance of Hanslick's ideas, came in the form of a small booklet authored by Robert Hirschfeld in 1885.

Just one year before he published his *Ed. Hanslick's Critical Method* (*Das kritische Verfahren Ed. Hanslick's*), Hirschfeld, a student of music of the fourteenth and fifteenth centuries, received his doctorate at the University of Vienna. There, under Hanslick's direction, he had completed a dissertation on the theoretical writings of the medieval polymath Johannes de Muris.[57] Upon his graduation, Hirschfeld embarked upon a multifaceted career as a teacher, critic, editor, and conductor who made an important debut before the Viennese public by directing a series of "Renaissance Evening" concerts of pre-Baroque choral music in the autumn of 1884. After one such concert held in March of the following year, Hirschfeld awoke to find a stinging review of the event on the pages of the *Neue freie Presse*. The author of the review was his former teacher. These are Hanslick's thoughts about Hirschfeld's series:

> Bach and Handel, the colossal foundations of our music history, are in a certain sense gatekeepers at the entryway of the same. With them begins that portion of German music that leads an actual life within the nation. No objection to this statement, such as that which has recently been attempted, can change the facts; the place of Bach and Handel will in no way be altered by the desire that their predecessors will, in time, be brought nearer to us through public performances. Their predecessors, regardless of their individual merits, have fallen to the level

55. Jacob Burckhardt, *The Civilization of the Renaissance in Italy*, ed. Ludwig Goldscheider (London: Phaidon, 1945), 1.

56. White, *Metahistory*, 243.

57. On Hirschfeld's life and work, see Botstein, "Music and Its Public," esp. 889–926 and 1018–75.

of objects for study and antiquarian hobbies. Before Handel and Bach there were indeed living musicians, but for us none of their music still lives.[58]

Hirschfeld, who was not only a brilliant student but also a gifted writer, responded with pen in hand. In what would become his polemical tract, he attacked the elder writer on historiographical, indeed ideological grounds. In casting his judgment not against the artistic merits of the performance he attended but against the goals that had motivated the inauguration of the concert series as a whole, Hirschfeld argued, Hanslick betrayed an essential conviction that underlay Hanslick's own teachings as a university professor: that all art is worthy of study, of having "its nature probed and its development traced" (*deren Wesen zu erforschen und deren Entwicklung zu verfolgen*).[59] Hirschfeld observed with irony that within Hanslick there seemed to "reside, as in a peculiar bifurcation, *two souls!*" In contrast to the professor Hanslick, who sought to instill within his students a respect for all artistic styles and idioms, the *critic* Hanslick

> happily throws overboard all seriousness in favor of clever antitheses and a kind of quick-wittedness. He strives to impress us not with a dignified and scholarly approach to art but with mere stylistic grace. ... That soul—or, as we shall henceforth call the man it inhabits, the music critic Ed. H.—has said the most unbelievable things and condemned out of hand in the *feuilleton* just cited an *entire, great, and marvelous artistic epoch* with a few soul-shaking sentences.

Hirschfeld closed his case with these damning lines: "*how sharply and unsparingly would the professor himself condemn the music critic in this case* were he to see in this way the peculiar duality of the soul we have described."[60]

In these passages, Hirschfeld's outrage is palpable. Yet when he wrote these words he must surely have known that Hanslick's remarks about his Renaissance

---

58. Hanslick's review appeared in the *Neue freie Presse* (March 5, 1885); cited in Robert Hirschfeld, *Das kritische Verfahren Ed. Hanslick's* (Vienna: R. Löwit, 1885), 8: "Bach und Händel, die Kolossalgestalten unserer Musikgeschihchte, stehen in gewissen Sinne als riesige Pförtner am Eingange derselben. Mit ihnen beginnt, was von deutscher Musik ein wirkliches Leben führt in der Nation. Dagegen gilt kein Einwand, wie kürzlich einer versucht worden; an dieser thatsächlichen Stellung Bach's und Händel's wird nichts geändert durch den Wunsch, es möchten auch die Vorläufer der Beiden durch öffentliche Aufführungen uns allmälig näher gerückt werden. Diese Vorläufer sind—unbeschadet ihrer Bedeutung im Einzelnen—als Objecte des Studiums oder als antiquarische Liebhaberei dem historischen Interesse verfallen. Vor Händel und Bach gab es lebendige Musiker, gibt es aber für uns keine lebendig gebliebene Musik."

59. Hirschfeld, *Das kritische Verfahren*, 6.

60. Hirschfeld, *Das kritische Verfahren*, 6–7: "...in merkwürdigem Zweispalt *zwei Seelen* ach! in dessen Brust wohnen. Nicht nur die Seele *ersten* Ranges nach Plato, der wir mit gebührender Hochachtung begegnen, sondern leider auch die Seele *achten* Ranges, welche den *Professor* verleugnet und den *Musikreferenten* Ed. H. bedeutet. Diese Theilseele achter Ordnung wirft gern zu Gunsten einer geistreichen Antithese, eines schlagfertigen Witzes allen Ernst über Bord; will nicht durch kunstwissenschaftliche Würde imponiren, sondern durch stylistische Anmuth gefallen... Diese Seele oder—nennen wir fortan den Mann, welchen sie erfüllt—der Musikreferent Ed. H. hat auch das Unglaublichste geleistet und in dem citirten Feuilleton über eine *ganze grosse, herrliche Kunstepoche* mit wenigen geistschillernden Sätzen den Stab gebrochen. ...*wie scharf und unerbittlich dieser Professor selbst den Musikreferenten in diesem Falle verurtheilen würde*, wenn der geschilderte eigenthümliche Seelendualismus solchen zuliesse."

Evenings were not the first that he had published about the place of pre-Baroque musics in late nineteenth-century society. Moreover, in comparing Hanslick's critical remarks to the impartial views of his remembered teacher, Hirschfeld sought to hold Hanslick's statements to a standard that the elder writer had rejected years ago, shortly after he had completed the first volume of his *History of Concert Life in Vienna*. As Hanslick had argued as early as 1870, when embarking upon his "living history" project, undertakings such as Hirschfeld's Renaissance Evenings indeed had a laudable aim: to enable long-forgotten works by neglected masters "to acquire," once again, "living, individual physiognomies" in the minds of contemporary listeners.[61] When considered from the perspective of the concert attendee, however, such events were, in Hanslick's view, highly problematic. In a discussion of a similar historical concert offered by the Vienna Singakademie in 1870, he observed:

> We are indeed, as terrible as this sounds, modern and worldly men. In art we sympathize more readily with poetic than churchly interests. We may indeed be uplifted by artistic pilgrimages to the abandoned abodes of earlier centuries, but we are no longer able to settle there wholeheartedly. Even compared with far greater ages, ours always seems the best. And the *only* art that can bring us *complete* fulfillment is that which springs from the general current of our ideas and emotions.[62]

However great the works of pre-Baroque composers might have sounded in their time, Hanslick argued, and however important the study of such works might be for our understanding of music's history, most members of contemporary society are simply unmoved by their performance. The emotional worlds conjured by those artists' music will invariably sound naive and old-fashioned to the modern listener. While the technical means by which such works are constructed are indeed of interest to historians, he explained, they are nevertheless representative of those once-beautiful forms that, as he wrote in *On the Musically Beautiful*, had been "worn out" by the passing of time.

In Hanslick's view, Palestrina, though undeniably one of the "truly great figures of music history," nevertheless embodied the spirit of an age when

> Music was, to such a great extent, cultivated one-sidedly, as polyphonic artifice, and this was considered beautiful art. Things that have become indispensable since Bach, Handel, and Mozart, and that have since become almost inseparable from

---

61. Hanslick, *Aus dem Concertsaal*, 209: "Die alten katholischen Meister...sind uns seit dem Wirken des 'Singvereins' und der 'Sing-Akademie' keine bloßen Namen mehr. Sie haben lebendig individuelle Physignomien bekommen."

62. Hanslick, *Aus dem Concertsaal*, 209: "Wir sind nun einmal, so entsetzlich dies klingt, moderne und weltliche Menschen. In der Kunst sympathisiren wir wärmer mit dem poetischen als mit dem kirchlichen Interesse, und erbauen wir uns auch gerne durch künstlerische Wallfahrten nach den verlassenen Stätten früherer Jahrhunderte—uns dort ungetheilten Herzens anzusiedeln, vermögen wir nicht mehr. Auch weit größeren Zeiten gegenüber erscheint unsere Zeit uns doch immer als die beste, und *ganz* vermag uns nur *die* Kunst auszufüllen, welche durch den gemeinsamen Strom unserer Ideen und Empfindungen hindurchging."

the very notion of music itself, were lacking in Palestrina's time. For this reason it takes a certain amount of effort for us moderns to truly feel, and not just to state out of habit, that he is a great composer and an original musical inventor.[63]

Hanslick even argued that Johann Sebastian Bach, whose music he himself adored, presented difficulties for many late-century listeners. Part of the problem, he explained, was that Bach's complex polyphony, freely employed in his choral works, tends too often to render his texts incomprehensible. Writing of an 1860 Singakademie performance of one of Bach's motets,[64] he observed that

> Studying the score, we are overcome with wonder for the magnificently thought-out and artistically fashioned construction. In performance of the same, we are, at best, uplifted by the playing of the organ and the strings. All enjoyment disappears when we see such a great number of human voices clambering with breathless haste up and down this enormous contrapuntal ladder. To the listener, the point of all these exertions is neither musically nor poetically clear, since the instrumental figurations executed by the voices in the chorus make it impossible to follow the fundamental idea of the music or to understand even a single syllable of text.[65]

Even in cases where Bach's texts *can* be understood, Hanslick continued, modern listeners are often unable to relate emotionally to their messages. This, he noted, was the case with one of his own favorite works, the cantata *Christ Lay in the Bonds of Death* (BWV 4). "The number of concert-goers who feel the same way that Bach did in his time about the 'sacrificial lamb prepared in the fire of love' is already very small," he remarked. "Indeed, many will become quietly irritated by this kind of poetry. Luther's Cantata, with Bach's music, remains an abiding monument to a great sacred art that has long since faded, a

---

63. Hanslick, *Concerte*, 261: "Die Musik lag damals, so sehr sie nach *einer* Seite, der künstlich polyphonen, ausgebildet war, doch als schöne Kunst in ihren Anfängen; Elemente, die uns seit Bach, Händel und Mozart unentbehrlich, fast untrennbar von dem Befriff Musik sind, fehlten ihr noch zu Palestrinas Zeit. Es kostet uns Modernen deshalb eine gewisse Anstrengung ihn als einen großen Componisten, als einen originalen musikalischen Erfinder nicht blos nachzubeten, sondern zu empfinden."

64. Hanslick identifies the motet as "J. S. Bach's 49. Psalm"—a psalm that Bach never set. It seems likely that the work Hanslick heard was the motet *Singet dem Herrn ein neues Lied*, BWV 225, which opens with text from Psalm 149. Hanslick's apparent reference to Psalm 49, in other words, may be the result of a typographical error. Few of Bach's motets set psalm texts, and, like the one described by Hanslick, *Singet dem Herrn* is composed for double choir, a configuration rarely used by Bach. If this hypothesis is correct, the string and organ parts to which Hanslick refers would most likely have doubled the vocal parts, as was common practice in performances of the period. I wish to thank Stephen Crist for suggesting this hypothesis.

65. Hanslick, *Aus dem Concertsaal*, 210: "Beim Studium der Partitur werden wir bewundernd in diesen großartig gedachten, kunstreich gethürmten Bau uns versenken, wir können uns allenfalls an einer Ausführung deselben durch Orgel und Streich-Instrumente erbauen; allein es flieht uns jeder Genuß, wenn wir eine große Zahl Menschenstimmen in athemloser Hast an diesen contrapunktischen Riesenleitern auf- und niederklettern sehen. Das Ziel dieser Anstrengungen wird dem Hörer weder musikalisch noch poetisch kalr, weil das instrumentale Figuriren der Chorstimmen es unmöglich macht, dem musikalischen Grundgedanken zu folgen oder auch nur eine Sylbe vom Text zu verstehen."

monument whose true effectiveness can only be appreciated completely in worship, churchly worship."[66]

But in spite of the claims he made in his review of Hirschfeld's Renaissance Evenings, the musics of Baroque and pre-Baroque composers were not, in Hanslick's view, mere "objects for study or antiquarian hobbies." Indeed, as many of his other statements on the subject make clear, Hanslick objected not to the music Hirschfeld programmed but to the *use* that he and others had sought to make of it. The works of Bach and Palestrina were not, Hanslick believed, historical artifacts that one ought to honor by memorializing them in special concerts, as the inauguration of Hirschfeld's series seemed to imply. Rather, they were—as Hirschfeld himself felt compelled to acknowledge in his response to Hanslick's critique—musics to be renewed and vocabularies to be modernized in the work of contemporary composers. This, Hanslick felt, was the special gift of one, incomparably talented musician, the young Johannes Brahms.[67]

In his initial consideration of his first encounter with Brahms and his work, published in *History of Concert Life in Vienna*, Hanslick described the artist with the even-handedness of a cultural historian striving for objective impartiality in his account of history-making events. Brahms was, for the Hanslick of 1869, an impressive, perhaps unrivaled, talent.[68] Revisiting this same encounter from his newly embraced critical perspective of one year later, Hanslick hailed the composer as a unique figure who promised "the brilliant modernization of the canon and the fugue." This gift, he argued, might have been nurtured in Brahms by the departed Robert Schumann, but "the common well from which they both have drawn is *Sebastian Bach*."[69] Reflecting upon Brahms's contributions from the perspective of the mid-1880s, Hanslick exclaimed:

> In the area of spiritual music in the grandest sense, nothing has appeared since Bach's Passions, Handel's oratorios, and Beethoven's *Festmesse* that stands so close to these works in magnificence of conception, sublimity of expression, and power of polyphonic composition as Brahms's Requiem and *Triumphlied*. Influences of all three masters—of Bach, Handel, and Beethoven—are at play in Brahms, but they have been so dissolved within his blood and they have reemerged as part of such a unique and independent individuality that one cannot derive Brahms from any of

66. Hanslick, *Concerte*, 87: "... sehr klein ist bereits die Zahl von Concertbesuchern, die für das 'in heißer Lieb' gebratene Opferlamm' empfinden, was seinerzeit Bach dafür empfand. Viel eher werden sie an dieser Art Poesie stilles Aergerniß nehmen. Luthers Cantate mit Bachs Musik bleibt ein unvergängliches Denkmal einer längst abgeblühten, großen geistlichen Kunst, ein Denkmal, zu dessen voller und ganzer Wirkung die Andacht, die kirchliche Andacht, hinzutreten muß."

67. Writing in reply to Hanslick's review of 1885, Hirschfeld conceded this point and, moreover, implicated Brahms in the same way that Hanslick did. See his *Das kritische Verfahren*, 17. For further consideration of Hirschfeld's response to Hanslick, see Botstein, "Music and Its Public," 894–900.

68. Hanslick, *Geschichte*, 417–18.

69. Hanslick, *Aus dem Concertsaal*, 256: "Hier liegt *Brahms'* Stärke; die geistvolle Modernisirung des Canons, der Fuge, hat er von *Schumann*. Die gemeinschaftliche Quelle, an der Beide schöpften, ist *Sebastian Bach*."

these three alone. One can only say that in him something of this tripartite spirit is resurrected in modern form.[70]

To Hanslick's mind, Hirschfeld's attempts to resurrect in concert the works of Bach and his forebears were doomed to fail, not because of the worth of the music performed but on account of the misguided conception all such undertakings. For Hanslick, the issue was not only one of taste but one with profound implications for the spiritual health of contemporary culture as whole. As his comments of 1885 make clear, Hanslick detected in Hirschfeld's concerts an "antiquarian" tendency similar to that bemoaned by the young Friedrich Nietzsche, whose writings had found wide circulation in Vienna—and especially at the university—almost as soon as they were published in the 1870s.[71] In his "On the Uses and Disadvantages of History for Life" (1874), Nietzsche observed that the "antiquarian" tendency, manifested in an uncritical or exaggerated "veneration of the past," indeed has a place in every age, for it can foster a sense of security in one's culture, an awareness that "one is not wholly accidental and arbitrary but grown out of a past as its heir."[72] However, if the antiquarian tendency is indulged too broadly and one-sidedly, it invariably leads to trouble. As Nietzsche argued, "everything old and past that enters one's field of vision... is in the end blandly taken to be equally worthy of reverence, while... everything new and evolving is rejected and persecuted." More important, should the antiquarian tendency "grow too mightily and overpower the other modes of regarding the past," it can pose a great danger not only for the present and future of art, but for the future of one's culture as a whole. The antiquarian frame of mind "knows," Nietzsche wrote, "only how to *preserve* life, not how to engender it... it hinders any firm resolve to attempt something new."[73] In Hanslick's view, to protect one's audience from the dangers of the antiquarian mindset was one of the primary responsibilities of both critic and historian. As he explained just prior to the turn of the century,

> Indeed our age... cannot do without the new, through which *our* blood courses. Poems and musical works of the classical periods of art might still live on in the

70. Hanslick, *Concerte, Componisten und Virtuosen*, 51: "Auf diesem Gebiete geistlicher Musik im weitesten Sinne ist seit *Bachs* Passionsmusiken, *Händels* Oratorien und *Beethovens* Festmesse nichts erschienen, was an Großartigkeit der Conception, Erhabenheit des Ausdrucks und Gewalt des polyphonen Satzes jenen Werken so nahe steht, wie Brahms Requiem und Triumphlied. Von allen drei Meistern, von Bach, Händel und Beethoven, spielen Einflüsse in Brahms; sie sind aber so vollständig in sein Blut verflößt, zu so eigener, selbständiger Individualität aufgegangen, daß man Brahms aus keinem dieser Drei einfach herleiten, sondern nur sagen kann, es sei etwas von diesem dreieinigen Geist in moderner Wiedergeburt in ihm auferstanden."

71. On the reception of Nietzsche's early work at the University of Vienna in the 1870s and 1880s, see William J. McGrath, *Dionysian Art and Populist Politics in Austria* (New Haven: Yale University Press, 1974). This topic will be considered in greater detail in chapter 5.

72. Nietzsche, "On the Uses and Disadvantages of History for Life," in *Untimely Meditations*, ed. Daniel Breazeale, trans. R. J. Hollingdale, Cambridge Texts in the History of Philosophy (Cambridge: Cambridge University Press, 1997), 73–74. For a consideration of Nietzsche's essay within the context of late-century Wagnerism, to be considered in chapter 5, see also Walter Frisch, *German Modernism: Music and the Arts*, California Studies in 20th-Century Music, no. 3 (Berkeley and Los Angeles: University of California Press, 2005), 16–17.

73. Nietzsche, "On the Uses and Disadvantages of History," 74–75 (emphasis in original).

bright light of day, but only modern music reveals those colors that correspond to the magical light of sunrise and sunset. I consider it the critic's responsibility to avoid discouraging productivity, to acknowledge those works of our time that are truly felt and unaffectedly entertaining, and not to disparage such works contemptuously in favor of a vanishing "golden age."[74]

For Hanslick, Hirschfeld's Renaissance Evenings epitomized Nietzsche's antiquarian "species of history." By resurrecting in the ritual of the concert the works of artists long past, Hirschfeld's work threatened to open further a Pandora's box whose lid had been left ajar by the Singakademie and other organizations already engaged in similar pursuits. In Hanslick's view, the proper response to the musical heritage of one's cultural community is not antiquarian reverence but the creation of new, living works from out of the traces of that heritage. To modernize, to reenliven, and to build upon the musical inheritance bequeathed by one's predecessors was, for Hanslick, the only path forward. As we will see later in this study, it was with respect to this point that Hanslick's "living history" shared essential assumptions and goals with Guido Adler's otherwise very different work of the period. But while Adler saw—for a while at least—that path forward leading from the music of Gustav Mahler to that of Arnold Schoenberg and his circle, Hanslick argued that Brahms had, long before, already set out upon that course. Rather than recreating the musics of departed artists as they had left them long ago, Brahms transformed the art of his forebears into the living music of the present age. In doing so, he accomplished a kind of a double affirmation. He secured his place in the history of the art; and, by enabling the traces of musical antiquity to play again within the listener's imagination, he reaffirmed his contemporaries' connection to that history as well.[75]

So what, then, *was* the reception of Hanslick's "living history" within the society he sought to address? While it is surely difficult to assess the impact of his work upon the thinking of non-academic readers, statements by the likes of

74. Hanslick, *Aus meinem Leben*, 2:308: "Unsere Zeit...kann überhaupt das Neue nicht entbehren, in welchem *unsere* Blutwelle rauscht. Dichtungen und Tonwerke der klassischen Kunstperiode leben im hellen Tageslicht; für den Zauber der Morgen- und Abenddämmerungen hat erst die moderne Musik die entsprechenden Farben entdeckt. Ich halte es für Pflicht des Kritikers, die Produktion nicht zu entmutigen, das echt Empfundene und ungesucht Geistreiche unserer Zeit anzuerkennen und es gegen ein entschwundenes 'goldenes Zeitalter' nicht verächtlich herabzusetzen."

75. It may be worth noting that the interpretation offered here of Hanslick's arguments regarding Brahms and his music resonates with a number of recent analytical and historiographical studies of the composer's work. Kevin Korsyn, for instance, observes in a consideration of Brahms's String Quartet, Op. 51, no. 1, that "Brahms inscribes himself in history by inscribing history in his work... Brahms reaffirms the past while renewing it" (Korsyn, "Brahms Research and Aesthetic Ideology," *Music Analysis* 12, no. 1 [1993], 94–95). Along similar lines, Walter Frisch writes that "Brahms showed how techniques of the remote past could be put in the service of a musical language both expressive and original. ...for Brahms the music of the past was not a crutch but a creative stimulus" (Frisch, *German Modernism*, 150). Most recently, Margaret Notley has observed that Brahms, through his studies of parallel octaves and fifths in the music of other, mostly earlier composers, "effected his own, specifically nineteenth-century renewal of contrapuntal traditions" (Notley, *Lateness and Brahms*, 143).

Hirschfeld, the novelist Stefan Zweig, and the critic Max Graf provide us with some hints. For Hirschfeld, the opinion-making power of Hanslick's work was formidable enough to drive him to make his debut as a critic by turning, in the most public of ways, against his mentor of just one year earlier. Zweig elaborates a similar portrait, describing a writer so widely respected as to enjoy "pontifical" authority among the most cultured and highly educated segments of late-century Viennese society.[76] For Graf, a critic who socialized with Sigmund Freud and despised Hanslick and his influence, the situation was much the same. Recalling Hanslick's stature from the perspective of wartime exile in New York, Graf observed that

> The perfect harmony between Hanslick and the musical taste of Viennese society explains the hold he had upon his Viennese readers. ... Hanslick, then, represents the type of critic who is his readers' mouthpiece. He is the man who finds the finest formulas—even scientific ones—to express his readers' likes and dislikes, who transforms their most undistinguished opinions into intelligence, grace, and wit.[77]

There can be no doubt that Graf penned these lines in order to disparage Hanslick and his work. But this fact only makes the situation clearer. Hanslick's writings, as even Graf was compelled to admit, indeed preserve, as if frozen in a photographer's frame, a representative expression of the experiences and attitudes of a sizeable portion of the society of which he was a part. In this respect, his "living history" succeeded remarkably in accomplishing its author's goals.

As we have seen, however, Hanslick's achievement in this regard did not translate into success for his more ambitious attempt to erode the disciplinary boundaries within which his scientifically-minded colleagues were working to define the musicological field. As Adler's appointment to Hanslick's university chair in 1898 made clear, Jodl, Mach, and their colleagues at the institution ultimately succeeded in expelling from the academy an approach to historical research and writing that threatened to undermine musicology's claims to academic legitimacy. Indeed, it has only been in recent decades that historians of Western classical music have begun to return to positions like those that Hanslick pioneered, to "acknowledge"—in Rose Rosengard Subotnik's words—"their own presence in their acts of scholarship and thereby the limitations of pure objectivity and universal validity that are entailed in their results by their particular outlook and decisions."[78] But although Hanslick's "living history" seems to have been quickly forgotten after his death, we must not lose sight of the fact his project was only a single, unusually theorized manifestation of a broader, diffuse phenomenon. As we will see in the chapters to come, the impulse to record one's subjective impressions—even, as Spitta disdainfully observed, to identify aspects of one's

---

76. Stefan Zweig, *The World of Yesterday*, anonymous trans. (Lincoln: University of Nebraska Press, 1964), 100.

77. Max Graf, *Composer and Critic: Two Hundred Years of Musical Criticism* (New York: W. W. Norton, 1946), 246.

78. Rose Rosengard Subotnik, "Musicology and Criticism," in *Developing Variations: Style and Ideology in Western Music* (Minneapolis: University of Minnesota Press, 1991), 87–97 (cited at 92).

self in the objects of one's research—was widely and powerfully felt. Though few writers followed Hanslick's lead in openly proclaiming the subjective nature of their analytical or historical arguments, many assumed, in their work, the deeply subjective stances he described. We see this in the work of Heinrich Schenker, whose studies of musical structure and the compositional process provided vehicles for his own creative self-explorations. And we encounter it in Adler's work as well, where demands for a scientific approach to music study stand side by side with anxious negotiations of cultural identity and attempts to advance a program of cultural renewal in the spirit of Nietzsche and Wagner. For a great many inhabitants of Hanslick's Vienna, there was simply no separating music scholarship from the critical impulse. Each was deeply inscribed within the other.

PART II

HEINRICH SCHENKER
AND THE CHALLENGE
OF CRITICISM

Heinrich Schenker, circa 1900. Undated photograph with inscription to his friend
Moriz Violin, "To his dearest Floriz in loyalty." Used by permission of Special
Collections, University of California, Riverside Libraries, University of California,
Riverside.

CHAPTER THREE

MUSIC ANALYSIS AS CRITICAL METHOD

Though its leading figures are known today primarily for their work as historians, the positivist movement in music research touched upon more than source studies and philological criticism. As we saw in chapter 1, the inductive, four-stage process that Adler prescribed for music study in his "Scope, Method, and Goal of Musicology" (1885) was dominated, in its first two stages, by analysis. Before one can assess a work's place and significance in the historical development of the art, Adler argued, one must acquire a thorough understanding of the manifest character of the artwork itself. "We begin," he wrote,

> with the *rhythmic* features: whether and in what way the music is barred, what temporal relationships are found in each section, and how these are grouped and arranged periodically. Likewise, we could have begun with *tonality*—by considering the tonal character, first of the individual voices and then of the whole... After this, individual sections are studied in terms of their cadences, transitional passages, and accidentals, and these too are considered in relation to the whole. At that point the *polyphonic structure* can be examined: the range and spacing of the voices; the intervals of imitation between themes and motives and the temporal displacement between entrances; the appearance of themes in augmented, diminished, inverted, and retrograde forms; the use of consonances and dissonances and their preparation and resolution or lack thereof. The way in which the different voices unfold in relation to each other must be traced, considering the relationship between primary and secondary themes, the presence or absence of a *cantus firmus*, and whether or not the *cantus firmus* is broken. The development of themes and motives will be charted and assessed. If the composition has an accompanying *text*, then that too must be examined critically, at first only as poetry and then in relation to its setting and its connections with the melody.[1]

---

1. Guido Adler, "Umfang, Methode und Ziel der Musikwissenschaft," *Vierteljahrsschrift für Musikwissenschaft* 1 (1885), 6: "Wir beginnen mit den *rhythmischen* Merkmalen: ob eine Taktart und welche vorliegt, welche zietlichen Verhältnisse in den Gliedern zu finden, wie diese periodisirt und gruppirt sind. Es könnte auch mit der *Tonalität* begonnen werden und zwar die tonliche Beschaffenheit einzelner Stimmen und dann erst die des Ganzen... Die einzelnen Theile werden nach ihrer Cadenzirung, den Übergängen, Accidentien untersucht und zum Ganzen

In this passage, Adler made clear that he conceived of analysis as a "scientific" endeavor, in the terms of Ian D. Bent's classic study of nineteenth-century analytical writings. To Adler's mind (and in Bent's words), music analysis was an exercise "imbued with the impulse to describe exactly, to measure, to quantify, the material attributes of music."[2] Such an approach, Adler reasoned, was the only one appropriate for a scholar who wished to attain what Adler considered the ultimate goal of musicological inquiry: the uncovering of objectively verifiable "artistic laws" (*Kunstgesetze*) that govern the evolution of musical forms and styles across different historical periods.[3] Embracing such a view of the analyst's task, Adler followed in the footsteps of his mentor, Hanslick. Writing on Beethoven's overture to *The Creatures of Prometheus* in the first edition of *On the Musically Beautiful* (1854), Hanslick provided a detailed, technical account of the unfolding of melodic line and harmonic structure in the overture's opening bars. ("The C-major triad of the first four bars corresponds to the four-two chord in the fifth and sixth bars, then to the six-five chord in the seventh and eighth," Hanslick wrote of the work.)[4] Hanslick acknowledged that such a "dissection" of Beethoven's overture threatened to "make a skeleton out of a radiant body." But he nonetheless recommended such an approach for its promise "to destroy all misguided speculation"—to relieve the scholar of the temptation to make claims for a work that cannot be verified via empirical observations.[5]

From the time of his first attempts as a writer on music, Heinrich Schenker was of a different mind concerning the promise and practice of analysis, and he did not share Adler's views about the goal of music study. Indeed, in his first published essay, an analytical review of Brahms's Op. 107 songs that appeared in the Leipzig *Musikalisches Wochenblatt* in October 1891, he expressed profound unease with the

---

gestellt. Nunmehr wird die Construction der *Mehrstimmigkeit* klargelegt: Umfang und Vertheilung der Stimmen, die Nachahmung der Themen und Motive je nach den Eintritten in verschiedenen Intervallen und ihrer verschiedenen zeitlichen Aufeinanderfolge, ob die Themen vergrößert, verkleinert, umgekehrt oder entgegengesetzt sind, ferner die Führung der Con- und Dissonanzen, deren Vorbereitung und Auflösung oder freier Eintritt. Die Art der Bewegung der einzelnen Stimmen untereinander wird verfolgt: das Verhältniß von Haupt- und Nebenstimmen, die Herübernahme eines Cantus firmus, seine Verwendung und Gliederung, die Durchführung der Themen und Motive wird erwogen und fixirt. Hat die Composition einen *Worttext*, so wird dieser kritisch untersucht: zuerst nur als Dichtung, hierauf in Bezug auf die Unterlegung oder Verbindung mit der Melodie." For an alternative translation of this passage, see Bojan Bujić, ed., *Music in European Thought, 1851–1912*, Cambridge Readings in the Literature of Music (Cambridge: Cambridge University Press, 1988), 349.

2. Ian D. Bent, ed., *Music Analysis in the Nineteenth Century*, 2 vols., Cambridge Readings in the Literature of Music (Cambridge: Cambridge University Press, 1994), 2:1.

3. Adler, "Umfang, Methode und Ziel," 9. Further discussion of this aspect of Adler's argument is provided in chapter 1.

4. Hanslick/Strauß, 1:50; Hanslick/Payzant, 13: "...dem *C-dur*-Dreiklang in den vier ersten Takten entspricht der Secundaccord im fünften und seschsten, dann der Quintsext-Accord im siebenten und achten Takt."

5. Hanslick/Strauß, 1:50; Hanslick/Payzant, 14: "Solche Zergliederung macht ein Geripe aus blühenden Körper, geeignet, alle Schönheit, aber auch alle falsche Deutelei zu zerstören." On analysis as "dissection" and the use of metaphors drawn from the biological sciences to describe the activity, see Bent, *Music Analysis*, 1:7–8.

effects that these and other scientifically inspired programs of research had had upon the critical discourse on the art. He opened his debut essay by castigating those among his fellow critics who had been swayed by arguments such as Adler's:

> For some time now, critics and the public have been whispering to each other that Brahms has entered into his third and weakest creative period. These days, when *feuilletonistic* criticism, instinctively recognizing the greatness of the composer but seldom providing proof, is trying to work its way toward the study of music history and to occupy itself with the construction of historical periods, even the most brilliant rallies of the Brahmsian genius will hardly be proof enough. What can a Violin Sonata in A Major, a String Quintet, Op. 111, or a Fourth Symphony in E Minor achieve against such a proclamation?! Criticism sticks to what has already been decided. Otherwise, there would indeed be no aesthetic in whose name it still speaks. Nevertheless, I will attempt, in the most recent songs, Op. 107 (which Brahms wrote for a solo voice with piano accompaniment), to provide proof that a brilliant strength of invention and powerful artistic reasoning still work together undiminished in him to create perfect artworks.[6]

In Schenker's view, the lackluster reception lately greeting Brahms in the critical press in no way reflected the effectiveness or worth of the composer's recent music. Instead, it revealed the sorry state of music criticism in his time. Too many critics, Schenker charged, had failed to appreciate the creative genius evident in Brahms's late compositions in their rush to "construct historical periods" within the span of the artist's output. And predictably, he observed, the periods into which that output was typically divided traced a familiar trajectory from youthful apprenticeship to mature mastery and ultimately to elderly decline.[7]

Yet for all of the shortcomings of such approaches to writing about Brahms's music, Schenker noted, those critics who adopted them simply followed upon the heels of contemporary music historians. In the wake of the disciplinary polemics of Adler, Spitta, and their scientifically inspired colleagues, historical musicology had emerged as that branch of music study to which all others aspired methodologically. And that branch, Schenker observed sarcastically,

---

6. Heinrich Schenker, "Kritik. Johannes Brahms. Fünf Lieder für eine Singstimme mit Pianoforte, Op. 107," *Musikalisches Wochenblatt* 22 (1891); repr. in *Schenker*, 2–8 (cited at 2): "Seit geraumer Zeit schon flüstern sich Kritik und Publicum zu, Brahms sei in seine dritte und schwächste Schaffensperiode getreten. Wenn nun die feuilletonistische Kritik, instinctiv die Grösse des Componisten erkennend (Beweise liefert sie selten), der Musikgeschichte vorarbeiten und sich mit Periodisirungen befassen will, so werden ihr selbst die Hinweise auf die glänzendsten Kundgebungen des Brahms'schen Geistes in dieser Periode kaum Beweis genug sein. Was kann einem Justament! gegenüber eine Violinsonate in Adur, ein Streichquintett op. 111, eine 4. Symphonie in Emoll u.s.w. ausrichten? Es bleibt dabei, was beschlossen wurde. Sonst gäbe es ja keine Aesthetik, in deren Namen doch die Kritik spricht. Indessen will ich versuchen, an den letzten Liedern, op. 107, die Brahms für eine Singstimme mit Pianofortebegleitung geschrieben, den Nachweis zu liefern, dass noch immer in ihm glänzende Erfindungskraft und mächtiger Kunstverstand ungeschwächt zusammenwirken, um vollkommene Kunstwerke zu schaffen."

7. A recent and thoughtful consideration of critical attempts to assign periods to Brahms's life and work from the 1860s to the present, with particular emphasis upon efforts to define Brahms's "late period" and "late style," is provided in Margaret Notley, *Lateness and Brahms: Music and Culture in the Twilight of Viennese Liberalism*, AMS Studies in Music, no. 3 (Oxford: Oxford University Press, 2007), chapter 2.

was dominated by writers preeminently concerned with the development of musical form and style over time, obsessed with the elegance of laws induced to account for that development, and oblivious to the unique effectiveness and worth of individual works of art. Indeed, the critical discourse that Schenker described adhered closely to the ideal of music study outlined in Adler's "Scope, Method, and Goal of Musicology." It valorized theorizing about stylistic development and relegated to the sidelines or dismissed entirely the kinds of subjective engagement with musical works that Schenker held most dear.

As we saw in the previous chapter, Hanslick, after his break from Herbartianism, also expressed profound unease about the effects of positivist scholarship upon the popular discourse on music, and he attempted to pioneer, with his "living history," a historiographical alternative. Schenker, in contrast, found his own alternative to Adlerian scholarship in analysis. And significantly, the mode of analysis that Schenker espoused could hardly have been more different from the "scientific" one that Adler prescribed. At a time when approaches such as those he would advocate were widely derided as hopelessly unscientific, Schenker held that there existed no better means than *hermeneutic* analysis to account for the impact of a musical work upon the mind of the listener. And it was precisely that impact, he insisted, rather than the dispassionate study of music's formal or stylistic development, that made the experience of music meaningful to a multitude of late-century listeners.

But as we will see, Schenker's experiments with hermeneutic analysis would prove to be short-lived. In the end, he would prove to be a more deeply ambivalent figure than Hanslick ever was. For in his search for a mode of critical inquiry capable of accounting for music's worth, Schenker found himself powerfully drawn to the theoretical contributions of Richard Wagner, a figure whose work he would soon come to despise. And before long, he would turn his back on his youthful experiments altogether, rejecting hermeneutic analysis as a critical tool and coming to embrace an empiricist ideal of music research before the end of the decade. In chapter 4, we will take a close look at Schenker's brush with empiricism. But first we must consider the hermeneutic, indeed Wagnerian, origins of his earliest analytical endeavors.

THE PROMISE OF ANALYSIS

That Schenker chose to approach his work as a critic from an analytical perspective would have come as no surprise to his readers, not because he had already secured a reputation as an analyst but because analytical essays such as his had been staples of the critical press for decades. The very journal for which he wrote, the Leipzig *Musikalisches Wochenblatt*, included in its inaugural issue of 1870 the first installment of a serialized analytical review, complete with examples in musical notation, of Brahms's German Requiem.[8] The

---

8. A. Maczewski, "Ein deutsches Requiem. Nach Worten der heiligen Schrift für Soli, Chor und Orchester von J. Brahms," *Musikalisches Wochenblatt* 1 (1870), 5, 20–21, 35–36, 52–54, 67–69.

high point of such writing for the *Wochenblatt* seems to have come the following decade, when the Viennese critic Theodor Helm published analytical discussions of all of Beethoven's string quartets in a serialized essay spanning seventy-two issues over ten years.[9] Yet the tradition was still alive and well when Schenker began writing in 1891. During the year preceding Schenker's debut, the *Wochenblatt* published analytical reviews by Georg Riemenschneider of Aleksandr Glazunov's First Symphony, Andreas Hallén's Swedish Rhapsody, and Edvard Grieg's *Peer Gynt*.[10] Similar essays also appeared regularly in the *Wochenblatt*'s principal Viennese competitors, the *Neue musikalische Presse* and the *Österreichische Theater- und Musikzeitung*.

Significantly, many of the essays mentioned above took the form of what Bent has characterized as "hermeneutic" or "elucidatory" analyses. In a manner described in general terms around 1800 by the philosopher and theologian Friedrich Schleiermacher and elaborated more fully by Wilhelm Dilthey in the 1880s, all of these critics sought to "describe" the musical work under consideration in terms of its formal characteristics, and, in turn, to "*interpret* rather than to describe" what they heard.[11] The former, the "objective" side of analysis, required a writer to draw upon the illustrative potential of musical notation and the descriptive language of music theory in order to provide an empirical, prose account of the structure of a composition as preserved in score. This was, in essence, the same mode of analytical investigation for which Adler called in his "Scope, Method, and Goal of Musicology." In contrast, the "subjective" side of the critic's task was concerned with "the *inner life* of the music rather than with its outward, audible form." It was, Bent explains, an attempt "to transcend that outer form and penetrate the non-material interior" of a work. The critic engaged in such a project moves back and forth between objective and subjective modes of analysis in an attempt to understand the object of his study ever more deeply and clearly. And significantly, the entire hermeneutic endeavor is motivated by an inherent assumption of value: the listener's perception of the greatness of a work justifies the "empirical" analysis for which Adler called.

As Bent has shown, hermeneutic modes of analysis, often informed by idealist or Romantic conceptions of musical meaning, appear throughout the nineteenth-century literature on music. Indeed, they underlie much of the critical work of some of century's most famous writers on the art, including E. T. A. Hoffmann, Hector Berlioz, Robert Schumann, and

9. Helm's essays, originally published between 1873 and 1882, were reprinted as *Beethoven's Streichquartette. Versuch einer technischen Analyse dieser Werke im Zusammenhange mit ihrem geistigen Gehalt*, 2d ed. (Leipzig: C. F. W. Siegel, 1910; first edition, 1885). Helm's analysis of the Quartet in A minor, Op. 132, is translated in Bent, *Music Analysis*, 2:242–66.

10. Georg Riemenschneider, "Kritik. Alexander Glazounow. 1. Symphonie für grosses Orchester," *Musikalisches Wochenblatt* 21 (1890), 266–68; "Kritik. Andréas Hallén. Schwedische Rhapsodie No. 2, Op. 23, für grosses Orchester," *Musikalisches Wochenblatt* 21 (1890), 435–36; "Kritik. Edvard Grieg. Orchestersuite aus der Musik zu Ibsen's dramatischer Dichtung 'Peer Gynt', Op. 16," *Musikalisches Wochenblatt* 21 (1890), 447–48.

11. The discussion in this paragraph is largely summarized from Bent, *Music Analysis*, 2:1–19; all citations are from page 1 (emphasis in original).

Hermann Kretzschmar.[12] Closer to the world of Schenker's debut essay, the objective/subjective paradigm of hermeneutic analysis was acknowledged explicitly by Theodor Helm in the introduction to his volume of collected essays on Beethoven's string quartets, reprinted from his contributions to the *Musikalisches Wochenblatt* published in the 1870s and 1880s. The effectiveness of the quartets, Helm observed with reference to the analytical approach taken in his book, "can only be demonstrated through the most rigorous technical analysis of the scores as they relate to the poetic mood, so far as that can be ascertained."[13] Here Helm promises first to broach the "descriptive" side of critical inquiry by way of empirical, "technical" analysis. Once that task is accomplished, however, he will strive to penetrate the "non-material interior"—the poetic mood—of Beethoven's compositions. As Bent points out, such an approach to the analyst's task was embraced even by the young Philipp Spitta, in the preface to the first volume of his *Johann Sebastian Bach* (1873), written ten years before his positivist manifesto, "Art and the Study of Art" ("Kunstwissenschaft und Kunst"). "I have naturally placed the greatest weight on the formal aspect, in proportion to the extent that this is more amenable to exact scientific measurement than is the ideal aspect," Spitta wrote with regard to his discussions of the works he considered.

> However, to neglect the latter altogether seemed to me unwarranted. . . . In instrumental music the writer faces the choice either of baldly confronting his reader with an anatomical exhibit, or of attempting by way of a word here and there to capture the atmosphere which alone can awaken that exhibit to burgeoning life. I have adopted the latter approach. . . . I can only hope I shall not be reproached for acting with undue subjectivity.[14]

Given its pervasiveness in the critical discourse of nearly the whole of the nineteenth century, it should come as no surprise that Schenker too was deeply indebted to this methodological trend. But here it seems that comments he made later in life, especially with regard to the hermeneutic analyses of his despised Hermann Kretzschmar, have tended to obscure this aspect of his intellectual history from the view of most commentators.[15] Nonetheless, in the concluding lines of the prefatory paragraph of his review of Brahms's Op. 107 songs, Schenker situated his own consideration squarely within the hermeneutic tradition:

> I will attempt, in the most recent songs, Op. 107 (which Brahms wrote for a solo voice with piano accompaniment), to provide proof that a brilliant strength of

12. Hermeneutic analyses by all of these figures are provided in English translation in Bent, *Music Analysis*, 2:31–57 (Berlioz on Meyerbeer's *Les Huguenots*), 2:106–17 (Kretzschmar on Bruckner's Fourth Symphony), 2:141–60 (Hoffmann on Beethoven's Fifth Symphony), and 2:161–94 (Schumann on Berlioz's *Symphonie fantastique*).

13. Helm, *Beethoven's Streichquartette*, iii (from the foreword to the first edition of 1885): "Dieser mir als künstlerische Lebensfrage erscheinende Nachweis konnte nur durch die gründlichste technische Analyse der Partituren im Zusammenhalten mit deren poetischer Stimmung—soweit sie eben erkennbar—erzielt werden."

14. Spitta, *Johann Sebastian Bach*, vol. 1 (1873); cited in Bent, *Music Analysis*, 2:82.

15. This situation is considered in Bent, *Music Analysis*, 2:12–13.

invention and powerful artistic reasoning still work together undiminished in him to create perfect artworks. I will apply a method here that possesses compelling strength when it remains purely objective, but that does not spurn subjective inter-pretation so long as the latter does not presume to be objective.[16]

But although his approach to Brahms's music was deeply rooted in critical tradition, Schenker carried out the subjective side of his analytical project in an unusually provocative manner. In his essay on Brahms's songs, and again in his review of Brahms's choral pieces, Op. 104, likewise published in the Leipzig *Wochenblatt* (1892), he attempted to elucidate the poetic essence of Brahms's com-positions by exploring the correspondence of musical events and the emotions or ideas depicted and implicit in the texts they set. Generally speaking, ample precedent exists in the literature for a critical orientation such as Schenker's, as many writers of the period were fond of highlighting moments of particularly effective text setting in the songs they studied.[17] But Schenker was unusually reflective about the issue, arguing at times that Brahms's music clarifies emo-tional relationships that his poets had intended to convey but had been unable to communicate effectively to their readers on account of the inherent constraints of the poetic medium. Indeed, he even argued, in his essay on Op. 104, that Brahms deliberately subjugated his own creative will to his poets' expressive desires—desires that could not be realized by artists working with words alone. Like many critics of his time, Schenker was furthermore prone to supplying dramatic narratives to account for the unfolding of the works he considered. But whereas the construction of such narratives was often motivated by abstract, ide-alist conceptions of musical meaning,[18] Schenker's comments were motivated by a distinctly different critical agenda. The point of Schenker's analytical inquiry, as he himself described it, was not the *construction* of elucidatory narratives but the *uncovering* of narratives that he posited to have inspired, whether consciously or not, Brahms's own creative work. Moreover, Schenker suggested that we as lis-teners must likewise endeavor to uncover such narratives if we are to understand and appreciate the effectiveness of Brahms's music.

With respect to these issues, I would argue, Schenker's claims exhibit an aes-thetic sensibility that is conspicuously Wagnerian, quite possibly deriving from

16. *Schenker*, 2: "Indessen will ich versuchen, an den letzten Liedern, op. 107, die Brahms für eine Singstimme mit Pianofortebegleitung geschrieben, den Nachweis zu liefern, dass noch immer in ihm glänzende Erfindungskraft und mächtiger Kunstverstand ungeschwächt zusammenwirken, um vollkommene Kunstwerke zu schaffen. Ich wende hierbei eine Methode an, der zwingende Kraft innewohnt, wenn sie rein objectiv bleibt, die aber die Subjectivität nicht verschmäht, so lange sich dieselbe von der Anmaassung frei hält, Objectivität zu sein."

17. This subject has recently been explored by Heather Platt in "Hugo Wolf and the Reception of Brahms's Lieder," in *Brahms Studies 2*, ed. David Brodbeck (Lincoln: University of Nebraska Press, 1998), 91–111; and "Jenner versus Wolf: The Critical Reception of Brahms's Songs," *Journal of Musicology* 13, no. 3 (1995), 377–403.

18. For a recent and illuminating treatment of this issue, see Mark Evan Bonds, "Idealism and the Aesthetics of Instrumental Music at the Turn of the Nineteenth Century," *Journal of the American Musicological Society* 50 (1997), nos. 2–3, 387–420 (esp. 413–14); and Bonds, *Music as Thought: Listening to the Symphony in the Age of Beethoven* (Princeton: Princeton University Press, 2006).

Wagner's writings themselves, and in any case indebted to a complex of ideas that Wagner articulated, famously and persuasively, as he laid the aesthetic foundations for the music drama in *Opera and Drama* and other midcentury essays. To put this another way, in seeking to defend Brahms's late work—whether vocal or instrumental, he would insist—against its critical detractors, Schenker enlisted the help of a composer widely regarded as Brahms's musical antithesis. And in response to the positivist movement in music research and what he considered its deleterious effects upon the critical discourse, he invoked the work of the spiritual father of some of the period's most notoriously irrationalist aesthetic movements.

ENCOUNTERS WITH BRAHMS, ENCOUNTERS WITH WAGNER

Schenker began his discussion of "An die Stolze" ("To Pride"), the first song of Op. 107, by noting that the structure of Brahms's music does not correspond to the poetic structure of the text it sets. Instead, he argued, the form of the song corresponds perfectly to the poetic *idea*, which itself transcends the manifest form of Paul Flemming's verse. He observed:

> To be sure, the composer binds two strophes together into a period. But through the postponement of the decisive point of articulation—namely, of the dominant-seventh chord—until after the first line of the second and fourth strophes, the relationship between the textual ideas is developed far more sharply than through the form of the poem alone. In truly declamatory fashion, the music strides forward from "und gleichwohl kann ich anders nicht" [and in any case I can do nothing else (line 1)] to "ich muss ihr günstig sein" [I must win her favor (line 2)], and it reaches its formal high point in the passionate, penetrating setting of "ich will, ich soll, ich muss dich lieben" [I will, I shall, I must love you (line 5)]. As a result, the touching message of the remaining lines in the pair of strophes is rendered much more sharply in the musical form of the consequent phrase [*Nachsatz*].[19]

As shown in Table 3.1, the fourth line of the first quatrain of "An die Stolze" concludes in m. 11 ("mir mußgönnt seinen Schein"). Apparently assuming that the paired quatrains of Flemming's verse would more typically have been set in a simple binary form, Schenker explained that the primary musical interruption, demarcating the end of the antecedent phrase (*Vordersatz*), would normally be expected at the end of m. 11—at the juncture between the first and the second quatrains. However, he observed, Brahms postponed this interruption, an "articulating" dominant-seventh chord (as Schenker called it), until m. 17, by

---

19. *Schenker*, 2: "Je zwei Strophen bindet der Componist zu einer Periode zusammen. Durch Verlegung des entscheidenden Wendepunctes aber—des Dominantseptaccordes nämlich—hinter die erste Zeile der 2., respective 4. Strophe prägt sich die Beziehung der textlichen Gedanken weit schärfer aus, als selbst durch die Form des Gedichtes. Treu declamierend schreitet die Musik vom 'und gleichwohl kann ich anders nicht' zum 'ich muss ihr günstig sein' vor und erhält ihren formellen Gipfelpunct erst in der durchdringend leidenschaftlichen Vertonung des 'ich will, ich soll, ich muss dich lieben.' Dadurch erscheint noch weiter die rührende Pointe der übrigen Zeilen des Strophenpaares viel schärfer umrissen in der musikalischen Form des Nachsatzes."

TABLE 3.1.   Schenker's analysis of Brahms, "An die Stolze," Op. 107, no. 1

First Quatrain	Line 1	Und gleichwohl kann ich anders nicht,	I	mm. 1–3	
	Line 2	ich muß ihr günstig sein,		mm. 3–5	
	Line 3	obgleich der Augen stolzes Licht		mm. 7–9	antecedent
	Line 4	mir mißgönnt seinen Schein.		mm. 9–11	
Second Quatrain	Line 5	Ich will, ich soll, ich muß dich lieben,	V^7	mm. 12–17	
	Line 6	dadurch wir Beid uns nur betrüben,	V^7	mm. 17–21	
	Line 7	weil mein Wunsch doch nicht gilt,		mm. 21–23	consequent
	Line 8	und du nicht hören wilt.	I	mm. 23–28	

(And in any case I can do nothing else;/I must win her favor,/though the proud light of her eye/begrudges me its light.//I will, I shall, I must love you,/though we only make each other sad,/because my wish comes to nothing,/and you do not wish to hear.)

which point the voice has not only begun the second quatrain but completed its first line (Example 3.1). In this way, he argued, Brahms imposed a structural division upon Flemming's text that differed from the poet's own.[20]

To appreciate the peculiar nature of Schenker's reading of "An die Stolze," one need only compare his statements to those made by Eduard Hanslick in a review of the same work published two years earlier. In the latter essay, Hanslick

---

20. Before considering the implications of Schenker's reading, we should note some curious aspects of his analysis. First, the generic structure on which Brahms seems to play in "An die Stolze" is not, as Schenker suggests, a simple binary form but rather what James Hepokoski has described as a through-composed "lyric-binary," which can, in this case, be characterized schematically as AA'BC. In Brahms's song, the first poetic quatrain (mm. 1–11) is set as a parallel period AA', concluding on the dominant (albeit with perfect authentic cadence evaded via inversion in m. 11). In its normative guise, a lyric-binary setting would continue by presenting lines 5–6 in a contrasting manner; this section (B) would end with a strongly articulated dominant harmony, serving as the primary interruption in the song. Lines 7–8, concluding the second quatrain, would be cadential in nature, preparing for and realizing a perfect authentic cadence in the tonic (section C). Of particular interest here is the fact that the "decisive point of articulation"—the strongly articulated dominant that marks both a momentary interruption of forward momentum and the dramatic turning point in the narrative—would typically occur after line 6. In "An die Stolze," we find this interruption after line 5. One could therefore argue that the event that Schenker describes as "postponed" in this song in fact arrives one line *earlier* than expected. Of course, Schenker's argument about the essential *displacement* of this interruption is nonetheless valid. On the lyric-binary form, see Hepokoski, "*Ottocento* Opera as Cultural Drama: Generic Mixtures in *Il trovatore*," in *Verdi's Middle Period 1849–1859: Source Studies, Analysis, and Performance Practice*, ed. Martin Chusid (Chicago: University of Chicago Press, 1997), 147–96 (esp. 150–60).

EXAMPLE 3.1

EXAMPLE 3.1   (continued)

likewise drew his readers' attention to the unexpected pairing of music and text in Brahms's song. For Hanslick, however, this unusual arrangement only reinforced his own previously voiced conviction that a musical work cannot be said to express an emotional message in any precise way.[21] Observing that Flemming's "bourgeois [*bürgerlichen*] words get in the way of the passionate music," Hanslick argued that "one can consider this song yet another example of the ambiguity of music—a thing rarely encountered with Brahms. The music snuggles up faultlessly [*schmiegt sich tadellos*] to the distressing words of Flemming's poem, but the words of a *hopeful* lover could underlie this straightforward A-major melody as well."[22]

21. Hanslick advanced this argument in the first edition (1854) of *On the Musically Beautiful* (see Hanslick/Strauß, 1:55–60; Hanslick/Payzant, 16–20).

22. Hanslick, *Musikalisches und Litterarisches* (*Die moderne Oper*, vol. 5) (Berlin: Allgemeiner Verein für Deutsche Litteratur, 1889), 144 (emphasis added): "Die bürgerlichen Worte stellen sich leidenschaftlicher Musik in den Weg. ... Man kann an diesem Liede—ein sesltener Zufall bei Brahms—wieder einmal eine Probe auf die Vieldeutigkeit der Musik machen. Die Musik schmiegt sich tadellos dem schmerzlichen Gedichte Flemmings an, aber auch die Worte eines hoffnungsvoll Liebenden dürften sich dieser klaren A-dur-Melodie unterlegen lassen."

With regard to the significance of Brahms's setting, Schenker's conclusions could not have been further removed from Hanslick's. For Schenker, the formal division that Brahms imposed upon Flemming's poem, while undermining the structure intended by the poet, in fact corresponds perfectly to the *meaning* of the verse. Indeed, he argued, the structure of Brahms's music makes that meaning more explicit than the text alone can: the antecedent, lines 1–5, describes the poet's love, while the consequent, lines 6–8, depicts his sorrow. Flemming, working within the constraints of poetic convention, could not reconcile the tension between the outward form of the poem he constructed and the ideas he sought to convey. But Brahms, who faced no such constraints, was able resolve this tension faultlessly. Composing a setting that contravened against the manifest structure of the poetic text, Brahms successfully set the meaning of Flemming's words free, so to speak. He was able to bring out, as Schenker remarked, "the relationship between the textual ideas...far more sharply than [was possible] through the form of the poem alone." Here we find the first of many instances where Schenker's thinking crosses paths with Wagner's.

In *Opera and Drama* (1851), the most extensive and probably most widely read of all his polemical essays, Wagner identified a pair of formal parameters by which poets had for ages arranged their materials in what was, he argued, a misguided attempt to communicate effectively with their readers: meter and rhyme. The real effect of these devices, Wagner explained, was in fact just the opposite; metrical patterns destroy the natural rhythm of speech, and rhyme is by nature foreign to linguistic expression. Summarizing his arguments with regard to this point, Wagner decried poetry's "impoverished outward setting, which distorts the proper expressiveness of speech and obscures its meaningful content."[23] On the other hand, Wagner explained, a musical setting whose structural characteristics are made to correspond to poetic *ideas* rather to a poem's form will reveal with utmost clarity the emotional content of that poem, its meaning in the deepest sense. Coordinating the melodic and harmonic structure of his work with the emotional unfolding of a poetic text rather than with its manifest structure, "the musician attains vindication for his work...from the poet's intention—an intention that the latter could only hint at, or at best realize only partially and for a fraction of his message...but the full realization of which is possible for the musician alone."[24] This, it seems, is precisely what Schenker argued with respect to "An die Stolze."

Schenker provided a similar reading of "Mädchenlied" ("Girl's Song"), the fifth song of Op. 107. Referring to the opening strophe of the work (and apparently borrowing a turn of phrase from Hanslick's review of "An die Stolze" cited above), he observed that "in the most meager form of an eight-measure phrase, the music snuggles up [*schmiegt sich*] to the words. Absorbing [their] content

23. Wagner, 4:112: "...sein ärmliche, den richtigen Sprachausdruck entstellende, seinen sinnvollen Inhalt verwirrende äußere Fassung." For an alternate translation, see Wagner/Ellis, 2:249.

24. Wagner, 4:153; Wagner/Ellis, 2:293: "Die Rechtfertigung für sein Verfahrung...erhält der Musiker daher aus der Absicht des Dichters, – aus einer Absicht, die dieser eben nur andeuten oder höchstens nur für die Bruchtheile seiner Kundgebung...annähernd verwirklichen konnte, deren volle Verwirklichung aber eben nur dem Musiker möglich ist."

within itself, it is raised to the most wondrously beautiful height of expression."[25] Here again, Schenker argued that Brahms's music serves as a vehicle for poetic content—for the emotions and ideas that are expressed in a poem and often transcend its manifest structure. He illustrated this point by elaborating upon the harmonic progression underlying this passage.

> The harmonies appearing within this phrase are simple; they create a lasting effect with their powerful ability to support [the melody], and they take turns peaceably with one another. Although they progress far away from the [tonic] B-minor triad,[26] they always make their way back to—and, after their quiet wanderings, eventually arrive at—the triad for which they strive, and of which we have had, inwardly, a premonition [i.e., they return to the tonic]. They make the impression of a complete cycle, an ellipse, I would say. The agreement (even better, the analogy) between the melodic line and the progression of harmonies on the one hand, and the character of melancholy on the other, is obvious. Indeed, true melancholy, monotonous in its color and quiet by nature, always strikes in very small waves.[27]

Here Schenker describes the character of the harmonic progression underlying the first strophe of "Mädchenlied" as analogous to that of the emotion portrayed in its text: melancholy. In Paul Heyse's poem, a young woman, unloved, works away her days at a spinning wheel while all the other women of her village marry. For Schenker, the circularity of the progression, with its play between the tonic B minor and both B- and D-major sonorities, mirrors perfectly the waves of melancholy afflicting the protagonist (Example 3.2). Again, Schenker calls attention to the ways in which Brahms's music makes vividly apparent to the listener the emotional reality underlying events depicted in the verse. Whereas readers of Heyse's text alone must infer for themselves the emotional state of the protagonist from the actions and situations described, Brahms's setting makes the listener immediately and intuitively aware of the mood intended by the poet. Indeed, Schenker observed, the analogy between musical structure and prevailing emotion is "obvious" in Brahms's song.

As in his analysis of "An die Stolze," one is immediately struck, when reading Schenker's remarks on "Mädchenlied," by the similarities between the ways in which he describes his observations and Wagner's own statements on the setting

25. *Schenker*, 7: "In der knappsten Form eines achttaktigen Satzes schmiegt sich die Musik an die Worte an, und, den Inhalt in sich aufnehmend, schwingt sie sich zu wunderschöner Höhe des Ausdrucks empor."

26. The original reads "Gmoll-Dreiklang." In his review, Schenker made use of a transposed score—a decision, he later recalled, for which he was chastised by Brahms himself; see Schenker, "Erinnerungen an Brahms," *Deutsche Zeitschrift* 46 (1933), 477. In the translation, I have indicated the original key, B minor.

27. *Schenker*, 7: "Die Harmonien, die in diesem Rahmen auftreten, sind einfach, besitzen Ausdauer in der Tragkraft und lösen still einander ab. Indem sie ferner von einem Gmoll-Dreiklang ausgehen, nach einem solchen wieder streben und nach ruhiger Wanderung den erstrebten und von uns innig vergeahnten Dreiklang auch erreichen, machen sie den Eindruck eines geschlossenen Cyklus, einer Ellipse, möchte ich sagen. Die Uebereinstimmung, besser das Analoge der Zeichnung der Melodie und der Bewegung der Harmonien auf der einen und des Charakters der Schwermuth auf der anderen Seite ist offenbar—; denn das ist es ja, dass wahre Schwermuth, monoton in der Farbe, ruhig im Wesen, nur sehr kleine Wellenkreise schlägt."

EXAMPLE 3.2

of texts, published in *Opera and Drama* and elsewhere. Reflecting upon what he regarded as the elucidative capacity of harmonic structure in a vocal work, for instance, Wagner argued that "the musician becomes perfectly understandable precisely through the technique of quite markedly returning to the first tonality [*Tonart*], thus firmly establishing the unity of the underlying emotion. This is a feat impossible...for the poet. The poet could only hint at the underlying emotion through the *sense* of the verses; he therefore longed for its full realization in feeling, and left it for the musician to fulfill."[28] In this passage, Wagner described precisely the kind of situation that Schenker explored in his analysis of "Mädchenlied." Moreover, the arguments advanced by both writers were essentially the same.

In his next essay on Brahms's work, a review of Brahms's a capella choral pieces, Op. 104, published in the *Wochenblatt* in August and September 1892,

28. Wagner, 4:153; Wagner/Ellis, 2:293: "der Musiker gerade dadurch vollkommen verständlich wird, daß er in die erste Tonart ganz merklich zurückgeht, und die Gattungsempfindung daher mit Bestimmtheit als eine einheitliche bezeichnet, was dem Dichter...nicht möglich war. – Allein der Dichter deutete durch den *Sinn* beider Verse die Gattungsempfindung an: er verlangte somit ihre Verwirklichung vor dem Gefühle, und bestimmte den verwirklichenden Musiker für sein Verfahren."

Schenker elaborated in greater detail along the lines he pioneered in his review of Op. 107. And once again, he drew upon Wagnerian theories of musical structure and meaning to defend the effectiveness of Brahms's music. In his review of Op. 104, however, Schenker seems to fixate especially upon one idea in particular: the capacity of poetic ideas to regulate and even determine the unfolding of musical form—perhaps, he suggested, even within the mind of the composer itself. He began his discussion of "Nachtwache I" ("Night Watch I"), the first piece in the collection, by describing what he called the "antiphonal" structure of the work. Throughout most of Brahms's setting of this text by Friedrich Rückert, the choir is divided into two halves, consisting of soprano and altos on the one hand and tenor and basses on the other. These two subchoirs alternate in their presentation of the harmonized melodic line, with the upper subchoir leading the lower by one measure. This antiphonal arrangement, Schenker suggested, may be understood as representing two characters, and he described this arrangement in dramatic terms. "The deliberate retention of the antiphonal structure," he observed, "enables the choir to represent, as it were, two individuals, embodied in the soprano and the tenor."[29] He continued by postulating a hypothetical dramatic scenario, based upon the poetic text, that could have given rise to the antiphonal setting. "It is like two lovers," he wrote, "who have not yet confessed their love for each other, but who, separated by a great distance, dedicate to each other their 'tones of the breast awakened by the breath of love' [vom Odem der Liebe geweckten Töne der Brust]. It is as if their tones and sighs cross paths in the air that separates them."[30]

There was, however, a problem with this interpretation, as Schenker himself was quick to admit. Namely, the poem itself does not allude to the presence of two individuals, but suggests instead the thoughts of a single, hopeful protagonist:

Leise Töne der Brust
Geweckt vom Odem der Liebe,
Haucht zitternd hinaus,
Ob sich euch öffn' ein Ohr,
Öffn' ein liebendes Herz,
Und wenn sich keines euch öffnet,
Trag' ein Nachwind euch
Seufzend in meines zurück.

(Soft tones of the breast, / awakened by the breath of love, / whisper forth tremulously / if an ear or loving heart / should open to you; / and should none open, / let a night wind bear you back, / sighing, to mine.)

29. Schenker, "Kritik. Johannes Brahms. Fünf Gesänge für gemischten Chor a capella, Op. 104," Musikalisches Wochenblatt 23 (1892); repr. in Schenker, 14–26 (cited at 14): "Das principielle Festhalten am Wechselgesang...lässt den Chor gleichsam zwei Individuen repäsentieren, die im Sopran und im Tenor verkörpert erscheinen."

30. Schenker, 15: "Es ist, als wären es zwei Liebende, die sich ihre gegenseitige Liebe zwar noch nicht gestanden, aber, fern von einander, ihre 'vom Odem der Liebe geweckten Töne der Brust' einander widmen, und als kreuzten sich die Töne und Seufzer in der Luft, die sie trennt." My translations of the texts of Op. 104 are based on those by Lionel Salter, published with the recording Brahms: Choral Works (Philips CD 432 512–2).

EXAMPLE 3.3

As soon as he acknowledged this problem, however, Schenker responded to those who might raise objections on these grounds. Although a dramatic scenario involving two lovers might have inspired Brahms's antiphonal setting, Schenker reasoned, the *poet's* intention to portray the experience of a *single* individual might in turn to have inspired Brahms to score each of the antiphonally opposed subchoirs in a homophonic manner. Example 3.3, mm. 1–4 of "Nachtwache I," shows the homophonic and antiphonal structures that Schenker described.

Admitting the apparent conflict between Rückert's intentions and Brahms's setting (a conflict vividly embodied in Schenker's interpretation), Schenker argued that the antiphonal structure seems to represent Brahms's own contribution to the dramatic whole. He explained: "The system of two individuals, each represented in a homophonic manner (about which I spoke above), furthermore seems to me to reveal an independent idea on the part of the composer, going beyond the idea of the poet."[31]

At this point in our investigation, we must pause to note that Schenker's arguments do not rely upon Wagnerian precepts alone. Indeed, in this instance he is clearly indebted to a line of aesthetic thinking that preceded both his work

---

31. *Schenker*, 15: "Das mit Zugrundelegung der Homophonie erfundene System der zwei Individuen, von denen ich oben Näheres sagte, scheint mir weiter eine eigene selbständige, über die Idee des Dichters hinausgehende Pointe des Componisten zu offenbaren."

and Wagner's by decades. Throughout the whole of the nineteenth century, the creative process had been among the most widely examined topics among writers on music aesthetics, and the ability of a composer of songs to add a layer of meaning to that provided by a poetic text was frequently discussed. Reflecting upon this well-worn theme in his *The Boundaries of Music and Poetry* of 1855, August Wilhelm Ambros observed that "it is the manner of robust spirits to compose a piece of music to some verbal text or other, the intellectual content of which leaves the accompanying words—although it was suggested by them and follows their tendency—so far behind it in depth of thought that they seem, as it were, like a mere point of departure, whence the mind of the composer has lifted itself up to something quite different from and higher than what the scanty word says."[32] Three decades later, in his *Music as Expression* (1885), Friedrich von Hausegger similarly argued that "a new process of creation, aroused [in the composer's mind] by the poetry, must provide the basis for his artistic product. And so, the poet and the musician admittedly find themselves at the same fount, but they part ways as soon as they prepare to quench their thirst."[33] The German literature on music aesthetics abounds with statements such as these.

The moment he attempts to reason his way out of the interpretive knot in which he has found himself thus far, however, Schenker's departure from such statements becomes clear. Admitting that Rückert's poetic text cannot account, on its own, for the structure of Brahms's setting, he conceded that "one will consider this impression of mine a mere hypothesis, in which I, for my part, find an explanation for the two individuals." Nevertheless, Schenker insisted that "without it, the division of the choir would remain inexplicable to me, since the content of the poem seems by nature to revolt against it."[34] Though freely admitting his inability to prove that an imagined dialogue between two lovers had *actually* motivated Brahms's choices when composing "Nachtwache I," Schenker argued that we, as listeners, must assume that it did if we are to understand the otherwise perplexing structure of Brahms's musical setting. Once again, on this point, Schenker's thinking crosses paths with Wagner's.

On several occasions in *Opera and Drama*, Wagner asserted, much like Schenker, that musical structures and processes can be incomprehensible to an audience unless those processes themselves have been determined by the

---

32. August Wilhelm Ambros, *Die Grenzen der Musik und Poesie: Eine Studie zur Ästhetik der Tonkunst* (1855); trans. John Henry Cornell as *The Boundaries of Music and Poetry: A Study in Musical Aesthetics* (New York: G. Schirmer, 1893), 100–101 (I have modified Cornell's punctuation in this passage).

33. Friedrich von Hausegger, *Die Musik als Ausdruck*, 2d ed. (Vienna: Carl Konegen, 1887), 185–86: "Ein Neuschaffungsproceß aus dem in ihm durch die Dichtung wachgerufenen Drange heraus muß seinem Kunstgebilde die Gestalt geben. Und so finden sich Dichter und Musiker zwar an der gleichen Quelle, entfernen sich aber sogleich wieder, wenn wie sich anschicken, ihren Trank zu credenzen."

34. *Schenker*, 15: "Diesen meinen Eindruck wolle man blos als Hypothese betrachten, in der ich für meinen Theil die Erklärung der beiden Individuen finde. Sonst bleibe mir die Spaltung des Chores umso unerklärlicher, als ja der Inhalt des Gedichtes sich von Haus aus gegen sie aufzulehnen scheint."

requirements of a dramatic event or scenario. In a discussion of harmonic progression, for instance, Wagner argued that harmonic structures lacking dramatic
motivations "have worked only numbingly and bewilderingly upon the feelings, and their most muddled excursions have, in this sense, provided satisfaction only to a certain opulence of musical intellect on the part of our musicians
themselves, but not to the layman who does not understand [the inner workings
of] music."[35] In contrast, he explained, a harmonic progression determined by
either the demands or the implications of a poetic text will be perceived by all
"as something instinctively knowable, to be seized upon without any distract-
ing effort, quickly and readily comprehensible for the feelings."[36] At another
point in *Opera and Drama*, Wagner expounded upon this idea in more general
terms, in a manner encompassing all aspects of musical construction: "In the
exercise of its highest faculty"—in Wagner's view, its ability to communicate
feelings to listeners—"musical expression will remain entirely vague and uncertain so long as it does not absorb within itself the poetic intention described
above."[37] From this Wagnerian point of view, to explain the antiphonal structure of "Nachtwache I" in terms of a dramatic scenario, even one invented post
facto, and moreover to insist that we must accept the validity of such a scenario
if we are to understand the structure of the work, was an obvious, perhaps even
inevitable interpretive strategy.

In his discussion of "Nachtwache II," the second piece of Op. 104, Schenker
returned to another subject that had occupied him in his earlier review of the
Op. 107 songs. He considered the ways in which even the finest details of
Brahms's setting appear to have been composed in order to make clear to the
listener emotions intimated yet left undefined by the poet's words. Tracing the
evolution of melodic contour, motivic development, and harmonic progression
in mm. 10–13 of the piece, he explained how nearly all of the musical events in
this passage were constructed so as to serve the demands of the poetic idea.

> The way the passages loses itself in the key of A-flat major (I say it *loses itself*
> because of its gentle gliding over the C-minor triad, and because of the F triad
> that saturates the first part of the second measure); the rhythm and the sequence of
> harmonies, and especially the placement of the tonic and dominant triads together;
> the melodic line at the word "Stimmen" [*voices*] and the dynamic intensification
> of the melody to a gentle height with this word—how willingly all of these ele-
> ments are bound together in order to serve the poetic idea, which seeks to capture
> and hold down, as it were, a more remote thought with the gentle strength of
> the mood. [These elements are furthermore united] in order to satisfy the form

---

35. Wagner, 4:157; Wagner/Ellis, 2:298: "So weit sie diesem ihren Ursprunge ganz getreu
blieb, hat sie auf das Gefühl auch nur betäubend und verwirrend gewirkt, und ihre buntesten
Kundgebungen in diesem Sinne haben nur einer gewissen Musikverstandesschwelgerei unserer
Künstler selbst Genuß geboten, nicht aber dem unmusikverständigen Laien."

36. Wagner, 4:158; Wagner/Ellis, 2:298: "...als einen unwillkürlich kenntlichen, ohne alle
zerstreuende Mühe zu erfassenden, dem Gefühle leicht und schnell begreiflich zuführen."

37. Wagner, 4:189; Wagner/Ellis, 2:334: "Der Ausdruck der Musik wird, bei der Verwendung
dieser äußersten Fähigkeit, so lange ein gänzlich vager und unbestimmender bleiben, als er nicht
die soeben bezeichnete dichterische Absicht in sich aufnimmt."

dictated by the poet, with its fine and soft questioning, just like that of this own imagination![38]

Observing that the most salient aspects of compositional artistry evident in "Nachtwache II" owe their existence to the expressive requirements of the poetic idea, Schenker proclaimed that Brahms created the work with "the most perfectly characteristic will, as if he served that of the poet alone."[39] Not unlike the ideal composer described in *Opera and Drama*, Schenker's Brahms carried out his work in the service of the poet's art.

Before considering the broader implications of Schenker's approach to Brahms's music, we must consider one more example from these early reviews: Schenker's remarks on "Letztes Glück" ("Last Bliss"), the third piece from Op. 104, with a text by Max Kalbeck. For Schenker, this work exemplifies, even more than the others, the ways in which a poetic idea can not only determine the unfolding of isolated musical events but prescribe, virtually as an agent in itself, large-scale formal designs. As he observed at the outset of his discussion, "the most remarkable thing about this six-part choral work is the freedom with which the poetic idea has created its own musical form corresponding precisely to itself."[40] As shown in Table 3.2, Schenker heard "Letztes Glück" as divisible into four large sections, each in a different key. And he regarded the large-scale form of the work, defined both tonally and in terms of melodic design, to have arisen as a product of the emotional content of Kalbeck's poem, in which each pair of lines suggests a different mood.[41]

Upon examining the melodic structure of "Letztes Glück" in greater detail, however, Schenker made one of the most provocative observations in the entire essay. Describing the ways in which melodic motives can be made to conjure

---

38. *Schenker*, 19: "Die Entrückung des Satzes in die Asdur-Tonart—sanft möcht ich die Entruckung nennen wegen des Hinweggleitens über den Cmoll-Dreiklang und wegen des an erster Stelle des 2. Taktes verwendeten weichen F-Dreiklangs—, der Rhythmus und die Ordnung der Harmonien, insbesondere die Stellung des Haupt- und des Dominantdreiklanges innerhalb derselben, der Tonfall der Melodie bei dem Worte 'Stimmen' und endlich die dynamische Hebung der Melodie zu einer sanften Höhe gegen dieses Wort hin, wie willig verbinden sich all diese Elemente, um der dichterischen Idee zu dienen, die ja einen entlegeneren Gedanken mit der sanften Kraft der Stimmung gleichsam herabholen und fesseln will, und um der Form des Dichters zu genügen, der fein und leise frägt, als würde seine eigene Phantasie ihn selbst erst befragen!"

39. *Schenker*, 19: "Aber Brahms, mit ureigenem Wollen geradezu, als bediente er sich dabei nur des Dichters."

40. *Schenker*, 21: "Am bemerkenswerthesten ist in diesem sechsstimmigen Chor die Freiheit, mit welcher die dichterische Idee sich eine eigene, eben nur ihr entsprechende musikalische Form erschuf."

41. As Kevin Korsyn has observed, Schenker's interest in Wagner's ideas about mood and its musical representations persisted throughout much of the decade. Schenker would return to this issue in his well-known essay from 1895, "Der Geist der musikalischen Technik," though he would assume a more critical stance toward Wagner's ideas at that time. See Korsyn, "Schenker's Organicism Reexamined," *Intégral* 7 (1993), 82–118 (esp. 104–7). For further discussion of Schenker's analysis of the motivic structure of "Letztes Glück" and "Nachtwache II," see Allan Keiler, "Melody and Motive in Schenker's Earliest Writings," in *Critica Musica: Essays in Honor of Paul Brainard*, ed. John Knowles (Amsterdam: Gordon and Breach, 1996), 186–91.

TABLE 3.2.   Schenker's analysis of Brahms, "Letztes Glück," Op. 104, no. 3

	Text	Key	Melodic group	Mood
Part 1	Leblos gleitet Blatt um Blatt Still und traurig von den Bäumen; (Lifelessly, leaf after leaf glides quietly and sorrowfully from the trees;)	F minor	A (related motivically to D)	Serious shadow of the autumnal (related to mood of Part 4)
Part 2	Seines Hoffens nimmer satt, Lebt das Herz in Frülingsträumen. (its hopes never fulfilled, the heart persists in a dream of spring.)	A-flat major	B (related motivically to C)	The dream of spring (related to mood of Part 3)
Part 3	Noch verweilt ein Sonnenblick Bei den späten Hagerosen— (A ray of sun lingers on the late, wild roses—)	F major	C (related motivically to B)	A ray of sun lingering on the late, wild roses (related to mood of Part 2)
Part 4	Wie bei einem letzten Glück, Einem süßen, hoffnungslosen. (as on a single last bliss, a sweet one, without hope.)	F minor	D (related motivically to A)	A last, hopeless bliss (related to mood of Part 1)

specific emotions the mind of a listener, he argued that the recurrence of such motives over the course of a work can suggest dynamic interconnections in the emotional world of a dramatic protagonist. He described, in other words, a musical phenomenon similar to that widely known as Wagner's system of *Leitmotiven*.

One will allow me to say the following about the motivic replications and repetitions appearing in the melody. In one's experience of a mood imparted through the senses or only indirectly through the imagination, opposing feelings seem to combat each other, but in reality one feeling exerts a lasting effect on the next. Ultimately, all [of these feelings] work together, contributing to the overall character of the mood. In order to re-create the complicated nature of a mood that one will readily consider "unified," motivic replications and repetitions, if operating in the service of ideas, can function like materials for binding together skillfully assembled thought constructions, since they can replicate certain effects of one idea within opposing ones. It is possible (ultimately every individual must decide for himself) that the partial repetition of the first melodic group in the fourth part of our piece portrays perfectly the idea of the "letztes Glück" [the last bliss; part 4], since it implies a connection with the image, "leblos gleitet Blatt um Blatt still und traurig von dem Bäumen" [lifelessly, leaf after leaf glides quiety and sorrow-fully from the trees; part 1]. It is equally possible that similarities in the melodic construction of the two middle sections bring these closer together as well, with symbolic strength, so to speak.[42]

For Schenker, no emotional state is simple. Rather, each consists of a complex interaction of a multitude of feelings. Motivic recurrence and development, he argued, can replicate both the underlying complexity of a single emotional state and the relationships among the various emotional states characteristic of diverse moods. The motivic similarities between the first and fourth parts of "Letztes Glück," he explained, suggest an affinity between two shades of an autumnal mood. A similar relationship, he asserted, exists between parts two and three.

In this passage, Schenker's discussion of motivic processes and their emo-tional signification is remarkably similar to Wagner's own initial formulation of the idea behind the *leitmotive* technique. For Wagner too (though he did not use the term), musical motives can be made to signify specific feelings through their association with a poetic text. And just as Schenker would observe in his review of "Letztes Glück," the processes of motivic development and replication, Wagner argued, can thus be used to portray the complex, dynamic nature of human thought and emotion. As he explained in *Opera and Drama*,

> The musical motive into which the thought-filled poetic verse of a dramatic actor is poured (before our eyes, so to speak) is a thing conditioned by necessity. With its return, a *definite* emotion is perceptibly communicated to us. Indeed, we find that this emotion is in turn derived from another one, which had previously found itself longing toward the expression of a new one (the prior emotion is no longer voiced by the actor, but is made perceptible to our senses by the orchestra). The sounding of this motive therefore unites for us a non-present cause with its own effect—an emotion just now beginning to be expressed. And whereas we and our feelings are made enlightened witnesses to the organic growth of one definite emotion from out of another, we endow our feeling with a capacity greater than thinking—with the instinctive knowledge of thought realized in emotion.[43]

42. *Schenker*, 21–22: "Zu den in der Melodie auftretenden motivischen Nachbildungen und Wiederholungen erlaube man mir Folgendes zu bemerken. Wie in dem durch die Sinne vermittelten oder nur mittelbar durch die Phantasie angeregten Erleben der Stimmung die Gegensätze zwar ein-ander zu bekämpfen scheinen, in Wahrheit aber der Eine in dem Anderen nachwirkt und so endlich Alle zusammenwirken, um die Complicirtheit einer Stimmung zu begründen, die man für eine 'Einheitlichkeit' auszugeben beliebt, so können motivische Nachbildungen und Wiederholungen, wenn sie im Dienste der Gedanken auftreten, ebenso sehr Bindemitteln für gewandte gedankliche Erscheinungen werden, als sie das gewisse Nachwirken des einen Gegensatzes in dem anderen wiedergeben können. Es ist möglich—in letzter Instanz entscheidet jedes einzelne Individuum—, dass die theilweise Wiederholung der ersten melodischen Gruppe unseres Chores in der vierten den Gedanken 'des letzten Glückes' satter darstellt, weil sie die Verbindung mit dem Bilde 'leblos gleitet Blatt um Blatt still und traurig von den Bäumen' wieder anregt. Ebenso ist es möglich, dass Aehnlichkeiten der Melodiebildung in den beiden mittleren Lichtpartien diese sozusagen mit sym-bolischer Kraft einander näher rücken."

43. Wagner, 4:185; Wagner/Ellis, 2:329–30: "Das musikalische Motiv aber, in das—so zu sagen vor unseren Augen—der gedankenhafte Wortvers eines dramatischen Darstellers sich ergoß, ist ein nothwendig bedingtes; bei seiner Wiederkehr theilt sich uns eine *bestimmte* Empfindung

For Wagner and Schenker alike, the processes of motivic development and recurrence can provide, in the hands of a skilled composer, a musical analogue to emotion and thought. They can mirror the inherent, dynamic complexity of an emotional state and also the underlying connections and affinities between two or more distinct moods.

At the end of his discussion of "Letztes Glück," Schenker anticipated the skepticism that his claims might inspire among readers—both on account of his lack of documentary evidence pertaining to Brahms's creative motivations and also because of his own narrow focus upon a handful of Brahms's vocal works. He countered both of these potential objections by asserting that "all of this is possible within the mind of each individual, even if it goes beyond the intentions of the composer, who would perhaps claim only a formal function for the similarities and repetitions in his melodic construction, as one generally does in purely instrumental music."[44] With regard to his lack of documentary evidence, Schenker took pains to remind his readers that he made no claim to provide his audience with authoritative, objective insights into Brahms's creative thinking. Relying upon neither sketch studies nor any other kind of documentary research, his arguments were hardly products of scientific inquiry as Adler and others had defined it. Rather, Schenker conceived of his essays, first and foremost, as guides for listeners—as aids to understanding and appreciating the effectiveness of Brahms's music. In this way, his essays are similar—in spirit, if not in detail—to those most famous of late-century listening guides, Hans von Wolzogen's elucidatory analyses of Wagner's music dramas.[45] Moreover, by placing the composer's presumed intentions at the center of his interpretive agenda while simultaneously acknowledging that Brahms himself might have seen things somewhat differently, Schenker situated his remarks, as we will see in the final part of this chapter, firmly within the nineteenth-century German hermeneutic tradition.

---

wahrnehmbar mit, und zwar wiederum als die Empfindung Desjenigen, der sich soeben zur Kundgebung einer neuen Empfindung gedrängt fühlt, die aus jener—jetzt von ihm unausgesprochenen, uns aber durch das Orchester sinnlich wahrnehmbar gemachten—sich herleitet. Das Mitklingen jenes Motives verbindet uns daher eine ungegenwärtige bedingende mit der aus ihr bedingten, soeben zu ihrer Kundgebung sich anlassenden Empfinding; und indem wir so unser Gefühl zum erhellten Wahrnehmer des organischen Wachsens einer bestimmten Empfindung aus der anderen machen, geben wir unserem Gefühle das Vermögen des Denkens, d. h. hier aber: das über das Denken erhöhte, unwillkürliche Wissen des in der Empfindung verwirklichten Gedankens."

44. *Schenker*, 22: "Alles Das ist in der Empfindung des einzelnen Individuums möglich, auch wenn es über die Absicht des Componisten hinausginge, welcher von den Aehnlichkeiten und Wiederholungen seiner Melodiebildung vielleicht blos formale Dienste beanspruchte, nicht anders, als man es in der Regel in der reinen Instrumentalmusik thut."

45. Indeed, Schenker's essays were, in this respect, exemplary models of late-century music criticism as defined by Leon Botstein. They were written to serve as a "guiding medium," as "prose translations of the musical experience." See Botstein, "Music and Its Public: Habits of Listening and the Crisis of Musical Modernism in Vienna, 1870–1914 (Ph.D. diss., Harvard University, 1985), 878 (the source of the citation here); and Botstein, "Listening through Reading: Musical Literacy and the Concert Audience," *19th-Century Music* 16, no. 2 (1992), 129–45.

And although Schenker's essays touched explicitly upon only a small number of vocal works, Schenker made clear, in his closing remarks, his belief that the interpretative strategies he employed can apply just as well to the entirety of Brahms's output, whether vocal or instrumental. Since Brahms might have conceived of the composition of Op. 104 in a manner similar to that of an instrumental work, Schenker reasoned, it must be just as valid to interpret Brahms's instrumental music in a similar fashion—in poetic, even dramatic terms. Admittedly, Schenker does not explain, precisely, just how such a strategy might play out in practice. One might imagine, for instance, a descriptive association of melodic lines in a symphony or string quartet with the kinds of dramatic ideas explored in his discussion of "Nachtwache I"—a strategy perhaps not far removed from the work of Hermann Kretzschmar, whose narrative accounts of music's unfolding would later provoke Schenker's notorious scorn.[46] But what *is* clear in Schenker's parting remarks is his sense of fulfillment of the promise he made in the introduction to his review of the Op. 107 songs: to elucidate for his readers the effectiveness and worth of Brahms's late output as a whole.

WAGNERISM, DIVINATION, AND SCHENKER'S SEARCH FOR ALTERNATIVES

In the end, what seems to point so provocatively in these reviews to Wagner and his theoretical work is not an explicit statement of allegiance to the latter but a wealth of details in the critic's language and argumentation. Indeed, Schenker makes no mention of Wagner himself, and it is possible that his understanding of the Wagnerian ideas he invoked owed as much to other writers on the composer—to Hanslick, Ambros, or Hausegger, for instance—as it did to Wagner's statements themselves.[47] But whatever his sources, it is significant to note that Schenker's Wagnerian readings of Brahms's songs and choral works were greeted enthusiastically by prominent supporters of Brahms and Wagner alike. These included Max Kalbeck, one of Brahms's staunchest defenders in the critical press; Maximilian Harden, a friend of Wagner's widow Cosima and Schenker's editor at the Berlin weekly *Die Zukunft*; and Ernst Wilhelm Fritzsch, the original publisher of Wagner's collected prose works. Undoubtedly, the enthusiasm displayed by such a range of individuals suggests that there were many figures in Schenker's time who likewise believed that the aesthetic gulf widely posited to separate

46. See, for instance, Schenker's remarks in his "Beethoven's Fifth Symphony (Continuation)" (1923), trans. William Drabkin, in Schenker, *Der Tonwille: Pamphlets in Witness of the Immutable Laws of Music, Offered to a New Generation of Youth*, ed. William Drabkin, 2 vols. (Oxford: Oxford University Press, 2004–5), 1:193–95.

47. Indeed, as Thomas S. Grey has shown, many ideas widely regarded as Wagnerian in the final decades of the century are traceable to other writers and earlier periods than those in which Wagner wrote and to contexts far removed from those that Wagner considered. See Grey, "...*wie ein rother Faden*: On the Origins of 'leitmotif' as Critical Construct and Musical Practice," in *Music Theory in the Age of Romanticism*, ed. Ian D. Bent (Cambridge: Cambridge University Press, 1996), 187–210; and Grey, *Wagner's Musical Prose: Texts and Contexts*, New Perspectives in Music History and Criticism (Cambridge: Cambridge University Press, 1995).

Brahms's music from Wagner's aesthetics was little more than a myth perpetuated by partisan critics.[48] But it is also possible that at least some of Schenker's supporters sympathized as well with his broader endeavor: to demonstrate the value of hermeneutic analysis as a means of elucidating music's meaning and worth in an age when that approach was roundly dismissed as unscientific and subscholarly within the musicological community.

Whatever the reasons that lay behind the positive reception of Schenker's essays, however, the fact that those essays invoked ideas bearing the unmistakable stamp of Wagnerian thinking is hardly surprising, given his intentions. For when he announced, in the opening lines of his review of the Op. 107 songs, that he would "provide proof that a brilliant strength of invention and powerful artistic reasoning still work together undiminished" in Brahms "to create perfect artworks," Schenker made clear his concern for something more essential than the composer's music. He proclaimed his intention to defend the vitality of Brahms's creative *thinking*. As Schenker had argued in the introduction to his debut essay, the problems of reception recently besetting the artist had arisen because critics, striving to emulate the methodologies of music historians ("trying to work [their] way toward the study of music history"), had failed to appreciate and take sufficient account of, in his words, "the Brahmsian genius." And as Allan Janik has recently shown, it was Wagner's work, more than that of any other, that kept alive a Romantic fascination with creative genius well into the final years of the nineteenth century.[49]

At the time when Schenker entered the critical fray in 1891, the Romantic "cult of genius," as Friedrich Nietzsche had described it, was under attack from nearly every side. Thirteen years earlier, Nietzsche, whose *Birth of Tragedy* (1872) and other early essays had provided philosophical inspiration for an array of irrationalist aesthetic movements, had gone on to take a "positivist" turn of his own in his *Human, All Too Human* of 1878.[50] There, in an attempt to step out from

48. For further discussion of the contemporary reception of Schenker's reviews, see Kevin C. Karnes, "Another Look at Critical Partisanship in the Viennese *fin de siècle*: Schenker's Reviews of Brahms's Vocal Music, 1891–92," *19th-Century Music* 26, no. 2 (2002), 73–93. On the complexities of critical partisanship in Schenker's Vienna, and on the Brahms/Wagner polarity in particular, see also Notley, *Lateness and Brahms*, esp. chapter 1; and Notley, "Late-Nineteenth-Century Chamber Music and the Cult of the Classical Adagio," *19th-Century Music* 23, no. 1 (1999), 33–61.

49. See Allan Janik, "Ebner Contra Wagner: Epistemology, Aesthetics, and Salvation in Vienna, 1900," in *Wittgenstein's Vienna Revisited* (New Brunswick, NJ: Transaction, 2001), 85–104.

50. A useful overview of the historiography of Nietzsche's work, along with a discussion of the widespread use of the term *positivist* to describe his *Human, All Too Human*, is provided in Maudmarie Clark, "On Knowledge, Truth, and Value: Nietzsche's Debt to Schopenhauer and the Development of His Empiricism," in *Willing and Nothingness: Schopenhauer as Nietzsche's Educator*, ed. Christopher Janaway (Oxford: Clarendon Press, 1998), 37–78. On this issue, see also Walter Frisch, *German Modernism: Music and the Arts*, California Studies in 20th-Century Music, no. 3 (Berkeley and Los Angeles: University of California Press, 2005), 15–28. The influence of Nietzsche's early writings upon diverse antimodern movements in late-century Austria and Wilhelmine Germany is examined in, respectively, William J. McGrath, *Dionysian Art and Populist Politics in Austria* (New Haven: Yale University Press, 1974); and Fritz Stern, *The Politics of Cultural Despair: A Study in the Rise of the Germanic Ideology* (New York: Anchor Books, 1961). This topic will be considered in greater detail in chapter 5.

beneath the Wagnerian shadow under which he had penned his own earlier work, the philosopher called for excising the very notion of genius from the center of aesthetic debate. Genius, the post-Wagnerian Nietzsche argued, was not some unfathomable, divine gift, but an imagined product of "our vanity." When examined rationally, he observed, "the activity of the genius does not at all appear to be something fundamentally different from the activity of the inventor in mechanics, of the astronomer or the historical scholar, of the master tactician."[51] The Romantic cult of artistic genius, Nietzsche charged, was a cult built around a myth.

In his attempts to debunk the myth of genius in music and the arts, Nietzsche was bolstered, as Walter Frisch has shown, by the work of a musicologist, Gustav Nottebohm. In his pioneering studies of Beethoven's sketches begun in the 1860s, Nottebohm presented provocative evidence that even this most brilliant of artists was not a figure possessed of unfathomable creative powers but simply "a great worker, tireless not only in inventing, but also in rejecting, sifting, reshaping, ordering."[52] The skepticism of both philosopher and musicologist was duly echoed in Adler's "Scope, Method, and Goal of Musicology." Weary of the Romantic associations conjured by the very idea of genius, Adler made clear his aversion to all research that placed an artist's personality and working methods at the center of attention. In his view, studies of the creative process and even biography did not belong to the domain of musicology proper but were instead no more than "auxiliary disciplines" (*Hilfswissenschaften*). The primary focus of the musicologist's work, he argued, must always remain fixed upon the structure, style, and historical transmission of musical works. "Above all else," Adler wrote, "the history of music will consider artistic creations in and of themselves. [It will examine] the ways in which they are related to one another and have influenced each other, without special consideration being given to the life and activities of the individual artists who contributed to this course of development."[53] Given this trend in music study in the final decades of the century, it is no wonder that Schenker would fault his fellow critics for paying little heed to Brahms's genius.

For this same reason, it is also unsurprising that Schenker would turn, in his attempt to illuminate that genius, to aspects of Wagnerian aesthetics. For Wagner had displayed an unwavering fascination for the very topic that interested Schenker most. In *Opera and Drama*, Wagner celebrated Mozart's operatic contributions as testimony to the latter composer's innate and spontaneous creative gifts. "Nothing is more characteristic of Mozart," he argued, "in his work as an operatic composer, than the lack of concern and deliberation with which

51. Friedrich Nietzsche, *Human, All Too Human: A Book for Free Spirits*, trans. Gary Handwerk, The Complete Works of Friedrich Nietzsche, vol. 3 (Stanford: Stanford University Press, 1995), 122–26 (cited at 123).

52. Frisch, *German Modernism*, 18–19. The quotation, from page 119 of *Human, All Too Human*, is given on page 19 of Frisch's study.

53. Adler, "Umfang, Methode und Ziel," 8: "In höchster und letzter Instanz aber wird die Geschichte der Musik die künstlerischen Schöpfungen als solche betrachten, in ihrer gegenseitigen Verkettung, dem wechselseitigen Einfluß ohne besondere Rücksicht auf das Leben und Wirken einzelner Künstler, die an dieser stetigen Entwicklung Theil genommen haben."

he applied himself to his work."[54] To Wagner's mind, Mozart was an inspired, almost mythical figure, for whom (in the words of Gustav Schilling) the most complex music "pours out from within in what is called free fantasy."[55] Two decades later, drawing upon his recent readings of Schopenhauer's metaphysics, Wagner described a similarly nonrational creative endowment in his influential essay "Beethoven" (1870). There, and in spite of Nottebohm's evidence to the contrary, Wagner portrayed the departed artist as figure capable of giving himself over to a subconscious state, experiencing in that state the Schopenhauerian will, and returning to the phenomenal world bearing copies of the will in the guise of his compositions.[56] To be sure, the philosophical trappings in which Wagner framed his accounts of genius varied over time. But those accounts were largely consistent with respect to their essential features. In Wagner's view, it was innate creative genius, rather than Nietzsche's deliberate sifting and shaping, that accounts for the greatness of an artwork. Moreover, he argued, the workings of genius are wholly unconscious and irrational and therefore unsusceptible to the modes of empirical investigation that Adler and Spitta prescribed.

As we will see in chapter 4, Schenker did not follow Wagner very far down this path. Indeed, within only a handful of years, he, like Nietzsche, would make a radical turn and begin to espouse an empiricist vision of art-historical study. But to invoke Wagner's ideas at all within the context of a consideration of genius in the final decade of the nineteenth century was to stake one's position firmly in the midst of what Allan Janik has identified as one of the period's principal "critical modernist paths."[57] It signaled Schenker's deep distrust of the scientific worldview, no matter how powerfully he might have been attracted to aspects of it. To Schenker's mind, empirical descriptions of musical structure and the induction of laws posited to govern the historical development of form and style cannot, on their own, account for the meaning and significance of the musical experience. For that experience did not consist only in the aural (or visual, when reading a score) perception of music's formal parameters but also, and even more essentially, in subjective, imaginative engagements with the mind of the artist as revealed in

54. Wagner, 3:246; Wagner/Ellis, 2:36: "Von *Mozart* ist mit Bezug auf seine Lufbahn als Opernkomponist nichts charakteristischer, als die unbesorgte Wahllosigkeit, mit der er sich an seine Arbeiten machte."

55. Gustav Schilling, *Encyclopädie der gesammten musikalischen Wissenschaften*, 2d ed. (1840–42); trans. in Peter Le Huray and James Day, eds., *Music and Aesthetics in the Eighteenth and Early-Nineteenth Centuries*, Cambridge Readings in the Literature of Music (Cambridge: Cambridge University Press, 1981), 468.

56. See Wagner, 9:66–71; Wagner/Ellis, 5:65–71. For further discussion of Wagner's views on creativity and his indebtedness to the work of Schopenhauer with respect to this issue, see Janik, "Ebner Contra Wagner"; and Bryan Magee, *The Tristan Chord: Wagner and Philosophy* (New York: Henry Holt, 2000), esp. 126–73 and 228–36. For Schopenhauer's statements on musical creativity and music itself as a copy of the will, see Schopenhauer, *The World as Will and Representation*, trans. E. F. J. Payne, 2 vols. (Indian Hills, CO: Falcon's Wing Press, 1958), 1:255–67.

57. Janik, "Ebner Contra Wagner," 103. Further elaboration of Janik's idea of critical modernism is provided in his *Wittgenstein's Vienna Revisited*, 15–36; and in Janik, "Vienna 1900 Revisited: Paradigms and Problems," in *Rethinking Vienna 1900*, ed. Steven Beller, Austrian History, Culture, and Society, no. 3 (New York and Oxford: Berghan, 2001), 27–56.

the musical work. Wagner, as Janik has shown, embraced a Romantic conception of creativity and vehemently rejected attempts to reduce the work to its empirically describable form despite his modernist musical language and attraction to the promise of scientific inquiry to dispel all sorts of myth and illusion. As Janik has characterized the work of Wagner and other critical modernists, so also Schenker's statements on Brahms constituted an "immanent critique" of the "limits" of scientifically inspired discourse. Like the positions of many creative Germans of his time, Schenker's essays evinced "a peculiarly skeptical healthy reaction against the spellbinding power that modernity exerts upon us."[58]

But before we turn away from Schenker's essays to examine his more general statements on the creative process, we must pause to consider one more aspect of his early analyses—one that will enable us to appreciate the seriousness of the challenge that his essays posed to music study in his time. As we have seen, Schenker drew liberally upon Wagnerian ideas to elucidate the effects of Brahms's genius in his music. But the means by which he sought to apprehend that genius *itself* predated Wagner's work by decades. Indeed, I would suggest that Schenker's approach to the latter task was *divinatory* in a sense first described by the philosopher and theologian Friedrich Schleiermacher (1768–1834) shortly after the turn of the nineteenth century.

Underlying Schleiermacher's highly influential work on textual exegesis, collected and posthumously published as *Hermeneutics and Criticism* (*Hermeneutik und Kritik*, 1838), was the conviction that one's hopes for arriving at a meaningful understanding of any text can best be met if one pursues simultaneously two distinct yet overlapping modes of analysis. The first or *grammatical* mode is one by which a critic endeavors to understand and describe a text's unique linguistic—or musical—configurations. In essence, it is the same approach to analytical work that Ian Bent calls "scientific," that Schenker called "objective," and that Adler advocated in his "Scope, Method, and Goal of Musicology." In contrast, Schleiermacher's second mode of analysis, which he called the *psychological*, is one by which a critic attempts to uncover the authorial intentions and understandings that gave rise to a work in the mind of its creator. As Bent has described a general hermeneutics entailing a reiterative alternation between objective and subjective modes of inquiry, giving rise to the famous image of a "hermeneutic circle," so also Schleiermacher prescribed a reiterative alternation of grammatical and psychological approaches to a text.[59]

As for how a reader might actually undertake such a hermeneutic critique, Schleiermacher offered an extensive catalogue of advice. One's understanding

58. Janik, "Vienna 1900 Revisited," 40.

59. Friedrich Schleiermacher, *Hermeneutics and Criticism and Other Writings*, ed. and trans. David Bowie, Cambridge Texts in the History of Philosophy (Cambridge: Cambridge University Press, 1998), 8–11. On Schleiermacher's hermeneutics, see also Bowie, *Aesthetics and Subjectivity from Kant to Nietzsche*, 2d ed. (Manchester: Manchester University Press, 2003), 183–220; and Terry Pinkard, *German Philosophy, 1760–1860: The Legacy of Idealism* (Cambridge: Cambridge University Press, 2002), 148–58. The impact of Schleiermacher's ideas upon the nineteenth-century discourse on music is considered in Bent, *Music Analysis*, 2:2–10.

of the structure of a text, attained through grammatical analysis, can be honed by adopting what the philosopher called a *comparative* approach to one's material. By comparing the artistic work under consideration to similar works by the same author and by others, one can gain an appreciation for the ways in which its structural or linguistic characteristics are unique as opposed to reflective of broader conventions of linguistic usage and style. With respect to the psychological aspect of interpretation, Schleiermacher advocated divination. "The *divinatory* method," he explained, "is the one in which one, so to speak, transforms oneself into the other person and tries to understand the individual element directly."[60] As Andrew Bowie has argued, however, Schleiermacher did not intend his statements on divination to be read as invitations to arbitrary psychological speculation. Rather, divinatory criticism was, for the philosopher, literally subjective; it was, in Bowie's terms, an exercise "grounded in ourselves."[61] Its efficacy, as Schleiermacher explained, depends "on the fact that every person, besides being an individual themselves, has a receptivity for all other people. But this itself seems only to rest on the fact that everyone carries a minimum of everyone else within themselves, and divination is consequently excited by comparison with oneself."[62] The idea, as Schleiermacher described it, is to approach the question of how an artist created his work by asking *myself* how *I* would have created it, what would have prompted *me* to do it that way. All the while, however, I must bear in mind that the author, as an individual different from me in some fundamental respects, quite likely did it somewhat differently.

Significantly, the divinatory method described in *Hermeneutics and Criticism* was precisely the means by which Schenker attempted to apprehend Brahms's creative thinking. As we have seen, Schenker argued, when discussing "Nachtwache I," that the nested antiphonal and homophonic textures shown in Example 3.3 seemed to "reveal an independent idea on the part of the composer himself, going beyond the idea of the poet." He admitted that this statement was only a "hypothesis, in which I, for my part, find an explanation" for the peculiar structure of the work. But he went on to explain that "without it, the division of the choir would remain inexplicable to me, since the content of the poem seems by nature to revolt against it." In this passage, Schenker made clear the mode of inquiry that underlay his interpretive efforts. His analyses, in Schleiermacher's terms, were "excited by comparison with oneself." They were, in this classic sense, exercises in divination.

That Schenker adopted a divinatory approach to account for Brahms's genius is significant for two reasons. First, Schleiermacher's divination, as Terry Pinkard has shown, provided the theoretical foundation upon which members of a circle of highly influential writers active in Berlin and Jena made some of their first attempts at literary criticism in the years around 1800. As one among them, Friedrich Schlegel, wrote in the literary journal *Athenäum*, "the romantic kind of

---

60. Schleiermacher, *Hermeneutics and Criticism*, 92 (emphasis in original).
61. Bowie, *Aesthetics and Subjectivity*, 2; Bowie considers Scheleirmacher's notion of divination on pages 207–8.
62. Schleiermacher, *Hermeneutics and Criticism*, 93.

poetry . . . . . . can be exhausted by no theory and only a divinatory criticism would dare try to characterize its ideal."[63] In other words, divination was a mode of criticism widely associated in the popular consciousness with the apex of German literary Romanticism—and thus, by extension, with the Romantic traditions of aesthetic theorizing from which Spitta, Adler, and their like-minded colleagues sought to distance music study in their positivist polemics. Second, divination was a mode of inquiry had had been specifically targeted by at least one influential positivist scholar as irrelevant and even antithetical to the scientific endeavor as a whole. As the art historian Moriz Thausing wrote in his seminal polemic, "The Status of Art History as a Science" ("Die Stellung der Kunstgeschichte als Wissenschaft," 1873), "imagination or divination" (*Eingebung oder Divination*) can offer nothing to an individual who seeks to attain a scientifically rigorous understanding of art. "Above all else," Thausing argued, "our studies must be concerned with the precise estimation of the monuments of art. To arrive at this requires no sort of special imagination or divination. Rather, it requires that one follow only the path of exacting study and unrelenting comparison, similar to that blazed by the most real of our sciences, the natural sciences."[64] In light of arguments such as Thausing's, if a late-century writer wished to make clear his rejection of the positivist movement and its aspirations to transform the study of music into a science, he could find no better means of doing so than by embracing a divinatory approach to his work.

In recent decades, Schenker's contributions to music analysis have been widely regarded as laying the foundation for an array of radical structuralist experiments, from the systematized (and Americanized) Schenkerian analyses of Arthur Komar to the post-tonal theories of Milton Babbitt.[65] But this image of Schenker must be complicated, to say the least, by our recognition of the fact that his first attempts at analytical work revealed a profound distrust of the influence of positivist scholarship upon the critical discourse on music. Indeed, Schenker's entry into the critical arena was prompted, at least in part, by his conviction that if music criticism were to retain a meaningful place in an increasingly rationalistic culture, critics would need to greet with skepticism calls to emulate the methods of the natural sciences in their work. The critic, Schenker held, must embrace subjective impression, indulge the hermeneutic impulse, and even

63. Cited and discussed in Pinkard, *German Philosophy*, 163.

64. Moriz Thausing, "Die Stellung der Kunstgeschichte als Wissenschaft," in *Wiener Kunstbriefe* (Leipzig: E. A. Seemann, 1884), 11: "Auf der genauen Anschauung der Denkmäler beruht aber vor Allem unser Studium. Um zu dieser Kenntniss zu gelangen, bedarf es jedoch keiner besonderen Eingebung oder Divination. Vielmehr ist es nur ein Weg genauer Prüfung und fortwährender Vergleichung, ähnlich demjenigen, den die realsten unserer Wissenschaften, die Naturwissenschaften einzuschlagen pflegen."

65. See, for instance, Joseph Kerman, "How We Got Into Analysis, and How to Get Out," *Critical Inquiry* 7, no. 2 (1980), 311–31; repr. in *Write All These Down: Essays on Music* (Berkeley and Los Angeles: University of California Press, 1994), 12–32 (on Komar); and Alastair Williams, *Constructing Musicology* (Aldershot: Ashgate, 2001), 21–27 (on Babbitt and others).

probe the depths of the creative mind in his attempts to elucidate the effectiveness and worth of the artworks he considers. It is only in this way, he believed, that one might effectively convey to one's readers what really matters in the musical experience: the workings of genius upon the imagination of the listener through the medium of the musical work.

But to conclude from Schenker's essays on Brahms that he was steadfastly opposed to the whole of the positivist movement would be mistaken. For while he lamented its influence upon some aspects of the critical discourse, he embraced its tenets with respect to others. As we will see, Schenker's early fascination with Wagnerian aesthetics and his experiments with divinatory analysis would soon give way to an approach to studying the problem of creativity that was avowedly rationalist, even empiricist. Like many critical modernists, Schenker did not reject the positivist movement in its entirety. Wary of its portents, he was drawn to its promise, and he was ambivalent to the end.

CHAPTER FOUR

COMPOSER, CRITIC, AND THE
PROBLEM OF CREATIVITY

When Schenker attempted, in his review of Brahms's choral pieces, Op. 104, to account for the effects of Brahms's genius by way of hermeneutic analysis and divination, he did not theorize explicitly about the nature of genius itself. In other essays from 1890s, he did just that, pursuing, to an extent unusual in his day, a topic that had fascinated writers on the arts for centuries. And if his invocations of aspects of Wagnerian aesthetics within the context of such discussions signaled his skepticism about the positivist endeavor to demystify the musical experience in all of its aspects, he soon found himself, by way of that same investigation, moving ever closer to the intellectual camp of Adler, Spitta, and Thausing.

In the years immediately following his 1891 debut in the critical press, Schenker explored an array of speculative, even irrationalist theories of the creative process similar to those outlined by Wagner, E. T. A. Hoffmann, and a host of Romantic writers. We find such explorations in a series of early essays focusing on some of the most prominent musicians of his time, from Anton Bruckner to the pianist and composer Eugen d'Albert.[1] But Schenker's own experience as a practicing composer—he did not give up his dreams of becoming a successful artist until after the turn of the century—kept him from embracing such theories wholeheartedly. For a while, he sought to temper them in order to take account of the considerable amount of deliberating work that he knew the compositional act to require. By the end of the decade, however, he would give up on that project altogether. He would renounce all forms of speculation about the creative process and embrace instead a self-consciously realistic, even empiricist approach to the study of the subject, taking account only of those experiences recorded in documentary accounts left by practicing composers. As we have seen, Schenker began his career expressing profound unease about the influence of scientifically oriented scholarship upon the critical discourse on music. Yet he found himself,

---

1. For instance, Heinrich Schenker, "Kritik. Anton Bruckner. Psalm 150 für Chor, Soli und Orchester," *Musikalisches Wochenblatt* 24 (1893); "Anton Bruckner," *Die Zukunft* 5 (1893); and "Eugen d'Albert," *Die Zukunft* 9 (1894); all repr. in *Schenker*, 41–42, 57–61, 117–21.

within only a handful of years, preaching the merits of rational, deliberating, empirical study as an indispensable critical tool.

However, Schenker's turn to an empiricist position with respect to the problem of creativity was neither straightforward nor definitive. Indeed, less than a decade after he disavowed the speculative tradition in the late 1890s, he would embrace it once again. Toward the end of his life, he would even suggest that his early faith in scientifically oriented approaches to research was not inspired by his own experiences with rationalistic modes of inquiry but instead reflected the revealed wisdom of a onetime mentor, Brahms. To be sure, we have good reason to doubt the accuracy of Schenker's elderly recollections of his studies with Brahms, and it is quite possible that his exchanges with the composer never occurred as he described them. Nevertheless, Schenker's hints at revelatory rather than reasoned causes for his fleeting embrace of positivist scholarship testify to the depth and persistence of the ideological dilemmas posed by the positivist challenge for writers of his generation.

EXPLORING THE CRITICAL TRADITIONS

Throughout the first decade of his career as a critic, Schenker was fascinated with the creative process. Among late-century writers on music, only Wagner seems to have rivaled Schenker in the extent to which he was prone to theorizing about the issue. Yet Schenker's debt to Wagner in this regard was ambivalent and troubled, and many of the critic's earliest statements on the subject seem to have been motivated by a desire to reconcile the tenets of Wagner's arguments with what he knew to be the complex realities of the composer's craft.

As we saw in chapter 3, Wagner had outlined, most extensively in "Beethoven" (1870), a theory of the creative process by which the act of composition is posited to take place entirely within the unconscious reaches of the artist's mind. For Wagner, the creative genius of a Mozart or a Beethoven was spontaneous and irrational and thus wholly unsusceptible to the scientifically oriented modes of inquiry that Adler and his like-minded colleagues advocated.[2] In a biographical sketch of his friend, the composer and pianist Eugen d'Albert, published in the Berlin cultural weekly *Die Zukunft* in 1894, Schenker acknowledged the theoretical plausibility of this Wagnerian paradigm. "There are works in the musical literature that arose when the flash of an idea suddenly descended through the endless chaos of fantasy and immediately illuminated and created the whole work with the most dazzling light," Schenker wrote. "Such works were conceived and born as a whole, and the entire destiny of [their] creation, life, growth, and death already resided pre-formed and well defined in the first seed. A flash occurred, and the creation just lay there, admittedly stark naked, but solidly formed."[3]

---

2. See Wagner, 9:66–71; Wagner/Ellis, 5:55–71.

3. Schenker, "Eugen d'Albert," in *Schenker*, 117: "Es giebt in der Musikliteratur Werke, die so entstanden, daß durch das unendliche Chaos der Phantasie plötzlich der Blitz eines Gedankens darniederfuhr, der mit grellstem Licht sofort auch das ganze Werk beleuchtete und erschuf. Solche Werke wurden in Einem empfangen und geboren und schon im ersten Keim lag das ganze Schicksal der Schöpfung, Leben, Wachsthum und Ende, bestimmt vorgezeichnet. Es kam jener Blitz und die Schöpfung lag da, zwar splitternackt, aber fest geformt."

However, Schenker's uncertainty about Wagner's theory becomes apparent immediately after one reads these words. Continuing, he argued that, in reality, such a spontaneous, unconscious event hardly ever seems to occur. Even the greatest works by the most brilliant composers must bear at least some marks of deliberating, conscious reflection. He expressed his doubts as follows:

> On the other hand, a certain dust of reflection [*Staub der Reflexion*] covers most artworks. On the true masterworks there is so little that the most skillful observer can hardly discern it. But on other works, to the contrary, there is all too much, and it can be discerned all too clearly. Since such a work could not have been produced in an atmosphere free of reflection, some dust settled in the midst of its creation. This was just as unavoidable as with any object immediately surrounded by air.[4]

In his essay on D'Albert, Schenker broached an aesthetic dilemma that would dog him throughout his early years. On the one hand, he acknowledged the possibility of a creative act in which the entirety of an artwork takes shape spontaneously, as if under its own volition, within the unconscious reaches of the mind. But he also felt compelled to admit that this kind of wholly unconscious compositional event rarely, if ever, occurs. As an active composer who did not yet display Wagner's inclination toward cultivating a mythology of origins with respect to his own work, Schenker acknowledged that nearly all composers must rely at times upon their conscious, deliberating sensibilities as they work to shape their musical materials into compelling, coherent wholes. In an attempt to reconcile theory and reality, he argued that the effectiveness of a finished composition reflects the degree of skill with which its creator has disguised the audible traces of his deliberating sensibilities. Echoing in this way a line of aesthetic argument that extends back to Immanuel Kant's *Critique of Judgment* (1790), Schenker stressed that the work of art, regardless of its imaginative origins, must appear not artificial but like a product of nature. It must be perceived like something untouched by the hands that crafted it—like something created not by rational man but by an unconscious, natural process.[5]

Yet in spite of his hedging on this issue, it is important to note that Schenker's answer to the Wagnerian paradigm was hardly a "scientific" proposition as Adler and Spitta had defined the term. Despite his attempts to take account of the realities of the composer's work, Schenker held fast to a speculative conception of the creative act that was indebted, as its echoes of Kant suggest, to a line of critical theorizing that originated more than a century before he picked up his pen. As Carl Dahlhaus, Ian D. Bent, and many others have shown, the notion of the creative process as a dynamic interplay of conscious and unconscious creative

---

4. *Schenker*, 117–18: "Auf den meisten Kunstwerken aber liegt einiger Staub der Reflexion, auf den echten Meisterwerken gar so wenig, daß ihn die geschicktesten Nachempfinder kaum noch wahrnehmen, auf den übrigen Werken dagegen allzu viel, allzu deutlich. Da ein solches Werk eben nicht in reflexionfreier Luft erzeugt werden konnte, so kam mitten im Werden und Schaffen ein Staub angeflogen, und Das war eben so wenig zu verhüten, wie irgend ein Gegenstand vor Staub zu bewahren ist, den die Luft unmittelbar umgiebt."

5. For a detailed consideration of this aspect of Kant's aesthetics, see Terry Pinkard, *German Philosophy, 1760–1860: The Legacy of Idealism* (Cambridge: Cambridge University Press, 2002), 66–75.

faculties was deeply rooted in Romantic discourse about music, literature, and the visual arts. It underlay, for example, E. T. A. Hoffmann's famous review of Beethoven's Fifth Symphony, published in Leipzig in 1810.[6] As Hoffmann observed, "it is usual to regard [Beethoven's] works merely as products of a genius [*Genie*] who ignores form and discrimination of thought and surrenders to his creative fervour and the passing dictates of his imagination"—as someone, in other words, for whom the creative act unfolds spontaneously within the unconscious mind. But in reality, Hoffmann continued, Beethoven "is nevertheless fully the equal of Haydn and Mozart in rational awareness [*Besonnenheit*], his controlling self detached from the inner realm of sounds and ruling it in absolute authority."[7]

Closer to Schenker's day, this speculative, conscious/unconscious paradigm of creativity can be detected in Eduard Hanslick's review of Bruckner's Psalm 150 for chorus and orchestra, published in the 1896 installment of Hanslick's "living history" series. There, Hanslick argued that Bruckner's work sounded more like the product of an "uncontrolled wandering of the imagination" than a coherent, well-balanced whole. The structural problems evident in the piece revealed, to Hanslick, Bruckner's inability to direct rationally the spontaneous outpourings of his creative mind.[8] Six years earlier, this same paradigm was evoked more explicitly by the Viennese critic Emil Ritter von Hartmann, when he charged that Brahms suffered from precisely the opposite intellectual shortcoming from that detected by Hanslick in Bruckner. To Hartmann, Brahms's tendency to develop elaborate musical textures out of seemingly insignificant thematic materials testified to the composer's overindulgence in conscious deliberation and insufficient fount of spontaneous invention. Writing of a performance of Brahms's First Symphony in 1890, Hartmann observed:

> This time too, as at its first performance, Brahms's C-Minor Symphony has interested us more than won us over or filled us with enthusiasm. Brahms is indeed a brilliant musician, whose serious, reflective nature and extraordinary skill impress

6. On Hoffmann's understanding of the creative process, see Ian D. Bent, ed., *Music Analysis in the Nineteenth Century*, 2 vols., Cambridge Readings in the Literature of Music (Cambridge: Cambridge University Press, 1994), 1:12–13; and Carl Dahlhaus, *Ludwig van Beethoven: Approaches to His Music*, trans. Mary Whittall (Oxford: Clarendon Press, 1991), 68–71. More general considerations of nineteenth-century theories of artistic creativity and the conscious/unconscious paradigm in particular are provided in Harold Osborne, *Aesthetics and Art Theory: An Historical Introduction* (London: Longmans, Green, 1968), 131–54; and Lilian R. Furst, *Romanticisim in Perspective: A Comparative Study of Aspects of the Romantic Movement in England, France, and Germany* (London: Macmillan, 1979), 119–35. For a discussion of such theories as invoked in the discourse on music, see Edward E. Lowinsky, "Musical Genius: Evolution and Origins of a Concept," *Musical Quarterly* 50, no. 3 (1964), 321–40; repr. in *Music in the Culture of the Renaissance and Other Essays*, 2 vols., ed. Bonnie J. Blackburn (Chicago: University of Chicago Press, 1989), 1:87–105.

7. Cited, from the Leipzig *Allgemeine musikalische Zeitung*, in Bent, *Music Analysis in the Nineteenth Century*, 2:147.

8. Hanslick, *Fünf Jahre Musik* (*Die moderne Oper*, vol. 7) (Berlin: Allgemeiner Verein für Deutsche Litteratur, 1896), 204: "Die absolute Freiheit der Instrumental-Komposition erscheint bei Strauß und Bruckner als ein meisterloses Schweifen der Phantasie, welche, des organischen Zusammenhanges spottend, sich gern ins Ungemessene verliert."

most of his works with the stamp of sublimity and nobility, and whose musical working often arouses a sense of wonder in us. He is, however, by no means a gifted inventor or a creator of great and original ideas. Where, in Brahms's symphonies, can we find even a single idea such as those that Bruckner has given us with truly sumptuous and abundant generosity in his eight symphonic works?[9]

Along similar lines, the conductor Felix Weingartner went so far as to suggest that Brahms and Bruckner seemed to reside at opposite ends of an imagined spectrum of creativity, respectively exemplifying, entirely conscious and wholly unconscious approaches to the creative act. "I was once asked my opinion of the rivalry of Bruckner and Brahms," Weingartner wrote in his 1897 book *The Symphony after Beethoven* (*Die Symphonie nach Beethoven*). "I replied, 'I should like nature to give us a musician reuniting in himself the qualities of the two composers, the immense imagination of Bruckner, with the knowledge of Brahms. From such a combination would arise an artistic figure of the highest possible value.' "[10]

It is within this critical and rhetorical context that we should read Schenker's most elaborate and systematic discussion of creativity from the early years of his career. This came in the midst of a lecture he delivered before a meeting of the University of Vienna's Philosophical Society in 1895, entitled "The Spirit of Musical Technique" ("Der Geist der musikalischen Technik").[11] In the published version of this lecture, which appeared in the Leipzig *Musikalisches Wochenblatt* later that year, Schenker began his discussion of the issue by elaborating upon the properties of a musical work crafted in the kind of overly deliberating, reflective manner that Hartmann detected in Brahms. "Now it can happen," Schenker wrote,

that the composer's imagination...surveys the complete content from a bird's-eye perspective, as it were, and he comparatively assesses and arranges the character

9. Originally published in the *Neue Wiener Musik-Zeitung*; repr. in *Brahms-Kongress Wien 1983. Kongressbericht*, ed. Susanne Antonicek and Otto Biba (Tutzing: Hans Schneider, 1988), 507: "Die *C-moll*-Symphonie von *Brahms* hat uns, wie ehedem bei ihrer ersten Aufführung, auch diesmal mehr interessirt als erwärmt und begeistert. Brahms ist eben ein geistvoller Musiker, dessen ernst reflectirendes Wesen und ausserordentliches Können den meisten seiner Werke den Stempel des Erhabenen, Vornehmen aufdrückt, dessen musikalische Arbeit uns häufig Bewunderung abringt: ein starker Erfinder und Schöpfer grosser origineller Ideen ist er nun einmal nicht. Wo findet sich in Brahms' Symphonieen auch nur ein einziger solcher Gedanke, wie sie uns Bruckner in seinen acht symphonischen Werken mit wahrhaft verschwenderischer Freigebigkeit in Hülle und Fülle geschenkt hat?"

10. Felix Weingartner, *The Symphony since Beethoven*, trans. Arthur Bles (New York: Scribners, n. d.), 67. Further consideration of contemporary critical understandings of the creative intellect of Brahms and Bruckner is provided in Sandra McColl, *Music Criticism in Vienna, 1896–97: Critically Moving Forms*, Oxford Monographs on Music (Oxford: Clarendon Press, 1996); Margaret Notley, "Bruckner and Viennese Wagnerism," in *Bruckner Studies*, ed. Timothy L. Jackson and Paul Hawkshaw (Cambridge: Cambridge University Press, 1997), 54–71; Notley, "Brahms as Liberal: Genre, Style, and Politics in Late Nineteenth-Century Vienna," *19th-Century Music* 17, no. 2 (1993), 107–23; and Constantin Floros, *Brahms und Bruckner. Studien zur musikalischen Exegetik* (Wiesbaden: Breitkopf und Härtel, 1980).

11. Schenker, "Der Geist der musikalischen Technik," *Musikalisches Wochenblatt* 26 (1895); repr. in *Schenker*, 135–54; trans. by William Pastille as "The Spirit of Musical Technique," *Theoria* 3 (1988), 86–104 (hereafter cited as Schenker/Pastille). On this event, see Federhofer, *Heinrich Schenker. Nach Tagebüchern und Briefen in der Oswald Jonas Memorial Collection*, Studien zur Musikwissenschaft, no. 3 (Hildesheim: Georg Olms, 1985), 12–15.

and significance of each individual mood contained within it, in spite of their natural orderings. And yet, as much as this procedure seems to be a logical process, it is not motivated by either logical or organic causes. Rather, the ordering of the moods and the relative significance of the parts and the whole reveal most clearly the personal character of the composer and his will to persuade the listener of [the effectiveness of] this ordering as it was determined by the composer himself—that is, to deceive the listener in subtle ways.[12]

For Schenker, all compositional choices made by way of conscious reflection must inevitably lack, by their very definition, the sort of natural, organic necessity that Kant and others demanded. For this reason, the best that such a reflective artist can achieve is the "deception" of his listeners with regard to the imaginative origins of his work, his music being indelibly tainted by his personal, subjective desires.[13]

As in his essay on Eugen d'Albert, however, Schenker went on, in "The Spirit of Musical Technique," to describe another side of the compositional act. He argued that the unimpeded functioning of the unconscious faculties of mind, in contrast to the "inorganic" process just considered, may indeed give rise to a work that sounds intuitively coherent and organic to the listener. That is, he defended, once again, the theoretical plausibility of the Wagnerian paradigm. He wrote:

> Nonetheless, I know of one phenomenon in the musical imagination that seems to match the scientific notion of the "organic" in a strict sense. The existence of this phenomenon can be verified only with great difficulty, but I am personally convinced that it is real. I find that the imagination, after it brings forth a certain construction, is absolutely besieged by many other constructions of a similar nature, and that the power that these similar constructions exert over the composer is often so irresistible that he includes them in the musical content he is constructing without even becoming aware of their similarity. Often (one guesses it only after a penetrating examination of the artwork), the composer would have preferred to bring about a completely dissimilar construction. But one can see how his imagination did not deviate from its initial course, and forced a similar construction upon him.[14]

12. *Schenker*, 148–49: "Nun kann es geschehen, dass die Phantasie des Componisten…den gesammten Inhalt, trotz dem natürlichen Nacheinander desselben, gleichsam aus der Vogelperspective überschaut und Charakter und Maass aller einzelnen darin enthaltenen Stimmungen gegen einander ordnet und abwägt, und doch hat dieses Verfahren, so sehr es eine logische Arbeit zu sein scheint, weder einen logischen, noch einen organischen Gesichtspunct zur Ursache, vielmehr enthüllen sich in den Stimmungen und Maassen der einzelnen Theile, sowie des ganzen Inhaltes, am deutlichsten der persönliche Charakter des Componsiten und der starke Wille, den Zuhörer zu der Stimmung- und Maassordnung, wie er selbst sie geschaffen, zu bekehren und sie, die Ueberzeugung des Zuhörers täuschend, einzuschmuggeln." For an alternate translation, see Schenker/Pastille, 99.

13. As Kevin Korsyn has argued in a consideration of these same passages from Schenker's essay, Schenker's arguments about the "inorganic" nature of the artwork and its creative origins might profitably be read as a critique of the "organicist ideology" that pervaded much of the nineteenth-century discourse on music. See Kevin Korsyn, "Schenker's Organicism Reexamined," *Intégral* 7 (1993), 82–118.

14. *Schenker*, 150; Schenker/Pastille, 100: "Indessen kenne ich eine Erscheinung in der musikalischen Phantasie, auf die der naturwissenschaftliche Begriff des 'Organischen' ganz streng zu

In the end, and as before, Schenker remained torn between his faith in spontaneous creativity as a guarantor of organic coherence on the one hand, and his personal knowledge of the complexities of the composer's work on the other. Immediately after reasserting his faith in the validity of the Wagnerian paradigm, he qualified his account of it, acknowledging that such a creative act never actually seems to occur. "This organic process," Schenker admitted, referring to the latter,

> is naturally organic only so long as it is not tainted by consciousness. In the moment when the composer supplants his imagination with the search for similarities, that which would otherwise readily seem organic to us devolves into the merely *thematic*—that is, to *willed similarity*. For this reason, the term organic must be treated with care, and only hypothetically. It assumes that the composer has *not willed* this similarity, and that it actually arose *organically* in the imagination.[15]

"Ultimately," Schenker wrote, "the hypothetical organic does not at all suffice for the construction of complete content."[16] In light of what he acknowledged to be the unavoidably "willed" nature of the compositional act, Schenker concluded his discussion by arguing that whatever a composer must do in order to assemble his materials in a coherent manner, he must take care to assure that the result never sounds unnatural to the listener. Acknowledging that the "deception" that he noted earlier is an inescapable part of the compositional process, he argued that it must be carried out with the most artful slight of hand. "The material of musical content," he explained, "never arises completely organically, yet the teleology of the composer desires that the significance and ordering of the moods, as he created them and ultimately shaped them into their definitive form, be assessed according to the standards of the organic."[17] That is, they must be heard and evaluated as if they were the products of an unimpeded outpouring

---

passen scheint. Es ist das eine nur sehr schwer controlirbare Erscheinung, aber ich persönlich halte sie für eine Tatsache. So finde ich, dass die Phantasie, nachdem sie ein bestimmtes Gebilde hervorgebracht hat, von vielen Gebilden ähnlicher Natur förmlich belagert ist, und es ist die Macht dieser ähnlichen Gebilde über den Componsiten oft so unwiderstehlich, dass er sie in den zu bauenden Inhalt einschliesst, ohne sich deren Aehnlichkeit gar zum Bewusstsein geführt zu haben. Oft— man erräth es nur bei einer ganz hingebenden Betrachtung des Kunstwerkes—hätte der Componist lieber ein vollständig unähnliches Gebilde heraufbeschwören wollen, und siehe da,—die Phantasie weicht von ihrer erstgefundenen Art nicht ab und drängt ihm nur ein Aehnliches auf."

15. *Schenker*, 150; Schenker/Pastille, 100: "Jedoch ist dieses Organische natürlich nur so lange organisch, so lange es vom Bewusstsein nicht befleckt worden, und im Augenblick, wo der Componist seiner Phantasie den Weg und die Suche nach Aehnlichkeiten anbefohlen hat, sinkt, was uns leicht sonst organisch scheinen könnte, zu blos 'Thematischem' d. h. *ähnlich Gewolltem* herab. Was organisch ist, ist deshalb vorsichtigerweise immer nur hypothetisch zu behandeln: vorausgesetzt, dass der Componist jene Aehnlichkeit *nicht gewollt* hat, ist sie in der Phantasie wirklich *organisch* entstanden."

16. *Schenker*, 152; Schenker/Pastille, 102: "...schliesslich reicht das hypothetisch Organisch zum vollständigen Inhaltsbau gar nicht aus."

17. *Schenker*, 149–50; Schenker/Pastille, 100: "Niemals ist das Material des musikalischen Inhaltes im Ganzen organisch entstanden, wohl aber will es die Teleologie des Componisten so haben, dass die von ihm geschaffene und endlich dem definitiven Zustand übergebene Maass- und Stimmungsordnung nach Gesichtspuncten des Organischen beurtheilt werde."

of spontaneous invention. As with all forms of compositional artifice (Schenker's term for all compositional activity beyond the invention of melody), the composer must strive to employ his deliberating sensibilities in such a way as "to preserve the impression of this unconscious condition in which the artificial whole can be most readily perceived and heard as something arising naturally."[18]

To be sure, many of Schenker's early remarks about the organic work and its imaginative origins can seem inconsistent and philosophically problematic, as nearly a quarter-century of debate about his intentions and sources attests.[19] But with respect to his position on the creative process, the broad outlines of his argument are clear enough. In Schenker's view, the spontaneous functioning of the creative unconscious can theoretically give rise to organic-sounding musical works. But even the greatest artists seem unable to compose through unconscious inspiration alone. Given this situation, he concluded, the composer must employ his deliberating sensibilities with utmost discretion, so that the finished work sounds to the listener as if it had arisen spontaneously. Indeed, Schenker's arguments made clear his skepticism with regard to the Wagnerian theory of creativity, and in that respect they were undoubtedly shaped by his own experiences as a practicing composer.[20] Yet his arguments remained firmly grounded in speculative tradition nonetheless.

SCHENKER'S TURN

At some point between the completion of "The Spirit of Musical Technique" in the spring of 1895 and the publication of his next extensive statement on creativity in November of the following year, something changed in Schenker's mind. While he had earlier embraced an abstract theory of the compositional process indebted to over a century of aesthetic speculation, he somehow became convinced, over the course of 1895–96, that the creative act had been fundamentally misunderstood by nearly all who had written about it previously. He came to believe that only practicing composers, rather than critics or philosophers, can accurately assess the complexities of the creative experience, and he argued that critics, if they wish to understand the process, must dedicate themselves to studying carefully documentary evidence left by creative artists. He ceased calling upon composers to hide the evidence of conscious deliberation in their finished works, and he argued instead that honing one's rational and deliberating

---

18. *Schenker*, 147; Schenker/Pastille, 98: "...um für die Empfindung jenen unbewussten Zustand durchaus zu retten, in dem das künstliche Ganze als ein scheinbar natürlich Geborenes am glücklichsten empfangen und gehört werden konnte."

19. For representative positions and arguments, see Korsyn, "Schenker's Organicism Reexamined"; Allan Keiler, "The Origins of Schenker's Thought: How Man is Musical," *Journal of Music Theory* 33, no. 2 (1989), 273–98; and Pastille, "Heinrich Schenker, Anti-Organicist," *19th-Century Music* 8, no. 1 (1984), 29–36.

20. For further consideration of ways in which Schenker's experiences as a composer might have affected his positions on various issues, see Keiler, "The Origins of Schenker's Thought," 287; and Stephen Hinton, "Musikwissenschaft und Musiktheorie oder Die Frage nach der phänomenologischen Jungfräulichkeit," *Musiktheorie* 3, no. 3 (1988), esp. 202–3.

sensibilities is the most important pursuit of the aspiring artist. Disavowing all speculation and lobbying his readers to assume a self-consciously realistic, even empirical approach to the study of the subject, Schenker departed abruptly from convictions he had recently espoused. This departure constituted his first substantive break from the critical mainstream of his time with respect to any issue of widespread concern. And it also made clear his newfound sympathies with Adler, Gustav Nottebohm, and others who believed that the most promising modes of inquiry into matters of art and the spirit were empirical and experiential rather than speculative. It signaled, in other words, a significant change in his attitude toward the positivist challenge. At the end of this chapter, we will consider some possible causes for Schenker's turn. First, however, we must take a close look at the new position he assumed.

The first indications of a new current in Schenker's thinking about the problem of creativity appeared in an essay entitled "Routine in Music" ("Routine in der Musik"), published in the Viennese cultural weekly *Neue Revue* in November 1896. There, Schenker brought a new vocabulary to his discussion of the inadequacy of spontaneous inspiration in a way that revealed a subtle but important shift in his conception of the problem. He no longer aimed his critique at the workings of conscious and unconscious mental faculties; instead, he targeted the extent to which artistic learning contributes to the development of the creative personality. Schenker admitted that a certain degree of innate creative genius, responsible for the spontaneous production of musical ideas, is indispensable for an artist of the first rank. But he argued that it cannot account for the *evolution*— and thus, for Schenker, the perfecting—of a musician's talents over the course of his or her life. He wrote:

> Genius can never bridge the gap between youth and true mastery. Even the first products of the most brilliant composers do not exhibit at length the degree of cultivated artistic sensibility that the masters who are older in years and experience …obtained before them. Neither the earliest Mozart nor the earliest Beethoven (before Op. 1) nor Schubert achieved the self-assurance with their first creations that already characterized the older masters, of their own time and of those prior to them.[21]

The key to achieving the sort of mastery attained by Schubert and Beethoven, Schenker held, is not locked away in the hidden recesses of the unconscious mind. Instead, it is to be found in disciplined work and practice and in a methodical exploration of the full array of expressive means at one's disposal. It is only through such diligent study, he argued, that one can discover one's unique

---

21. Schenker, "Routine in der Musik," *Neue Revue* 7 (1896); repr. in *Schenker*, 205–9 (cited at 206): "…nicht einmal das Genie kann eine Brücke schlagen von der Jugend zur wahren Meisterschaft. Die ersten Producte selbst der genialsten Componisten wiesen lange nicht jenen Grad von künstlerischer Durchbildung auf, den die an Jahren und Erfahrung älteren Meister… vor ihnen erzielt habe. Weder der früheste Mozart, noch der früheste Beethoven (vor opus 1) oder Schubert erreichten in ihren Erstlingsgedanken jene Haltung, die die älteren Meister vor und zu ihrer Zeit schon charakterisirte, trotzdem ihnen oft die genaue Nachahmung derselben allein das Ziel gewesen."

creative voice. "He for whom nature has reserved a new word in art must, in the beginning, mint it slowly and laboriously," he explained.

> It will unfold as it must, until it appears as something both new and newly essential [*neu-typisch*]! For a long time, such an original artist will torment himself and his art, trying this path and that, until he finds one that he can comfortably follow. Once he has found it, he may happily stick with it or he may set out yet again to carve out a new one. This new path is his compositional method.[22]

To be sure, Schenker's remarks in "Routine in Music" were addressed to would-be composers. But the way in which he framed his discussion also had important implications for the study of the problems he considered. No composer, Schenker argued, however endowed with innate genius, can create a meaningful artwork unless he first learns to understand and respect the conventions of the musical art itself. And whereas the workings of genius and unconscious faculties of invention were—as Wagner stressed repeatedly—inaccessible to rationalistic inquiry, the kinds of diligent practice and methodical exploration emphasized by Schenker could be verified, described, and analyzed. Indeed, this is precisely what Gustav Nottebohm had accomplished in his pioneering studies of Beethoven's sketches, which, begun in the 1860s, were widely regarded as one of the positivist movement's earliest and most stunning achievements.[23] In his next extensive statement on the subject, Schenker too would endorse such an approach to studying the creative process.

In an essay entitled "More Art!" ("Mehr Kunst!"), published in the *Neue Revue* in October 1897, Schenker elaborated upon the theme of "Routine in Music" in a manner that vividly revealed his newfound antagonism toward the whole of the critical discourse on the subject of creativity as it had unfolded during the preceding century. Asserting once again that even the greatest of musicians must strive to hone their artistic sensibilities through diligent work and practice, Schenker opened "More Art" with a quote from Goethe's *Maximen und Reflexionen* (posth., 1833). "In all arts, there is a certain level that one can reach with so-called natural talent alone," Goethe wrote. "At the same time, it is impossible to surpass that level if art does not come to its aid."[24] Schenker glossed Goethe's statement as follows:

> Not everyone has natural talent for a particular art. Not everyone who has natural talent strives to reach the highest level of art attainable through [natural talent]

---

22. *Schenker*, 206: "Aber wem die Natur vorbehielt, ein neues Wort in der Kunst mitzusprechen, der muß es erst langsam, mühsam prägen. Denn es muß, soll es wirken, neu-typisch dastehen! Ein solcher originaler Künstler nun quält sich, auch seine Kunst, versucht bald diesen, bald jenen Weg und es dauert recht lange, bis er einen sich gemäßen findet. Da er ihn gefunden, freut es ihn, darauf zu bleiben, oder wieder einen neuen zu bahnen. Der neue Weg ist seine eigene Compositionsmethode."

23. Gustav Nottebohm, *Ein Skizzenbuch von Beethoven* (Leipzig: Breitkopf und Härtel, 1865); and *Beethoveniana* (Leipzig: Breitkopf und Härtel, 1872).

24. Schenker, "Mehr Kunst!," *Neue Revue* 8 (1897); repr. in *Schenker*, 248–52 (cited at 248): "In allen Künsten gibt es einen gewissen Grad, den man mit den natürlichen Anlagen sozusagen allein erreichen kann. Zugleich aber ist es unmöglich, denselben zu überschreiten, wenn nicht die Kunst zu Hilfe kommt." Schenker quotes Goethe's *Maxime* number 1160.

alone. And finally, not everyone strives to exceed this level once he has attained it. In order to call upon the help of art (as Goethe said), it is necessary, above all else, to possess a clear understanding of its objectives [*Beruf*], requirements, and effects. And neither the need for art nor an understanding of its nature can mature within us before we have felt how incomplete everything is that our "natural talents" can achieve for us on their own. It is certain that the endpoint of natural talent, the starting-point of art, the interpenetration and working-together of both elements, and the creation of true art (that art which is, in equal measure, artificial and natural) are all things that are revealed, in fundamental ways, only to the few. And even those few have felt the comfort of art only after they have first suffered bitterly the painful feeling of being abandoned by it.[25]

At first glance, Schenker's take on Goethe's statement seems merely to affirm the widely held view that both natural talent and knowledge of art play essential roles in the development of the creative personality. But the extent of his break with his earlier statements becomes clear toward the end of this passage. In "More Art," Schenker argued that only a handful of individuals are capable of appreciating the complexities of the creative process and the degree to which artistic learning, as opposed to natural talent, plays a decisive role in one's creative development. And significantly, those few whom Schenker had in mind were not Hanslick, Hartmann, or other critics, and they were not those musicians like Wagner and Weingartner who were inclined to philosophizing about the subject in their published writings. Indeed, he observed, such writers' tendency to indulge in abstractions had only hindered the public's understanding of the artist's work. "Goethe's truth," Schenker asserted, "is most difficult to understand in the realm of music, since music is the art in which the most natural and simple things are least visible of all. For this reason, it is an art about which the most bizarre metaphysical exclamations are always believed."[26] Instead, Schenker argued, the only sources from which one can learn about the realities of the creative act are the documentary testimonials and manuscript evidence left by practicing composers. "No one aside from a few musicians can say how much or how little the strongest natural talent can achieve in music without the help

---

25. *Schenker*, 248–49: "Nicht Jeder hat doch zu irgend einer Kunst natürliche Anlagen, nicht Jeder, der die natürlichen Anlagen besitzt, sucht schon den höchsten, durch sie allein erreichbaren Grad von Kunst überhaupt zu erreichen, und schließlich sucht nicht Jeder diesen Grad zu überschreiten, selbst nachdem er ihn erreicht hat. Um die Kunst, wie Goethe meinte, zu Hilfe zu rufen, gehört vor Allem doch die deutliche Erkenntniß von ihrem Beruf, ihren Nothwendigkeiten und Wirkungen. Und nun kann weder das Bedürfnis nach der Kunst, noch die Erkenntniß ihrer Natur in uns eher reifen, als bis wir gefühlt, wie unvollkommen Alles ist, was unsere 'natürlichen Anlagen' ganz allein uns leisten. Es ist gewiß, der Endpunkt der natürlichen Anlagen, der Anfangspunkt der Kunst, das Zusammenfließen und Ineinanderwirken beider Elemente und das Entstehen der wahren Kunst, jener Kunst, die im selben Maße künstlich wie natürlich ist—das sind Alles Dinge, die im Grunde sich nur den Wenigsten offenbaren, und selbst diese Wenigsten haben den Trost der Kunst empfunden, nachdem sie das peinliche Gefühl erst bitter durchgekostet haben, von ihr verlassen zu sein."

26. *Schenker*, 249: "Am schwersten läßt sich Goethe's Wahrheit gerade in der Musik einsehen. Wie ja überhaupt die Musik jene Kunst ist, in der selbst das Natürlichste und Einfachste am allerwenigsten eingesehen und dafür immer noch ein Niederschlag der seltsamsten Metaphysik geglaubt wird."

of art," he observed. "And again with the exception of musicians, no one can explain the ways in which that help is manifested and what it can mean for the impotence of natural talent."[27]

Emphasizing the distinction between his own, realistic approach to the subject and the speculative orientation still prevalent in his day, Schenker explained that the ideal of musical "craftsmanship" (*Handwerkerthum*) had been wrongly disparaged by generations of writers who granted innate creative genius too privileged a position. "The Romantics," Schenker noted in example, "were always inclined to put off, as it were, the starting-point of art, and to push the boundaries of natural talent ever farther outwards."[28] In contrast, Schenker was convinced that the fallacy of such arguments had been recognized even by some of the "last Romantic" (*letzte Romantiker*) composers themselves: Mendelssohn, Schumann, and Schubert. Each of these figures, Schenker explained, had acknowledged, at some point in his life, the limitations of his natural talents. And in response to that realization, each had sought to learn as much as he could about the art he strove to practice—about its history, materials, expressive potential, and limitations.

Drawing upon statements left by Schumann, Schenker elaborated a portrait of that composer as an artist who began his career in thrall to the whims of his creative genius. But Schumann achieved true greatness, Schenker explained, only after learning, from Mendelssohn's example, to subjugate his creative desires to the higher dictates of musical laws and traditions.[29] In a similar vein, Schenker described the young Franz Schubert as an artist who proudly believed that he had mastered the art of composition through intuition alone. However, Schenker continued, Schubert realized later in life that he longed intensely for the help of "that great art that reigns over moods and thoughts." It was only after coming to terms with this realization and addressing the deficiencies in his childhood education that he was able to muster his talents and set to work upon his "Unfinished" B-minor symphony.[30] Schenker concluded "More Art" by considering a final, contemporary example, the recently departed Johannes Brahms. For Schenker, Brahms was the finest and perhaps only recent composer who had comprehended

27. *Schenker*, 249: "Es weiß Niemand außer wenigen Musikern zu sagen, wie viel oder wie wenig in der Musik die kräftigste natürliche Anlage ausdrücken kann, noch ohne die Zuhilfenahme der Kunst, und die Musiker wieder ausgenommen, weiß sonst Niemand zu erklären, worin die Hilfe der Kunst besteht und was sie einer Ohnmacht der natürlichen Anlage bedeuten kann."

28. *Schenker*, 250: "... die Romantiker immer geneigt waren, den Anfangspunkt der Kunst gleichsam hinauszuschieben und der natürlichen Anlage die Grenze weiter zu stecken..."

29. *Schenker*, 250: "Man denke an Robert Schumann. Am Anfang eine Mißachtung aller Erfahrungen der Kunst, ein schrankenloses Hingeben an die natürliche Anlage, aber schon mit 25 Jahren sieht er das einzig Wahre ein und drückt die Erkenntniß des Mendelssohn'schen Wesens mit den Worten aus: 'Er ist der beste Musiker der Zeit, zu dem ich aufschaue wie zu einem hohen Gebirge.' Ein anderes mal sagt er: 'In ähnlichen Verhältnissen, wie er (Mendelssohn) aufgewachsen, von Kindheit an zur Musik bestimmt, würde ich euch sammt und sonders überflügeln.' Besser konnte er den Schaden, den er an seiner Größe gelitten hat, nicht bezeichnen. So viel er konnte, machte er den Schaden später gut."

30. *Schenker*, 250–51: "Nicht unähnlich war der Fall Schubert's. Trotzdem er, kaum acht Jahre alt, bereits so viel wußte, daß sein erster Lehrer sagte: 'Wenn ich ihm was Neues beibringen wollte, hat er es schon gewußt, folglich habe ich ihm eigentlich keinen Unterricht gegeben, sondern

and assimilated the creative lessons of those who had come before him. In sharp contrast to his contemporaries Hector Berlioz and Franz Liszt, Brahms did not allow himself to be ruled by the whims of his creative imagination. Instead, he deliberately worked to cultivate his artistic sensibilities through the very sort of diligent study and practice that Schenker advocated. He wrote:

> It was therefore of the most profound significance for our time that, until recently, an artist worked among us who maintained a consciousness of art in the midst of the most Romantic (one could also say most modern) atmosphere. From the beginning, his natural talent bowed down before the greater splendor of art. Because of this, it was endowed with the most beautiful reward. ... He alone understood the great sermon of art and practiced what it preached. Now Brahms is dead. What will come now?[31]

For the Schenker of "More Art" and "Routine in Music," what made a musician into a great one was not natural talent or innate creative genius. Instead, it was a commitment, into which one must consciously enter, to work diligently at honing one's craft and internalizing whatever lessons might be gleaned from the experiences of one's predecessors. And if a critic who is not also a composer wishes to understand the creative process, he has only one way to proceed. He must dedicate himself to examining, in a careful and deliberate manner, those records of the creative experience left by practicing artists. He must shun metaphysical speculation and Romantic poetics and dedicate himself to a course of empirical, rationalistic inquiry.

THE PROBLEM OF SCHENKER'S BRAHMS

Assessing this turn in Schenker's thinking over the course of 1895–96, one is struck by an essential question. What could have prompted him to revise his position so radically and in so short a period of time? It does not seem that Schenker's turn to an empiricist position was inspired by criticism of his earlier views. Indeed, his university lecture on "The Spirit of Musical Technique," in which he expounded upon the conscious/unconscious paradigm of creativity, seems to have been well received. Even such an illustrious figure as the physicist

---

mich mit ihm bloß unterhalten und stillschweigend gestaunt', trotzdem er ferner, elf Jahre alt, als Capellknabe im Orchester der Convictisten die symphonischen Meisterwerke der Classiker genau kennen gelernt, empfand er dennoch in reiferen Jahren, zum letzten Male kurz vor seinem Tode, die Sehnsucht nach jener großen Kunst, die über den Stimmungen und Gedanken herrscht, und die Stimmungen nur um so reiner, stoffloser und lustiger und die Gedanken um so körperhafter schafft, je mehr Einfluß sie darin erhält. Er raffte sich auf, seine Sehnsucht nach der Beherrscherin der Stimmungen und Gedanken zu befriedigen und konnte die h-moll-Symphonie schreiben!"

31. *Schenker*, 252: "Für unsere Zeit war es daher von höchster Bedeutung, daß bis vor Kurzem unter uns ein Künstler schuf, der inmitten der romantischesten, man sagt auch modernsten Stimmungen, sozusagen Besinnung zur Kunst hatte, der von Anfang an die natürliche Anlage unter die größere Herrlichkeit der Kunst beugte und darum den schönsten Lohn davontrug. ... Er allein begriff die große Predigt der Kunst und übte, was sie befahl. Nun ist Brahms todt. Was folgt jetzt?"

and philosopher Ernst Mach wrote to Schenker after the event to say that he had found a "healthy kernel" (*gesunden Kern*) in his talk.[32] As Kevin Korsyn has suggested, Mach probably responded, in his note to Schenker, to what he perceived as the critic's skepticism regarding such pervasive, irrationalist treatments of his material such as those found in Wagner's writings.[33] But as we have seen, Schenker's statements in his lecture were likewise highly speculative. And while Schenker did arrive, in "More Art," at views more closely in line with positions Mach held, it seems unlikely that this fleeting encounter with Mach—the only one of which records survive—could have prompted Schenker's complete reevaluation of his earlier views.

Significantly, however, Schenker himself left a handful of clues about the origins of his turn scattered throughout his work. As we have seen, in the closing lines of "More Art," he associated the substance of his remarks on creativity with the recently departed Johannes Brahms. Thirty-six years later, in an article published to commemorate the centennial of Brahms's birth, he revealed that he had completed what amounted to an informal course of study with the composer shortly before he penned "More Art."[34] From his surviving correspondence with Maximilian Harden, his editor at the Berlin weekly *Die Zukunft*, we know that Schenker visited Brahms's apartment in the spring of 1894 to conduct an interview for the paper.[35] Recalling that assignment in his 1933 centennial essay, Schenker explained that he and the composer got along well, that a relationship soon developed, and that the two met occasionally from that point forward, until the onset of Brahms's terminal illness became apparent in the summer or fall of 1896. Recounting Brahms's advice regarding his music criticism, compositions, and piano playing, the elderly Schenker directed his readers to the published memoirs of Gustav Jenner, Brahms's only long-term student. In Jenner's volume, Schenker explained, one finds "the most beautiful echo" (*den schönsten Widerhall*) of advice and wisdom that the master imparted to him as well.[36] And indeed,

32. Mach's note to Schenker, in a postcard of December 2, 1896, is preserved in the Oswald Jonas Memorial Collection of the Special Collections Library, University of California, Riverside (hereafter cited OJMC), box 12, folder 47. It is the only surviving record of their correspondence. It is transcribed and discussed in Federhofer, *Heinrich Schenker*, 14–15; and transcribed by Martin Eybl, trans. Geoffrey Chew, in Ian D. Bent, ed., *Schenker Correspondence Project*. [Online] 2004–. Available at http://mt.ccnmtl.columbia.edu/schenker/ (accessed September 23, 2007).

33. See Korsyn, "Schenker's Organicism Reexamined," 109–16.

34. Schenker, "Erinnerungen an Brahms," *Deutsche Zeitschrift* 46, no. 8 (1933), 475–82.

35. Schenker's assignment is outlined in an unpublished letter sent by Harden to Schenker, dated May 11, 1894 (OJMC, box 11, folder 42). Schenker recounted this assignment in detail in a letter to the pianist and composer Julius Röntgen, dated April 13, 1901. This document is preserved in the Nederlands Muziek Instituut (The Hague), item NMI C 176–01; it is transcribed and translated by Kevin C. Karnes in Bent, *Schenker Correspondence Project*.

36. Schenker, "Erinnerungen an Brahms," 476. For further consideration of Schenker's reported interactions with Brahms, see Karnes, "Schenker's Brahms: Composer, Critic, and the Problem of Creativity in Late Nineteenth-Century Vienna," *Journal of Musicological Research* 24, no. 2 (2005), 145–76 (some of the arguments advanced in this article are revised in the discussion that follows); and Pastille, "Schenker's Brahms," *American Brahms Society Newsletter* 5, no. 2 (1987), 1–2.

when one turns to Jenner's memoirs, one finds that many of Brahms's recorded teachings echo closely Schenker's statements on creativity put forth in "Routine in Music" and "More Art." The source of the ideas that prompted Schenker's turn to an empiricist position, Schenker seemed to suggest, was his onetime mentor, Brahms.

In his memoirs of his period of study, *Johannes Brahms as Man, Teacher, and Artist* (*Johannes Brahms als Mensch, Lehrer und Künstler*), Jenner recalled his initial encounter with Brahms as a humbling experience, in which the composer made him acutely aware of his lack of knowledge about the art he sought to practice. He wrote:

> Brahms turned my attention away from the superficiality of mere dreamy feelings to the deeper realization (of which I had only a presentiment) that, along with feeling, another factor must also be active: reasoning. On account of my lack of skill and knowledge, I could make use of the latter only quite imperfectly. I came to recognize not only the fact that I still had a great deal to learn, but above all those areas upon which I would have to concentrate. I lacked first and foremost a solid foundation of knowledge.[37]

Like Schenker, who emphasized in "More Art" that the devoted study of art is of crucial importance for every composer's creative development, so also Brahms stressed to Jenner the importance of mastering the disciplines of harmony, counterpoint, and orchestration before pursuing further compositional studies.[38] It is such technical skill, Brahms counseled his student, that "first enables the composer to arrange his ideas freely and to bring them to paper."[39]

Time and again, Jenner recalled Brahms's assurances that all great artists must hone their talents through diligent study and disciplined practice. Not one of them, Brahms assured his student, had been able to rely upon his innate creative talents alone. In a passage that recalls Schenker's "Routine in Music," Jenner remembered Brahms proclaiming that "Natural talent is, of course, very important here, but even the greatest talent cannot substitute for an appropriate and

37. Gustav Jenner, *Johannes Brahms als Mensch, Lehrer und Künstler. Studien und Erlebnisse*, 2d ed. (Marburg an der Lahn: N. G. Engelwert'sche Verlagsbuchhandlung, 1930), 8–9: "So lenkte Brahms meinen Blick von der Oberfläche einer traumseligen Empfindung hinunter in Tiefen, wo ich nur ahnen konnte, dass neben der Empfindung auch ein anderer Faktor tätig sein müsse, der aus Mangel an Können und Wissen bei mir nur sehr unvollkommen mitarbeitete: der Verstand. Ich sah nicht allein, dass ich zu lernen habe, sondern vor allem gleichzeitig, wo ich zu lernen habe. Mir fehlte zunächst eine solide Grundlage des Wissens." An alternate translation of this passage is found in Jenner, "Johannes Brahms as Man, Teacher, and Artist," trans. Susan Gillespie, in *Brahms and His World*, ed. Walter Frisch (Princeton: Princeton University Press, 1990; hereafter cited as Jenner/Gillespie), 188.

38. Jenner, *Johannes Brahms*, 45–46; Jenner/Gillespie, 201–2.

39. Jenner, *Johannes Brahms*, 43–44; Jenner/Gillespie, 201: "Noch ein anderes Hindernis, das sich dem jungen unerfahrenen Komponisten entgegenzustellen pflegt, kann nicht frühe genug beiseite geräumt werden, wenn es sich darum handelt, überhaupt 'schreiben' zu lernen, d. h. jene Technik zu erringen, die dem Komponisten überhaupt erst ermöglicht, seine Gedanken frei auszugestalten und zu Papier zu bringen."

proper education. Even Mozart first had to learn to write."[40] Like the Schenker of 1896 and 1897, Jenner's Brahms believed that disciplined work plays a key role in every composer's creative development. As the elder artist advised his student, "You must learn to work. You must write a lot, every day, and you must not believe that what you write always has to be something meaningful. ... How many songs must one write before a useable one emerges!"[41] Furthermore, Jenner remembered Brahms advising that before one can develop one's own compositional voice, one must study the works and creative experiences of the great artists of the past and strive to internalize the lessons garnered from them. This, Brahms counseled, was the way in which Bach, Mozart, and Beethoven had all learned.[42] Jenner summarized Brahms's views as follows:

> How often did I hear Brahms, in anger, proclaim ironically: "Everyone knows that one must learn in all other fields. Only in music is it unnecessary; one can make music or one can't!" It is clear that an artist should, above all, work to understand his time and its art. We call a man a great one only if he, in tune with the spirit of his time, has the strength and the skill to hit the nail on the head. But pity the strong man whose tools of the trade are not in order. For him the hammer will miss its mark.[43]

To be sure, it is easy to spot the similarities between Schenker's statements and Jenner's recollections of Brahms's teachings. Both Jenner's Brahms and the young Schenker stressed that refined artistic sensibilities, honed by disciplined work and practice, are indispensable for the creation of great musical works. Both believed that studying the music and experiences of past masters is essential for discovering one's own compositional voice. Both felt that the importance of innate genius and natural talent had been greatly overestimated by their predecessors and peers. And both lamented the fact that their conception of the ideal creative musician seemed to be vanishing among their contemporaries. To conclude from this situation that the turn we have charted in Schenker's thinking was prompted by his personal interactions with Brahms would be to confirm the profound significance of a relationship proudly recalled toward the end of Schenker's life. It would also account for the unanticipated appearance of those

---

40. Jenner, *Johannes Brahms*, 44; Jenner/Gillespie, 201: "Die natürliche Begabung tut hier selbstverständlich viel zur Sache, aber selbst die höchste Begabung vermag gerade in diesem wichtigen Punkte eine zweckmässige vernünftige Erziehung nicht überflüssig zu machen. Auch Mozart hat sich die Technik des Schreibens erst erringen müssen..."

41. Jenner, *Johannes Brahms*, 44–45; Jenner/Gillespie, 202: "Sie müssen arbeiten lernen. Sie müssen viel schreiben, Tag für Tag, und nicht glauben, es müsse immer etwas bedeutendes sein, was Sie schreiben. ... Wie viele Lieder muss man machen, ehe ein brauchbares entsteht!"

42. Jenner, *Johannes Brahms*, 57–58 (this passage is not included in Jenner/Gillespie).

43. Jenner, *Johannes Brahms*, 58–59 (this passage is not included in Jenner/Gillespie): "Wie oft habe ich Brahms im Zorn ironisch ausrufen hören: 'Dass man in allen anderen Dingen zu lernen hat, weiss jeder, nur in der Musik ist es nicht nötig; das kann man, oder man kann es nicht!' Dass ein Künstler vor allem seine Zeit und ihre Kunst verstehen lerne, ist klar. Denn nur den nennen wir einen grossen Mann, der, durchdrungen vom Geist seiner Zeit, die Kraft und das Geschick hat, den Hebel am rechten Fleck einzusetzen und zu bewegen. Wehe aber auch der starken Natur, deren Handwerkzeug nicht in Ordnung ist: der Hebel wird versagen."

ideas in Schenker's writings from 1896 to 1897. For as his correspondence with another of his editors, Hermann Bahr, makes clear, Schenker began drafting "Routine in Music"—the essay in which he unveiled these ideas—during the summer of 1895, precisely when the critic was, by his own account, in the midst of his studies with Brahms.[44]

But it is perhaps significant that Schenker's remarks recall not only those of Jenner's Brahms. Indeed, many of Schenker's statements echo, just as vividly, observations made by Friedrich Nietzsche during a period in which the once-Wagnerian philosopher was likewise reevaluating his own position on the problem of creativity. Just as Schenker emphasized the importance of honing one's artistic sensibilities through diligent study and practice, so too Nietzsche published the following remarks in his *Human, All Too Human* of 1878:

> Artists have an interest in our believing in sudden flashes of insight, in what we call inspirations; as if the idea for a work of art, for a poem, for the fundamental thought of a philosophy shone down like a gleam of grace from heaven. In truth, the imagination of a good artist or thinker continually produces good, mediocre, and bad things, but his *power of judgment*, highly sharpened and practiced, rejects, selects, ties together.[45]

In his memoirs, Jenner recounted Brahms's assurances that all artists, however gifted, must tirelessly work to hone their skills; "even Mozart first had to learn to write," he remembered Brahms explaining. In a similar vein, Nietzsche, in *Human, All Too Human*, counseled that "The genius, too, does nothing other than learning first to set stone upon stone."[46] The philosopher continued with a passage that echoes Brahms's angry outburst about the necessity of musical learning:

> Just don't talk to me about natural gifts or innate talents! We could name great men of every kind who were only slightly gifted. But they *acquired* greatness, became "geniuses" (as we say), by means of qualities, of which when they are lacking, those who are aware of them do not readily speak: they all had that diligent earnestness of the artisan, which learns first to shape the parts perfectly before it dares to make any great whole.[47]

And like Jenner's Brahms, who directed his student to compose a little something every day and who assured him that, if he proceeded in that way, a usable song would eventually emerge, so also Nietzsche advised his readers on the writing of effective prose:

---

44. Letter sent by Hermann Bahr to Schenker, dated July 4, 1895, located in OJMC, box 9, folder 10a; transcribed by Eybl, trans. Chew, in Bent, *Schenker Correspondence Project*: "The article on 'Routine in Music' can naturally be serialized over two issues, if you wish, although that always carries various disadvantages."

45. Friedrich Nietzsche, *Human, All Too Human: A Book for Free Spirits*, trans. Gary Handwerk, The Complete Works of Friedrich Nietzsche, vol. 3 (Stanford: Stanford University Press, 1995), 118 (emphasis in original).

46. Nietzsche, *Human, All Too Human*, 123.

47. Nietzsche, *Human, All Too Human*, 124 (emphasis in original).

The recipe for how someone can become a good novelist can easily be given...but following it presupposes qualities that we tend to overlook when we say "I do not have enough talent." Just make a hundred or more outlines for novels, none longer than two pages, yet of such clarity that every word in them is necessary; write down anecdotes daily until you learn to find their most pregnant, effective form. ... Allow some ten years to go by in practicing these various things: what is then created in the workshop can even be permitted out into the light of day.[48]

In *Human, All Too Human*, we find another echo of Brahms's teachings as remembered by his student. And we also find yet another consideration of the creative act that anticipates Schenker's statements.

This is not to say, of course, that it was Nietzsche rather than Brahms who inspired Schenker's turn. (Although we should note, as Korsyn has demonstrated, that Schenker was evidently familiar with Nietzsche's work.)[49] But the situation does make clear that we must read Schenker's hints at Brahmsian origins with caution. After all, there exists scant documentary evidence to establish unambiguously more than a casual relationship between composer and critic. Neither of the principal publications by Brahms's contemporaries devoted to recording the composer's activities during his final years mentions Schenker's studies with the artist.[50] Kalbeck's diaries, which likewise illuminate Brahms's elderly activities, also include no mention of these meetings, despite the fact that Kalbeck and Schenker appear to have corresponded since the 1880s.[51] In one of Schenker's surviving letters to Kalbeck, he does allude to contact with Brahms in a way that might corroborate his statements of 1933, when he reports that Brahms was "very, perhaps overly appreciative" of his attempts at composition.[52] But Schenker's extensive correspondence with the pianist Moriz Violin, his closest personal friend, makes no mention of such contact. Schenker's diary, begun in 1896, likewise sheds no light on the issue.[53]

48. Nietzsche, *Human, All Too Human*, 124.

49. See Korsyn, "Schenker's Organicism Reexamined," 95–104.

50. Richard Heuberger, *Erinnerungen an Johannes Brahms. Tagebuchnotizen aus den Jahren 1875 bis 1897*, ed. Kurt Hofmann, 2d ed. (Tutzing: Hans Schneider, 1976); Max Kalbeck, *Johannes Brahms*, 4 vols. (Berlin: Deutsche Brahms-Gesellschaft, 1904–14).

51. Kalbeck's diaries are, however, incomplete, covering only 1895 and 1897. They are held in private collection. I am grateful to Sandra McColl for providing detailed information about their contents. Schenker's correspondence with Kalbeck, which includes drafts of two letters from Schenker to Kalbeck penned during Schenker's university years (1884–89), is preserved in OJMC, box 5, folder 9 (Schenker to Kalbeck), and box 12, folder 7 (Kalbeck to Schenker). One of these early letters is transcribed and discussed in Federhofer, *Heinrich Schenker*, 8–9.

52. Unpublished letter drafted by Schenker to Kalbeck, dated May 10, 1897 (OJMC, box 5, folder 9): "Sehr geehrter Herr! Ich darf mir wohl nicht schmeicheln, anzunehmen, dass Sie meine schriftstellerischen Versuch in Harden's 'Zukunft,' in der Wiener 'Neue Revue' oder in der 'Zeit' beachtet haben? Es läge aber mehr daran, wenn, Sie mir die Ehre erweisen wollten, Compositionen von mir anzuhören, über die sowohl Brahms, als Goldmark, d'Albert u Busoni sehr, vielleicht allzusehr anerkennend sich aussprachen? Ich bitte Sie, durch den Gedanken sich gar nicht zu beunruhigen, als bäte ich implicite um Ihre markante schriftstellerische Hilfe. Mir ist nur darum zu thun, im Kreis der Allerbesten mich hier als Komponisten einzuführen, noch ehe d'Albert von mir Einiges spielt. Darf ich hoffen? In ausgezeichneter Hochachtung Dr Heinrich Schenker."

53. Schenker's correspondence with Violin is preserved in OJMC, boxes 6–8 and box 14, folder 45; his diary is preserved in OJMC, box 1, folder 1.

In the end, what may be most important to take from this situation is not that Brahms might have provided the impetus for Schenker's early brush with an empiricist position. Rather, it is that Schenker hinted at such a situation in the first place. For when he reflected upon his youthful activities in his essay of 1933, he had long ago abandoned the position he had espoused in "Routine in Music" and "More Art," and he had embraced once again a metaphysical view of creative genius that was as irrationalist as anything that Wagner ever espoused. Indeed, the publication of Schenker's *Harmony* (*Harmonielehre*) in 1906—the first installment of what would become his principal theoretical contribution, the *New Musical Theories and Fantasies* (*Neue musikalische Theorien und Phantasien*)— made clear that he had, by that time, already rejected his empiricist experiments of a decade earlier. In *Harmony*, Schenker described the compositional act not by way of the personal recollections of Schubert, Schumann, or Brahms but in Wagnerian, even Schopenhauerian terms.[54] Considering a hypothetical circumstance in which an artist sets out to compose a passage of music in a church mode, only to find his music drifting, as if inevitably, toward major or minor, he wrote:

> A great talent or a man of genius, like a sleepwalker, often finds the right way, even when his instinct is thwarted by one thing or another or...by the full and conscious intention to follow the wrong direction. The superior force of truth—of Nature, as it were—is at work mysteriously behind his consciousness, guiding his pen, without caring in the least whether the happy artist himself wanted to do the right thing or not. If he had his way in following his conscious intentions, the result, alas! would often be a miserable composition. But, fortunately, that mysterious power arranges everything for the best.[55]

Summing up his newfound view regarding such a situation, he observed: "many works, consciously or intentionally written in the church modes, spontaneously came out as major or minor. ... This happened whenever the genius of the artist was so strong that Music could use him as a medium, so to speak, without his knowledge and quite spontaneously."[56] As it happened, Schenker's advocacy of an empiricist position was only a brief diversion from convictions he harbored throughout most of his life. In his writings from 1906 onward, he would repeatedly describe musical works shaping themselves, of their own volition, within the mind of the genius, and the greatest of composers as those who were driven by deepest, unconscious instinct.[57] This fact, I would argue, provides an important key to understanding Schenker's conflicted response to the positivist challenge as evinced in his turn-of-the-century writings.

54. The Schopenhauerian foundations of Schenker's statements, post-1900, on the compositional process are considered in Nicholas Cook, "Schenker's Theory of Music as Ethics," *Journal of Musicology* 7, no. 4 (1989), 420–24.

55. Schenker, *Harmony*, ed. Oswald Jonas, trans. Elisabeth Mann Borgese (Chicago: University of Chicago Press, 1954), 60. For Schopenhauer's famous analogy between composer and sleepwalker, see *The World as Will and Representation*, trans. E. F. J. Payne, 2 vols. (Indian Hills, CO: Falcon's Wing Press, 1958), 2:255–67.

56. Schenker, *Harmony*, 69.

57. See, for example, Schenker, *Counterpoint*, vol. 2 (orig. 1922), ed. John Rothgeb, trans. John Rothgeb and Jürgen Thym (New York: Schirmer, 1987), xx: "The sum total of my works present

In his essay on Brahms of 1933, Schenker hinted that his youthful attraction to empirical research was not prompted by his personal experience of the strength and nature of evidence gathered through the scientifically inspired study of documentary sources. Rather, he suggested, it was prompted by the revealed wisdom of a onetime mentor, Brahms. And significantly, to do that—to hint at revelatory rather than reasoned causes for his fleeting embrace of an empiricist position—was to deny that the work of Adler, Nottebohm, and other scientifically oriented scholars had ever played a role in his intellectual development. It was to deny that he had ever been swayed by the positivist movement, which valorized empirical observation and inductive reasoning and had little use for the kinds of metaphysical theorizing in which he indulged in *Harmony* and his subsequent theoretical works. In this way, Schenker's elderly recollections had the effect of smoothing over a significant bump in his intellectual development, and thus they indulged a carefully honed mythology of Schenker's creative work. That mythology, which held that even his earliest attempts as a writer had "clearly hinted at" (*deutlich durchblicken lassen*) the synthesis of his mature analytical theories, would only be stoked by Schenker's students in the years following his death in 1935.[58] Yet in publishing his centennial essay on Brahms, Schenker also acknowledged, ironically and surely unwittingly, the strength of the pull that the positivist challenge had once exerted upon his imagination. For without attraction to its promises and claims, there would be no need for denial. This too, it seems, was part and parcel of Schenker's conflicted history.

Compared with Schenker, Eduard Hanslick found an easy answer to the positivist challenge. Once he had become convinced that musical beauty can only

---

an image of art as self-contained, as growing of itself—but, despite all infinitude of appearance, as setting its own limits through selection and synthesis"; and Schenker, *Free Composition* (orig. 1935), ed. and trans. Ernst Oster (New York: Longman, 1979), xxiv: "The phenomenon of genius signifies a breath drawn from the unconscious, a breath which keeps the spirit ever young." For further discussion of Schenker's mature notion of genius, see Ian Bent, "Heinrich Schenker e la missione del genio germanico," *Rivista Italiana di Musicologia* 26, no. 1 (1991), 3–34.

58. See, for instance, Felix Salzer, "Die Historische Sendung Heinrich Schenkers," *Der Dreiklang* 1, no. 1 (1937), 2–12 (cited at 7). This is not the only instance of such historical refashioning in Schenker's Brahms essay. To take another example: Schenker recalled that after he had played through his Op. 1 at the piano during one of his meetings with Brahms, the composer replied with the typically abrupt and ambiguous quip, "Sie spielen wohl sehr gut Klavier." Schenker's supposed response to Brahms's statement, however, reflects his thinking as it stood about thirty years later, around the time he wrote his *Tonwille* essays: "So oft mein Spiel in der Öffentlichkeit oder in privaten Kreisen Beifall fand oder meine Vortragsanweisungen Interesse erregten, die ich in Erkenntnis des Kunstwerkes als einer Einheit in Synthese, Schreibart und Vortrag seit einem Vierteljahrhundert allen analytischen Arbeiten beigab, gedachte ich beglückt jener ersten an mich gerichteten Worte des Meisters" (Schenker, "Erinnerungen an Brahms," 476–77). For further discussion of various mythologies cultivated by Schenker and others around his work, see Joseph Lubben, review of *The Masterwork in Music: A Yearbook. Volume I (1925)* by Heinrich Schenker, *Journal of the American Musicological Society* 52, no. 1 (1999), 145–56; and Roberg Snarrenberg, "Competing Myths: The American Abandonment of Schenker's Organicism," in *Theory, Analysis and Meaning in Music*, ed. Anthony Pople (Cambridge: Cambridge University Press, 1994), 30–58.

be described within specific cultural and historical contexts, Hanslick realized that he would have to abandon his work as an aesthetic philosopher and reinvent himself as a historian. And once he had decided to dedicate himself to documenting the contemporary unfolding of his society's "living history," he realized that scientifically oriented modes of research could not answer the questions he pondered. While doubtlessly fraught with deep introspection and moments of personal crisis, Hanslick's rejection of the positivist enterprise was straightforward and resolute. The same cannot be said of Schenker.

To Schenker's mind, the challenge posed to music study by Spitta, Adler, and their like-minded peers raised a host of important questions but offered few clear-cut answers. Like Hanslick, Schenker recognized that scientifically inspired modes of research cannot account for the listener's experience of music's beauty, effectiveness, and worth. In response to that realization, he sought, in his reviews of Brahms's songs and choral works, to revive a besieged, hermeneutic approach to analysis and a Romantic poetics of genius. But as a practicing composer, he also felt compelled to acknowledge the impossibility of explaining the complexities of the creative act by means of philosophical speculation. Eventually, he recognized the promise of empirical study to demystify the process. And if he then went on to abandon his empiricist convictions within a decade after he first espoused them, that fact does not detract from the significance of this early shift in his thinking. For it signaled not only his early attraction to positivist scholarship and its promise but also his first substantive break from the critical mainstream of his time. Moreover, with respect to the ambivalence with which he greeted the positivist challenge, Schenker was, as we are finding, perfectly typical of his age.

In the final part of this book, we will turn to Adler's own late-century work, in which we discover that even he greeted aspects of the positivist movement with uncertainty. Over the course of the 1890s, while Schenker was working to establish himself as one of Vienna's leading music critics, Adler was emerging as one of Central Europe's most prominent historians of the art. But during that decade, Adler's vision of his discipline was undergoing significant changes. By the time he was appointed Hanslick's successor at the University of Vienna in 1898, the variety of *Musikwissenschaft* that he preached and practiced had become something quite different from what he had described in his "Scope, Method, and Goal of Musicology." Indeed, Adler's work from the turn of the century makes clear that the positivist movement was not monolithic but vigorously contested from within.

PART III

GUIDO ADLER AND THE PROBLEM OF SCIENCE

Guido Adler and his wife Betti in 1887. Courtesy of the Hargrett Rare Book and Manuscript Library/University of Georgia Libraries.

CHAPTER FIVE

A SCIENCE OF MUSIC FOR AN
AMBIVALENT AGE

If the positivist movement in music study provoked such deeply felt and con-flicted responses from figures as dissimilar in their interests and outlooks as Schenker and Hanslick, it is only natural to ask whether such ambivalence was not in some way felt by leading figures in the movement itself. After all, if Hanslick maintained that what really matters about the musical experience is the impact of the work upon the listener's imagination, and if Schenker insisted that the "objective" analysis of musical structure can yield only a partial appreciation of its significance, then one must suspect that there were many others as well who felt that the empirical description of historical sources and the induction of laws regarding formal construction cannot satisfy the sensitive listener's longing to understand what he or she hears. Might it be, one might ask, that such polemi-cizing positivists as Spitta and Chrysander somehow sensed that their own pro-grammatic statements offered only partial or tentative solutions to the problem of how to study and write about the art? And what about Adler, the figure whose work is widely regarded as epitomizing the positivist endeavor as a whole?

To be sure, nearly all late-century attempts to impose positivist agendas upon the study of art betray a degree of anxiety. As we have seen, Chrysander, writing in the *Jahrbücher für musikalische Wissenschaft*, fretted about whether his colleagues would ever accept that such a "vague" art as music could be sub-jected to "the strictest demands of science."[1] A decade later, Moriz Thausing voiced similar misgivings with regard to his work as an art historian when he noted that "artistic phenomena are not as easily grasped as natural objects... for us, there are no experiments, much less a *corpus vile*."[2] Even Spitta, whose "Art and the Study of Art" ("Kunstwissenschaft und Kunst," 1883) provided

---

1. Friedrich Chrysander, "Vorwort und Einleitung," *Jahrbücher für musikalische Wissenschaft* 1 (1863), 10; trans. in Bojan Bujić, ed., *Music in European Thought 1851–1912*, Cambridge Readings in the Literature of Music (Cambridge: Cambridge University Press, 1988), 345–46.
2. Moriz Thausing, "Die Stellung der Kunstgeschichte als Wissenschaft," in *Wiener Kunstbriefe* (Leipzig: E. A. Seemann, 1884), 11: "...die Kunstgegenstände nicht so leicht erreichbar sind wie Naturobjecte...für uns absolut kein Experiment, und am wenigsten ein *corpus vile* gibt."

Hanslick's detractors with a store of ideological ammunition at the time of his retirement from the University of Vienna, conceded that transforming the study of art into a science posed formidable methodological challenges. The discipline as a whole, Spitta observed, lacked "a solid tradition," was "uncertain of its methods," and was often "questionable with regard to its conclusions." Indeed, he admitted, it was still "considered by many educated people . . . [to] lack the strength to stand on its own."[3]

For Adler too, the positivist movement posed considerable problems for his field. And his own career-making disciplinary polemic, "The Scope, Method, and Goal of Musicology" (1885), is no less anxiety-ridden than those of his contemporaries. But the anxiety evident in Adler's essay is of a different sort from that encountered with Thausing, Spitta, and Chrysander. Unlike those evinced by his colleagues, the doubts Adler adduced about the success of his endeavors did not concern the susceptibility of music to the demands of empirical research or the ability of music scholars to emulate the methodological rigor of their naturalist peers. Rather, they concerned the continued vitality of the creative arts in an increasingly scientific age. "It has been said," Adler observed in this essay, "that the spread of the scientific study of any art is a sure sign that art is in decline."[4] And while one can imagine a figure like Spitta dismissing such concerns out of hand, Adler took them seriously enough to dedicate a significant part of his disciplinary manifesto to an attempt to assuage such fears. "So long as the study of art remains within its natural boundaries and assists artists in clearly defined enterprises," he wrote, "it can pose no threat to musical production."[5] In spite of his own assurances, however, Adler's sympathy with his unnamed skeptics was such that he chose to address their concerns even in his parting words to his audience. There, he defined a pair of goals for his discipline that might have lent some comfort to his critics but could only have confounded many of his positivist peers. The first of these goals, "the investigation of truth" (*Erforschung des Wahren*), was one with which few historians could quarrel. The second, "the promotion of beauty" (*Förderung des Schönen*), was another matter altogether.[6] To appreciate just how remarkable the second of these goals was, we need only recall Spitta's assertion,

---

3. Philipp Spitta, "Kunstwissenschaft und Kunst," in *Zur Musik. Sechzehn Aufsätze* (Berlin: Gebrüder Paetel, 1892), 3: "Ohne den Rückhalt einer festen Tradition, schwankend in ihrer Methode und vielfach fragwürdig in ihren Resultaten, gilt sie selbst unter den Gelehrten mehr nur als ein Anhängsel anderer wissenschaftlicher Disciplinen, dem die Kraft fehlt, auf eigenen Füßen zu stehen."

4. Guido Adler, "Umfang, Methode und Ziel der Musikwissenschaft," *Vierteljahrsschrift für Musikwissenschaft* 1 (1885), 19; trans. in Bujić, *Music in European Thought*, 352: "Man hat behauptet, daß es ein sicheres Anzeichen des Verfalles der Kunst sei, wenn die Kunstwissenschaft sich auszubreiten beginne."

5. Adler, "Umfang, Methode und Ziel," 19; trans. in Bujić, *Music in European Thought*, 352: "Bleibt die Kunstwissenschaft in den natürlichen Grenzen und vereinigt sie sich zu bestimmten Aufgaben mit Künstlern . . . so kann sie unmöglich die Kunstproduction gefährden."

6. Adler, "Umfang, Methode und Ziel," 20; trans. in Bujić, *Music in European Thought*, 353: "Je aufrichtiger der Wille, desto wirksamer in der Folge, je umfassender das Können, desto bedeutungsvoller das Product, je mehr gemeinschaftlich das Vorgehen, desto tiefgreifender die Wirkung, welche hohe Güter in sich birgt: Erforschung des Wahren und Förderung des Schönen."

in "Art and the Study of Art," that the historian of music "must ignore beauty in all its abundance, as it can find no place in his system"; or Thausing's, that "the best history of art is one in which the word *beautiful* never appears."[7]

Adler's decision to end his manifesto by declaring that the musicologist must work for the promotion of beauty raises a host of questions about the discipline he envisioned and the broader cultural discourse to which he responded. First, just who were those figures whose concerns he addressed when he proclaimed that the advent of science need not spell the demise of art? And more fundamentally, can it be that Adler's relationship to the positivist movement was more complex and troubled than we have tended to suspect? As I will suggest in the final chapters of this book, when one looks beyond "The Scope, Method, and Goal of Musicology" to consider Adler's critical editions, biographical studies, and journalistic criticism, one encounters an unfamiliar side of a historian who never shed his youthful concern for an array of problems regarding science, art, and the challenges of modernity that he first confronted during his student years. To be sure, Adler spent the first decade of his career trying to win for music study a respected place in an increasingly scientific academy. But once he was securely ensconced in his professorship in Prague, and—even more significantly—once he was tenured by the University of Vienna, he turned his attention back to earlier concerns, in which the figures of Nietzsche and Wagner loomed large. And as he did that, he embarked upon a search for means of assuring the vitality of contemporary art in an ideologically divided, deeply ambivalent age.

WAGNER, BATKA, AND THE PROBLEM OF SCIENCE

Adler's engagement with music and its histories followed a circuitous if unsurprising path. Having spent his youth at the Vienna Conservatory and the University of Vienna, he was drawn in his twenties to the intellectual ferment stoked in that city by Wagner and the young Friedrich Nietzsche. He associated with the likes of the poet Siegfried Lipiner and the future political organizer Victor Adler (no relation) and, more broadly, with members of the circle of artists and intellectuals surrounding the writer Engelbert Pernerstorfer—a group that dedicated itself, among other things, to advancing the career of the young Gustav Mahler.[8] Even within this community of activists, Adler's activism stood out. In 1873, with a pair of friends from the conservatory, he cofounded the Viennese Academic Wagner Society (Wiener akademischer Wagner-Verein), an organization dedicated to providing financial support to the Bayreuth festival and to "spreading the Wagnerian idea of reform in music and drama."[9] Three years later, while

7. Spitta, "Kunstwissenschaft und Kunst," 9; Thausing, "Die Stellung," 5. These writers' views on this issue are considered in detail in chapter 1.

8. On the activities of the Pernerstorfer circle, see William J. McGrath, *Dionysian Art and Populist Politics in Austria* (New Haven: Yale University Press, 1974).

9. From the "Geschäfts-Bericht" published in the *Erster Jahres-Bericht des Wiener akademischen Wagner-Vereines für das Jahr 1873* (Vienna: Selbstverlag des Vereines, 1874), 31. For Adler's account of his activities during this period of his life, see his *Wollen und Wirken. Aus dem Leben eines*

enrolled in law school at the university, he made the inaugural pilgrimage to Bayreuth. Back in Vienna, he lectured in 1877 on the festival and its meanings to the university's Reading Society for German Students (Leseverein für deutsche Studenten).[10] At one point, he even drafted a letter to Wagner, wondering whether "I might be the one to proclaim, with his humble voice, the noble substance" of the master's work.[11] During these years, Adler sensed that he had a higher calling in life than the career in civil service for which his legal studies were preparing him. He had dedicated himself, as Nietzsche had urged, to "struggl[ing] on behalf of culture" by promoting "the production of the genius." For Adler, that genius was Wagner.[12]

When Adler returned to the world of academe in the late 1870s to study music history after a brief and unhappy stint as a lawyer, he made a professionally apposite decision. He resolved to focus his attention on the history of harmony and polyphony, a more politically innocuous field of inquiry than Wagnerian art and aesthetics. Completing his dissertation under Hanslick's supervision in 1880 and publishing it at the end of that year, he embarked upon an academic career propelled rapidly upward by a series of positivist polemics and a steady stream of publications related to his doctoral research.[13] Adler lectured at the University of Vienna until 1885, when he accepted a professorship at the German University in Prague. There, as we saw in chapter 1, he devoted himself to work as founding editor of the *Vierteljahrsschrift für Musikwissenschaft* and the *Monuments of Music*

Musikhistorikers (Vienna: Universal Edition, 1935), 2–17 (unless otherwise noted, all biographical information supplied in the discussion that follows is taken from this source). On the history and activities of the Wagner-Verein, see Margaret Notley, "Musical Culture in Vienna at the Turn of the Twentieth Century," in *Schoenberg, Berg, and Webern: A Companion to the Second Viennese School*, ed. Bryan R. Simms (Westport, CT: Greenwood Press, 1999), 55–58.

10. Adler's lectures to the Leseverein are noted in the *Jahresbericht des Lesevereines der deutschen Studenten Wien's über das VI. Vereinsjahr 1876–77* (Vienna: Selbstverlag des Leseverein der deutschen Studenten Wien's, 1877; hereafter cited as *Leseverein Jahresbericht 1876–77*), 29. Entitled "Bayreuth 1876," they were delivered on April 14 and 21, 1877; the text is not known to survive.

11. From a manuscript draft letter found in a loose-leaf gathering of papers whose first page bears the inscription "Skizzen u Auszüge über Musiktheori, Gesch: u Musikaufführungen in Wien Guido Adler 1878 I. Heft." The letter is marked, apparently in Adler's hand, "An RW / nicht geschickt 1878?"; it is preserved in the Guido Adler Papers (MS 769; hereafter cited GAP) of the Hargrett Rare Book and Manuscript Library/University of Georgia Libraries, box 1, folder 4: "vielleicht ich derjenige bin…seine schwache Stimme für die edle Sache erschallen zu lassen." Courtesy of the Hargrett Rare Book and Manuscript Library/University of Georgia Libraries.

12. Friedrich Nietzsche, "Schopenhauer as Educator," in *Untimely Meditations*, ed. Daniel Breazeale, trans. R. J. Hollingdale, Cambridge Texts in the History of Philosophy (Cambridge: Cambridge University Press, 1997), 163. For a detailed consideration of Adler's early indebtedness to Wagner and the Viennese Wagnerian movement that differs from the one elaborated here, see Leon Botstein, "Music and Its Public: Habits of Listening and the Crisis of Musical Modernism in Vienna, 1870–1914" (Ph.D. diss., Harvard University, 1985), 1317–92.

13. In addition to "Umfang, Methode und Ziel," Adler's disciplinary polemics include the unpublished lectures "Das Studium der Musikwissenschaft" (undated) and "Das Studium der Musikwissenschaft auf der Universitaet" (dated, apparently in Adler's hand, "?1881 1885"), both preserved in GAP, box 1, folder 16.

in Austria (*Denkmäler der Tonkunst in Österreich*) series of critical editions. In 1898, following Hanslick's retirement, he returned to his alma mater as a tenured, full (*ordinarius*) professor. At that point, after spending two decades occupied with the history of music theory, research on medieval repertoires, and a variety of administrative projects, he turned his attention back to the artist who had inspired him to music study in the first place. He dedicated himself to writing the lectures that would evolve into his first book, *Richard Wagner* (1904).[14] And he began to publish critical essays on Wagner and his music in Vienna's *Neue freie Presse*, the prestigious liberal daily paper from which Hanslick had recently retired.

Among the reasons Adler had for entering the critical fray shortly after 1900, one seems to have been to justify his turn, as a respected scholar of musical antiquity, to the nineteenth century's most notorious modernist composer. One of the ways in which he did this was to trumpet his activism of a quarter-century earlier on behalf of Wagner's art. But while it was easy for him to declare that he had been an "eager apostle" (*eifriger Apostel*) of the master during his student years and had been "educated and molded" (*erzogen und gebildet*) by Wagnerian music, such invocations of youthful idealism were often difficult to reconcile with his more recently proclaimed scholarly ideals.[15] In the spring of 1903, an exchange between Adler and the Prague-based historian Richard Batka, played out on the pages of two of the empire's leading daily papers, made clear just how messy and unsatisfying Adler's attempts at negotiating the Wagnerian legacy could be. And buried beneath the rhetoric of Adler's arguments and Batka's responses, we find revealed an important source of Adler's anxiety with regard to the positivist challenge.

Adler's dispute with Batka, an ardent Wagnerian and Bayreuth insider, was touched off by one of Adler's *Neue freie Presse* essays from 1903, entitled "Richard Wagner and Science."[16] The controversy to which the latter article responded, however, can be traced back several months earlier, to another of Adler's critical essays, "A Bayreuth Protest," published in the *Neue freie Presse* in January of that year. In "A Bayreuth Protest," Adler argued that the denunciation by a handful of "Bayreuth adepts" of a recent, unstaged performance of *Parsifal* did not detract from what he considered the considerable artistic merit of the event. Whatever Wagner himself might have thought about unstaged performances of his works, the time had long since passed when anyone, including the departed composer or his family, could speak in a proprietary manner on matters concerning his art. "Today," Adler proclaimed, "Wagner's work is the common property of the German nation. Soon, it will be the common property of all."[17] *Parsifal*, he argued, may rightfully be performed by any and all who care to do so, in whatever manner they see fit.

---

14. Adler, *Richard Wagner. Vorlesungen gehalten an der Universität zu Wien* (Leipzig: Breitkopf und Härtel, 1904).

15. Adler, "Ein Bayreuther Protest (Zur Parsifal-Frage)," *Neue freie Presse* (January 11, 1903), 10; Adler, "Richard Wagner und die Wissenschaft. Erwiderung," *Bohemia* (May 19, 1903), Beilage, 2.

16. Adler, "Richard Wagner und die Wissenschaft," *Neue freie Presse* (May 10, 1903), 12–13.

17. Adler, "Ein Bayreuther Protest," 10: "Wagner's Werke sind heute Gemeingut der deutschen Nation und werden bald kosmopolitisches Gemeingut werden."

Picking up on this argument four months later in "Richard Wagner and Science," Adler took aim at the figure whom he considered the arch Wagnerian himself, the conductor Hans Richter. Specifically, Adler sought to discredit Richter's statements about an issue that lay close to the historian's heart. Speaking of the pending unveiling of a Wagner memorial in Berlin, Adler reported, Richter had argued that it would be inappropriate to commemorate the event with an academic conference. The reason, Richter adduced, was that Wagner was deeply skeptical of science. For Adler, the conductor's position was preposterous. First, he explained, in the manner of his "Bayreuth Protest," a figure like Richter had no authority to speak on Wagner's behalf, either on *Parsifal* or on the merits of academic research. And second, Wagner's ideas about science and historical study had no significance for the modern world. After all, Adler reasoned, referring to the composer's *Opera and Drama* and other midcentury writings, "the whole of art history is for Wagner only a ladder leading upward to his own artistic creations."[18] And that, he observed, was hardly a scientific position. Indeed, it made clear the composer's misunderstanding of the scientific endeavor as a whole. "One celebrates Wagner as an artist," Adler wrote. "Wagner's views on science are irrelevant."[19]

Given the nature of Adler's assertions and the target of his attack, it comes as no surprise that "Richard Wagner and Science" provoked an immediate response from a dedicated Wagnerian like Batka. And Batka, writing three days later in the Prague daily *Bohemia*, would prove to be a formidable antagonist, for he recognized at once the oversimplification that lay at the heart of Adler's argument.[20] To begin, Batka countered, Wagner was neither ignorant nor a foe of science. On the contrary, the composer was widely regarded as exceptionally well versed in an array of humanistic disciplines, and he was keenly interested in many branches of the natural sciences as well. But although Wagner appreciated both the rigor and the promise of the sciences, Batka explained, he was deeply suspicious of what he took to be the views and ambitions of many scientists. An uncritical veneration of scientific achievement, Wagner believed, had led many to place too great a stake in the certainties promised by rationalistic inquiry. And that, in turn, had had a stifling effect on imagination, feeling, and creativity—an effect that was readily apparent in all too many aspects of modern life. Referring to Wagner's well-known hostility to the "science" of musicology in particular, Batka declared that the composer had sought "to drum up suspicion of musicology on account of its pretense to godliness, and to shake down to its roots its claims of infallibility."[21] Continuing, Batka argued (here speaking for Wagner) that "there is something inherent to the great genius of which

---

18. Adler, "Richard Wagner und die Wissenschaft" (*Neue freie Presse*), 13: "Die ganze Kunstgeschichte ist für Wagner nur die Stufenleiter, die zu seinem Kunstwerk führt."

19. Adler, "Richard Wagner und die Wissenschaft" (*Neue freie Presse*), 13: "Man feiert Wagner als Künstler. ... Wagner's Anschauungen über Wissenschaft sind irrelevant."

20. Richard Batka, "Richard Wagner und die Wissenschaft," *Bohemia* (May 13, 1903), 17.

21. Batka, "Richard Wagner und die Wissenschaft," 17: "Gerade der Fall Wagner ist dazu geeignet, der Musikwissenschaft vor ihrer Gottähnlichkeit bange zu machen und ihren Unfehlbarkeitsglauben bis auf den Grund zu erschüttern."

philological wisdom cannot even dream." That something, in Batka's terms, was *apperception* (*Schauen*), "not with a scholar's glasses but from the clearer, higher vantage point of an elevated sensitivity to life." Only from such a perspective, Batka explained, can one hope to understand "the *great* connections between things" (*Zusammenhänge*) and acquire "moral and artistic conviction."[22] Wagner, Batka argued, had no bones with science itself. But he strongly objected to those scientists and academics who would claim that rationalistic inquiry can provide answers to all of life's uncertainties and satisfy humankind's spiritual needs.

Adler's response to Batka appeared six days later in the same journal for which the latter wrote, and his "Reply" (*Erwiderung*) to "Richard Wagner and Science" is revealing of more than he intended. Rather than offering a sensitive response to Batka's attempt to complicate Wagner's position, Adler dug in his heels, and adduced for his readers passages from Wagner's writings that ostensibly attest to the composer's ignorance of and hostility toward the scientific endeavor as a whole. "We know well the contradictions of Wagner's statements," Adler wrote,

> but on science he expressed himself clearly and concisely in *The Artwork of the Future* and later repeated and elaborated upon these statements. There we read: ". . . Science absorbs within itself the arbitrariness of man's notions in their totality, while alongside it life, in *its* totality, follows an instinctive and necessary course of development. Science thus bears the sins of life, and atones for them through its self-destruction. It ends up [evolving into] its precise opposite: the knowledge of nature and the acknowledgement of the unconscious and the instinctive—thus, of the necessary, the true, and the sensual. The nature of science is therefore finite, and that of life eternal, just as the nature of error is finite and that of truth eternal. But only that which is perceived through the senses and bows to the demands of the sensual is true and living. The arrogance of science in its denial and contempt of the sensual is the pinnacle of error. On the other hand, its greatest victory consists in overcoming that arrogance, which [science] itself brings about, through the acknowledgement of the sensual. . . ."[23]

22. Batka, "Richard Wagner und die Wissenschaft," 17: "Und etwas gibt die Nähe bedeutender Genies, wovon die Philologenweisheit sich nichts träumen läßt: ein Schauen, nicht mit gelehrter Brille, sondern von klarer, hoher Warte ein erhöhtes Lebensgefühl, einen Blick für die *großen* Zusammenhänge, eine sittliche und künstlerische Ueberzeugung."

23. Adler, "Richard Wagner und die Wissenschaft. Erwiderung" (*Bohemia*), 2 (ellipses in original): "Wir kennen die Widersprüche der Wagnerschen Thesen. Allen über die Wissenschaft als solche hat er sich klar und bündig in seiner Abhandlung 'Das Kunstwerk der Zukunft' aus-gesprochen und die gleichen Sentenzen auch später wiederholt und ausgeführt. Es heißt da: '. . . Die Willkürlichkeit der menschlichen Anschauungen in ihrer Totalität nimmt die Wissenschaft auf, während neben ihr das Leben selbst in seiner Totalität einer unwillkürlichen, notwendigen Entwicklung folgt. Die Wissenschaft trägt somit die Sünde des Lebens und büßt sie an sich durch ihre Selbstvernichtung: sie endet in ihrem reinen Gegensatze, in der Erkenntnis der Natur, in der Anerkennung des Unbewußten, Unwillkürlichen, daher Notwendigen, Wirklichen, Sinnlichen. Das Wesen der Wissenschaft ist sonach endlich, das des Lebens unendlich, wie der Irrtum endlich, die Wahrheit unendlich ist. Wahr und lebendig ist aber nur, was sinnlich ist und den Bedingungen der Sinnlichkeit gehorcht. Die höchste Steigerung des Irrtums ist der Hochmut der Wissenschaft in der Verläugnung und Verachtung der Sinnlichkeit; ihr höchster Sieg dagegen der, von ihr selbst herbeigeführte, Untergang dieses Hochmutes in der Anerkennung der Sinnlichkeit. . . .'" Adler's citation is from Wagner, 3:45; trans. in Wagner/Ellis, 1:72.

In Wagner's view, as Adler presented it, science and its rationalistic modes of inquiry can provide a person with nothing more than a partial and misleading view of the world. True knowledge, Wagner purportedly believed, cannot be attained through scientific investigations but only through immediate, sensual experience—by way of the sort of intuitive knowing that Batka called *apperception*. It was for this reason, Adler explained, that Wagner considered science an epistemological dead end. "Now I am certainly the last person to proclaim the omnipotence of science," Adler declared. "But I do believe that Wagner's denial of its place in our culture is quite out of line."[24]

Yet as Batka pointed out the following day in the final installment of this exchange, Adler took Wagner's words out of context, and the complexity of Wagner's argument is lost in Adler's gloss.[25] Indeed, as Batka made clear in his initial response to his colleague, Wagner's condemnation of science, in the very passage cited by Adler, is anything but absolute. When read in context, the composer's statement is fundamentally ambivalent: it *celebrates* the promise of science to dispel error and superstition, while condemning the inflated claims made for scientific inquiry by some of its practitioners. At the time when Adler sparred with Batka, he had nearly completed his monograph on the composer and had surely read the whole of Wagner's argument. So it seems odd that he would insist on the dogmatism of Wagner's views when confronted directly with their complexity and ambivalence. On this point, Batka too seemed flummoxed, noting that Adler's assertions threatened to revive the sort of reductive partisan bickering encountered all too often during the "by-gone era of Hanslick."[26] But whatever Adler's reasons for framing his response as he did, the stubbornness with which he held to his position in the face of abundant complicating evidence suggests that he was, in fact, deeply troubled by what he found in Wagner's argument. Indeed, Adler's response reveals with utmost clarity the source of one broad-reaching and powerfully articulated critique of science with which he himself had wrestled, and that he sought to answer in his "Scope, Method, and Goal of Musicology."

In *The Artwork of the Future* (1849), Wagner began his first extended statement on his art with a broad-based discussion of the implications of his culture's increasingly scientific world-view for the vitality of its artistic and spiritual life. For Wagner, recent advances in the natural sciences and the new modes of thinking that they had fostered were unquestionably positive developments that promised to demolish the long-held illusion that humanity must live and work "in subservience to a power that is external and imaginary"—a power like that

---

24. Adler, "Richard Wagner und die Wissenschaft. Erwiderung" (*Bohemia*), 2: "Ich bin nun allerdings der letzte, eine Omnipotenz der Wissenschaft anzunehmen; allein ich glaube, daß durch diese Negation Wagners ihrer Stellung in unserer Kultur wohl nicht Genüge geleistet ist."

25. Batka, "Richard Wagner und die Wissenschaft," *Bohemia* (May 20, 1903), Beilage, 2.

26. Batka, "Richard Wagner und die Wissenschaft" (May 13), 2: "Diesen Coup aus der Verflossenen Aera der Hanslick und Konsorten brauchte sein Nachfolger wahrlich nicht nachzubeten."

commonly vested in the church, the nation, and the state.[27] In organized religion, Wagner explained, man finds "codified ... those notions he has gathered from his arbitrary views of nature." Science, in contrast, erodes such notions by making them "objects of deliberate, conscious contemplation and investigation." Through such contemplation, illusions are dispelled. And as that happens, the ground will be laid for humankind's spiritual reunion with the naturally ordered universe of which it is a part. In this way, Wagner explained, "the path of science proceeds from error to knowledge, from appearance to reality, from religion to nature."[28]

But Wagner also recognized a darker, even dangerous side to science, and it is here that we encounter what Walter Frisch has called the "ambivalent modernism" characteristic of so much of his work: faith in the promise of modernity coupled with a deeply held suspicion of its portents.[29] It was from this aspect of Wagner's discussion that Adler drew his polemical ammunition. For all of its promise, Wagner warned, scientific inquiry must not be pursued as an end in itself, but only as a means to a higher goal. Scientific rationalism, he explained, constitutes only a kind of halfway point on the philosophical path toward a higher mode of understanding both mankind and the world. And significantly, that higher mode of understanding can only be attained through the immediate, intuitive, and sensual experience of art. Indeed, Wagner argued, if scientific inquiry is pursued with this higher goal in mind, it will naturally evolve into artistic creativity. "The pinnacle of error is the arrogance of science in its denial and contempt of the sensual [*Sinnlichkeit*]," Wagner observed, bewailing his contemporaries' misplaced faith in the limitless power of rationalistic investigations.[30] "The activities of consciousness attained through science, the portraying of the life that one comes to know through it, the reflection of its necessity and truth: this is art itself."[31] Reflecting hypothetically upon the consequences of his society's infatuation with science, he mused: "The redemption of thought and

27. Wagner, 3:44; Wagner/Ellis, 1:71: "Der Mensch wird nicht eher das sein, was er kann und sein soll, als bis sein Leben der treue Spiegel der Natur, die bewußte Befolgung der einzig wirklichen Notwendigkeit, der *inneren Naturnotwendigkeit* ist, nicht die Unterordnung unter eine *äußere*, eigenbildete und der Einbildung nur nachgebildete, daher nicht notwendige, sondern *willkürliche Macht*."

28. Wagner, 3:44–45; Wagner/Ellis, 1:72: "Gestaltet der Mensch das Leben unwillkürlich nach den Begriffen, welche sich aus seinen willkürlichen Anschauungen der Natur ergeben, und hält er den unwillkürlichen Ausdruck dieser Begriffe in der Religion fest, so werden sie ihm in der Wissenschaft Gegenstand willkürlicher, bewußter Anschauung und Untersuchung. Der Weg der Wissenschaft ist der vom Irrtum zur Erkenntnis, von der Vorstellung zur Wirklichkeit, von der Religion zur Natur."

29. Walter Frisch, *German Modernism: Music and the Arts*, California Studies in 20th-Century Music, no. 3 (Berkeley and Los Angeles: University of California Press, 2005), 7–12.

30. Wagner, 3:45; Wagner/Ellis, 1:72: "Die höchste Steigerung des Irrtumes ist der Hochmut der Wissenschaft in der Verleugnung und Verachtung der Sinnlichkeit."

31. Wagner, 3:43–44; Wagner/Ellis, 1:71: "die Betätigung des durch die Wissenschaft errungenen Bewußtseins, die Darstellung des durch sie erkannten Lebens, das Abbild seiner Notwendigkeit und Wahrheit aber ist – die *Kunst*."

science in the artwork would be impossible if life itself could be made dependent upon scientific speculation. If conscious, deliberating thought could completely govern life... then life itself would be negated. It would be swallowed up by science."[32] Fortunately, as Wagner's *if*'s reveal, the latter had not yet come to pass. But he considered the extinguishing of art and life by an unbridled enthusiasm for scientific advance to be a very real threat facing the modern world.

In his exchange with his colleague from Prague, Adler presented this latter aspect of Wagner's argument as constituting the entirety of his position, ignoring the composer's declared enthusiasm for the promise of science to dispel illusion. And in doing this, Adler was not only misleading but in good company. For he portrayed the composer in the very manner of a large number of late-century German writers who gave voice to what Fritz Stern has famously called the "idealism of antimodernity." In contrast to Frisch's *ambivalent* modernism, which embraced some aspects of the modern age while viewing others with suspicion, Stern's idealism of antimodernity represented a wholesale rejection of modernity and its trappings in favor of the revival of an imagined, premodern past. And significantly, many of the period's most influential antimodern polemicists considered Wagner their intellectual father.[33]

As Stern documents, the final years of the nineteenth century saw the publication of a torrent of skeptical and irrationalist polemics condemning science, technology, and rationalistic inquiry as antithetical to mankind's spiritual essence and German cultural values particularly. Chief among these latter values were creativity and (in Stern's words) "childlike simplicity, subjectivity, individuality."[34] In the 1870s, such a view was voiced in Adler's circle by the poet Siegfried Lipiner, who lectured to the University of Vienna's Reading Society for German Students on the need for a "Renewal of Religious Ideas in the Present" and who drew extensively upon Wagner's work to support his assertions.[35] In his stunningly successful *Rembrandt as Educator* (*Rembrandt als Erzieher*, 1890), the polemicist Julius Langbehn similarly described a German nation "being destroyed by science and intellectualism," and declared that it could be "regenerated only through the resurgence of art and the rise to power of great, artistic individuals in a new society."[36] By the time Adler penned his *Neue freie Presse* essays, it

---

32. Wagner, 3:46; Wagner/Ellis, 1:73–74: "Die Erlösung des Denkens, der Wissenschaft, in das Kunstwerk würde unmöglich sein, wenn das Leben selbst von der wissenschaftlichen Spekulation abhängig gemacht werden könnte. Würde das bewußte, willkürliche Denken das Leben in Wahrheit vollkommen beherrschen...so wäre das Leben selbst verneint, um in die Wissenschaft aufzugehen."

33. Fritz Stern, *The Politics of Cultural Despair: A Study in the Rise of the Germanic Ideology* (New York: Anchor Books, 1961), 52–60.

34. Stern, *The Politics of Cultural Despair*, 132. See also Frisch, *German Modernism*, esp. 12–15.

35. Siegfried Lipiner, *Über die Elemente einer Erneuerung religiöser Ideen in der Gegenwart. Vortrag gehalten im Lesevereine der Deutschen Studenten Wiens am 19. Januar 1878* (Vienna: Carl Gerold's Sohn, 1878); Lipiner cites from Wagner on pages 12–13. For discussion of this essay, see McGrath, *Dionysian Art*, 79–82.

36. Julius Langbehn, *Rembrandt als Erzieher*, 31st ed. (Leipzig: C. L. Hirschfeld, 1891), esp. 57–121. The quoted text is from Stern, *The Politics of Cultural Despair*, 160.

had become fashionable to entertain such views even in the mainstream press, where programs of cultural "regeneration" espoused by Langbehn, Constantin Frantz, and other antimodern polemicists were frequently linked to Wagner and his work.[37] In his 1903 exchange with Batka, Adler followed in the footsteps of writers such as these, elaborating an image of Wagner as the artist-philosopher invoked in their antimodern tirades.

Given this situation, one might suspect that Adler's selective reading of Wagner was prompted by something other than his concern for science alone. Indeed, I would suggest that the virulent anti-Semitism of many late-century Wagnerians might well have played a role. As Leon Botstein has observed, Adler recalled, late in life, having been deeply distraught upon his return to Vienna from Prague in 1898 by the divisiveness that he newly encountered in the rhetoric of many Viennese, and especially by what he regarded as a general tolerance for anti-Semitic views.[38] At the time of his return, the circle of Wagnerians surrounding Wagner's widow Cosima had distinguished itself as a point of origin for some of the most caustic literature on cultural regeneration ever to appear in print. Batka himself had contributed to this literature with an 1892 biography of J. S. Bach, in which he invoked Wagner's statements in order to bolster his case for German cultural supremacy throughout modern history.[39] As an assimilated Jew with strongly liberal political sympathies and a cosmopolitan worldview, Adler could only have felt deep distaste for such a radical position as Batka's. It may be that his exaggeration and subsequent rejection of Wagner's antimodern views reflected, however unwittingly, his distress and alarm at this broader state of affairs.

But though he claimed, in his *Neue freie Presse* essays, to have rejected Wagner's position on science in toto, the bulk of Adler's writings from the 1880s onward reveals that he was in fact deeply committed to responding sensitively and creatively to the critique Wagner advanced in *The Artwork of the Future*. As we will see, during his time in Prague, and especially once he had returned to Vienna, Adler distanced himself from his positivist colleagues and his own early polemics and embarked upon a quest to define and model an approach to music study that responded to Wagner's concerns. The terms in which he framed that response, however, were not those of Wagner himself. Rather, they were those of Nietzsche, whose ambivalent statements on science and modernity captured the imagination of many members of Adler's generation more powerfully than those of any other writer. To delve more deeply into the sources and significance of Adler's troubled statements on science, we must therefore turn away from the fin de siècle and revisit the period in which he first confronted such issues. We must turn, that is, to the politically and socially turbulent world of the Viennese 1870s.

---

37. An illuminating discussion of the trope of regeneration in the late-century cultural discourse is provided in Shearer West, *Fin de Siècle: Art and Society in an Age of Uncertainty* (Woodstock, NY: Overlook, 1994), 122–38.

38. Botstein, "Music and Its Public," 1341–44.

39. Batka, *J. S. Bach*, Musiker-Biographien, no. 15 (Leipzig: Philipp Reclam, 1892).

FRIEDRICH NIETZSCHE AND THE
PROBLEM OF HISTORY

As William J. McGrath has observed in his classic study of Viennese student culture during Adler's university years, the problems of knowledge, science, and art on which Wagner wrote provided countless young artists and intellectuals with a philosophical locus that many never outgrew. Indeed, the same questions that Wagner raised in *The Artwork of the Future*, framed in similar terms, would surface in the creative work of many of Adler's contemporaries throughout the final quarter of the century.[40] In the 1870s, when Adler was a student at the university and at the Vienna Conservatory, the twin social foci for artists and others concerned with such questions were the Reading Society for German Students and the Viennese Academic Wagner Society. Adler cofounded the Wagner Society in 1873 with a pair of friends from the Conservatory. He joined the Reading Society during the 1876–77 academic year and thereafter played an active role in its work.[41]

The Reading Society for German Students was founded in 1871 on a culturally nationalist, *großdeutsch* or "Greater German" platform. It sought to celebrate the shared cultural heritage of all of Europe's German speakers, who had been divided politically by the founding of Bismarck's German state to the exclusion of Austria in the year of the society's establishment. In its first annual report, the society's members declared their intention "to gather German students of all factions under a *single* banner, not for the purpose of [indulging in] high-spirited aggression toward other nationalities but to uphold, in serious, worthy, and determined ways, the *German* spirit and *German* learning at the second-oldest university of the German people [*Volk*]."[42] In keeping with its *großdeutsch* ideals, the society's meetings were dedicated to exploring philosophical and artistic paths by which a host of lost unities might be restored to contemporary society: of Austria and Bismarck's Germany in particular, and of the German spirit that had been rent by recent political events. Among the society's proclaimed spiritual fathers were Wagner and Arthur Schopenhauer. But its primary "educator," to whom its members declared their devotion in a collectively authored letter of 1877, was Nietzsche.[43] In the Nietzschean discourse on science and art, eagerly discussed at the society's meetings, we find stated unambiguously those anxieties that Adler acknowledged in his "Scope, Method, and Goal of Musicology." And we find pondered an array of questions that would occupy the historian throughout the rest of his life.

---

40. McGrath, *Dionysian Art*.

41. *Leseverein Jahresbericht 1876–77*, 26.

42. *Leseverein Jahresbericht 1871–72*, 3: "...galt es doch, die deutschen Studenten aller Fractionen um *ein* Banner zu schaaren, nicht zu übermüthigen Aggression gegenüber den anderen Nationalitäten, sondern um in ernster, würdiger, aber auch entschlossener Weise den *deutschen* Geist und die *deutsche* Wissenschaft aufrecht zu halten an der zweitältesten Universität des deutschen Volkes!" On the goals and activities of the Reading Society, see McGrath, *Dionysian Art*, esp. 63–71.

43. This letter is discussed in McGrath, *Dionysian Art*, 69–70.

To be sure, as McGrath has shown, Nietzsche and Wagner were not the only writers whose statements on the cultural implications of scientific advance captured the imagination of the society's members. The Viennese physician Karl Rokitansky, for instance, famously attempted, in his writings of these years, to link Darwinian theories of evolution to the existential suffering of man. And the esteemed psychologist Theodor Meynert struggled to reconcile the desirable products of scientific rationalism with its potentially dehumanizing effects. For their efforts, both were honored by the Reading Society with lecture invitations and honorary memberships, and the society even staged a Rokitansky festival in January 1874.[44] But for many of its members active during the second half of the 1870s, the more distant figure of Nietzsche was the greatest source of fascination. And unlike in Germany, where Nietzsche's work remained largely unappreciated until the 1890s and a wave of popular philosophizing about problems of science did not take hold until the turn of the century, Nietzsche's critiques of science and its attendant cultural dilemmas were hotly debated in Adler's Vienna almost as soon as they appeared in print.[45]

With respect to their implications for our understanding of Adler's musicological program, Nietzsche's early writings on the challenges and perils of scientific inquiry can be understood in terms of three intersecting lines of thought. The first is a Wagnerian critique of scientific rationalism similar to that elaborated in *The Artwork of the Future*. The second is a set of cautionary reflections upon attempts to transform the study of history into a science. The third is a set of directives for Nietzsche's readers about how they must dedicate themselves to nurturing contemporary art and culture if they wish to stave off the decline of both in an increasingly rationalistic age. Although Nietzsche's fascination with scientific inquiry has recently been probed in detail, his debt to Wagner in this regard seems to have passed unnoticed.[46] Nevertheless, his discussion of science in *The Birth of Tragedy Out of the Spirit of Music* (1872), a volume dedicated to Wagner, makes the origins of at least some of his arguments clear.

---

44. Meynert's first lecture to the Reading Society was delivered in March 1872; he was named an honorary member during the 1871–72 academic year. The Rokitansky festival was held in January 1874; Rokitansky was awarded an honorary membership during the 1876–77 academic year. See *Leseverein Jahresbericht 1871–72*, 7, 11; *Leseverein Jahresbericht 1873–74*, 6; *Leseverein Jahresbericht 1876–77*, 18. On the work of these figures, see McGrath, *Dionysian Art*, 40–44. On Rokitansky, see also William M. Johnston, *The Austrian Mind: An Intellectual and Social History 1848–1938* (Berkeley and Los Angeles: University of California Press, 1972), 224–25.

45. For a recent consideration of the late-century Wilhelmine discourse on science and of the work of the philosophers Hermann Rudolf Lotze and Hans Vaihinger in particular, see Alexander Rehding, *Hugo Riemann and the Birth of Modern Musical Thought*, New Perspectives in Music History and Criticism (Cambridge: Cambridge University Press, 2003), 82–88.

46. Studies of the philosophical foundations of Nietzsche's statements on science from the early period of his career include Babbette E. Babich, *Nietzsche's Philosophy of Science: Reflecting Science on the Ground of Art and Life* (Albany: State University of New York Press, 1994); Babich, "Nietzsche's Critique of Scientific Reason and Scientific Culture: On 'Science as a Problem' and Nature as Chaos," in *Nietzsche and Science*, ed. Gregory Moore and Thomas H. Brobjer (Aldershot

In *The Birth of Tragedy*, Nietzsche described a modern phenomenon whose roots he traced to ancient Greece: "the influence of Socrates," which has "spread over posterity like a shadow that keeps growing in the evening sun."[47] In an earlier age, the philosopher explained, that society that gave rise to Attic tragedy struck a balance between the instinctual passion of Dionysus and the rational clarity of Apollo. In contrast, modern Germany had fostered a "Socratic" culture, in which "theoretical man...finds the highest object of his pleasure in the process of an ever happy uncovering that succeeds through his own efforts"— that is, in a rationalistic search for concrete knowledge about man and the world he inhabits.[48] In the terms of Wagner's *Artwork of the Future*, Nietzsche's Germany had succumbed to the "pinnacle of error"; it had been spellbound by the "arrogance of science."

And there was, Nietzsche proceeded to observe, a "profound *illusion*" at the heart of the present Socratic optimism: "the unshakable faith that thought, using the thread of causality, can penetrate the deepest abysses of being." That illusion, he argued, "accompanies science as an instinct." Indeed, it is the very thing that provides rationalism with its authority. But the authority of reason, Nietzsche continued, is an illusion nonetheless, and as such it must eventually be dispelled. And as that happens, he predicted, science will be pushed "to its limits, at which it must turn into *art*."[49] As Wagner had argued in *The Artwork of the Future*, so too Nietzsche proclaimed in *The Birth of Tragedy*: science and rationality can take a person only so far in his quest to understand himself and the world. A deeper understanding can only be attained through the experience of art, which must pick up where science leaves off. If modern society is not to exist forever enveloped in illusion, Nietzsche argued, it must allow its rational inquiries to evolve into creative, artistic work.

As the historian of philosophy Babette E. Babich has argued, Nietzsche, contrary to popular belief, did not intend his work to be read as merely a catalogue of the ills of modernity. Rather, he considered the true philosopher a "physician of culture"—one capable of providing a cure for what ails it.[50] In his work of the early 1870s, Nietzsche did not rest content after disparaging rationalistic inquiry, and unlike Langbehn and other writers on German "regeneration," he did not believe that his society's best hope for the future lay in revival of a mythical,

---

and Burlington, VT: Ashgate, 2004), 133–53; Thomas H. Brobjer, "Nietzsche's Reading and Knowledge of Natural Science: An Overview," in *Nietzsche and Science*, 21–50; and Maudemarie Clark, "On Knowledge, Truth, and Value: Nietzsche's Debt to Schopenhauer and the Development of His Empiricism," in *Willing and Nothingness: Schopenhauer as Nietzsche's Educator*, ed. Christopher Janaway (Oxford: Clarendon Press, 1998), 37–78. My understanding of Nietzsche's arguments, elaborated below, is indebted to these sources.

47. Friedrich Nietzsche, *The Birth of Tragedy Out of the Spirit of Music*, in *The Birth of Tragedy and the Case of Wagner*, trans. Walter Kaufmann (New York: Vintage, 1967), 93.

48. Nietzsche, *The Birth of Tragedy*, 94. The original, which reads "in dem Prozeß einer immer glücklichen, durch eigene Kraft gelingenden Enthüllung," might also be rendered as "in the process of an ever-contented" or "ever-fortuitous uncovering."

49. Nietzsche, *The Birth of Tragedy*, 95–96 (emphasis in original).

50. Babich, "Nietzsche's Critique of Scientific Reason," 151.

premodern past. Rather, he sought to provide his contemporaries with constructive advice about how they might work to ensure their nation's cultural vitality in what was destined to be an increasingly scientific age. To be sure, in *The Birth of Tragedy* Nietzsche spoke of overturning the Socratic order through the Dionysian power of Wagner's music dramas. But elsewhere he outlined less revolutionary, more realistic alternatives. It was in these latter writings, serially published as *Untimely Meditations* (*Unzeitgemässe Betrachtungen*), that Adler and the Reading Society found much of their philosophical inspiration. It is also here that we encounter the second key thread in Nietzsche's critique of science: a consideration of the challenges of historical scholarship, and of contemporary calls to refashion the study of historical phenomena after the model of the natural sciences.

At the heart of his second *Untimely Meditation*, entitled "On the Uses and Disadvantages of History for Life" (1874), Nietzsche outlined his now-famous typography of attitudes toward historical study. He did this in response to what he perceived as a "consuming fever of history" (*verzehrenden historischen Fieber*), evinced in the oft-heard "demand that history should be a science."[51] What made this enthusiasm a "fever" to Nietzsche's mind was widespread ignorance of the essential fact that amassing historical knowledge as an end in itself is hardly an ethically neutral act. Like any endeavor claiming the status of a science, it must be greeted with skepticism. For just as historical knowledge can provide a powerful stimulus for new creative work, so too can it foster antipathy toward the present, toward the cultural achievements of one's own age, and toward those of future generations. Like Wagner writing on science in 1849, Nietzsche had no bones with historical study itself. But he did have grave concerns about some of the *uses* to which it might be put. The purpose of Nietzsche's typography of "species of history" was to explore this essential ambivalence.

If one conceives of history "monumentally," Nietzsche argued, as a succession of isolated heroic accomplishments, then one might arrive at the productive realization that "the greatness that once existed was once *possible* and may thus be possible again" (69). But, he continued, the monumental perspective might just as easily give rise to a selective and willfully forgetful historiography, in which "whole segments" of one's past—those deemed unworthy of emulation—"are forgotten, despised, and flow away in an uninterrupted colourless flood" (70). On the other hand, if one adopts an "antiquarian" point of view, regarding the past as an undifferentiated mass of innumerable venerable deeds, then one might profitably acquire a detailed understanding of the cultural heritage of one's community. But one who assumes the antiquarian perspective might also be inclined to regard present-day achievements with antipathy, since the deeds and works of living men and women can easily appear isolated and feeble when compared with the untold riches of past glories (72–75). Finally, a person who adopts a "critical" stance toward his history might succeed in freeing himself from the emotional burden of past mistakes. But such a person is also likely to forget that

51. Nietzsche, "On the Uses and Disadvantages of History for Life," in *Untimely Meditations*, 60, 77 (subsequent references will be given in the text with emphasis as in original).

just as "we are the outcome of earlier generations, we are also the outcome of their aberrations, passions and errors, and indeed of their crimes" (76). A person who turns a blind eye to the ugliness of his past, Nietzsche warned, is only too likely to repeat it.

Given the inescapable ethical complexities of historical study, Nietzsche argued, modern man, if he wishes to lead a productive life, must strive to maintain a balance between historical and "unhistorical" modes of regarding the world. Seeking to identify "the boundary at which the past has to be forgotten if it is not to become the gravedigger of the present," Nietzsche stressed that "the unhistorical and the historical are necessary in equal measure for the health of an individual, of a people and of a culture" (62–63). Nietzsche freely admitted that ensuring the vitality of a nation's culture—sustaining the "unity of artistic style in all the expressions of the life of a people," as he wrote in his first *Untimely Meditation*—requires that its creative members pay considerable attention to their community's cultural heritage.[52] But he also warned that an undue obsession with amassing historical knowledge can spell the end of cultural productivity. What the modern age therefore requires is a mode of historical study that will inspire the creation of new philosophies and new art—one cultivated not for purely academic ends but "in the service of the future and the present."[53]

This latter point brings us to the third key thread in Nietzsche's critique of science: a call to action on the part of the young to promote the cultural achievements of the present. For if anyone is capable of maintaining the vitality of contemporary culture, Nietzsche reasoned, it is the young artist, writer, composer, and scholar—all of those who have not yet been corrupted by institutionalized faith in the limitless promise of scientific inquiry. "Let us never weary in our youth of defending the future against these iconoclasts who would wreck it," Nietzsche urged. As Wagner had warned of the ambitions of some scientists to extinguish creative life through their work, so Nietzsche declared that "we shall have to discover...*that the excesses of the historical sense from which the present day suffers are deliberately furthered, encouraged and—employed.*"[54] "Here I recognize," the philosopher proclaimed, "the mission of that *youth* I have spoken of... I know that they understand all these generalities from close personal experience, and will translate them into a teaching intended for themselves."[55] In the third installment of his *Untimely Meditations*, entitled "Schopenhauer as Educator" (1874), Nietzsche outlined a specific program of action. "The fundamental idea of *culture*," he counseled, "sets for each one of us but one task: *to promote the production of the philosopher, the artist and the saint within us and without us and thereby to work at the perfecting of nature.*" "Mankind must work continually at the production of individual great men," he declared; "that and nothing else is its task."[56] If a historian of culture does not wish to contribute to his own

52. Nietzsche, "David Strauss, the Confessor and the Writer," in *Untimely Meditations*, 5.
53. Nietzsche, "On the Uses and Disadvantages of History," 77.
54. Nietzsche, "On the Uses and Disadvantages of History," 115 (emphasis in original).
55. Nietzsche, "On the Uses and Disadvantages of History," 121 (emphasis in original).
56. Nietzsche, "Schopenhauer as Educator," 160, 161 (emphasis in original).

culture's decline, Nietzsche suggested, he has no choice but to dedicate himself to fostering its continued vitality. And the only way in which to do that is to encourage the creative endeavors of contemporary men through the medium of one's scholarly work.

As McGrath has observed, the founding members of the Reading Society for German Students took Nietzsche's sermon to heart. When the young Gustav Mahler, an artist of unquestionable creative genius, appeared in their midst in the late 1870s, the society's members went to extraordinary lengths to ensure his material security and professional success.[57] Adler himself, as a member of the society, became an ardent champion of Mahler and his music during this same period. Having befriended the composer, five years his junior, during their conservatory years, Adler welcomed Mahler into the Wagner Society in 1877 and immediately sought to secure work for the artist as a conductor and choirmaster. Moreover, Adler's devotion to Mahler was not limited to the 1870s. During his time in Prague, Adler championed Mahler's accomplishments as conductor at that city's German Theater at every opportunity. And once both figures had settled in Vienna just prior to 1900, Adler spearheaded an effort to raise funds for the publication of Mahler's early symphonies.[58] As Edward R. Reilly has observed in his documentary history of their relationship, "The story of this friendship is essentially a story of recommendations, interventions and projects that the musical scholar designed for the benefit of the composer."[59] In his substantial and persistent efforts on behalf of Mahler's professional and personal life, Adler answered, wittingly or not, Nietzsche's call to the young. And indeed, once Mahler's reputation was firmly established around the turn of the century, Adler turned his attention to another young artist of indisputable genius, Arnold Schoenberg. Soon, he would apply his considerable social clout to promoting Schoenberg's work as well.[60]

It is, however, important to note that Adler's response to Nietzsche need not have been inspired by a literal encounter with the philosopher's work. Indeed, Adler does not mention Nietzsche's name in any of his surviving statements, published or otherwise, from this period. But Nietzsche's ideas pervaded the creative endeavors of many of those with whom Adler associated, and encounters with Nietzsche's thought, mediated through a host of others, would have been all but unavoidable for the historian. To take one example, we may consider briefly the case of the poet Siegfried Lipiner. Lipiner, like Adler, was a member of Mahler's inner circle. He spoke on Nietzsche's "Schopenhauer as Educator" at

---

57. McGrath reports that Victor Adler's efforts included purchasing a piano for his home on which Mahler could practice. See McGrath, *Dionysian Art*, 89.

58. The most detailed chronicle of this relationship is Edward R. Reilly, *Gustav Mahler and Guido Adler: Records of a Friendship* (Cambridge: Cambridge University Press, 1982). On Adler's efforts to secure a subvention for the publication of Mahler's symphonies, see also Henry-Louis de La Grange, *Mahler*, vol. 1 (Garden City, New York: Doubleday, 1973), 465–66 and 475–76.

59. Reilly, *Gustav Mahler and Guido Adler*, 79.

60. On Adler's relationship with Schoenberg, see Reilly, *Gustav Mahler and Guido Adler*, 99–100; and Joseph Auner, ed., *A Schoenberg Reader: Documents of a Life* (New Haven: Yale University Press, 2003), esp. 114–15.

a meeting of the Reading Society's intimate Lecture Club (Redeclub) just two weeks after Adler addressed the same group on the Bayreuth festival in the spring of 1877.[61] As reported in Vienna's *Neue musikalische Presse*, Lipiner took enough of an interest in Adler's work as a scholar to attend the historian's inaugural address to the faculty of the University of Vienna after his return to the institution in 1898.[62] In 1876, at the height of Adler's involvement with the Reading Society, Lipiner made a stunning debut before the public with an epoch poem, *Unbound Prometheus (Der Entfesselte Prometheus)*. There, the poet elaborated, in dramatic and unmistakable terms, upon the primary threads of Nietzsche's critique of science.

In Lipiner's poem, we follow the meandering Titan Prometheus, who, freed from his mythical tethers, seeks to reacquaint himself with a world of men who have lost touch with their god, forsaken their culture, and turned against each other. Among those encountered by the wandering Titan is a figure who calls himself "Pure Science" (*reine Wissenschaft*) and who proclaims to an uncomprehending Prometheus that an excess of learning is the best deterrent from a life of creative action. But what if youth, Prometheus asks, invoking the lesson of Nietzsche's *Meditation* on history, feels inspired to creative work when pondering the deeds of the past? "How, then, can you hold back these rising tides?" "Sir," replies Pure Science, "through *science*! If the strong, youthful spirit can find satisfaction only in deeds, it is to be expected! But it must not *attempt* deeds like those that were done before; it should understand them, sir, and *describe* them."[63] "I tell you, sir," Pure Science intones, "a book can bind lions, and contemplation [*Betrachtung*] can dull the strongest spirits. Oh, if only our fathers had taught this to the young, our age would not be so wild and chaotic!"[64] As for himself, Pure Science exclaimed, "I stand by the side and merely watch; it makes one wise, without pain and discomfort."[65] In Lipiner's poem, and without mention of Nietzsche, we find recast central themes of the philosopher's critique. And

---

61. Lipiner's lecture, entitled "Ueber Nietzsche's unzeitgemässe Betrachtungen: Schopenhauer als Erzieher," was delivered on April 28, 1877. As noted in the Leseverein's annual report, the Redeclub had only thirty members during the 1877–78 academic year; no figures are available for 1876–77. See *Leseverein Jahresbericht 1876–77*, 29; *Leseverein Jahresbericht 1877–78*, 26. On Mahler and Lipiner, see McGrath, *Dionysian Art*, chapter 4; and La Grange, *Mahler*, vol. 1, 68–69 and *passim*.

62. See the anonymous essay "Antrittsverlesung des Professors Guido Adler an der Wiener Universität," *Neue musikalische Presse* (October 30, 1898), 2. Lipiner's attendance was first identified by Reilly, in *Gustav Mahler and Guido Adler*, 92.

63. Lipiner, *Der Entfesselte Prometheus. Eine Dichtung in fünf Gesängen* (Leipzig: Breitkopf und Härtel, 1876), 50: " 'Wie wollt ihr dann die hohen Fluten dämmen?' // 'Herr, durch die *Wissenschaft*! Wenn nur an Thaten / Der Jugendstarke Geist sich sätt'gen kann, / So sei es ihm gewährt! Doch muss er nicht / Die Thaten, die doch schon gethan sind, *thun*, / Er soll sie wissen, Herr, und sie – *beschreiben*.' "

64. Lipiner, *Der Entfesselte Prometheus*, 48: "Ich sag' euch, Herr, ein Buch kann Löwen bänd'gen, / Und stärkste Geister zügelt die Betrachtung. / O! hätten unsre Ahnen so die Jugend / Gebildet, nimmermehr wär' unsre Zeit / So wild und wüst."

65. Lipiner, *Der Entfesselte Prometheus*, 49: "Ich stehe abseits und betrachte nur, / Da wird man weise ohne Schmerz und Schaden."

the message of Lipiner's poem is clear. If a nation's culture is to remain vital and alive, it requires more than abstract learning and rational inquiry. It requires of its members lives of action, led in dedication to the fostering of genius and the production of new artistic and spiritual work.[66]

As we will see in the final part of this chapter, convictions similar to those espoused in Lipiner's poem underlie Adler's musicological project as it evolved over the early decades of his career. Indeed, when considering that project against the backdrop of the intellectual world of Adler's youth, it becomes clear that the unnamed skeptics addressed in his "Scope, Method, and Goal of Musicology" were legion. They included, in addition to Wagner and Nietzsche, Lipiner and Rokitansky, Victor Adler and Theodor Meynert, and a host of others whose conflicted positions regarding the promise and perils of scientific inquiry reflected the concerns of so many members of Adler's generation. In contrast to Spitta, Thausing, and many other scientifically inspired scholars of art, Adler did not dismiss such concerns out of hand. On the contrary, his work was shaped as much by the Nietzschean critique of science as it was by the positivist movement itself.

A SCIENCE OF MUSIC FOR AN
AMBIVALENT AGE

As we saw in chapter 1, Adler spent much of his time in Prague elaborating a positivist program for music study in response to Hanslick's legacy. Yet his work from that period provides numerous hints that he was concerned, even then, with contemporary critiques of rationalistic inquiry and with defending and exemplifying the ways in which historical research can serve as a catalyst for new creative work. In a lecture of 1885 on Bach and Handel, published in the journal of Vienna's Academic Club (Wissenschaftlicher Club), Adler observed that "Artists ponder and think in order to construct works that correspond to their creative needs. In the service of art, they make use of the experience of their predecessors."[67] All talented composers, Adler explained, have a profound desire for historical knowledge, which inevitably informs the ways in which they carry out their creative work. Thus infused with the spirit of history, their musical creations constitute spiritual links between a nation's past and its future. "Just as Pindar's works fill us with feelings of reverence and admiration today," he wrote, "so too will subsequent generations gaze with wonderment at our poets. But they will do more than that. They will also follow in the path of that

---

66. For further discussion of Lipiner's poem within the context of Nietzsche's work and its reception, see McGrath, *Dionysian Art*, 62–63 and 69.

67. Adler, "Johann Sebastian Bach und Georg Friedrich Händel. Ihre Bedeutung und Stellung in der Geschichte der Musik," *Monatsblätter des Wissenschaftlichen Club* 12 (1885) (offprint, Vienna: Adolf Holzhausen, 1885), 1: "Künstler sinnen und denken, um das ihren Kunstbedürfnissen entsprechende Gewerke zu errichten, sie benützen die Erfahrungen ihrer Vorgänger im Dienste der Kunst."

art about which we speak today."[68] In the preface to the inaugural volume of the *Monuments of Music in Austria* series of critical editions, Adler commented more explicitly upon the historian's role in this creative process. He argued that even such a scholarly pursuit as editorial work—that very field of research advocated by Count Leo Thun-Hohenstein and many other midcentury Austrian empiricists—can contribute in important ways to the vitality of contemporary art. The volume in hand, Adler explained in his prefatory essay, will provide present-day composers with a store of historical materials from which to draw as they endeavor to create new musics. In launching the *Monuments* series, he declared, "We are not only fulfilling a sense of duty aroused in us by thankfulness and piety. We are also purifying and refreshing our modern artistic life. Historical knowledge not only brings to light the beautiful from past ages, but also works as a stimulant upon artists and the public of the present and the future."[69]

In these statements, we find an attitude toward historical study that resonates not only with Nietzsche's attempts to unite historical research and creative activity but also with an array of remarks made by a host of others in the final decades of the century. We have already encountered similar statements made by Hanslick and ascribed to Brahms, and indeed both of these figures, as members of the *Monuments* board, were cosignatories of Adler's preface.[70] Moreover, as Walter Frisch has observed, Brahms was just one among many artists of the period who looked to the past for inspiration. Such a tendency, Frisch suggests, was in fact characteristic of a common late-century attitude toward the creative act, which he calls "historicist modernism": viewing "musical techniques from the remote past" as means by which to "achiev[e] a distance from late Romantic styles."[71] At first glance, this seems to be precisely what Adler advocated in the 1880s and early 1890s, during his years in Prague. But once he was securely ensconced in a tenured professorship at the University of Vienna, Adler took advantage of his newfound professional security to elaborate these relatively common sentiments into a provocative and novel program for his discipline. That program, which he boldly announced in his inaugural lecture to the university's faculty in 1898, was different in subtle yet important respects from the historicist modernism of

68. Adler, "Johann Sebastian Bach und Georg Friedrich Händel," 10–11: "...wie uns heute Pindar's Werke mit Ehrfurcht und Bewunderung erfüllen, so werden nachkommende Geschlechter unsere Tondichter anstaunen, Aber nicht nur anstaunen, auch ausüben mögen sie die Kunst, in der wir heute sprechen." For a more detailed consideration of Adler's essay that makes a similar point, though without situating Adler's statements within the context of the Nietzschean discourse, see Botstein, "Music and Its Public," 1332–35.

69. Preface to Johann Joseph Fux, *Messen*, ed. Johannes Evangelist Habert and Gustav Adolf Glossner (*Denkmäler der Tonkunst in Österreich*, vol. 1) (Vienna: Artaria, 1894), v: "Wir erfüllen nicht nur eine Schuld des Dankes und der Pietät, sondern wir läutern und erfrischen dadurch unser modernes Kunstleben. Die geschichtliche Erkenntniss fördert nicht allein das schöne Alte zu Tage, sondern wird auch anregend wirken auf Künstler und Publicum der Gegenwart und Zukunft."

70. The preface is cosigned by C. August Artaria, Johannes Brahms, Eduard Hanslick, Wilhelm Ritter von Hartel, Albert Ritter von Hermann, Engelbert Mühlbacher, Hans Richer, and Wilhelm Baron Weckbecker.

71. Frisch, *German Modernism*, 139; this subject is considered in detail in chapter 4 of Frisch's study.

Brahms and others. And it responded as directly and forcefully to the Nietzschean critique of science as to positivist ideologies of art-historical study.

In the tradition of the seminal polemics of Spitta, Thausing, and his own "Scope, Method, and Goal of Musicology," Adler began his 1898 lecture, entitled "Music and Musicology" ("Musik und Musikwissenschaft"), by describing the disciplinary ambitus of scientifically oriented research.[72] Like his predecessors, he defined the boundaries of scholarly work by contrasting it with the activities and attitudes of creative artists. But whereas his colleagues had insisted that the scientific study of music and art can have nothing in common with the production of paintings or symphonies, Adler announced, in his lecture's opening pages, his strong opposition to their vision. Thirteen years earlier, in his "Scope, Method, and Goal of Musicology," he declared that the most urgent goal (*Ziel*) of musicological research was to solidify the scientific rigor of its methods. By 1898, he had revised his view of both his discipline and its aims. He now proclaimed that "The highest goal [*Ziel*] to which I aspire in the study of art is to work on behalf of art through the knowledge of art" (*durch die Erkenntnis der Kunst für die Kunst zu wirken*).[73]

In Thausing's own inaugural lecture to the university's faculty in 1873, the pioneering historian of the visual arts had argued that the methods and goals of historians and artists "stand in distinct opposition to each other, corresponding to two entirely different paths. ... [T]he goals of their activities are of such different natures that a correspondence of their results cannot even be considered."[74] As if to refute a figure who had served as a model for his own early efforts, Adler argued in 1898 that "the more closely we look into the field of musicology and consider its associated auxiliary disciplines, the more strongly we become convinced of its connections with living, progressive art."[75] Spitta, another of Adler's early models, had proclaimed in his own disciplinary polemic, "Art and the Study of Art," that "Knowledge has its own power, and science is an end in itself ...the working methods of art and the study of the same may never run hand in hand."[76] Adler, in contrast, insisted that the responsible musicologist must not cloister himself in library or lecture hall. Rather, he must remain intensely committed to responding sensitively, through his research, to the creative needs of the present day. "In both its historical and its systematic parts," Adler wrote, "in

---

72. Adler, "Musik und Musikwissenschaft. Akademische Antrittsrede, gehalten am 26. Oktober 1898 an der Universität Wien," *Jahrbuch der Musikbibliothek Peters* 5 (1898), 27–39.

73. Adler, "Musik und Musikwissenschaft," 31.

74. Thausing, "Die Stellung," 13–14: "Praxis und Theorie sind nicht blos auseinander zu halten, sie bilden auch einen sehr entschiedenen Gegensatz zu einander, entsprechend den beiden ganz verschiedenen Wegen... die Ziele ihres Strebens sind aber so verschiedener Natur, dass an eine Uebereinstimmung der Resultate nirgends gedacht werden kann."

75. Adler, "Musik und Musikwissenschaft," 33: "Je genauer wir das Gabiet der Musikwissenschaft untersuchen, die von ihr herangezogenen Hilfsmittel betrachten, desto mehr überzeugen wir uns von dem Konnex mit der lebendig fortschreitenden Kunst."

76. Spitta, "Kunstwissenschaft und Kunst," 13: "Das Wissen hat seine Macht für sich; Wissenschaft ist Selbstzweck... Die Arbeitswege der Kunstwissenschaft und der Kunst dürfen niemals ineinander laufen."

its philosophical and philological and physical-mathematical sides, musicology is not only dependent upon the conditions of its own genetic development but also guided—following willingly an inner need—by the demands of the art of its time."[77]

From such responses to the work of his predecessors, Adler turned to the Nietzschean discourse directly. Addressing Nietzsche's concerns about the "antiquarian" mode of historical awareness, he assured his audience that there were few people alive who displayed the sort of uncritical veneration of past achievements that so worried the philosopher and his followers. While Nietzsche had argued that in a culture enamored with historical study "everything new and evolving" would be "rejected and persecuted,"[78] Adler insisted that "the majority of modern listeners are, with respect to their convictions and needs, most at home with the art of their own age." Indeed, he continued, "There is not much danger that the sympathies of a person historically trained will remain stuck in a past epoch, and that he will, on account of that prejudice, be intolerant toward the works of his contemporaries or other epochs."[79] But although Adler attempted to blunt Nietzsche's argument, he was not dismissive of the philosopher's concerns. Though the risks posed by the antiquarian mindset might be slight, Adler considered it of crucial importance to discourage such a mindset at every opportunity. Acknowledging the activities of the "Caecilianer," members of the All-German Cecilia Society (Allgemeiner deutsche Cäcilien-Verein) dedicated to reforming the Catholic church by reviving the music of Palestrina and his contemporaries, Adler insisted that such antiquarian reverence was characteristic only of "uneducated" and "half-educated" (Halbgebildeten) segments of society.[80] Nevertheless, he argued that the historian of music must do everything in his power to combat such an attitude. "As a child of the times, one has the right—and I would add, even though I am a historian, the duty as well—to greet the works of present-day artists with love and respect, and not to crush them by making inappropriate comparisons with works of the past."[81]

---

77. Adler, "Musik und Musikwissenschaft," 33: "...sowohl in ihrem historischen, wie in ihrem systematischen Teile, sowohl nach ihrer philosophischen, als ihrer philologischen und der physikalisch-mathematischen Seite ist die Musikwissenschaft nicht nur abhängig von den Bedingungen ihres eigenen genetischen Ganges, sondern richtet sich, einer inneren Notwendigkeit freiwillig folgend, nach den Anforderungen der jeweiligen Kunst ihrer Zeit."

78. Nietzsche, "On the Uses and Disadvantages of History," 74.

79. Adler, "Musik und Musikwissenschaft," 35: "Der grössere Teil der modernen Hörer bleibt in seinen Gesinnungen und Anforderungen bei der Kunst seiner Zeit, geht mit ihr. Die Gefahr ist nicht gross, dass der Einzelne, der historisch geschult ist, in irgend einer Epoche der Vergangenheit mit seinen Sympathien stecken bleibe und in dieser seiner Voreingenommenheit intolerant werde gegenüber der Produktion seiner Zeitgenossen oder anderer Epochen."

80. Adler, "Musik und Musikwissenschaft," 35. On the activities of the Cecilia Society, see James Garratt, *Palestrina and the German Romantic Imagination: Interpreting Historicism in Nineteenth-Century Music*, Musical Performance and Reception (Cambridge: Cambridge University Press, 2002), esp. chapter 4.

81. Adler, "Musik und Musikwissenschaft," 39: "Als Kind der Zeit hat man das Recht, und ich sage, obzwar ich Historiker bin, auch die Pflicht, den Werken der mitlebenden Künstler mit Liebe und Achtung zu begegnen, sie nicht durch unpassende Vergleiche mit den Werken der Vergangenheit zu erdrücken."

Following the line of reasoning that animated Nietzsche's *Meditation* on history to a distinctly Nietzschean conclusion, Adler closed his address by reminding his audience that the vitality of a nation's cultural life can be assured only through a careful balance of historical and ahistorical thinking. Historians of music, he argued, must bear this in mind, and they must never lose sight, in their enthusiasm for their research, of their responsibilities to living artists and modern art. "I would consider Voltaire's assertion that 'One must respect the living; one owes nothing but the truth to the dead,' which conforms to my own view, not merely an assertion born of politeness," he wrote. "Indeed, with regard to the living, one must allow, along with fairness, truth and justice to prevail. And one must take care to avoid the great danger that rears its head so often: to be either too attentive to the one or too inattentive to the other."[82] In his parting words to the university's faculty, Adler recapitulated these points. The historian of music must carry out his research in the service of modern art, and the lines that some had attempted to draw between scholarship and creative work must be emphatically erased:

> The duty of the musical scientist is not to hate but to love, to advise, and to help. Art and the study of art do not reside in separate domains with sharply drawn boundaries. Rather, only their methods of working are different, and these change with the times. The more closely science remains in contact with progressive art and living artists, the closer it comes to its goal: *to work on behalf of art through the knowledge of art.*[83]

It is not easy to imagine a statement on the ideal practice of musicological research that more closely answers Nietzsche's critique of science and historical inquiry than Adler's inaugural lecture. As Adler repeatedly emphasized, the historian of music, if he wishes to live in a culturally vibrant society, cannot rest content with amassing historical knowledge out of purely academic curiosity. In contrast to what he himself had argued in the early years of his career, advancing the fledgling "science of music" must never be regarded as an end in itself. Musicologists, Adler declared in 1898, must conduct their research in the service of present-day artists, who will work in turn to transform historical styles and idioms into the "living" art of the present. In this way, Adler's science of music dissolved itself, precisely as Wagner and Nietzsche had counseled, into the creative act.

---

82. Adler, "Musik und Musikwissenschaft," 39: "Den Satz Voltaire's '*On doit des égards aux vivants, on ne doit aux morts que la verité*', der meine Ansicht bestätigt, möchte ich nicht einzig als Ausfluss blosser Höflichkeit angesehen wissen. Nein, auch gegenüber den Lebenden, soll man nebst Billigkeit sowohl Gerechtigkeit als Wahrheit walten lassen, und die grosse Gefahr, die so oft eintritt, vermeiden, aus zu grossen Rücksichten für den einen zur Rücksichtslosigkeit gegen die anderen sich bestimmen zu lassen."

83. Adler, "Musik und Musikwissenschaft," 39: "Nicht mitzuhassen, sondern mitzulieben, mitzuraten, mitzuhelfen ist die Pflicht des Wissenschafters der Musik. Kunst und Kunstwissenschaft haben nicht getrennte Gebiete, deren Scheidelinie scharf gezogen wäre, sondern nur die Art ihrer Bearbeitung ist verschieden und wechselt nach den Zeitläuften. Je enger der Kontakt der Wissenschaft mit der forschreitenden Kunst und den lebenden Künstlern, desto näher kommt sie ihrem Ziele: *durch die Erkenntnis der Kunst für die Kunst zu wirken.*"

As Adler preached in 1898, so he carried out his subsequent work. His first large-scale project completed after his appointment in Vienna was a critical edition of the Trent Codices, six manuscript volumes of medieval music recently acquired by the Imperial Ministry of Culture and Education. In the prefatory essay appended to his edition, Adler made clear that he addressed his work not only to fellow historians but also, and just as importantly, to composers. He acknowledged that the repertoire contained in the manuscripts he edited—by DuFay, Dunstable, Binchois, and others—was of considerable and intrinsic historical interest. But he considered the creative stimulus that his edition might provide to artists to be of no lesser importance. Explaining his stance to the composers of his day, Adler urged them to delve into the volume and to take from it whatever they could use. He challenged them to respond by striving, in their own creative work, for something higher than the mere imitation of musical languages in the manner of the *Caecilianer*. He urged them to endeavor to understand the essence (*Kern*) or spirit of the Trent repertoire and to strive to resurrect that spirit in the musics of modernity. "I would like to make a call to our creative artists," Adler exclaimed. "After reading through and hearing [these] old works, strive to grasp their essence; do not believe, if you merely copy their surface features and use those as a leavening agent, that you will have seized upon what is truly of use in this art." On the other hand, he continued, if the essence of the musics contained in the codices is grasped and reenlivened in the creative act, "then the art of the past will be refreshing and work as a stimulus" for future creative endeavors.[84] In preparing his editions of historical musics, Adler believed, he carried out his work "in the service of the future and the present." Addressing his scholarship to present-day artists, he heeded Nietzsche's call to assume an active role in the nurturing of contemporary cultural life.[85] And he provided an answer to all of his contemporaries who struggled to reconcile the conflicting demands of a late-century society enamored with science yet deeply suspicious of its portents.

With respect to his ideas about the musicologist's necessary engagement with the creative world of his day, Adler's vision of his emergent discipline differed not only from that of Thausing and Spitta but also from that of his influential colleague to the north, Hugo Riemann. As Alexander Rehding has recently shown, Riemann had no ear for much of modern music, and he considered it the musicologist's duty "to instruct composers and listeners what music ought

---

84. Preface to Guido Adler, ed., *Sechs Trienter Codices* (*Denkmäler der Tonkunst in Österreich*, vol. 14) (Vienna: Artaria, 1900), ix: "Unseren schaffenden Künstlern möchte ich zurufen: wenn ihr die alten Werke leset und höret, so strebet darnach, den Kern zu erfassen; glaubet nicht, wenn ihr die Aeusserlichkeiten nachahmet und als Reizmittel verwendet, dass ihr euch damit des eigentlich Verwendbaren der alten Kunst bemächtigt habt. In diesem Sinne verarbeitet, werden die alten Kunstwerke erfrischend und bildend wirken."

85. Nietzsche, "On the Uses and Disadvantages of History," 77.

to be." Riemann, working primarily through the discourse on music theory, sought to shape contemporary musical practice along stylistic lines that he himself defined.[86] Adler, in contrast, held that the experiments and innovations of living artists were to be encouraged in whatever direction they might lead, provided only that composers proceed in their work with a carefully honed knowledge of the past. In this respect, Adler's attitude toward the musical culture of his time also differed from that of Max Reger, Hans Pfitzner, and others whom Frisch identifies as "historicist modernists," who tended to see the present age as "sick" and "corrupt" and who sought in the music of past epochs a kind of healing balm.[87] In Adler's view, all contemporary art created with historical understanding was worthy of respect. It was, he felt, up to Mahler, Schoenberg, and other composers to determine what the future course of music should be. Musicologists had no right to intercede. Indeed, they were to be "guided" in their scholarly work "by the demands of the art of their time."

But of course, the line between insisting that composers work from a historically informed perspective and interceding on stylistic questions is a fine one. And as Adler made clear in an essay of 1904 on the founding of Vienna's Society of Creative Musicians (Vereinigung schaffender Tonkünstler) by Schoenberg and Alexander Zemlinsky, his optimism regarding the direction that some of these artists' recent work had taken was decidedly guarded.[88] It is here, I would suggest, that we encounter a contradiction inherent in Adler's musicological program, which will have significant implications for our understanding of his writings on Wagner considered in the following chapter. For though he took pains to disassociate himself from a mode of scholarship like Hanslick's, inspired and directed by one's subjective impressions and opinions about what one studies, Adler's Nietzsche-inspired goal of working "on behalf of art" nonetheless rested a upon pair of essential value judgments. Namely, just what new musics are sufficiently rooted in the past as to deserve the musicologist's love, advice, and help? And, which historical repertoires are worthy of being proffered as models for young composers?

Moreover, just as Adler's ambivalence with regard to such questions permeates his early work, so too is that same body of writings marked by ambivalence of another sort. For like Nietzsche, who acknowledged in *The Birth of Tragedy* that the real focus of his inquiry into the history of Greek drama was "a seriously German problem,"[89] Adler was haunted, even obsessed, by the present-day fate of the German nation and his own uncertain place—as a Jew, a liberal,

---

86. Rehding, *Hugo Riemann*, esp. 63, 110–12, and 135–38 (cited at 63).

87. Frisch, *German Modernism*, 138–44 (cited at 139).

88. Adler, "Eine neue musikalische Vereinigung in Wien," *Neue freie Presse* (March 31, 1904), 1–3. This essay is discussed in Botstein, "Music and Its Public," 1345–51. For further consideration of Adler's support for Schoenberg in light of his ideas about historical study, see Wolfgang Rathert, "Das Neue und das Alte Neue. Tradition und Fortschritt im Denken Guido Adlers," in *Alte Musik im 20. Jahrhundert. Wandlungen und Formen ihrer Rezeption*, ed. Giselher Schubert (Mainz: Schott, 1995), 19–29.

89. Nietzsche, *The Birth of Tragedy*, 31.

and an Austrian civil servant—within it. As he traversed a path over the course of these decades from a *großdeutsch* nationalist to a distinguished representative of the supranational Habsburg Empire, Adler's work as historian and critic provided a principal means by which he negotiated the shifting cultural allegiances he forged. Like Riemann, Adler changed his positions and misread sources as he struggled to define the German and the Austrian in music. And as was the case with his colleague in Leipzig, Adler's crises of cultural identity resonated well beyond his age. No less than others, this aspect of his intellectual history comprised an essential component of the ideological foundations of the discipline he labored to found.

CHAPTER SIX

GERMAN MUSIC IN
AN AGE OF POSITIVISM

By the end of the twentieth century, it had become widely accepted that the discipline of musicology that Adler helped to found rested upon nationalistic assumptions about which musics merit the attention of scholars and which aesthetic values might be considered normative. Joseph Kerman suggested as much as early as 1980, when the identity of the "Germany" behind Adler's nationalism still seemed unproblematic.[1] In recent years, however, the outlines of what Adler and other nineteenth-century intellectuals understood by Germany—and the German in music—have begun to appear less clear. Richard Taruskin, for one, has called attention to two distinct conceptions of German identity overlapping within the cultural discourse of the second half of the century. One of these, Taruskin observes, was grounded in Enlightenment ideals of education or *Bildung*, the other in racialist ideologies.[2] In a similar vein, Daniel Beller-McKenna has drawn attention to competing visions of German nationhood in Brahms's vocal music, some of which exhibits significant tension between images of Germany rooted in the idea of state or *Reich* and others in notions of an imagined cultural community or *Volk*.[3] Looking further back toward the beginning of the century, the historian Hinrich Seeba has shown that even such a celebrated memento of German national awakening as Ernst Moritz Arndt's 1813 poem and song "What

1. Joseph Kerman, "How We Got into Analysis, and How to Get Out," *Critical Inquiry* 7 (1980), 314–15; repr. in *Write All These Down: Essays on Music* (Berkeley and Los Angeles: University of California Press, 1994), 15–16. For a thoughtful response to Kerman's argument, see Celia Applegate, "How German Is It? Nationalism and the Idea of Serious Music in the Early Nineteenth Century," *19th-Century Music* 21, no. 3 (1998), 274–96; and Applegate, "What is German Music? Reflections on the Role of Art in the Creation of the Nation," *German Studies Review* 15 (1992), 21–32.

2. Richard Taruskin, introduction to *repercussions* 5, nos. 1–2 (1996), 15. See also Taruskin, *The Oxford History of Western Music*, 6 vols. (New York: Oxford University Press, 2005), 3:127–29.

3. Daniel Beller-McKenna, *Brahms and the German Spirit* (Cambridge, MA: Harvard University Press, 2004). For further discussion of the distinction between ideas of nation and state in the nineteenth-century discourse on German identity, see James J. Sheehan, "Nation und Staat. Deutschland als 'imaginierte Gemeinschaft'," in *Nation und Gesellschaft in Deutschland*, ed. Manfred Hettling and Paul Nolte (Munich: C. H. Beck, 1996), 33–45.

is the German's Fatherland?" ("Was ist des Deutschen Vaterland?") constitutes "an implicit recognition of the fact that German identity is based on regional, cultural diversity."[4] In light of observations such as these, it now seems that there was no single, stable image of the German nation in the cultural and political discourse of the period. Indeed, the idea of Germany encompassed an array of distinct and competing visions of the nation's identity, members, and claims.

The difficulties one encounters when attempting to define the German in the nineteenth century are further compounded when one turns from artworks and broad fields of discourse to the positions of individuals. For as Celia Applegate has argued, conflicting senses of group affiliation and cultural belonging were present in the minds of many members of German-speaking society. Writing of E. T. A. Hoffmann's "nationalistic" assertions in his essays of the 1810s, she warns that "Hoffmann's political and cultural loyalties, like those of many of his contemporaries, often worked at cross-purposes and were marked by misconceptions and false hopes." And if, as she argues, Hoffmann's case "illustrates the difficulty of saying what was and what was not 'nationalistic' in this period," then we can be assured that similar cases abound in Adler's time as well.[5] To take one example, Carl E. Schorske has observed that the founding members of the University of Vienna's Reading Society for German Students, which we met in the previous chapter, awarded honorary memberships in 1878 to both the radical pan-German Georg von Schönerer and the liberal Anton Füster, hero of the 1848 Revolution. "This coincidence," Schorske notes, "reveals how difficult it was to distinguish 'forward' from 'backward' " in the culture of Adler's youth, "and how easily the older democratic nationalism could become reincarnated in new right-wing radical forms."[6] Indeed, one could argue that the complexities inherent in "the German question" were especially vexing in the Habsburg lands, where the traumatic events that followed in the wake of the 1848 Revolution—the war with Prussia of 1866, the division of the Empire with the Hungarian Compromise of 1867, and the founding of Bismarck's German state under Prussia in 1871—had the effect of splintering Austria's German-speaking subjects into Habsburg loyalists, *großdeutsch* nationalists, and numerous shades in between.[7]

4. Hinrich C. Seeba, " 'So weit die deutsche Zunge klingt': The Role of Language in German Identity Formation," in *Searching for Common Ground: Diskurse zur detuschen Identität 1750–1871*, ed. Nicholas Vazsonyi (Cologne: Böhlau, 2000), 49. A valuable survey of competing visions of German identity advanced throughout the century is provided in Sheehan, *German History, 1770– 1866*, Oxford History of Modern Europe (Oxford: Clarendon Press, 1989), 836–52.

5. Applegate, "How German Is It?" 279.

6. Carl E. Schorske, *Fin-de-Siècle Vienna: Politics and Culture* (New York: Vintage, 1981), 127. The honors bestowed on Schönerer and Füster are documented in the *Jahresbericht des Lesevereines der deutschen Studenten Wien's über das VII. Vereinsjahr 1877–78* (Vienna: Selbstverlag des Leseverein der deutschen Studenten Wien's, 1878), 8.

7. A detailed overview of the nineteenth-century discourse on Austrian national identity is provided in Friedrich Heer, *Der Kampf um die österreichische Identität* (Vienna: Böhlau, 1981). A concise summary of several key issues is found in Ernst Bruckmüller, "The National Identity of the Austrians," trans. Nicholas T. Parsons, in *The National Question in Europe in Historical Perspective*, ed. Mikuláš Teich and Roy Porter (Cambridge: Cambridge University Press, 1993), 196–227.

In a time and place where cultural allegiances were complex, elusive, and multiply determined, those evinced in Adler's work are as shifting and tangled as we might expect. Like many of his contemporaries, Adler was deeply concerned with defining the German and the Austrian in music, and his work as a scholar provided him with many opportunities to advance and explore an array of definitions. But the perspectives from which he approached the questions he pondered were unstable and often overlapped. For much of his life, he lived as an assimilated Jew in the reactionary Vienna of Schönerer, Count Eduard Taaffe, and a host of illiberal others—a circumstance that would normally lead us to expect his work to show few overt signs of the rhetoric of radical nationalism. But for over a decade—the very decade during which he established his reputation as a scholar—he lived in Prague, where he identified with an embattled German-speaking minority struggling to maintain its rights to cultural expression and its historical grip on power. An avid Wagnerian, Adler dedicated his early years to advancing a *großdeutsch* cultural agenda through his work with the Reading Society for German Students and the Viennese Academic Wagner Society. But he went on to build a career as an esteemed representative of the supranational Habsburg monarchy and its fragile, multiethnic empire.

Rather than attempting to impose order and coherence upon Adler's statements on music and nation, this chapter will examine the positions revealed in four facets of his work from the turn of the century: his early essays on the history of harmony; his lectures on Bach, Handel, and Mozart; his efforts to found the *Monuments of Music in Austria* (*Denkmäler der Tonkunst in Österreich*) series of critical editions; and his first book-length study, *Richard Wagner* (1904). Each of these cases illuminates Adler's response to a specific crisis that shook his society, from the death of Wagner and the rise of Czech political nationalism to the decline of popular faith in the Habsburg monarchy and the rise of an irrationalist ideology of regeneration. Taken as a whole, this body of Adler's work reminds us, as Applegate observes, that "calling oneself a German may not preclude hanging on to any number of other self-interpretations." At the same time, Adler's writings also testify, in Applegate's words, "to the tremendous flexibility and ambiguity of the national idea itself."[8]

ESSAYS ON THE HISTORY OF HARMONY

Before Adler cemented his reputation as a positivist historian with his "Scope, Method, and Goal of Musicology" (1885), he had already built an illustrious career as a scholar of medieval musics. Indeed, it was upon the strength of two early studies of the history of harmony—one the published version of his dissertation—that he was appointed to a professorship in Prague. In these theoretical essays, now neglected, and a follow-up article published in 1886, we find the historian at a troubled and revealing point in his intellectual development. For

8. Applegate, *A Nation of Provincials: The German Idea of Heimat* (Berkeley and Los Angeles: University of California Press, 1990), 12.

these studies reveal the young musicologist struggling to reconcile the methodological demands of positivist scholarship with the value judgments enshrined in the *großdeutsch* rhetoric that permeated the world of his youth, and his abiding faith in a German special path with the far more limited claims that the historical record would support from a "scientific" perspective.

Among all the topics that Adler could have chosen to study at the beginning of his career, the historical origins of harmonic singing were among the most sensitive with regard to the discourse on cultural identity that roiled much of German-speaking Europe. For as Alexander Rehding has shown, some of the period's most prominent music scholars—both Prussian and Austrian—went to considerable lengths to demonstrate that harmonic singing was a specifically Germanic contribution to European cultural history.[9] Locating its origins among the Celtic peoples of southern Britain, historians as diverse as Hugo Riemann in Leipzig and Richard Batka in Prague heralded the testimony of a twelfth-century monk, Giraldus Cambrensis (Gerald of Wales), as proof of the origins of triadic harmony amid a Germanic, if not literally German, people. Partly translated into English by the historian Edward Rimbault in the 1860s, Giraldus's writings included such provocative statements as "the Britons do not sing their tunes in unison, like the inhabitants of other countries, but in different parts."[10] And though there was nothing in Giraldus's testimony to suggest that the inhabitants of medieval Wales sang in thirds and sixths rather than in parallel octaves, this fact did nothing to prevent Adler's contemporaries from seizing upon it in order to bolster their theories of harmony's national beginnings.[11] Citing Giraldus, Riemann proclaimed in his *Handbook of Music History* (1905) that "there are numerous indications that the *musical culture* of the ancient *Celts* must have practiced harmonic singing [*die Mehrstimmigkeit*] during a period when the culture of southern Europe knew nothing whatsoever of it."[12] Likewise drawing upon Giraldus, Batka declared: "One accepts that the races [*Stämme*] of northern Europe, the Celts and the Germans, were the bearers of the harmonic conception of music, and that they brought it to all corners of our part of the world over the course of their migrations."[13] These are the sorts of assertions against which Adler's essays were read.

9. Alexander Rehding, "The Quest for the Origins of Music in Germany Circa 1900," *Journal of the American Musicological Society* 53, no. 2 (2000), 345–85; and Rehding, *Hugo Riemann and the Birth of Modern Musical Thought*, New Perspectives in Music History and Criticism (Cambridge: Cambridge University Press, 2003), 127–38.

10. Edward F. Rimbault, *The Rounds, Catches and Canons of England: A Collection of Specimens of the Sixteenth, Seventeenth and Eighteenth Centuries, Adapted to Modern Use* (London: Cramer, Wood, n. d. [ca. 1865]), vii–viii.

11. See Rehding, "The Quest for the Origins," 364–71; and Rehding, *Hugo Riemann*, 130–32.

12. Hugo Riemann, *Handbuch der Musikgeschichte*, vol. 1, part 2, *Die Musik des Mittelalters (bis 1450)* (Leipzig: Breitkopf und Härtel, 1905), 136: "Mancherlei Anzeichen weisen darauf hin, daß der uralten *keltischen Musikkultur* die Mehrstimmigkeit schon zu einer Zeit eigen gewesen sein muß, wo die südeuropäishe Kultur von derselben noch keine Ahnung hatte."

13. Batka, *Allgemeine Geschichte der Musik*, 2 vols. (Stuttgart: Carl Grüninger, n. d.), 1:161: "Man nimmt an, daß die nordeuropäischen Stämme, die Kelten und Germanen, die Träger der harmonischen Musikauffassung gewesen sind und sie während der Völkerwanderung in alle Winkel unseres Erdteils getragen haben."

To be sure, Adler, in spite of his positivist prescriptions, did not stand entirely above the fray when it came to locating the origins of harmonic singing among Europe's Germanic peoples. Indeed, as Rehding notes, his work in this area would provide a powerful catalyst for writers such as Riemann, who would, over the course of years to come, adopt more overtly national-specific stances than he did.[14] But even in his first contribution to the musicological literature, "The Basic Historical Classes of Western Christian Music Through 1600" ("Die historischen Grundclassen der christlich-abendländischen Musik bis 1600," 1880), Adler went to considerable lengths to lobby his colleagues not to place too great a stake in the national character or origins of the phenomena he described. In that essay, based upon his dissertation, Adler extrapolated from Theodoricus de Campo's fourteenth-century distinction between *musica naturalis* and *musica artificialis* a classificatory distinction of his own, between "music of nature" (*Naturmusik*) and "art music" (*Kunstmusik*), paralleling the common nineteenth-century division of humanity into "peoples of nature" (*Naturvölker*) and "peoples of culture" (*Kunstvölker*). Immediately after doing so, however, he took a step back from what might easily have lapsed into a search for the national character of those peoples who had played the greatest role in the development of harmonic music. He argued that the evidently national characteristics evinced in the phenomenal manifestation of *Naturmusik*—the folksong—can tell us very little about the origins and development of contemporary musical practice.[15] "A system for classifying music according to nations would not be justified," Adler wrote, addressing the influence of the folksong on the art song, "because, over the course of time, one nation or another is always stepping to the fore. Moreover, the purely musical effects of these fleeting national heydays are apparent only in musical trivialities—for example, in the crystalline cadences of the Dutch or the Italians." Indeed, he argued, "the reciprocal influence of national schools upon each other is so profound that a systematic partitioning [of the art] by nations is impossible."[16]

But Adler's efforts to limit his remarks to what he called music's "formal classes" (*formale Gruppen*)—defined, in the spirit of Hanslick's *On the Musically Beautiful*, by their "formal characteristics" (*formale Eigenschaften*) alone[17]—did not preclude his provocative conclusion that Germanic peoples had indeed played a

14. Rehding, "The Quest for the Origins," 360–64 and 364 n. 65; and Rehding, *Hugo Riemann*, 134 n. 71.

15. Guido Adler, "Die historischen Grundclassen der christlich-abendländischen Musik bis 1600," *Allgemeine musikalische Zeitung* 15 (1880) (offprint, Leipzig: Breitkopf und Härtel, 1880), 3–4. On the notions of *Naturvölker* and *Kulturvölker*, see Rehding, "The Quest for the Origins," 356–60.

16. Adler, "Die historischen Grundclassen," 4: "Nichtsdestoweniger wäre eine Hauptclassificirung der Tonkunst nach Nationen nicht gerechtfertigt, weil, wenn auch zu verschiedenen Zeiten, je eine oder die andere Nation mehr in den Vordergrund tritt, die rein musikalischen Wirkungen dieser temporären nationalen Blüthezeiten sich nur in gewissen tonlichen Idiotismen zeigen, wie z. B. in der krystallinischen Schlussform (Cadenz) der Niederländer oder der Italiener. Die gegenseitigen Wechselbeziehungen und Wechseleinflüsse der nationalen Schulen sind aber so bedeutend, dass eine systematischen Grundeintheilung nach Nationen sich nicht thunlich erweist."

17. Adler, "Die historischen Grundclassen," 13.

pivotal role in the evolution of the art. Narrating the history of music's development in terms of a dialectic process in which a teleological march toward the present day is correlated with increasing complexity of form, Adler plotted a course from the hymns and sequences of the middle ages to the polyphonic masses of the Renaissance. The pivotal historical moment in this development, he argued, had arrived around the turn of the fifteenth century, when the tenor became a middle voice in the polyphonic texture and the *discantus* assumed the leading melodic role. And it just so happened, he proceeded to explain, that the first recorded instances of such polyphonic practice arose among the Germans.[18]

Adler's other publications on the history of harmony exhibit a similar tension between, on the one hand, cautionary statements and insistence upon carefully reading one's documentary sources and, on the other, provocative conclusions that resonated broadly with late-century *großdeutsch* rhetoric. For instance, in his "Study on the History of Harmony" ("Studie zur Geschichte der Harmonie," 1881), the historian sought to push the origins of *fauxbourdon*—typically considered, in the late nineteenth century, a more "harmonic" style of singing than the earlier *discant*—well back into the middle ages. In doing so, as Rehding observes, he indulged a German philosophy of origins frequently harnessed for chauvinist agendas. If *fauxbourdon* could be proven to be coeval with *discant*, and if it could also be shown to be a wholly German phenomenon, then evidence could be had for an ancient German practice of singing that not only bypassed foreign influences but also pointed directly toward the language of modern harmonic music. Yet in this same essay, Adler warned against the tendency, evinced by Riemann and others, to read too much into etymological evidence that might suggest such German origins, supposedly evinced in the "faberdon" described by the fifteenth-century German poet Hanss Rosenplüt, in contradistinction to the clearly Latinate *discant* or *déchant*.[19]

Adler's ambivalence is most apparent, however, in his third essay on medieval topics, "Repetition and Imitation in Polyphony" ("Die Wiederholung und Nachahmung in der Mehrstimmigkeit," 1886). There, he confronted directly the source from which many writers had drawn their principal evidence: the testimony of Gerald of Wales. While freely admitting his personal belief that the monk's "essential argument cannot be mere fantasy," Adler nonetheless acknowledged that Giraldus's testimony "leaves the imagination of the historian with too much room to play."[20] From there, he proceeded to adduce for his read-

18. Adler, "Die historischen Grundclassen," 17–18.

19. Adler, "Studie zur Geschichte der Harmonie," *Sitzungsberichte der phil.-hist. Classe der kais. Akademie der Wissenschaften* 98, no. 3 (1881) (offprint, Vienna: Carl Gerold's Sohn, 1881), 8–9. *Fauxbourdon, discant*, and Adler's arguments about both are considered in light of German philosophies of origins in Rehding, "The Quest for the Origins," 360–64; and Rehding, *Hugo Riemann,* 132–34.

20. Adler, "Die Wiederholung und Nachahmung in der Mehrstimmigkeit. Studie zur Geschichte der Harmonie," *Vierteljahrsschrift für Musikwissenschaft* 2 (1886), 324–25 (cited at 325): "Man möge die Glaubwürdigkeit *Giraldus'* in kleinen Einzelheiten bezweifeln—die Grundbehauptung kann nicht bloßes Hirngespinst des Authors sein. ... Der Phantasie des Historikers läßt der Autor einen leider zu weiten Spielraum."

ers a number of potential problems of interpretation. And as he did that, his own position became increasingly uncertain.

In Adler's view, the chief trouble with Giraldus's testimony is that it includes an array of tantalizing and provocative statements that simply cannot be verified by way of corroborating documentary evidence. Adler noted, for example, that the monk "offered no grounds for his view that Danes and Norwegians brought harmony" to the Welsh. Adler admitted his belief that "it is possible, indeed probable, that these [Scandinavian] peoples also knew and practiced two- and three-part modes of singing," just as Giraldus had suggested. But he was troubled nonetheless by the heaping of supposition upon supposition that even he found tempting when reading this source. Immediately after observing that "it seems striking and significant that mention is made, in such a peculiar way, of several peoples [*Völker*]"—Danes and Norwegians—"belonging to a single race [*Stamm*]," Adler cautioned against reading too much into Giraldus's assertions, either about this or about any number of other issues that the monk addressed.[21] Noting that "in Great Britain, only the inhabitants of mountainous regions are mentioned" in Giraldus's account, Adler asked whether one should therefore "infer from this that the love for harmony derives from the joys of echo and imitation and from the comforting sound of reverberation." He dismissed such speculation out of hand. "Let us leave such nature-philosophy [*Naturphilosophie*] to the side," he declared. "Another person could say that it is the pleasure of the husband to accompany his wife harmonically or to call in her direction. A third could find motivation in the pleasures of the fullness of sound and its alternation."[22]

Indeed, Adler argued, the more deeply one looks into the evidence at hand, the more resolutely one becomes convinced that the earliest instances of harmonic singing were not the exclusive provenance of mountain dwellers, the

---

21. Adler, "Die Wiederholung," 325: "Seine Ansicht, daß Dänen und Norweger diese Harmonie verpflanzt hätten, begründet er nicht, wohl ist es möglich, ja wahrscheinlich, daß auch diese Völker diese zwei- und mehrstimmigen Weisen kannten und übten... Auffallend und bedeutsam erscheint, daß hier in so besonderer Weise mehrerer einem Stamme angehörigen Völker Erwähnung gethan wird."

22. Adler, "Die Wiederholung," 325: "in Großbritannien nur die Bewohner der Gebirgsländer hervorgehoben werden. ...sollen wir einen Erklärungsgrund für die Liebe an Mehrstimmigkeit aus der Freude an den Echo und der Nachahmung und der süßen Gewohnheit des Doppelklanges herleiten? Lassen wir solche Naturphilosophie bei Seite...ein zweiter könnte sagen, die Lust des Mannes, das Weib harmonisch zu begleiten, oder ihr entgegen zu singen, ein dritter könnte die Lust an Klangfülle und gegensätzlicher Abwechselung als Motiv ansehen." In referring disparagingly to *Naturphilosophie*, Adler voiced a disdain widely felt among late-century, scientifically minded German intellectuals. That branch of metaphysics, most commonly associated with F. W. J. Schelling and G. W. F. Hegel, strove, in the words of Terry Pinkard, "to give us an understanding of how the results of empirical natural science were in fact compatible and at one with our own subjective, more poetic, appreciation of nature." It constituted, Pinkard observes, a kind of "re-enchantment of nature," which "came to represent," for natural scientists and those who admired them, "all that was seemingly backward and mystical about post-Kantian philosophy, so completely out of touch with the realities of scientific practice and an industrializing world" (Terry Pinkard, *German Philosophy, 1760–1860: The Legacy of Idealism* [Cambridge: Cambridge University Press, 2002], 178, 179, 357).

Celtic people, or the Germanic *Stamm*. Rather, he suggested, the "harmonic instinct" (*harmonische Instinct*) is a thing apparently possessed by all "primitive" peoples of both the present and the past. Like many of his contemporaries, Adler considered harmonic singing a product of nature rather than of culture—of the people or *Volk* rather than of learned composers and institutions.[23] But among Europe's peoples, he insisted, that instinct seemed to be universal. It is even apparent, he observed in example, in the music-making practices of the present-day Russian peasantry. "In this [Russian] harmonic folksong singing, however foreign and half-barbaric it might sound to our ears," he wrote,

> one finds the seeds of multi-voiced composition [*vielstimmige Kunstsetzweise*]. And if this is the case with a people that has not yet experienced full artistic development, and whose artistic products are not on the same level of those of Western classical music, then one may readily accept that the original predisposition [toward harmonic singing] of our own people, and of those closely related to us, was of even greater significance—or at least that the primary products of our folk-muse [*Volksmuse*], whatever they might have been, were more significant than the works of composers.[24]

Adler's essays on the history of harmony evince palpable tension between the positivist methodologies advocated in his disciplinary polemics and the Greater German nationalist ideologies so deeply ingrained in his society. Indeed, while one senses him wrestling with both of these forces, one also finds him harnessing, at times, the former in service of the latter. To Adler's mind, the Germanic peoples had clearly played a special role in the development of modern music. But contrary to the assertions of Riemann and Batka, he insisted that the Germans did not stand alone. Granted, they might have been the first to leave records of harmonic singing in their learned compositions, and this circumstance was of crucial importance to Adler, given his insistence upon supporting one's assertions with empirically verifiable documentary evidence. Moreover, Adler candidly observed, the Germans had attained incomparable sophistication in their manipulation of harmonic materials. But he conceded that the historical record also makes clear that the Germans shared their innate aptitude for harmonic expression with a diverse array of other peoples residing throughout the world.

---

23. Adler first broached the idea of a universal *harmonische Instinct* in his "Studie zur Geschichte der Harmonie," 3. The tendency among Adler's contemporaries to look for evidence of ancient musical practices among "primitive" peoples of the present is discussed in Rehding, "The Quest for the Origins."

24. Adler, "Die Wiederholung," 345–46: "Es sind in diesem mehrstimmigen Volksgesange, so fremd und halbbarbarisch er unserem Ohre klingen möge, die Keime der vielstimmigen Kunstsetzweise enthalten; wenn dies bei einem Volke der Fall ist, welches eine durchaus nicht völlig selbständige Kunstentwickelung durchgemacht hat, dessen Kunstprodukte nicht auf der Höhe der abendländischen klassischen Musik stehen, so darf man wohl um so mehr annehmen, daß die originäre Anlage unseres Volkes und der ihm zunächst verwandten Völker von noch größerer Bedeutung war, mindestens aber daß selbst die primären Erzeugnisse unserer Volksmuse, wie immer sie geartet waren, gegenüber den Werken der Tonkünstler eine bedeutendere Stellung hatten."

LECTURES ON HANDEL, BACH, AND MOZART

Among the most troubled essays in Adler's *oeuvre* is a pair of lectures all but forgotten today: one on Bach and Handel, published in the journal of Vienna's Academic Club (Wissenschaftlicher Club) in 1885, and the other on Mozart, delivered in Prague in 1887 and published in Bohemia's German nationalist press nineteen years later.[25] These lectures reveal that while he was rising to prominence as a positivist historian of early musics, Adler was also cultivating a reputation, outside the academy, as a passionate polemicist on behalf of the spiritual heritage of an imagined *großdeutsch* cultural community.[26] In these essays, Adler extolled the virtues of the German spirit in the manner of Wagner and a host of radical provocateurs. He trumpeted Bach and Handel as artists capable of uniting mankind by spreading the fruits of the German genius to the farthest corners of the globe. And he heralded Mozart as the figure who had established decisively the supremacy of German music on the European cultural scene. To be sure, these lectures are hardly products of historical scholarship as Adler himself had defined it. There is no evidence in either essay that his statements are based upon original research, and so they might be dismissed as falling outside the purview of his methodological prescriptions. But I would argue that these documents are nonetheless important, for they illuminate ideas about German nationhood that lurk beneath Adler's statements on the medieval origins of harmony. And they make clear that Adler's positivist rhetoric did not prevent him from indulging in a variety of cultural chauvinism impervious to the sorts of rationalistic inquiry for which he himself had called.

At the start of Adler's "Johann Sebastian Bach and Georg Friedrich Händel: Their Significance and Place in the History of Music," written to commemorate the composers' shared bicentennial, Adler identified an aspect of their music that comprised, to his mind, its "fundamental idea" (*Grundidee*): its "choral lyricism" (*Chorlyrik*).[27] But by choral lyricism Adler did not mean a musical phenomenon susceptible to the sort of empirical study advocated in his "Scope, Method, and Goal of Musicology," also published in 1885. Rather, he used the term as a means of describing something patently unverifiable by way of documentary evidence: the community-building *experience* of singing and listening to the works of these composers.[28] "What I mean by the choir," Adler explained, "is a union of men who give voice in word and tone, at times together, at times following each other, to that which concerns the community and under which it suffers. It is a fundamental feeling common to the members of the community—in a word,

25. Adler, "Johann Sebastian Bach und Georg Friedrich Händel. Ihre Bedeutung und Stellung in der Geschichte der Musik," *Monatsblätter des Wissenschaftlichen Club* 12 (1885) (offprint, Vienna: Adolf Holzhausen, 1885); Adler, "W. A. Mozart," *Deutsche Arbeit* 5, no. 5 (1906), 300–4.

26. By *imagined community* I mean not one that is nonexistent but one that consists in shared experience, either historical or cultural, rather than in political activity or literal togetherness. In invoking this notion, I borrow from Benedict Anderson, *Imagined Communities: Reflections on the Origin and Spread of Nationalism*, rev. ed. (London: Verso, 1991).

27. Adler, "Johann Sebastian Bach," 4.

28. In spite of the title of Adler's essay, which suggests a general consideration of these artists' music, Adler's lecture considers only their vocal works.

its solidarity—that is expressed here." He continued, reflecting upon a singer's experience of these composers' polyphonic textures: "In how many, innumerable ways is this communal feeling divvied up! How colorfully is the fundamental idea [*Grundidee*] reflected in the minds of the individual representatives of this community of men!"[29] Both Bach and Handel, Adler argued, were blessed with the ability to unite individuals in spiritual communion through their works. The special quality of their music, its choral lyricism, encouraged singers and listeners alike to transcend the diversity of their individual concerns and to identify themselves as members of a coherent cultural community.

But although the community-building potential of the music of these artists might indeed be appreciated by all, Adler continued, their music retained, at its core, a distinctly national character. It constituted, he explained, a uniquely German gift bestowed upon mankind. "Just as the individual tone and the most artful melody speak to every heart without bias, so too the many-branched German choral character [*Chorbilde*] penetrates the farthest-flung corners of the civilized world."[30] Furthermore, the missionary quality that Adler ascribed to this music was not simply humanitarian. Rather, he described the influence of Bach and Handel spreading throughout Europe in a manner akin to divine conquest. "Rameau," he argued, "a contemporary of Bach and Händel, could still say, 'If you want to learn to compose, you must go to Naples.' But one can no longer say that after Bach and Händel. ... Since Bach and Händel the musical primacy [*Primat*], the true compositional and music-giving primacy, has belonged to Germany."[31] Continuing, Adler explained that the musical subjugation of the Italians by the Germans was not only a victory of style. It constituted nothing less than the salvation of modern musical culture from the materialism the Italians had fostered. "While German composers were busy assuming spiritual leadership, Italian composers were flooding the marketplace, where their lightweight wares were greeted with brisk sales," he wrote. In contrast, Bach and Handel, true to their German nature, had no taste for material success. Instead, they contented themselves with "inner fulfillment." Bach, Adler observed, "lived selflessly, in quiet seclusion, without grasping after success, only in the service of his godly music. And Händel, standing in the midst of the whirlwind of partisan passions, needed from the start to greet fleeting success with

---

29. Adler, "Johann Sebastian Bach," 4: "Den Chor möchte ich als eine Vereinigung von Menschen bezeichnen, die bald miteinander, bald nacheinander dasjenige in Wort und Ton aussprechen, wovon diese Gemeinde erfüllt ist, worunter sie leidet, was sie begeistert, was sie zu Thaten aneifert, was sie zu stiller Ergebenheit führt, ihre Theilnahme erweckt, sie mit banger Sorge erfüllt. Immer ist es ein Grundgefühl, welches den Mitgliedern der Gemeinschaft gemeinsam ist, es ist mit einem Worte eine solidarische Gemeinde, die sich hier künstlerisch ausdrückt. Wie mannigfaltig sind da die verschiedenen begleitenden Gefühle! In wie viele und unzählige kleinere Spielarten zertheilt sich da dieses Gemeingefühl!"

30. Adler, "Johann Sebastian Bach," 10: "...wie der einzelne Ton und wie die kunstvollste Melodie vom Herzen zum Herzen spricht ohne Tendenz, ohne versteckte Absicht, so dringen die vielverzweigten deutschen Chorgebilde in den entferntesten Winkel der civilisirten Welt."

31. Adler, "Johann Sebastian Bach," 10: "Während noch Rameau, der Zeitgenosse Bach's und Händel's, sagen konnte: 'Wollt Ihr componiren lernen, so geht nach Neapel'...konnte man dies, seit Bach und Händel gewirkt hatten, nicht mehr sagen. ...seit Bach und Händel war der musikalische Primat – der wahre tondichterische und tonangebende Primat – Deutschland zuzusprechen."

caution so as not to allow himself to be deterred in the end." For both of these artists, worldly riches were a secondary concern. Both, Adler argued, were motivated by a conviction that "their mission was holy."[32]

Picking up on this theme in his lecture on Mozart of 1887, Adler explained that whatever Bach and Handel had left unaccomplished at the time of their deaths, Mozart ultimately completed. Indeed, it was Mozart who "shook" to its core "the absolute rule of Italian music" (erschüttert die absolute Herrschaft der italienischen Musik).[33] As an artist, Adler argued, Mozart exhibited innumerable admirable traits, among them "an uninhibited manner with regard to both great and small, unqualified frankness, heartfelt devotion, loyal disposition, unshakeable trust in God...[and] touching sympathy for the joys and sorrows of his fellow men."[34] Naturally, these qualities were evident in his music. But that music, he continued, testified to something greater than Mozart's personal gifts. It exemplified the ability of the German genius to transform the national into the universal. Subjecting the musical language of Italian composers to his distinctly German sensibilities, Mozart revealed to the whole of the world the significance of the Italians' contributions. Stripping away the obscuring marks of their provincial Mediterranean origins, he unleashed the power of Italian opera to speak to the hearts of all men. "In composing Don Giovanni," Adler explained,

> Mozart realized the ideal of Italian opera and raised it to universal significance. In it, we find the quintessence of all dramatic art of the period; it constitutes the culminating point of the monodic school of composition, which had developed over the course of two centuries. It is this that accounts for the lasting importance and unquestionable significance of the work: forged by the power of history, hardened by the strength of the artist, [it was] animated by German spirit and sensibility.[35]

In Mozart's opera, Adler concluded, "there resides truth and depth. It delights us and lifts us upward toward true freedom... Though music has progressed significantly since Mozart's death and its means have been enriched, the lasting effects of Mozart's art will be felt so long as our culture exists."[36]

32. Adler, "Johann Sebastian Bach," 10: "Während die deutschen Tonsetzer die geistige Führerschaft übernahmen, überschwemmten die italienischen Tondichter den Markt und ihre leichte Waare fand reissenden Absatz. Ihnen gegenüber musste sich die Mehrzahl unserer Tondichter mit der inneren Befriedigung begnügen. Bach's Leben konnte ein leuchtendes Vorbild sein, er lebte in stiller Zurückgezogenheit selbstlos, ohne Haschen nach Erfolg, nur im Dienste seiner göttlichen Musik. Händel, im Wirbel der Parteileidenschhaft stehend, musste anfangs auf den momentanen Erfolg Rücksicht nehmen, liess sich aber schliesslich doch nicht beirren. Ihnen beider war ihre Mission heilig."

33. Adler, "W. A. Mozart," 301.

34. Adler, "W. A. Mozart," 302.

35. Adler, "W. A. Mozart," 303: "erreicht Mozart in der Komposition des 'Don Giovanni' das Ideal der zu universaler Bedeutung erhobenen italienischen Oper. In ihr ist die Quintessenz aller damaligen dramatischen Kunst enthalten; sie bildet den Kulminationspunkt einer zwei Jahrhunderte währenden Entwicklung seit dem Inslebentreten der monodischen Schule. Daher erklärt sich auch die dauernde Geltung und unbestrittene Bedeutung des Werkes: gefestet durch die Macht der Geschichte, gestählt an der Kraft des Künstlers, beseelt von deutschem Geist und Gemüt."

36. Adler, "W. A. Mozart," 304: "In seiner Kunst liegen Wahrheit und Tiefe, sie beglückt und erhebt uns zur wirklichen Freiheit... So sehr auch die Tonkunst seit Mozarts Tod fortgeschritten ist, ihre Mittel bereichert hat, das Kunstwerk Mozarts wird fortwirken, so lange unsere Kultur besteht."

After reading Adler's essays on Handel, Bach, and Mozart, one is left with little doubt about the identity of "our culture" to which he referred. Indeed, these lectures are remarkable not only for the lack of documentary evidence adduced to support their claims but also for their intensive use of language and imagery that appear as though culled from the panoply of classics of the literature on German cultural nationhood. From a century of activists of all political stripes, Adler borrowed statements on the community-building experience of choral singing. As early as 1789, Johann Abraham Peter Schulz, a lobbyist for peasant enlightenment, had argued that such singing can "soften manners, ennoble feelings, spread joy and sociability among the people, and in general have a great influence on the cultivation of the moral character."[37] Toward the middle of Adler's century, similar assertions abounded in the literature of the burgeoning choral movement, where they were often linked to hopeful remarks about Germany's spiritual or political unification. Writing in their founding charter of 1862, members of the German Singers' Club (Deutscher Sängerbund) declared their dedication to "the promotion of German feeling through the unifying power of German song." The mission of the club, its charter continued, was "to preserve and enhance the German national consciousness and [to foster] a feeling of solidarity among German tribes."[38]

In a similar vein, when Adler argued, in his essay on Bach and Handel, that German culture can work as a unifying, revivifying force for all of humanity, he invoked a central theme of Johann Gottlieb Fichte's *Addresses to the German Nation* (1806). In those addresses, Fichte famously urged Europe's German speakers to regard themselves as members of a nation (*Volk*) endowed with a unique historical mission: to assume the role of "regenerator and re-creator of the world."[39] In conjuring this image of a regenerative German mission, Adler was also in league with Wagner, who promised the rejuvenation of European culture at the hands of German artists.[40] "The further development of this influence, which we have foreseen, of artistic expression upon life," Wagner wrote in *Opera and Drama* (1851), "can in no way proceed from artworks whose linguistic basis resides in the Italian or the French language. Of all the languages of modern opera [*Opernsprachen*], only German is qualified for use in the project of reviving artistic expression in the manner we have recognized as necessary."[41]

37. Johann Abraham Peter Schulz, *Gedanken über den Einfluß der Musik auf die Bildung eines Volks* (1790); cited in David Gramit, *Cultivating Music: The Aspirations, Interests, and Limits of German Musical Culture, 1770–1848* (Berkeley and Los Angeles: University of California Press, 2002), 70.

38. Cited and discussed in Celia Applegate and Pamela Potter, "Germans as the 'People of Music': Genealogy of an Identity," in *Music and German National Identity*, ed. Celia Applegate and Pamela Potter (Chicago: University of Chicago Press, 2002), 18. On the topic of choral singing and the associated rhetoric of nation-building, see also Taruskin, *The Oxford History of Western Music*, 3:162–63.

39. Johann Gottlieb Fichte, *Addresses to the German Nation*, ed. George Armstrong Kelly, trans. R. F. Jones and G. H. Turnbull, European Perspectives (New York: Harper and Row, 1972), 215.

40. A detailed consideration of ideas of nation evinced in Wagner's writings is provided in Hannu Salmi, *Imagined Germany: Richard Wagner's Utopia*, German Life and Civilization, no. 29 (New York: Peter Lang, 1999). Salmi considers Wagner's relation to Fichte on pages 56–57.

41. Wagner, 4:211: "Jene vorahnende Entwicklung des Einflusses des künstlerischen Ausdruckes auf den des Lebens kann zunächst nicht von Kunstwerken ausgehen, deren sprachliche Grundlage

Indeed, in his essays on Bach, Handel, and Mozart, Adler's debt to Wagner ran deeper than this.

In *Opera and Drama*, Wagner, like Adler, identified Mozart's operatic work as a specifically German culmination of centuries of Italian musical reforms.[42] Wagner too railed against the market-driven forces that he posited to have shaped Italian musical life, and he also proffered German music as a spiritually untainted alternative.[43] As Adler argued in his lecture on Mozart, so also Wagner considered the essence of German genius to reside in its "universal" character and reach. And Wagner likewise celebrated the ability of German artists to strip the works of other nations of their localizing characteristics. "One may assert, without exaggeration," Wagner wrote in his polemical essay "What Is German?" ("Was ist Deutsch?") of 1878,

> that the universal, world-wide significance of the works of antiquity [*die Antike*] would have remained unknown if it had not been recognized and explained by German intellect. The Italian appropriated from such works whatever he could imitate and copy. The Frenchman, in turn, took from that imitation only what flattered his national sense for elegance of form. Only the German recognized their purely human originality and—turning his back on mere utility—their uniquely beneficial significance for rendering the purely human.[44]

"In the areas of aesthetics and critical or philosophical judgement," Wagner continued in this essay, "it may be shown—indeed, it is almost obvious—that the ability to grasp and appropriate, with the most highly objective purity of vision, that which is foreign and once distant was peculiar to the German spirit."[45] Unlike the Frenchman or the Italian, the German did not copy what he found in the artifacts of other nations; instead, he unmasked their universal meaning and proclaimed that meaning in his own creative work.[46] When Adler declared Mozart's genius to consist in "realizing the ideal of Italian opera and raising it to

---

in der italienischen und französischen Sprache liegt, sondern von allen modernen Opernsprachen ist nur die deutsche befähigt, in der Weise, wie wir es als erforderlich erkannten, zur Belebung des künstlerischen Ausdruckes verwandt zu werden." For an alternate translation, see Wagner/Ellis, 2:358.

42. Wagner, 3:244–45; Wagner/Ellis, 2:35–36.

43. See, for instance, Wagner's discussion, in *Opera and Drama*, of Rossini; in Wagner, 3: 248–55; Wagner/Ellis, 2:41–46.

44. Wagner, 10:40–41; Wagner/Ellis, 4:155: "Man kann ohne Übertreibung behaupten, daß die Antike nach ihrer jetzt allgemeinen Weltbedeutung unbekannt geblieben sein würde, wenn der deutsche Geist sie nicht erkannt und erklärt hätte. Der Italiener eignete sich von der Antike an, was er nachahmen und nachbilden konnte; der Franzose eignete sich wieder von dieser Nachbildung an, was seinem nationalen Sinne für Eleganz der Form schmeicheln durfte: erst der Deutsche erkannte sie in ihrer reinmenschlichen Originalität und der Nützlichkeit gänzlich abgewandten, dafür aber der Wiedergebung des Reinmenschlichen einzig förderlichen Bedeutung."

45. Wagner, 10:40; Wagner/Ellis, 4:155: "Auf dem Gebiete der Ästhetik und des kritisch-philosophischen Urteils läßt es sich fast zur Ersichtlichkeit nachweisen, daß es dem deutschen Geiste bestimmt war, das Fremde, ursprünglich ihm Fernliegende, in höchster objektiver Reinheit der Anschauung zu erfassen und sich anzueignen."

46. For further discussion of Wagner's statements on the universality of German culture, see Salmi, *Imagined Germany*, 52–61.

universal significance," he allied the artist with nothing less than the mission of the German genius that Wagner had described.

At first blush, Adler's invocations of such chauvinistic rhetoric might be dismissed as a reflection of his youthful involvement with the Reading Society for German Students and the Viennese Academic Wagner Society. After all, his association with these groups preceded the publication of these essays by nearly a decade. We have already considered the activities of the Reading Society, an organization dedicated to advancing an openly *großdeutsch* cultural agenda in deliberate contradistinction to the supranational vision of Austrian identity cultivated by Habsburg officialdom. The Wagner Society was likewise deeply concerned with national questions and with Wagner's contributions to the discourse on German cultural identity in particular. In its early years, that society published, in each of its annual reports, a single essay by one of its members addressing an issue of pressing concern for the organization as a whole. And in each of its first three years of operation, its featured essay considered Wagner's positions on German cultural nationhood. In its first annual report (1873), the society published "Richard Wagner and the National Idea," in which the future *gymnasium* teacher Adalbert Horawitz recounted Wagner's emerging consciousness of his German heritage during his years in Paris.[47] The report for the following year featured the essay "Richard Wagner and German Art," in which the architect Camillo Sitte argued that Wagner's music dramas had effected the "revival" (*Wiederbelebung*) and "reawakening" (*Erwachen*) of German art by casting themes and images of German mythology in a modern guise.[48] And in 1875, Hans von Wolzogen, in "German Folk Poetry as Foundation for a National Festival," described Wagner's Bayreuth festival as a phenomenon equivalent, in its nation-building potential, to the political unification of Germany under Otto von Bismarck. The festival, Wolzogen argued, is "an echo of the victorious period of 1870 and 1871 in that it celebrates and portrays a united and energetic expression of the national spirit [*Nationalgeist*] and a powerful awareness of its nature and effects."[49] Though Adler was not among the authors of the essays published in these reports, he was, as a guiding member of the society, certainly privy to the discussions from which they arose.

But while we might be tempted to account for Adler's lectures on Mozart, Bach, and Handel by emphasizing his early associations with a figure like Wolzogen, we must remember that those lectures were written long after he had ceased active participation in both the Reading Society and the Wagner Society. Indeed, both of those essays were published *after* he had laid out his positivist vision for music study in his "Scope, Method, and Goal of Musicology," whose

47. Adalbert Horawitz, "Richard Wagner und die Nationale Idee," in *Erster Jahres-Bericht des Wiener akademischen Wagner-Vereines für das Jahr 1873* (Vienna: Selbstverlag des Vereines, 1874; hereafter cited as *Wagner-Verein Jahresbericht 1873*), 1–28.

48. Camillo Sitte, "Richard Wagner und die deutsche Kunst," in *Wagner-Verein Jahresbericht 1874*, 1–41 (cited at 41).

49. Hans von Wolzogen, "Germanische Volksgrundgedichte als Nationalfeststoff," in *Wagner-Verein Jahresbericht 1875*, 3–13 (cited at 5): "Beide Ereignisse sind noch ein Nachklang der Siegeszeit von 1870 und 1871, indem sie die einheitlich thatkräftige Bekundung des Nationalgeistes und ein gestärktes Bewusstsein von seinem Wesen und Wirken feiern oder darstellen."

methodological prescriptions his lectures seem to ignore entirely. And so, if we wish to understand the context in which his lectures of 1885 to 1887 were penned and the complex of historical and ideological circumstances that informed the views expressed in them, we must look to other, very different corners of Adler's intellectual world.

To consider first Adler's statements on Bach: We begin to understand Adler's heavy reliance on Wagnerian rhetoric and imagery in this essay when we recall that the Bach bicentennial, for which it was written, occurred just weeks after the second anniversary of Wagner's death in February 1883. For many observers, the two events simply could not be separated. Ever since Johann Nikolaus Forkel had published his pioneering biography of Bach "for patriotic admirers of the true musical art" at the beginning of the nineteenth century, Bach and his music had widely been regarded as historical embodiments of a mythical German spirit.[50] Even Philipp Spitta, whose faith in the promise of empirical research eclipsed Adler's own by far, hinted at such an image in the prefatory remarks to his *Johann Sebastian Bach* of 1873.[51] In the wake of Wagner's death, however, a new urgency was felt by many to canonize Bach, Heinrich Schütz, and other long-departed artists as historical bearers of German cultural identity. This urgency was felt especially strongly with Bach, for Wagner himself had famously celebrated the composer as regenerator of a foundering German spirit after the Thirty Years' War.[52] At the time of the Bach bicentennial, celebrated in 1885, some prominent polemicists and even historians conflated their tributes to the latter artist with celebrations of Wagner and echoed in their bicentennial essays any number of Wagner's statements. In July of that year, the Leipzig *Neue Zeitschrift für Musik* honored Bach with an essay entitled "The National Significance of J. S. Bach and His Influence upon Richard Wagner's Art." The substance of that influence, its author argued, consisted in the essential fact that "Bach was a truly *German* artist."[53] In a similar vein, Richard Batka published a biography of Bach in 1892 that opened with extensive quotations from Wagner's "What is German?" Elaborating upon Wagner's statements, Batka declared that "Bach's lasting significance does not derive from the fact that he knew how to fuse new harmonies together...but from the fact that he was the rejuvenator

50. Johann Nikolaus Forkel, *Ueber Johann Sebastian Bachs Leben, Kunst und Kunstwerke für patriotische Verehrer echter musikalischer Kunst*, ed. Walther Vetter (Berlin: Henschelverlag, 1966). On this aspect of Forkel's work and legacy, see Applegate, "What is German Music?" 28; and Applegate and Porter, "Germans as the 'People of Music,'" 4–5.

51. Philipp Spitta, *Johann Sebastian Bach*, trans. Clara Bell and J. A. Fuller-Maitland, 3 vols. (New York: Dover, 1951), 1:i: "[Bach was] a man who forms, as it were, the focal point towards which all the music of Germany has tended during the last three centuries, and in which all its different lines converged to start afresh in a new period, and to diverge towards new results." With regard to his task as a biographer, Spitta observed: "The deeper and more ramified the roots by which he clung to the soil of German life and nature, the wider was the extent of the ground to be dug over in order to lay them bare."

52. See Wagner, "Was ist Deutsch?" in Wagner, 10:46–48; Wagner/Ellis, 4:161–64.

53. Wilhelm Kienzl, "Die nationale Bedeutung J. Seb. Bach's und dessen Einfluß auf das Kunstschaffen Richard Wagner's," *Neue Zeitschrift für Musik* 52, no. 27 (1885), 285–87 (cited at 285; emphasis in original).

[*Erneuerer*] of the German spirit."[54] Adler's assertions in his own bicentennial lecture were part of this tangled discourse.

A different set of historical circumstances informed Adler's statements on Mozart. A preface appended to the published version of his lecture on the artist explains that it was written and delivered in October 1887 to commemorate the centennial of the premiere of Mozart's *Don Giovanni* at the German Theater in Prague. Adler, as we saw in chapter 1, had moved to the Bohemian capital in 1885 to assume a professorship in music history at that city's German University. And by that time, both *Don Giovanni* and Prague's German Theater had taken on specific, symbolic significance in the city's political and cultural discourse. Both had become emblematic of the struggle of Prague's minority German-speaking community against social and cultural marginalization in an era of rapidly erod-ing political power.

Throughout the middle decades of the nineteenth century, the Habsburg state of Bohemia, a Czech-dominated province in the Austrian half of the Empire, had seen the coalescence of numerous groups demanding economic, cultural, and political rights for the majority, Czech-speaking populace.[55] In 1879, six years before Adler moved to Prague, the collapse of the Liberal majority in the Austrian Parliament brought the steadily building tensions in Czech-German relations to a point of crisis. That year, the reactionary government of Count Eduard von Taaffe solidified its power by building an anti-Liberal parliamentary coalition that was dependent upon the good will—assured by imperial con-cessions—of a conglomerate of Czech-nationalist groups. In the early 1880s, Bohemia's Germans lost their historical control of commerce and government in newly opened elections that were a direct outcome of these concessions. They endured the imposition of a series of increasingly restrictive language ordinances, and they watched over an explosion of ethnic violence at the University of Prague that led to its division into Czech and German campuses during 1881 and 1882. Feeling abandoned by authorities in Vienna and facing increasingly open hostility at home, many among the city's Germans saw themselves, in the words of one, as residing in "a game preserve whose ground was always shrinking."[56]

Among those who called upon members of Prague's beleaguered German community to assume an offensive stance in their struggles with the Czechs

---

54. Richard Batka, *J. S. Bach*, Musiker-Biographien, no. 15 (Leipzig: Philipp Reclam, 1892), 5–6: "Allein J. S. Bachs bleibende Bedeutung liegt wohl nicht darin, daß er neue Harmonien zusammenzusetzen wußte...sondern darin, daß er der Erneuerer des deutschen Geistes gewesen."

55. The most comprehensive study of the Prague German community during the second half of the nineteenth century remains Gary B. Cohen, *The Politics of Ethnic Survival: Germans in Prague, 1861–1914* (Princeton: Princeton University Press, 1981). For a recent consideration of the politi-cal background, see also Hugh LeCaine Agnew, *The Czechs and the Lands of the Bohemian Crown*, Studies of Nationalities (Stanford: Hoover Institution Press, 2004), 102–61. A valuable overview of political events and a provocative look at their implications for Viennese music criticism are pro-vided in David Brodbeck, "Dvořák's Reception in Liberal Vienna: Language Ordinances, National Property, and the Rhetoric of *Deutschtum*," *Journal of the American Musicological Society* 60, no. 1 (2007), 71–131. Unless otherwise noted, the discussion that follows is based upon these sources.

56. The philosopher Emil Utitz, cited in Scott Spector, *Prague Territories: National Conflict and Cultural Innovation in Franz Kafka's Fin de Siècle*, Weimar and Now: German Cultural Criticism, no. 21 (Berkeley and Los Angeles: University of California Press, 2000), 3.

was the university historian Philipp Knoll, who founded the Society for the Advancement of German Art, Science, and Literature in Bohemia (Gesellschaft zur Förderung deutscher Wissenschaft, Kunst und Literatur in Böhmen) in an attempt to foster popular enthusiasm for the German cause. As Adler's correspondence with his lifelong friend Alexius Meinong reveals, Adler too felt deeply troubled by the political situation he encountered in his new hometown, and he soon began to associate with Knoll and his group.[57] It was in the journal of Knoll's organization, *Deutsche Arbeit* (*German Work*), that his essay on Mozart was eventually published. In a lecture delivered to the German Bohemian Woods Club (Böhmerwaldbund) in 1885, Knoll made clear the ideological position of the society with which Adler sympathized. He implored his fellow Bohemian Germans to dedicate themselves to a program of "national education" by celebrating "the achievements of our great men and the great deeds of our nation." And he argued that "the knowledge of everything marvelous that the nation's spiritual heroes [*Geisteshelden*] have accomplished in art and science [can] arouse considerable pride in belonging to such a nation."[58] In penning his lecture on *Don Giovanni*, Adler answered Knoll's call. By 1887, Prague's German Theater, where the opera had premiered, had come to "represent," in the words of the historian Scott Spector, the hopes of many Bohemian Germans for "the continuing cultural integration of Prague with German-speaking Europe."[59] Moreover, the 1787 premiere of the opera was precisely the kind of local German cultural achievement that Knoll and his organization sought to celebrate. And once again, as Spector's work suggests, the Wagnerian tone of Adler's statements was unsurprising, given his intentions. For Wagner was regarded by many late-century German-speaking Bohemians as a principal source of spiritual sustenance and inspiration in an increasingly hostile age.[60]

MONUMENTS OF MUSIC IN AUSTRIA

If Adler's work through 1887 suggests ambivalence with respect to the national question and significant tension between his cultural sympathies and his passion for positivist modes of inquiry, then the next major project upon which

57. See the letters sent by Adler to Meinong dated November 12, 1887, December 29, 1889, and November 7, 1892, published in Gabriele Johanna Eder, ed., *Alexius Meinong und Guido Adler. Eine Fruendschaft in Briefen*, Studien zur österreichischen Philosophie, no. 24 (Amsterdam and Atlanta: Rodopi, 1995), 117–18, 134–45, 139–40.

58. Philipp Knoll, "Über Nationalgefühl und nationale Erziehung" (1885), in *Beiträge zur heimischen Zeitgeschichte* (Prague: J. G. Calve, 1900), 241–42: "Ein weiteres wichtiges Hilfsmittel der nationalen Erziehung besitzen wir in der Schilderung des Wirkens unserer großen Männer und der großen Thaten unserer Nation. Die Kenntnis der geschichtlichen Großthaten, durch welche das eigene Volk fördernd eingegriffen hat in die Entwicklung der Menschheit, und die Kenntnis von all dem Herrlichen, das die Geisteshelden der Nation in Kunst und Wissenschaft geschaffen, ist in hohem Maße geeignet, einen edlen Stolz auf die Zugehörigkeit zu einer solchen Nation zu erwecken."

59. Spector, *Prague Territories*, 15.

60. Spector, *Prague Territories*, 15.

he embarked only complicates this image further. In the spring of 1888, he and Eduard Hanslick wrote to the Austrian Ministry of Culture and Education to propose a series of critical editions of works by historical composers. Their project, as they initially envisioned it, would embrace the musics of the whole of German-speaking Europe. As Elisabeth Hilscher has documented, however, Adler and Hanslick were quickly compelled to restrict its scope, partly on account of their Prussian colleagues' decision to pursue a similar project on their own and partly as a result of the ministry's decision that their undertaking should be a "purely Austrian" (*rein österreichische*) affair.[61] When the inaugural volumes of both the Prussian and the Austrian series of critical editions appeared in the early 1890s, it immediately became clear that the differences between them were not only matters of repertoire. Rather, the series represented two starkly different ways of negotiating cultural identity in late-century German-speaking Europe. In Leipzig, there appeared the *Monuments of German Music* (*Denkmäler deutscher Tonkunst*), whose editors declared in their inaugural preface that "making the works of history's outstanding German composers accessible for art and the study of art has finally been recognized as a duty of our age."[62] Habsburg Vienna countered the Prussians with Adler's *Monuments of Music in Austria* (*Denkmäler der Tonkunst in Österreich*). And like the title of the series itself, with its use of the national modifier in the prepositional (*in Austria*) rather than attributive (*German*) form, Adler's prefatory essay carefully skirted the politically charged question of just what the term "Austrian" might mean. Austria itself, it goes without saying, could be found on any map. But *Austrian*, as a marker of identity, was deeply problematic. "Naturally," Adler wrote, "the works of composers who were born or worked in Austria will receive particular attention." But he promised that his series would also "encompass" the works of "all nations whose representatives and works took root in the classically consecrated soil of Austrian music."[63] If the Prussians' endeavor was specific with respect to its national scope, what, then, was to be the national substance of Adler's?

As Celia Applegate and Pamela Potter have recently shown, the Prussian *Monuments of German Music* was launched as part of an ambitious endeavor to

61. Elizabeth Theresia Hilscher, *Denkmalpflege und Musikwissenschaft. Einhundert Jahre Gesellschaft zur Herausgabe der Tonkunst in Österreich (1893–1993)*, Wiener Veröffentlichungen zur Musikwissenschaft, no. 33 (Tutzing: Hans Schneider, 1995), 41–50 (cited at 49). On this transformation, see also Hilscher, "Gesamtstaat versus Nationalitäten. Zur Verbindung von Politik und Musikwissenschaft bei Guido Adler," *Studien zur Musikwissenschaft* 46 (1998), 239–48.

62. Samuel Scheidt, *Tabulatura nova*, ed. Max Seiffert (*Denkmäler deutscher Tonkunst*, vol. 1) (Leipzig: Breitkopf und Härtel, 1892), unnumbered prefatory page: "Die Werke hervorragender älterer deutscher Tonmeister der Kunst und Kunstwissenschaft von neuem zugänglich zu machen, ist längst als eine Aufgabe unserer Zeit erkannt worden."

63. Preface to Johann Joseph Fux, *Messen*, ed. Johannes Evangelist Habert and Gustav Adolf Glossner (*Denkmäler der Tonkunst in Österreich*, vol. 1) (Vienna: Artaria, 1894), v, vii: "Naturgemäss sollen besonders Compositionen von Tonsetzern aufgenommen werden, die in Oesterreich geboren sind oder daselbst gewirkt haben. ... die 'Denkmäler der Tonkunst in Oesterreich' alle Nationen umfassen sollen, deren Vertreter und deren Werke auf dem classisch geweihten Boden der österreichischen Musik zu finden sind."

convert a century of enthusiasm about an imagined German cultural nation into political support for Bismarck's newly founded German state. The project, they write, reflected awareness among Hohenzollern officialdom that "certain music could usefully demonstrate the Germanness of the new state and its kings."[64] For nearly a century, writers and activists from Herder to Wagner had touted the musical heritage of Europe's German speakers as evidence of the coherence and strength of an imagined cultural community. But the founding of Bismarck's Germany in 1871, which excluded Austria's German-speaking inhabitants, exploded that vision of a language-based, pan-European German nation. From the perspective of Bismarck and others in power, the *Monuments of German Music* series provided a golden opportunity to demonstrate that an inviolable link existed between the historical German cultural nation and the modern, geographically narrower state. The fruits of the former would provide the musical substance of the series. And the modern state would provide financial and administrative backing for the project.

This same complex of cultural and political circumstances proved more vexing for Prussia's neighbor to the south, where tension between images of state and nation had been a topic of pressing concern since the immediate postrevolutionary years.[65] Among many other Habsburg officials, Count Leo Thun-Hohenstein, head of the Austrian Ministry of Culture and Education placed in charge of educational reform in the wake of the 1848 Revolution, was acutely aware that Austria's historical experience clashed with language-based images of German nationhood in ways that Prussia's, Bavaria's, or Saxony's did not. Unlike the situation in north-central Europe, which was politically fragmented yet linguistically homogeneous, the Habsburg Empire was politically united yet peopled by a diverse array of Germans, Slavs, Yiddish-speakers, and Hungarians. Indeed, German speakers, at midcentury, constituted less than half of the Empire's population. Given this situation, Thun-Hohenstein realized, the Romantic discourse on German cultural nationhood could only exert a culturally alienating—and, potentially, politically disintegrating—force within the Habsburg domain.

Amid the wave of educational reforms that brought Hanslick and Herbartianism to the University of Vienna, Thun-Hohenstein called upon the historian Josef Alexander Helfert to devise a way of denationalizing the popular and scholarly discourse on Austria's culture and history. The goal of this effort was to promote an image of Austria's historical identity that would counter the linguistically defined notions of national belonging that seemed, in the wake the 1848 Revolution, to portend nothing but sectarian division. For Helfert, the answer to the Ministry's dilemma was clear. Henceforth, he declared in his *On National History and the Present State of Its Cultivation in Austria* (1853), Austrian letters would need to abandon the notion that Austrian identity is rooted in language

---

64. Applegate and Potter, "Germans as the 'People of Music,'" 15–16 (cited at 15). My discussion in this paragraph is based upon this source.

65. See Alphons Lhotsky, "Geschichtsforschung und Geschichtsschreibung in Österreich," *Historische Zeitschrift* 189 (1959), 379–448 (esp. 427–31). My discussion in this paragraph and the one that follows is based primarily upon this source.

or cultural artifact. Instead, it must stress the historically—indeed, organically—unifying power of a benevolent Habsburg monarchy. "From the start," Helfert explained, "we must make clear that we do not use the word *national* in an ethnographic sense, but in a political one." He continued:

> For us, *national history* is not the history of any particular racially-defined group selected from among the many-tongued and many-colored peoples of the human species, but the history of a populace [*Bevölkerung*] that is united territorially and politically, that is embraced by the bonds of common authority, and that is bound by the protection of common laws. *Austrian national history* is, for us, the history of the whole Austrian state and the entire Austrian population [*Gesammtvolk*], in which people of diverse ancestries, customs, and levels of cultivation are entwined as if organically.[66]

To promote such a view of "national" identity, the Imperial Ministry of Culture and Education subsidized the publication of Helfert's monumental *Austrian History for the People* (*Österreichische Geschichte für das Volk*), in seventeen volumes, over the course of the following decade.[67]

Before Helfert's study was completed in 1867, however, a new round of troubles had begun to befall the empire. Austria's defeat in the war with Prussia, the Hungarian compromise of 1867, and the founding of Bismarck's German *Reich* all contributed to a deepening crisis of public confidence in the Habsburg monarchy. Indeed, many felt that the empire as a whole was losing its relevance in modern Europe. Against the backdrop of Georg von Schönerer's call for the union of Austria's German-speaking regions with Bismarck's German state, the political journal *Schwarzgelb* published an essay in 1888 in which an anonymous author appealed to the Austrian populace for their continued faith in the Habsburg crown. By virtue of its bitingly sarcastic tone, however, this document testifies perhaps most powerfully to the sense of cultural alienation and political inadequacy that gripped much of Austria's German-speaking population in the final decades of the century. "What have we achieved in the history of the world, and what has been achieved by the Prussians," the essay's author, widely believed to be the Habsburg Crown Prince Rudolf, asked. "Since when has there even existed a Prussian history? What a glorious past can Vienna claim, and what a laughable parvenu is Berlin in comparison! And *we* are supposed to bow our heads before this improvised great, which was born only yesterday and could

---

66. Josef Alexander Helfert, *Über Nationalgeschichte und den gegenwärtigen Stand ihrer Pflege in Oesterreich* (Prague: J. G. Calve, 1853), 1–2: "Voraus müssen wir erklären, dass wir den Ausdruck 'national' nicht im ethnografischen, sondern im politischen Sinne nehmen. ... *Nationalgeschichte* ist uns nicht die Geschichte irgend einer racenmäßig ausgezeichneten Gruppe aus den vielzüngigen und vielfarbigen Stämmen des Menschengeschlechtes, sondern die Geschichte einer territorial und politisch zusammengehörenden, von dem Bande der gleichen Autorität umschlungenen, unter dem Schutze des gleichen Gesetzes verbundenen Bevölkerung. *Österreichische Nationalgeschichte* ist uns die Geschichte des österreichischen Gesammtstaates und Gesammtvolkes, als dessen organisch in einander verschlungene Glieder all die nach Abstammung, Bildung und Gesittung verschiedenen Stämme erscheinen."

67. See Lhotsky, "Geschichtsforschung," 427–28.

very well collapse tomorrow? No, never!"[68] It was within this desperate political climate that Adler's *Monuments of Music in Austria* was launched.

Adler's initial inquiry to the Ministry of Culture and Education, submitted in the spring of 1888, was met with cautious interest and no official action. A serious commitment came only four years later, and it was sparked, as Hilscher observes, by a slight. When the first volume of the Prussian *Monuments of German Music* was published in Leipzig in 1891, the Prussian government sent the Austrian ministry a copy, along with an open invitation to Austrian scholars to contribute their efforts to the Prussians' series.[69] Within months of this embarrassing incident, the Austrian ministry gave Adler the go-ahead to convene a committee to oversee the preparation of a comparable series of its own, one that would be, in the ministry's terms, a "purely Austrian undertaking." In its statutes, submitted in the autumn of 1893, Adler's committee promised to represent proudly "the musical history of the fatherland" (*vaterländische Musikgeschichte*). The inaugural volume of *Monuments of Music in Austria*, consisting of four masses by Johann Joseph Fux, was published at the beginning of the following year.[70]

As it happened, the political exigencies that launched Adler's series also transformed it from one of *großdeutsch* purview into an endeavor celebrating the deliberately denationalized vision of Austria's historical identity described by Helfert in 1853 and embraced by Habsburg officialdom ever since. Just where Adler's own convictions lay with regard to this transformation, one cannot be sure.[71] But remarks he published in the series' inaugural preface echoed Helfert's assertions of forty-one years earlier. "In Austria," Adler wrote, "where music has been cultivated broadly for ages and where the artistic tastes of ruling dynasties found the heartiest echo in the natural disposition of the populace, we find an abundant store of works from music's history that deserve our veneration."[72] Such works, he explained, were among those things that had, for ages, united the diverse array of peoples who resided within the Habsburg lands. But the focal point of Austria's musical life, Adler continued, had always been Vienna, the spiritual hub and

---

68. From *Schwarzgelb. Politisches Journal. Organ für altösterreichische und gesamtstaatliche Ideen* (October 31, 1888); cited in Heer, *Der Kampf um die österreichischen Identität*, 254: "Was haben wir in der Weltgeschichte geleistet und was die Preußen? Seit wann gibt es überhaupt eine preußische Geschichte? Welche glänzende Vergangenheit hat Wien aufzuweisen und welch ein lächerlicher Parvenue ist Berlin dagegen? Und wir sollen uns beugen vor dieser improvisierten Größe, die gestern erst geboren worden und morgen schon zusammenbrechen kann? Nein, nimmermehr!"

69. Hilscher, *Denkmalpflege*, 53–55.

70. The committee's statutes are reprinted in Hilscher, *Denkmalpflege*, 221–23 (cited at 221). For an illuminating discussion of the rivalry between the Prussian and Austrian series as it stood a decade or so after the period considered here, see Rehding, *Hugo Riemann*, 138–49.

71. Adler's autobiography, which includes a lengthy discussion of the founding of the series, sheds little light on this matter. See Adler, *Wollen und Wirken. Aus dem Leben eines Musikhistorikers* (Vienna: Universal Edition, 1935), 47–76.

72. Preface to Johann Joseph Fux, *Messen*, v: "In Oesterreich, wo der Tonkunst seit jeher eine ausgebreitete Pflege zu Theil wurde, wo der Kunstsinn der regierenden Dynastien in der natürlichen Anlage der Bevölkerung den kräftigsten Widerhall fand, liegt ein überreicher Schatz ruhmwürdiger Tonwerke der Vergangenheit."

physical seat of the Habsburg dynasty. "Since the time of Kaiser Maximilian I, the royal Court Chapel in Vienna, which looked after music of all kinds—for chamber and opera—along with the churchly service, has been a sparkling mirror of Western art of the most distinguished sorts," he wrote. "Artists of all lands and kingdoms, often the best of their age, converged upon it seeking fame and glory." And just as those artists had once converged upon the Austrian Court, so too would Adler's *Monuments of Music in Austria* draw their works together again. In this way, it would celebrate anew the historical communion of the Habsburg peoples, and it would do so, as had happened in the past, through the medium of an imperial institution—in this case, not the royal chapel but the *Monuments* series itself. "The selection of works for publication," Adler promised, "will be as universal as art in Austria."[73]

With the founding of his series in 1893 and 1894, Adler found himself, unambiguously, on one side of the debate about Austria's national question. Whether he found himself there by choice or circumstance, however, is a question without a clear answer. Considering the positions he had assumed in his lectures on Bach and Mozart and his essays on harmony, one cannot help but suspect that he was at least a little troubled by the way in which things turned out. But in 1894, Adler was no longer an upstart musicologist and a sometime public speaker, and he could no longer afford to indulge such causes as Philipp Knoll's Bohemian rabble-rousing. In the intervening years, he had become a prominent member of the Habsburg civil service, occupying an important professorship at one of the empire's leading institutions of learning. By the time of the launch of his *Monuments* series, the radicalism of his early years had become a thing of the past.[74] But as we will see in the final part of this chapter, echoes of Adler's early concerns would surface yet again. And their effects upon his scholarly work would hardly be inconsequential.

RICHARD WAGNER (1904)

When Adler moved from Prague to Vienna to assume a full professorship in 1898, he turned his attention, as we saw in chapter 5, away from the history of harmony and polyphony and back to the figure who had first sparked his interest

---

73. Preface to Johann Joseph Fux, *Messen*, v: "Und gerade die kaiserliche Hofcapelle in Wien, welche neben dem Kirchendienste Musik aller Art in Kammer und Oper zu besorgen hatte, wurde seit Kaiser Maximilian I. ein leuchtender Spiegel der abendländischen Kunst vornehmster Art. Hier trafen sich Künstler aller Länder und Reiche, oft die Besten ihrer Zeit, um sich Ruhm und Verdienst zu schaffen. ... Universal wie die Kunst in Oesterreich soll auch die Auswahl der zur Veröffentlichung gelangenden Werke sein."

74. Indeed, as Margaret Notley has observed, in 1906 Adler celebrated a supranational image of Austrian instrumental music in a commemorative lecture on Mozart, in a manner that resonates with the imagery in his inaugural preface to the *Monuments* series. In the 1906 lecture, Adler drew an explicit parallel between Mozart's compositional style, in which "the customs of the Austrian peoples are interwoven in musical works," and his own hope that "statecraft [may] join the particularities of the various peoples [of the Habsburg Empire] into a higher unity." See Notley, *Lateness and Brahms: Music and Culture in the Twilight of Viennese Liberalism*, AMS Studies in Music, no. 3 (Oxford: Oxford University Press, 2007), 216–17 (cited at 217).

in music study during his student years. And as was the case with the essays on Wagner that he published in the *Neue freie Presse* and the Prague daily *Bohemia*, so too did he attempt to connect his first book-length study, *Richard Wagner* (1904), to his earlier concerns. As he wrote in the preface to that book, his studies of Wagner constituted "the fruit of thirty years of thought" (*die Frucht dreißigjähriger Denkarbeit*).[75] But over the course of those three decades, Adler's activism had lost much of its youthful edge. In 1904, Adler wrote on Wagner as a historian rather than as a polemicist, and he promised a reasoned, dispassionate look at the artist whose "ardent apostle" he had once declared himself to be.[76] *Richard Wagner*, its author promised, would consider the composer's artistic contributions in "strictly"—or "rigidly"—historical (*streng historischer*) terms. Wherever possible, the historian would let Wagner "speak for himself." He would avoid getting bogged down in the contentious secondary literature on the composer and his legacy. And he would likewise avoid paying heed to the views of "living personalities" so as to "remove all traces of personal coloring from the historical picture" developed in his book. Echoing the sentiment that had pervaded his inaugural lecture to the university's faculty six years earlier, Adler declared that he published *Richard Wagner* "in the service of art and its study" (*im Dienste der Kunst und ihrer Wissenschaft*). To be sure, he acknowledged the appropriation of Wagner's ideas by such radical polemicists as Constantin Frantz and Paul de Lagarde, and he wearily noted that Wagner was widely regarded as "a regenerator, a reformer, a philosopher, a politician, and the founder of a religion." In contrast to such positions, however, Adler promised to consider Wagner solely and exclusively as an *artist*.[77] In short, he pledged to carry out his work in the carefully reasoned, dispassionate manner advocated in his disciplinary polemics.

Yet, in spite of his promise to consider Wagner's artistic contributions apart from those forces that had shaped their reception, Adler opened his book with an attempt to expose the mythology that Wagner had cultivated about the origins and uniquely German qualities of his own creative work. With respect to Wagner's bluster in *Opera and Drama* about inventing a new musical language capable of revealing to the listener the inner thoughts of dramatic protagonists, Adler argued that the composer was hardly the pioneer he had claimed to be. Indeed, Adler observed, Wagner was, in this regard, in league with history's very first composers of opera: Jacapo Peri and members of the Florentine Camerata active at the turn of the seventeenth century. The same, he argued, could be said of Wagner's ambition to combine music, dance, and poetry into a "total artwork" or *Gesamtkunstwerk*. Considered from a broadly historical perspective, Adler explained, Wagner's supposedly revolutionary music drama is "not only an artwork of the future, but also an artwork of the past."[78] Elaborating upon this point, he wrote:

75. Adler, *Richard Wagner. Vorlesungen gehalten an der Universität zu Wien* (Leipzig: Breitkopf und Härtel, 1904), v.

76. Adler, "Ein Bayreuther Protest (Zur Parsifal-Frage)," *Neue freie Presse* (January 11, 1903), 10.

77. Adler, *Richard Wagner*, 2.

78. Adler, *Richard Wagner*, 3–8 (cited at 7): "Dies ist also nicht allein ein Kunstwerk der Zukunft, sondern es war auch ein Kunstwerk der Vergangenheit."

Many artists have sought to unite the grace of the melodic line with the strength of [verbal] expression. Such works were already created in opera's first century by M. A. Cesti, and then by Alessandro Scarlatti. Gluck's *Orpheus* is a typical work of this sort. After the Englishman Purcell and the Frenchman Rameau, our Mozart emerged as the ideal expositor of this ideal. And later, in the first period of German Romanticism, came Weber with his *Freischütz*. Wagner argued that the period in which Weber and the first Romantics were active saw the rebirth of the German *Volk* from out of the German spirit. Yet these developments did not occur, as he claimed, "in complete opposition to the general Renaissance of Europe's more recent peoples of culture [*Kulturvölker*]." Rather, they occurred in intimate connection with it. They constituted but one of its stages.[79]

Throughout the first nine chapters of his book, Adler cast a critical eye upon many of Wagner's claims of artistic originality, both for his own work and for the qualities of that culture that the artist had posited his work to represent. In case after case, Adler endeavored to demonstrate that Wagner was not a unique or pioneering figure but a brilliant synthesizer of trends and ideas that were already apparent in the creative endeavors of artists and cultures from years and even centuries past. "With respect to artistic practice," Adler summed up his argument on this issue, "Wagner is not a revolutionary, but one who built organically upon what had come before."[80]

Significantly, however, the critical stance that Adler assumed when discussing Wagner's musical contributions and claims on their behalf did not carry over into his substantial consideration of the composer's writings on contemporary culture and society. And this is important, for Wagner's prose—even more, perhaps, than his operas and music dramas—had made a profound impact upon virtually all aspects of cultural and political discourse in late-century German-speaking Europe.[81] Now taking literally his prefatory promise to strip the residue of reception from the texts he considered, Adler frequently reverted, when discussing Wagner's cultural criticism, to summary and paraphrase. He did this even when considering some of Wagner's most troubling and subsequently influential statements on race, religion, and German identity. Without any trace of

79. Adler, *Richard Wagner*, 5: "Manche Künstler suchten Anmut der melodischen Linien mit Kraft des Ausdrucks zu vereinen. Solche Werke wurden schon in dem ersten Jahrhundert der Oper geschaffen, so von M. A. Cesti, dann von Alessandro Scarlatti; ein typisches Werk dieser Art ist 'Orfeo' von Gluck. Nach dem Engländer Purcell und dem Fronzosen Rameau kommt da als höchstes Ideal unser Mozart und ferner in der ersten Epoche der deutschen romantischen Oper Weber mit seinem 'Freischütz'. Für diese Zeit, da Weber und die ersten Romantiker schufen, paßt die Behauptung Wagners, daß die eigene Wiedergeburt des detuschen Volkes aus dem deutschen Geiste hervorgegangen sei; dies vollzog sich nicht—wie er hinzufügt—'im vollen Gegensatze zu der übrigen Renaissance der neueren Kulturvölker Europas', sondern vielmehr im innigen Zusammenhange mit ihr als eine ihrer Etappen."

80. Adler, *Richard Wagner*, 118: "Wagner ist in der Kunstausübung nicht Revolutionär, sondern organischer Fortbildner."

81. The influence of Wagner's writings upon the cultural and political discourse of the period has been widely studied. See, for instance, Schorske, *Fin-de-Siècle Vienna*; McGrath, *Dionysian Art and Populist Politics in Austria* (New Haven: Yale University Press, 1974); and Allan Janik, *Wittgenstein's Vienna Revisited* (New Brunswick, New Jersey: Transaction, 2001).

critical engagement, he summarized, for instance, Wagner's arguments in "Art and Revolution" (1849) about the uniquely universal character of German culture. "From out of Germanic culture [*Germanentum*]," Adler wrote, "in which, despite its embrace of Christianity, there remained a powerful impulse toward productive work and a passion for daring undertakings, there could emerge an art directed toward and belonging to all men."[82] And of the composer's "German Art and German Politics" (1867), Adler reported, again without a hint of critical reflection, that Wagner "counseled the princes on the realization of those ideas that... gave rise to the resurrection of the German people from out of the German spirit... and that are intimately connected to that spirit's universality."[83]

Proceeding from these summaries to more general remarks about the "style and character" of Wagner's prose, Adler launched into a string of cautionary statements whose collective effect was to separate the artist from the troubled legacy of his work. To begin, Adler explained, "Wagner wrote as an artist, not as a theorist" of history or contemporary society. And "the fervent excitement that dominates his style lends his musings—as he himself acknowledged—more of a poetic than an academic or critical character."[84] "As a writer," Adler continued, "Wagner is most original and natural when laying out his theses on the music drama." In contrast, he asserted, the composer's statements on social and political issues were almost invariably derivative. Indeed, he argued, such statements can hardly be considered Wagner's own. "With respect to all other subjects about which he—as a spirit with a broad purview—spoke, wrote, and cast judgment," Adler observed, "the influences of many other authors is apparent." Referring implicitly to the work of Frantz, Julius Langbehn, and other polemicists of their ilk, Adler argued that this latter point "is especially the case with those ideas that, since Wagner's death, have been broadly disseminated in the ever-growing literature considering the 'regeneration' of mankind."[85] With the composer himself

82. Adler, *Richard Wagner*, 124–25 (cited at 125): "Aus dem Germanentum, in welchem trotz der Annahme des Christentums ein starker Tätigkeitstrieb, die Lust zu kühnen Unternehmungen geblieben sei, könne eine Kunst hervorgehen, welche sich an alle Menschen wende, allen Menschen zu eigen sei."

83. Adler, *Richard Wagner*, 127–28 (cited at 127): "Er ermahnt die Fürsten zur Durchführung jener Ideen, welche, gegründet auf dem klassischen Humanitätsprinzip, die Wiedergeburt des deutschen Volkes aus deutschem Geiste im achtzehnten Jahrhundert hervorgerufen haben und im Zusammenhang mit der Universalität des deutschen Geistes stehen."

84. Adler, *Richard Wagner*, 142: "Wagner schreibt nicht als Theoretiker sondern als Künstler. ... Die begeisterte Erregtheit, die seinen Stil beherrschte, gab—wie Wagner selbst hervorhebt—seinen Aufzeichnungen mehr einen dichterischen als wissenschaftlichen kritischen Charakter."

85. Adler, *Richard Wagner*, 144–45: "Am originellsten, am ursprünglichsten tritt Wagner als Schriftsteller bei der Aufstellung seiner Thesen über das musikalische Drama auf. ... In den Anschauungen auf allen übrigen Gebieten, über die er als weitausschauender Geist urteilte, sprach und schrieb, lassen sich die Einflüsse von diesem und jenem Autor nachweisen. Dazu gehören besonders jene Ideen, welche in der nach Wagners Tode sich auftürmenden Literatur unter dem Gesamtbegriffe der 'Regeneration' des Menschengeschlechtes breitgetreten werden." Further consideration of the trope of regeneration in turn-of-the-century German cultural and political discourse is provided in chapter 5 of the present study. For an illuminating discussion of this topic from a somewhat broader perspective, see Shearer West, *Fin de Siècle: Art and Society in an Age of Uncertainty* (Woodstock, NY: Overlook, 1994), 122–38.

thus pardoned for any misunderstandings to which his work had given rise, Adler turned his attention back to one of Wagner's most deeply problematic texts.

In his consideration of Wagner's notorious essay "Judaism in Music" (1851), Adler indeed seem tempted at times to break from the "rigidly historical" tack that he charted in the preface to his book. But as we witness him struggling to maintain what he took for scholarly composure, we also find him treading upon some troubling ethical terrain. Adler began his discussion of "Judaism in Music" with an account of Wagner's turbulent relationship with his onetime mentor, the French composer Giacomo Meyerbeer. He recalled how Wagner was "bitterly sickened" by the success of Meyerbeer's opera Le Prophète, in whose shadow the young composer felt his own work to recede in the public's view.[86] He explained that Wagner regarded the brilliant reception of Le Prophète as proof of a generalized critical insensitivity to great music, which Wagner considered a danger not only to the reception of his own operas but to German art as a whole. In response to that perception, Adler explained, Wagner lashed out against what he imagined to be an organized clique standing in opposition to his work. And that clique, Wagner famously insisted, was peopled by critics and listeners who were, like Meyerbeer, Jewish.[87]

At this point, Adler declared that "Wagner's suggestions are unjustified." But he did so for reasons that are revealing. Significantly, Adler did not examine the historical contexts, personal prejudices, or cultural circumstances that might have led Wagner to imagine a Jewish conspiracy aligned against him. And he did not attempt, as the essayist Eduard Bernsdorf had done a half-century earlier, to probe the cultural biases and broad societal implications of Wagner's inflammatory remarks.[88] Instead, Adler simply observed that none of the supposedly Jewish antagonists whose names Wagner adduced in his subsequently published "Explanation of Judaism in Music" were, in fact, Jewish. "Of all the enemies whom Wagner mentions by name or alludes to in his 'Explanation of Judaism in Music,'" he wrote, "not a single one is a Jew: Hans Bischoff, Moritz Hauptmann, Otto Jahn, Gustav Freytag, Eduard Hanslick."[89] "One would have expected more level-headedness, even from the agitated artist," Adler observed. Yet he immediately proceeded to make a case for pardoning Wagner's assertions. "But he has an excuse," the historian pleaded. "Or at least one can understand what he did, even if it was unjustified. For as he himself admitted, he was a person prone to extremes."[90]

86. Adler, Richard Wagner, 186–87 (cited at 187). For Wagner's essay, see Wagner, 5:66–85; Wagner/Ellis, 3:75–122.

87. Among recent contributions to the extensive literature on Wagner's "Judaism in Music" and the anti-Semitic positions evident in this and much of his work, see especially Frisch, German Modernism, esp. 11–12; Salmi, Imagined Germany, esp. 59–61; Taruskin, The Oxford History of Western Music, 3:227–30; and Bryan Magee, The Tristan Chord: Wagner and Philosophy (New York: Henry Holt, 2000), 343–80.

88. On Bernsdorf's reply to Wagner's essay, see Taruskin, The Oxford History of Western Music, 3:228.

89. Adler, Richard Wagner, 188: "Von all seinen Gegnern, die Wagner in den 'Aufklärungen' über das Judentum in der Musik' namentlich aufführt oder die er meint, ist aber nicht ein einziger ein Jude: Hans Bischoff, Moritz Hauptmann, Otto Jahn, Gustav Freitag, Eduard Hanslick. Die Hindeutungen Wagners sind unberechtigt."

90. Adler, Richard Wagner, 189: "Etwas mehr Maß hätte man auch von dem erregten Künstler erwarten dürfen. Doch für ihn gibt es eine Entschuldigung, vielmehr kann man sein Vorgehen verstehen, wenn auch nicht rechtfertigen; sagt er doch von sich selbst, er bewege sich in Extremen."

After thus dismissing "Judaism in Music" as a product of envy and naïve hot-headedness, Adler beat a hasty retreat from the essay, invoking the cover of his prefatory remarks to return to his focus on Wagner's music. "This is not the place," he wrote, "to engage in polemics about this theme, as that would lead us away from our primary charge, and because it has no significant, actual bearing upon our consideration of Wagner's art."[91] He appended to his discussion the following statement, attempting to turn his readers' attention back to more pleasant aspects of Wagner's legacy:

> We will not make any further attempts to refute Wagner's *belles lettres* on the topic of "regeneration," which have given rise to all sorts of confusion within the circles of his followers and far beyond them as well. This has already been attempted from many different sides and by voices far better suited to that purpose. May we permit ourselves only to observe that, in his consideration of this theme, [Wagner] sank to platitudes that do not seem worthy of the positions he took on other questions of artistic, social, and ethical import.[92]

With this, Adler took leave of Wagner's prose, to return to the safer, more comfortable world of the composer's musical achievements.

In *Richard Wagner*, the contradictions inherent in Adler's musicological program, first observed at the end of chapter 5, become readily apparent to the present-day reader and raise some troubling ethical questions. As he made clear in the preface to his book, Adler undertook his study in an attempt to attain what he called, in his "Music and Musicology" of 1898, the "highest goal" of musicological research: "to work on behalf of art through the knowledge of art."[93] That is, he hoped to shed light, by way of carefully reasoned, scholarly discourse, upon the contributions of a misunderstood figure and thereby to help a new generation of composers understand and subsume in their own creative work the creative substance of Wagner's. And so when he lapsed, under the cover of scientific objectivity, into paraphrase and a recitation of influences when discussing Wagner's most inflammatory statements on race, religion, and cultural identity, he seemed to retreat from the ethical responsibilities entailed in the pedagogical stance he took. After all, might not the historian's noncommittal remarks about Wagner's assertions signal his tacit approval of whatever his readers might make of them, or however they might respond to Wagner in their own creative endeavors?

At this point, one might, in Adler's defense, invoke another of the musicologist's bedrock disciplinary convictions, likewise voiced in his 1898 lecture:

91. Adler, *Richard Wagner*, 189: "Es ist hier über dieses Thema keine Polemik zu führen, weil wir sonst von unseren Hauptaufgaben abgeführt würden und es in keinem inneren, sachlichen Verhältnis steht zu dem, was über die Kunst Richard Wagners vorzubringen ist."

92. Adler, *Richard Wagner*, 189: "Wagners Belleitäten auf dem Gebiete der Regeneration, die in den Kreisen seiner Anhänger und darüber hinaus mancherlei Verwirrung anrichteten, haben wir hier nicht weiter zurückzuweisen. Es ist dies schon von verschiedenen Seiten aus geschehen, von Stimmen, die zu dieser Mission mehr berufen erscheinen. Es möge nur gestattet sein, zu bemerken, daß er in der Behandlung dieses Themas zu Gemeinplätzen herabsteigt, wie dies seiner sonstigen Haltung in Erörterung künstlerischer, sozialer, ethischer Fragen nicht ganz würdig erscheint."

93. Adler, "Musik und Musikwissenschaft. Akademische Antrittsrede, gehalten am 26. Oktober 1898 an der Universität Wien," *Jahrbuch der Musikbibliothek Peters* 5 (1898), 31.

that the scholar must respect the work of living artists, whatever its character might be. He insisted only that their musics exhibit a respect for tradition—that they be evidently rooted, in some way or other, in the cultural heritage of the nation. But here, I would argue, one encounters an essential contradiction. For in spite of Adler's declared aversion to Hanslick-like subjectivism, enshrined in his appeals for the musicologist's good-willed suspension of criticism and censure, his Nietzsche-inspired dedication to "struggl[ing] on behalf of culture" by promoting "the production of the genius" was predicated nonetheless upon a pair of essential value judgments.[94] Namely, which modern musics are sufficiently rooted in a culture's history to deserve the musicologist's respect and advocacy? And which aspects of a nation's historical experience are worthy of being transformed into the "living" art of the present? In light of these questions, and the latter especially, Adler's discussion of "Judaism in Music" can only seem evasive. To be sure, the historian did seem troubled at times by the methodological position staked out in the preface to his book. And in his consideration of Wagner's problematic essay, we witness him, in a rare moment, struggling to maintain a mode of discourse free of "all traces of personal coloring." But in concluding his discussion by directing his readers' attention away from moral quandaries raised and back to their rightful "primary charge" of studying dispassionately Wagner's music, Adler privileged empiricism over criticism, "scientific" objectivity over a critical engagement with German cultural history. In making this move, Adler turned his back upon the Nietzschean tradition that he ostensibly sought to uphold. And in doing that, as we will see in the epilogue to this study, he anticipated the position of a new generation of musicologists, dedicated to a brand of positivist scholarship more radical than anything openly advocated by the historian himself.

As Leon Botstein has suggested in his pioneering study of Adler's Vienna, when read against the backdrop of our knowledge of the tragedy that befell Adler and other German Jews in the 1930s and 1940s, Adler's position, as we have seen it evinced in *Richard Wagner*, "can only be considered...poignant, if naïve."[95] Indeed, the musicologist could only assume the stance that he did on account of his abiding faith in the power of reason to conquer the ignorance, bigotry, and irrationality that he already detected in the cultural and political discourse that surrounded him. In an age that had seen a flourishing of political anti-Semitism, racist polemics, and the rise of innumerable ideologies of social and cultural division, Adler could still declare, in response to "Judaism in Music," his intention "to leave to others the task of drawing further conclusions" from Wagner's

---

94. Friedrich Nietzsche, "Schopenhauer as Educator," in *Untimely Meditations*, ed. Daniel Breazeale, trans. R. J. Hollingdale, Cambridge Texts in the History of Philosophy (Cambridge: Cambridge University Press, 1997), 163.

95. Leon Botstein, "Music and Its Public: Habits of Listening and the Crisis of Musical Modernism in Vienna, 1870–1914" (Ph.D. diss., Harvard University, 1985), 1391.

remarks. He only appended some parting words about how he hoped the discussion would unfold:

> In considering these questions, those passions that have been so pathologically aroused in our time may play no role. Instead, they must be confronted in a candid, manly fashion and calmly discussed, and all points of disagreement must be considered circumspectly. We place our confidence in the judgment of history. We only trust that [those judgments] will be not be constructed upon false "foundations," which, proceeding from false premises, will lead to monstrous conclusions.[96]

"Adler," Botstein writes, "assimilated provincial Jew of middle-class professional origins, who rose to prominence through learning, turned to music and culture ... as an effective means of preserving the Imperial Austrian ideal" at a time when that ideal was under threat from a bewildering array of directions. Until the end, Botstein continues, Adler remained convinced that "culture and music in the classical tradition could combat barbarism, social conflict, decadence and decline."[97] Surely Adler believed that the same could be said for those scientifically inspired modes of research to which he dedicated his life. But as we know, the effectiveness of Adler's attempts to negotiate the cultural crises of his time through these means would ultimately prove nil. Science and rationalistic modes of inquiry were wholly ineffective weapons with which to combat the political realities of his age. In this regard, Adler shared his fate with many of his contemporaries. For his faith in the power of reason to triumph over irrationality—of tolerance to stamp out intolerance, of moderation to trump radicalism—was nothing other than enduring faith in the guiding tenets of Austrian liberalism. And by 1904, that liberal tradition was severely beleaguered—not quite extinguished, but drawing its last breaths.

96. Adler, *Richard Wagner*, 189–90: "Die weiteren Schlußfolgerungen zu ziehen, möge anderen überlassen bleiben. Bei diesen Fragen darf nicht die Empfindlichkeit eine Rolle spielen, die leider in unserer Zeit so krankhaft erregt ist; sondern offenes, mannhaftes Gegenübertreten, ruhige Erörterung und besonnene Erwägung aller Streitpunkte. Vertrauen wir ruhig dem Urteile der Geschichte. Nur darf diese nicht auf falsche 'Grundlagen' gestellt werden, die, von falschen Prämissen ausgehend, zu monströsen Schlußfolgerungen führen."

97. Botstein, "Music and Its Public," 1363.

INTO THE TWENTIETH CENTURY

When Adler turned away from Nietzsche's program for historical study at the end of *Richard Wagner*, he seemed to anticipate a variety of positivism that he himself never advocated. That radical variety, which rigidly shunned (or proposed to shun) all value judgments in the name of scientific objectivity, became, as Joseph Kerman has shown, a significant force in music study in the postwar years.[1] While the scholarship of Adler, Hanslick, and Schenker was deeply contested and fraught with ambivalence, the later phenomenon described by Kerman was distinctly self-assured. And though charting the emergence of the latter is a project for another book, it seems appropriate, in light of Adler's turn, to conclude the present one by suggesting some paths by which the positivism of Adler and his contemporaries came to assume a more radical guise in later decades. To this end, we might do well to consider a pair of responses to the late nineteenth-century discourse on music registered by two prominent writers active at the beginning of the twentieth: Arnold Schoenberg and Ernst Kurth. These two figures drew very different conclusions from the work of Adler and his colleagues, and their contributions suffered markedly different fates in the academic culture of the postwar era. In those responses and their fates, I would suggest, we find a hint at the origins of more recent developments.

When Schenker published "Routine in Music" and "More Art!" in 1896 and 1897, he indulged, as we saw in chapter 4, a fascination for scientifically oriented music study that was shared by many in his day. And though he abandoned the convictions espoused in those essays within a handful of years, his youthful effort to demythologize the creative process was taken up by Schoenberg, an acquaintance, after 1900. Through the medium of Schoenberg's writings, especially those collected and published in English under the title *Style and Idea*, that effort would become a central pillar of a decidedly modernist aesthetic of music that

---

1. Joseph Kerman, "How We Got Into Analysis, and How to Get Out," *Critical Inquiry* 7, no. 2 (1980), 311–31, repr. in *Write All These Down: Essays on Music* (Berkeley and Los Angeles: University of California Press, 1994), 12–32; and Kerman, *Contemplating Music: Challenges to Musicology* (Cambridge, MA: Harvard University Press, 1985).

would prove profoundly influential throughout much of the twentieth century.[2] In a series of essays published from the 1920s through the 1940s, Schoenberg combated his contemporaries' persistent faith in the same speculative theory of the creative process that Schenker had tried to refute in his late nineteenth-century work. Indeed, Schoenberg framed his arguments in terms that might be taken directly from "Routine in Music" and "More Art." In Schoenberg's statements on the creative act, Schenker's abortive experiments with an empiricist ideology of music study lived on.

To take one example, Schoenberg's desire to expose the "misconception" of the "general belief that the constituent qualities of music belong to two categories as regards their origin...to the heart or the brain" drove him, in 1946, to pen his "Heart and Brain in Music." There, he recounted his own experiences as a creative artist that confounded the attempts of critics and philosophers to formulate an abstract view of the creative process along the lines of the conscious/unconscious paradigm of creativity described by countless nineteenth-century writers. In that essay, Schoenberg recounted moments in which passages of extreme contrapuntal complexity seemed to pour forth directly from the unconscious reaches his mind, and other occasions when some of his most trivial-sounding passages required the greatest degree of rational deliberation to complete. Drawing evidence from such examples, Schoenberg proclaimed, like Schenker in "More Art," that the nature of the creative act is of such complexity that only practicing musicians can comprehend it.[3]

In another essay, "On the Question of Modern Composition Teaching" (1929), Schoenberg asserted, again like Schenker, that "the true art of composition (like true science) will always remain a secret science. It already counted as such at the time of the Netherlanders, for all the doubting scorn of graceless historians. It has to be so, not just because the initiated"—practicing composers—"are forbidden to make it known, but, particularly, because the others are unable to grasp it."[4] And in his famous essay "Brahms the Progressive" (1947), based on a radio lecture penned fourteen years earlier, Schoenberg portrayed the departed artist in terms that echo the concluding lines of Schenker's "More Art." "There is no doubt that Brahms believed in working out the ideas which he called 'gifts of grace,'" Schoenberg wrote;

> Hard labour is, to a trained mind, no torture, but rather a pleasure. As I have stated on another occasion: if a mathematician's or a chess player's mind can perform such miracles of the brain, why should a musician's mind not be able to do it? After all, an improviser must anticipate before playing, and composing is a slowed-down improvisation; often one cannot write fast enough to keep up with the stream of ideas. But a craftsman likes to be conscious of what he produces; he is proud of the ability of his hands, of the flexibility of his mind, of his subtle sense of balance, of his never-failing logic, of the multitude of variations, and last but not least of the

---

2. Arnold Schoenberg, *Style and Idea*, ed. Leonard Stein, trans. Leo Black (Berkeley and Los Angeles: University of California Press, 1984; orig. 1950).

3. Arnold Schoenberg, "Heart and Brain in Music," in *Style and Idea*, 53–76 (cited at 54).

4. Schoenberg, "On the Question of Modern Composition Teaching," in *Style and Idea*, 375.

profundity of his idea and his capacity of penetrating to the most remote consequences of an idea.[5]

As we have seen, Schenker, in *Harmony* (1906), turned his back upon such self-
consciously realistic views of the creative act and embraced once again a metaphysical conception of the process that flew in the face of those scientifically
oriented modes of research with which he had flirted in 1896 and 1897. However,
in the early decades of twentieth century, others, including Schoenberg, picked
up where Schenker had left off.

In sharp contrast, the Viennese theorist Ernst Kurth (1886–1946), once one of
Adler's favorite students, openly questioned the merits of scientifically inspired
music study during those same decades in which Schoenberg penned his essays
cited above. Indeed, Kurth's writings, considered as a whole, can be understood
to constitute an ambitious attempt to elaborate into a formalized approach to
musical inquiry some of the same, avowedly irrationalist statements on the aesthetic experience that Adler, Spitta, and the Schenker of 1896 and 1897 sought to
dispel from the discourse on the art. In a voluminous body of studies published
in the 1910s, 1920s, and 1930s, Kurth, a professor at the University of Berne,
outlined a highly influential if later neglected approach to music study that was
founded upon the inherently subjective experience of listening. Indebted to the
work of his friend and contemporary, the theorist August Halm (who considered
the untrained listener's aural sense of music's ebb and flow—its "motion," in
his terms—the essence of the art), Kurth identified the source of musical dyna-
mism in a play of creative energies within the composer's psyche.[6] In the first
part of his widely read *Foundations of Linear Counterpoint* (*Grundlagen des linearen
Kontrapunkts*, 1917), Kurth explained his views as follows:

> In order to establish a theory of music, it is not enough merely to "hear" and
> to inquire time and again about sonic phenomena, but rather [it is necessary] to
> plumb deeper into the primal processes within ourselves. All sonic activity lies on
> the uppermost surface of musical growth. The tremendous striving, the tensions
> of the infinitely rich interwoven play of forces which we call the musical substance
> in sound, ...lies beneath the sounds...and springs out of the undercurrents of
> melodic growth, out of psychic energies and dynamic tensions. Musical events

5. Schoenberg, "Brahms the Progressive," in *Style and Idea*, 439. This passage is not present
in the 1933 version of the essay; see Schoenberg, "Vortrag, zu halten in Frankfurt am Main am
12. II. 1933," trans. Thomas McGeary, *Journal of the Arnold Schoenberg Institute* 15, no. 2 (1992):
22–90. Margaret Notley has also considered Schoenberg's concern for the relative importance of
conscious and unconscious faculties of invention in the compositional act, and she points out that
Schoenberg's student, Alban Berg, likewise showed an interest in the subject. See Notley, "Brahms
as Liberal: Genre, Style, and Politics in Late Nineteenth-Century Vienna," *19th-Century Music* 17,
no. 2 (1993), 123. Berg's essay in question, "Die musikalische Impotenz der 'neuen Ästhetik' Hans
Pfitzners" (1920), is translated in Willi Reich, *The Life and Work of Alban Berg*, trans. Cornelius
Cardew (London: Thames and Hudson, 1965), 205–18.

6. A detailed consideration of Kurth's ideas and their relation to those of Halm is provided in
Lee A. Rothfarb, *Ernst Kurth as Theorist and Analyst*, Studies in the Criticism and Theory of Music
(Philadelphia: University of Pennsylvania Press, 1988), 5–9 (cited at 8).

merely manifest themselves in tones, but they do not reside in them. ... The origin of music, in the psychological sense, is a will toward motions.[7]

The significance of Kurth's work for the present discussion becomes apparent when we turn, as we did in the case of Schoenberg, to the subject of creativity, and when we compare Kurth's statements on that issue to those of Friedrich von Hausegger considered in chapter 1. In the manner of Kurth, Hausegger had identified, in the 1880s, a theoretical, instinctual, psychological stimulus (the "impulse") as the impetus for artistic creativity. And he too claimed that the coherence we sense when listening to a well-crafted composition reflects the fact that such a work arises "as the product of a single stimulus." As Kurth asserted that "it is not enough merely to...inquire time and again about sonic phenomena" and that we must "plumb deeper into the primal processes within ourselves," so too Hausegger argued that "it does not suffice that the parts of the form appear to the examining eye as a symmetrical construction." Rather, Hausegger continued, "we want to *feel* the unity and beauty of form. In the sympathetic vibrations of our body it becomes clear to us that the form has sprung from similar bodily vibrations, which have arisen as the necessary result of an arousing impulse, and thus as an inclination toward expressive motion."[8]

Though a comprehensive, comparative study of the work of Hausegger and Kurth remains to be undertaken, one immediately detects the similarities in their work—similarities of language and approach in their statements, and of the aesthetic theories that they adduced to underlie their claims about musical creativity and coherence. To be sure, Hausegger never dabbled in music analysis, the primary focus of Kurth's inquiries. But otherwise, as Stephen McClatchie has shown, the two had much in common. Both Kurth and Hausegger were deeply indebted to Schopenhauerian metaphysics for the formulation of their ideas. Both were inspired to creative work in large part by their experience of Wagner's music dramas. And both considered Bruckner's symphonies to provide contemporary validation of their abstract theories.[9] In his writings, Hausegger valorized the subjective experience of listening that Hanslick had sought to marginalize in *On the Musically Beautiful*. Kurth, in turn, proclaimed his distaste for the whole of the fashion for scientific inquiry that Hanslick's treatise had sparked. As Kurth wrote in the introduction to his first book, published in 1913, "it must be admitted at the outset that our entire music theory cannot do without a certain instinctive character alongside of an objective scientific one."[10]

7. Ernst Kurth, *Grundlagen des linearen Kontrapunkts* (1917); cited in Rothfarb, *Ernst Kurth as Theorist and Analyst*, 12–13.

8. Friedrich von Hausegger, *Die Musik als Ausdruck*, 2d ed. (Vienna: Carl Konegen, 1887), 197–98. For the original text, see chapter 1, n. 40 and 41.

9. See Stephen McClatchie, *Analyzing Wagner's Operas: Alfred Lorenz and German Nationalist Ideology*, Eastman Studies in Music (Rochester: University of Rochester Press, 1998), 27–41 (on Hausegger) and 52–56 (on Kurth). On these aspects of Kurth's work, see also Rothfarb, *Ernst Kurth as Theorist and Analyst*, 11–12.

10. Kurth, *Die Voraussetzungen der theoretischen Harmonik und der tonalen Darstellungssysteme* (1913); cited in Rothfarb, *Ernst Kurth as Theorist and Analyst*, 7.

As one early writer on Kurth's contributions approvingly remarked, "the over-coming of rationalistic music theory...has only now become a reality in the works of the Berne professor Ernst Kurth."[11] Another, however, responded to Kurth's "instinctive" tack with trepidation: "Heaven protect German musicol-ogy...from books like Kurth's becoming a school of thought."[12]

As Lee A. Rothfarb has observed in his classic study of the theorist, Kurth's aesthetics were profoundly shaped—as their echoes of Hausegger suggest—by those very same irrationalist and ambivalent currents of late nineteenth-century cultural discourse examined throughout this book. Indeed, Rothfarb argues, Kurth's writings must be read as contributions to an ambitious and broad-based attempt at educational reform in Wilhelmine Germany, in which a "subjective, intuitive understanding of the world" was proffered as a spiritually uplifting "alternative to the objective, calculative methods of physical science." In this respect, Kurth's work, Rothfarb notes, was undertaken in the spirit of what Fritz Stern calls the "idealism of anti-modernity"—an idealism that shaped, as we have seen, the outlook of so many turn-of-the-century writers on music, positivist and otherwise.[13]

And so, given the radically different, even diametrically opposed conclusions drawn by Schoenberg and Kurth from the late nineteenth-century discourse on music with respect to the problem of creativity, it may be revealing of more recent positions to review the reception of their statements in later years. For the same postwar academic culture that enthusiastically embraced Schoenberg's rationalistic prescriptions of the 1920s through the 1940s also rejected Kurth's self-conscious irrationalism of those same decades. As Rothfarb observes, "After World War II...a renewed wave of Positivism and rapid advances in scientific and humanistic fields put Kurth's work"—in spite of its initial popularity—"into a different, dimmer light."[14] And though Rothfarb does not pursue in detail the reasons for this postwar shunning of Kurth, a recent analysis of Schoenberg's "Brahms the Progressive" provides an illuminating point of contrast.

In a survey of the reception of Brahms's music in the years immediately following World War II, Daniel Beller-McKenna has documented a concerted if largely unacknowledged project undertaken by many German and German-émigré scholars to "de-Germanize" the image of the composer that had prevailed in German-language scholarship through 1945. That project, Beller-McKenna argues, "can be understood as an attempt to neutralize [Brahms's] legacy" in the wake of the Second World War. It was, he writes, "an endeavor born of the need to salvage something good, noble, and pure from the German cultural tradition in the wake of National Socialism." Schoenberg's revisionist essay on Brahms,

11. Ernst Bücken, in *Melos* (1924–25); cited in Lee A. Rothfarb, ed., *Ernst Kurth: Selected Writings*, Cambridge Studies in Music Theory and Analysis, no. 2 (Cambridge: Cambridge University Press, 1991), 3.

12. Georg Göhler, in the *Neue Zeitschrift für Musik* (1926); cited in Rothfarb, *Ernst Kurth: Selected Writings*, 31.

13. Rothfarb, *Ernst Kurth: Selected Writings*, 5–17 (cited at 7–8); Fritz Stern, *The Politics of Cultural Despair: A Study in the Rise of the Germanic Ideology* (New York: Anchor Books, 1961), 52–60.

14. Rothfarb, *Ernst Kurth: Selected Writings*, 4.

in which the artist is portrayed as largely free of the kinds of irrational passions celebrated in Wagner's essays and stoked in Hitler's speeches, constitutes, Beller-McKenna suggests, a seminal contribution to this endeavor.[15] And although one may question the extent to which Schoenberg himself would agree with that characterization of his essay, I would argue that the same complex of historical and ideological circumstances that have contributed to its reception in those terms also lay behind—at least in part—the postwar rejection of Kurth.

Throughout this book, I have cited from a pair of classic studies of nineteenth-century German irrationalist discourse published in the early 1960s by Fritz Stern and George L. Mosse.[16] It is important to note, however, that both of these authors conceived of their books as something other than dispassionate essays in cultural history. They were written, in Mosse's words, in an attempt to demonstrate that the "ideological bases of National Socialism" could be located in the work of such nineteenth-century writers as Nietzsche, Wagner, and Julius Langbehn. To Mosse's mind, the social and political "crisis" that culminated in Hitler's rise to power "had its actual starting point in the 1870s"—in those very same Wagner- and Nietzsche-inspired movements considered throughout the present book.[17] For Stern as well, to study the nineteenth-century "idealism of anti-modernity" was to confront the "origins, content, and impact of an ideology which not only resembles national socialism, but which the National Socialists themselves acknowledged as an essential part of their legacy."[18] As the attitudes enshrined in these classic histories unwittingly attest, those same irrationalist, "anti-modern" ideologies that deeply informed Kurth's pre-war work were widely interpreted, in the postwar years, as anticipating in direct and ominous ways the disastrous course of Germany's Nazi experience.[19]

Surely, this postwar frame of mind contributed to Kurth's midcentury neglect. And it just as surely lay behind, at least in part, the academic embrace of Schoenberg's Brahms, an imaginary composer unaffected by the irrationalist currents that surrounded him. Indeed, one might even suggest that this same frame of mind contributed to the rise of that broader phenomenon that Kerman decries:

---

15. Daniel Beller-McKenna, *Brahms and the German Spirit* (Cambridge, MA: Harvard University Press, 2004), 182–93. Beller-McKenna introduces the idea of "de-Germanification" on page 187; he considers Schoenberg's "Brahms the Progressive" on pages 188–89; the passage cited is on page 192. See also Beller-McKenna, "The Rise and Fall of Brahms the German," *Journal of Musicological Research* 20, no. 3 (2001), 187–210.

16. Stern, *The Politics of Cultural Despair*; George L. Mosse, *The Crisis of German Ideology: Intellectual Origins of the Third Reich* (New York: Grosset and Dunlap, 1964).

17. Mosse, *The Crisis of German Ideology*, 1, 4.

18. Stern, *The Politics of Cultural Despair*, 5.

19. It should be noted that much recent work on German history has attempted to provide a more nuanced, less teleological treatment of late nineteenth-century cultural criticism than that provided by Stern and Mosse. See, for instance, Kevin Repp, *Reformers, Critics, and the Paths of German Modernity: Anti-Politics and the Search for Alternatives, 1890–1914* (Cambridge, MA: Harvard University Press, 2000), which addresses the work of Mosse and Stern directly; and the essays collected in Steven Beller, ed., *Rethinking Vienna 1900*, Austrian History, Culture, and Society, no. 3 (New York and Oxford: Berghan, 2001), which respond to Carl E. Schorske's pioneering work on late nineteenth-century Vienna.

the explosive mid-twentieth-century growth of a positivist mode of music study far more radical than anything that Adler envisioned.[20] For as we have recently begun to acknowledge, Kurth was not the only figure whose legacy suffered for its ideological complexity in the postwar years. In the cases of Adler, Schenker, and Hanslick, their work was not shunned but reimagined. It is now widely recognized, for instance, that the systematized variety of Schenkerian analysis widely promulgated in North American universities bears little resemblance to the conflicted bulk of what Schenker actually published.[21] And while Adler is remembered and lauded for his achievement in his "Scope, Method, and Goal of Musicology," whole blocks of his late-century work, including the Nietzsche-inspired program for his discipline outlined in his "Music and Musicology" of 1898, have been all but forgotten. Perhaps most dramatically, the memory of Hanslick's "living history"—the avowedly subjective historiographical project to which he devoted the bulk of his life—has effectively been erased not only from the history of the discipline but from Hanslick's biography itself. At the end of our investigation, we might provisionally conclude that the positivist musicology of the postwar years was only a distant relative of its nineteenth-century precursor. While its lineage might indeed be traceable back to this earlier period, it was shaped not so much by the will of figures such as Adler, Schenker, and Hanslick but under the pressures of new and distinctly modern political and ideological agendas.

20. A similar argument has been advanced, drawing upon different materials, by Pamela M. Potter, who writes of postwar attempts to "denazify" German musicology by "purging the field of nationalistic implications, of pseudoscientific methods, of certain sensitive aesthetic questions, and above all of any racist ideas." "After 1945," she continues, "shifts in methodology gravitated toward objective, positivist approaches, such as chronologies and the careful analysis of source materials. These shifts might have been regarded as a departure from Nazi musicology, in that they abandoned the irrational in favor of the rational." See Potter, *Most German of the Arts: Musicology and Society from the Weimar Republic to the End of Hitler's Reich* (New Haven: Yale University Press, 1998), 253 and 263.

21. On this topic, see, for instance, Joseph Lubben, review of *The Masterwork in Music: A Yearbook. Volume I (1925)* by Heinrich Schenker, *Journal of the American Musicological Society* 52, no. 1 (1999), 145–56; and Robert Snarrenberg, "Competing Myths: The American Abandonment of Schenker's Organicism," in *Theory, Analysis and Meaning in Music*, ed. Anthony Pople (Cambridge: Cambridge University Press, 1994), 30–58. As Arved Ashby has shown, Arnold Schoenberg's legacy has likewise been subject to this sort of reimagining, with some of his early statements on twelve-tone composition having been recast in a more rigidly scientific guise by later theorists and composers. See Ashby, "Schoenberg, Boulez, and Twelve-Tone Composition as 'Ideal Type,'" *Journal of the American Musicological Society* 54, no. 3 (2001): 585–625.

BIBLIOGRAPHY

Unpublished Sources, Documentary Materials, and Archives

Österreichische Nationalbibliothek. *Jahresberichte des Lesevereines der deutschen Studenten Wien's*, 1872–78 (55267-B. Neu Mag.).

Private collection. Diaries of Max Kalbeck, 1895, 1897.

University of California, Riverside. Special Collections Library. Oswald Jonas Memorial Collection.

University of Georgia. Hargrett Rare Book and Manuscript Library. Guido Adler Papers (MS 769).

Wienbibliothek im Rathaus (formerly Wiener Stadt- und Landesbibliothek). *Jahres-Berichte des Wiener akademischen Wagner-Vereines*, 1874–78 (A 92701).

Books and Articles

Adler, Guido. "Die historische Grundclassen der christlich-abendländischen Musik bis 1600." *Allgemeine musikalische Zeitung* 15 (1880). Offprint, Leipzig: Breitkopf und Härtel, 1880.

———. "Studie zur Geschichte der Harmonie." *Sitzungsberichte der phil.-hist. Classe der kais. Akademie der Wissenschaften* 98, no. 3 (1881). Offprint, Vienna: Carl Gerold's Sohn, 1881.

———. "Johann Sebastian Bach und Georg Friedrich Händel. Ihre Bedeutung und Stellung in der Geschichte der Musik." *Monatsblätter des Wissenschaftlichen Club* 12 (1885). Offprint, Vienna: Adolf Holzhausen, 1885.

———. "Umfang, Methode und Ziel der Musikwissenschaft." *Vierteljahrsschrift für Musikwissenschaft* 1 (1885): 5–20.

———. "Die Wiederholung und Nachahmung in der Mehrstimmigkeit. Studie zur Geschichte der Harmonie." *Vierteljahrsschrift für Musikwissenschaft* 2 (1886): 271–346.

———. "Musik und Musikwissenschaft. Akademische Antrittsrede, gehalten am 26. Oktober 1898 an der Universität Wien." *Jahrbuch der Musikbibliothek Peters* 5 (1898): 27–39.

———, ed. *Sechs Trienter Codices*. Denkmäler der Tonkunst in Österreich, vols. 14–15. Vienna: Artaria, 1900.

———. "Ein Bayreuther Protest (Zur Parsifal-Frage)." *Neue freie Presse* (January 11, 1903): 10.

————. "Richard Wagner und die Wissenschaft." *Neue freie Presse* (May 10, 1903): 12–13.

————. "Richard Wagner und die Wissenschaft. Erwiderung." *Bohemia* (May 19, 1903): Beilage 2.

————. *Richard Wagner: Vorlesungen gehalten an der Universität zu Wien.* Leipzig: Breitkopf und Härtel, 1904.

————. "W. A. Mozart." *Deutsche Arbeit* 5, no. 5 (1906): 300–304.

————. *Wollen und Wirken. Aus dem Leben eines Musikhistorikers.* Vienna: Universal Edition, 1935.

Agnew, Hugh LeCaine. *The Czechs and the Lands of the Bohemian Crown.* Studies of Nationalities. Stanford: Hoover Institution Press, 2004.

Allen, Warren Dwight. *Philosophies of Music History: A Study of General Histories of Music, 1600–1960.* Rev. ed. New York: Dover, 1962.

Ambros, August Wilhelm. *The Boundaries of Music and Poetry: A Study in Musical Aesthetics.* Trans. John Henry Cornell. New York: G. Schirmer, 1893.

————. *Geschichte der Musik.* 3d ed. 5 vols. Leipzig: F. E. C. Leuckart, 1887–1909.

Anderson, Benedict. *Imagined Communities: Reflections on the Origin and Spread of Nationalism.* Rev. ed. London: Verso, 1991.

Antonicek, Susanne, and Otto Biba, eds. *Brahms-Kongress Wien 1983. Kongressbericht.* Tutzing: Hans Schneider, 1988.

Antonicek, Theophil. "Musikwissenschaft in Wien zur Zeit Guido Adlers." *Studien zur Musikwissenschaft* 37 (1986): 165–93.

"Antrittsverlesung des Professors Guido Adler an der Wiener Universität." *Neue musikalische Presse* (October 30, 1898): 2.

Applegate, Celia. "How German Is It? Nationalism and the Idea of Serious Music in the Early Nineteenth Century." *19th-Century Music* 21, no. 3 (1998): 274–96.

————. *A Nation of Provincials: The German Idea of Heimat.* Berkeley and Los Angeles: University of California Press, 1990.

————. "What Is German Music? Reflections on the Role of Art in the Creation of the Nation." *German Studies Review* 15, no. 1 (1992): 21–32.

Applegate, Celia, and Pamela Potter. "Germans as the 'People of Music': Genealogy of an Identity." In *Music and German National Identity,* ed. Celia Applegate and Pamela Potter, 1–35. Chicago: University of Chicago Press, 2002.

Ashby, Arved. "Schoenberg, Boulez, and Twelve-Tone Composition as 'Ideal Type.'" *Journal of the American Musicological Society* 54, no. 3 (2001): 585–625.

Auner, Joseph, ed. *A Schoenberg Reader: Documents of a Life.* New Haven: Yale University Press, 2003.

Babich, Babbette E. "Nietzsche's Critique of Scientific Reason and Scientific Culture: On 'Science as a Problem' and Nature as Chaos." In *Nietzsche and Science,* ed. Gregory Moore and Thomas H. Brobjer, 133–53. Aldershot and Burlington, VT: Ashgate, 2004.

————. *Nietzsche's Philosophy of Science: Reflecting Science on the Ground of Art and Life.* The Margins of Literature. Albany: State University of New York Press, 1994.

Batka, Richard. *Allgemeine Geschichte der Musik.* 2 vols. Stuttgart: Carl Grüninger, n.d.

————. *J. S. Bach.* Musiker-Biographien, vol. 15. Leipzig: Philipp Reclam, 1892.

————. "Richard Wagner und die Wissenschaft." *Bohemia* (May 13, 1903): 17.

————. "Richard Wagner und die Wissenschaft." *Bohemia* (May 20, 1903): Beilage 2.

Beller, Steven, ed. *Rethinking Vienna 1900.* Austrian History, Culture, and Society, no. 3. New York and Oxford: Berghan, 2001.

Beller-McKenna, Daniel. *Brahms and the German Spirit.* Cambridge, MA: Harvard University Press, 2004.

————. "The Rise and Fall of Brahms the German." *Journal of Musicological Research* 20, no. 3 (2001): 187–210.

Bent, Ian D. "Heinrich Schenker e la missione del genio germanico." *Rivista Italiana di Musicologia* 26, no. 1 (1991): 3–34.

———, ed. *Music Analysis in the Nineteenth Century*. 2 vols. Cambridge Readings in the Literature of Music. Cambridge: Cambridge University Press, 1994.

———, ed. *Schenker Correspondence Project*. 2004–. Online. Available at http://mt.ccnmtl. columbia.edu/schenker/ (accessed September 25, 2007).

Blackmore, John T. *Ernst Mach: His Work, Life, and Influence*. Berkeley and Los Angeles: University of California Press, 1972.

Blaukopf, Kurt. *Pioniere empiristischer Musikforschung. Österreich und Böhmen als Wiege der modernen Kunstsoziologie*. Wissenschaftliche Weltauffassung und Kunst, no. 1. Vienna: Hölder-Pichler-Tempsky, 1995.

Boisits, Barbara. "Ästhetik versus Historie? Eduard Hanslicks und Guido Adlers Auffassung von Musikwissenschaft im Lichte zeitgenössischer Theorienbildung." In *Das Ende der Eindeutigkeit. Zur Frage des Pluralismus in Moderne und Postmoderne*, ed. Barbara Boisits and Peter Stachel, 89–108. Studien zur Moderne, no. 13. Vienna: Passagen, 2000.

Bonds, Mark Evan. "Idealism and the Aesthetics of Instrumental Music at the Turn of the Nineteenth Century." *Journal of the American Musicological Society* 50, nos. 2–3 (1997): 387–420.

———. *Music as Thought: Listening to the Symphony in the Age of Beethoven*. Princeton: Princeton University Press, 2006.

Botstein, Leon. "Listening through Reading: Musical Literacy and the Concert Audience." *19th-Century Music* 16, no. 2 (1992): 129–45.

———. "Music and Its Public: Habits of Listening and the Crisis of Musical Modernism in Vienna, 1870–1914." Ph.D. diss., Harvard University, 1985.

Bowie, Andrew. *Aesthetics and Subjectivity from Kant to Nietzsche*. 2d ed. Manchester: Manchester University Press, 2003.

Brobjer, Thomas H. "Nietzsche's Reading and Knowledge of Natural Science: An Overview." In *Nietzsche and Science*, ed. Gregory Moore and Thomas H. Brobjer, 21–50. Aldershot and Burlington, VT: Ashgate, 2004.

Brodbeck, David. "Dvořák's Reception in Liberal Vienna: Language Ordinances, National Property, and the Rhetoric of *Deutschtum*." *Journal of the American Musicological Society* 60, no. 1 (2007): 71–131.

Bruckmüller, Ernst. "The National Identity of the Austrians." Trans. Nicholas T. Parsons. In *The National Question in Europe in Historical Perspective*, ed. Mikuláš Teich and Roy Porter, 196–227. Cambridge: Cambridge University Press, 1993.

Bujić, Bojan, ed. *Music in European Thought, 1851–1912*. Cambridge Readings in the Literature of Music. Cambridge: Cambridge University Press, 1988.

Burckhardt, Jacob. *The Civilization of the Renaissance in Italy*. Ed. Ludwig Goldscheider. London: Phaidon, 1945.

Burford, Mark. "Hanslick's Idealist Materialism." *19th-Century Music* 30, no. 2 (2006): 166–81.

Chrysander, Friedrich. "Vorwort und Einleitung." *Jahrbücher für musikalische Wissenschaft* 1 (1863): 9–16.

Chrysander, Friedrich, Philipp Spitta, and Guido Adler. "Vorwort." *Vierteljahrsschrift für Musikwissenschaft* 1 (1885): 3.

Chua, Daniel K. L. *Absolute Music and the Construction of Meaning*. New Perspectives in Music History and Criticism. Cambridge: Cambridge University Press, 1999.

Clark, Maudemarie. "On Knowledge, Truth, and Value: Nietzsche's Debt to Schopenhauer and the Development of His Empiricism." In *Willing and Nothingness: Schopenhauer as Nietzsche's Educator*, ed. Christopher Janaway, 37–78. Oxford: Clarendon Press, 1998.

Cohen, Gary B. *The Politics of Ethnic Survival: Germans in Prague, 1861–1914*. Princeton: Princeton University Press, 1981.

Collingwood, R. G. *The Idea of History*. Oxford: Clarendon Press, 1946.

Cook, Nicholas. "Schenker's Theory of Music as Ethics." *Journal of Musicology* 7, no. 4 (1989): 415–39.

Dahlhaus, Carl. "Eduard Hanslick und der musikalische Formbegriff." *Die Musikforschung* 20, no. 2 (1967): 145–53.

———. *Esthetics of Music*. Trans. William W. Austin. Cambridge: Cambridge University Press, 1982.

———. *Foundations of Music History*. Trans. J. Bradford Robinson. Cambridge: Cambridge University Press, 1983.

———. *The Idea of Absolute Music*. Trans. Roger Lustig. Chicago: University of Chicago Press, 1989.

———. *Ludwig van Beethoven: Approaches to His Music*. Trans. Mary Whittall. Oxford: Clarendon Press, 1991.

Danz, Joachim. *Die objektlose Kunst. Untersuchungen zur Musikästhetik Friedrich von Hauseggers*. Kölner Beitrag zur Musikforschung, no. 118. Regensburg: Gustav Bosse, 1981.

Eder, Gabriele Johanna. *Alexius Meinong und Guido Adler. Eine Fruendschaft in Briefen*. Studien zur österreichischen Philosophie, no. 24. Amsterdam: Rodopi, 1995.

———. "Eduard Hanslick und Guido Adler. Aspekte einer menschlichen und wissenschaftlichen Beziehung." In *Kunst, Kunsttheorie und Kunstforschung im wissenschaftlichen Diskurs. In memoriam Kurt Blaukopf (1914–1999)*, ed. Martin Seiler and Friedrich Stadler, 107–42. Wissenschaftliche Weltauffassung und Kunst, no. 5. Vienna: ÖBV/HPT, 2000.

Federhofer, Hellmut. *Heinrich Schenker. Nach Tagebüchern und Briefen in der Oswald Jonas Memorial Collection*. Studien zur Musikwissenschaft, no. 3. Hildesheim: Georg Olms, 1985.

Fichte, Johann Gottlieb. *Addresses to the German Nation*. Ed. George Armstrong Kelly. Trans. R. F. Jones and G. H. Turnbull. European Perspectives. New York: Harper and Row, 1972.

Floros, Constantin. *Brahms und Bruckner. Studien zur musikalischen Exegetik*. Wiesbaden: Breitkopf und Härtel, 1980.

Forkel, Johann Nikolaus. *Ueber Johann Sebastian Bachs Leben, Kunst und Kunstwerke für patriotische Verehrer echter musikalischer Kunst*. Ed. Walther Vetter. Berlin: Henschelverlag, 1966.

Frisch, Walter. *German Modernism: Music and the Arts*. California Studies in 20th-Century Music, no. 3. Berkeley and Los Angeles: University of California Press, 2005.

Fulda, Daniel. *Wissenschaft aus Kunst. Die Entstehung der modernen deutschen Geschichtsschreibung 1760–1860*. European Cultures: Studies in Literature and the Arts, no. 7. Berlin: Walter de Gruyter, 1996.

Furst, Lilian R. *Romanticism in Perspective: A Comparative Study of Aspects of the Romantic Movement in England, France, and Germany*. London: Macmillan, 1979.

Fux, Johann Joseph. *Messen*. Ed. Johannes Evangelist Habert and Gustav Adolf Glossner. Denkmäler der Tonkunst in Österreich, vol. 1. Vienna: Artaria, 1894.

Garratt, James. *Palestrina and the German Romantic Imagination: Interpreting Historicism in Nineteenth-Century Music*. Musical Performance and Reception. Cambridge: Cambridge University Press, 2002.

Graf, Max. *Composer and Critic: Two Hundred Years of Musical Criticism.* New York: W. W. Norton, 1946.

Gramit, David. *Cultivating Music: The Aspirations, Interests, and Limits of German Musical Culture, 1770–1848.* Berkeley and Los Angeles: University of California Press, 2002.

Green, Burdette, and David Butler. "From Acoustics to *Tonpsychologie.*" In *The Cambridge History of Western Music Theory,* ed. Thomas Christensen, 246–71. Cambridge: Cambridge University Press, 2002.

Grey, Thomas S. *Wagner's Musical Prose: Texts and Contexts.* New Perspectives in Music History and Criticism. Cambridge: Cambridge University Press, 1995.

———. "*...wie ein rother Faden*: On the Origins of 'leitmotif' as Critical Construct and Musical Practice." In *Music Theory in the Age of Romanticism,* ed. Ian D. Bent, 187–210. Cambridge: Cambridge University Press, 1996.

Gubser, Michael. *Time's Visible Surface: Alois Riegl and the Discourse on History and Temporality in Fin-de-Siècle Vienna.* Kritik: German Literary Theory and Cultural Studies. Detroit: Wayne State University Press, 2006.

Hall, Robert W. "Hanslick and Musical Expressiveness." *Journal of Aesthetic Education* 29, no. 3 (1995): 85–92.

Hanslick, Eduard. *Aus meinem Leben.* 2 vols. Berlin: Allgemeiner Verein für Deutsche Litteratur, 1894.

———. *Concerte, Componisten und Virtuosen der letzten fünfzehn Jahre. 1870–1885.* Berlin: Allgemeiner Verein für Deutsche Litteratur, 1886.

———. *Geschichte des Concertwesens in Wien.* Vol. 1, Vienna: Wilhelm Braumüller, 1869. Vol. 2, *Aus dem Concertsaal,* Vienna: Wilhelm Braumüller, 1870.

———. *Die moderne Oper.* Vol. 1, Berlin: A. Hofmann, 1875. Vol. 2, *Musikalische Stationen,* Berlin: A. Hofmann, 1880. Vol. 3, *Aus dem Opernleben der Gegenwart. Neue Kritiken und Studien,* Berlin: A. Hofmann, 1884. Vol. 4, *Musikalisches Skizzenbuch. Neue Kritiken und Schilderungen,* Berlin: Allgemeiner Verein für Deutsche Literatur, 1888. Vol. 5, *Musikalisches und Litterarisches. Kritiken und Schilderungen,* Berlin: Allgemeiner Verein für Deutsche Litteratur, 1889. Vol. 6, *Aus dem Tagebuche eines Musikers. Kritiken und Schilderungen,* Berlin: Allgemeiner Verein für Deutsche Litteratur, 1892. Vol. 7, *Fünf Jahre Musik (1891–1895). Kritiken,* Berlin: Allgemeiner Verein für Deutsche Litteratur, 1896. Vol. 8, *Am Ende des Jahrhunderts (1895–1899). Musikalische Kritiken und Schilderungen,* Berlin: Allgemeiner Verein für Deutsche Litteratur, 1899. Vol. 9, *Aus neuer und neuester Zeit. Musikalische Kritiken und Schilderungen,* Berlin: Allgemeiner Verein für Deutsche Litteratur, 1900.

———. *On the Musically Beautiful: A Contribution towards the Revision of the Aesthetics of Music.* Trans. Geoffrey Payzant. Indianapolis: Hackett, 1986.

———. *Suite. Aufsätze über Musik und Musiker.* Vienna and Teschen: Karl Prochaska, 1884.

———. *Vom Musikalisch-Schönen. Ein Beitrag zur Revision der Ästhetik in der Tonkunst.* Ed. Dietmar Strauß. 2 vols. Mainz: Schott, 1990.

Hausegger, Friedrich von. *Gedanken eines Schauenden. Gesammelte Aufsätze.* Ed. Siegmund von Hausegger. Munich: F. Bruckmann, 1903.

———. *Die Musik als Ausdruck.* 2d ed. Vienna: Carl Konegen, 1887.

Heer, Friedrich. *Der Kampf um die österreichische Identität.* Vienna: Hermann Böhlau, 1981.

Heinz, Rudolf. *Geschichtsbegriff und Wissenschaftscharakter der Musikwissenschaft in der zweiten Hälfte des 19. Jahrhunderts. Philosophische Aspekte einer Wissenschaftsentwicklung.* Studien zur Musikgeschichte des 19. Jahrhunderts, no. 11. Regensburg: Gustav Bosse, 1968.

Helfert, Josef Alexander. *Über Nationalgeschichte und den gegenwärtigen Stand ihrer Pflege in Oesterreich*. Prague: J. G. Calve, 1853.

Helm, Theodor. *Beethoven's Streichquartette. Versuch einer technischen Analyse dieser Werke im Zusammenhange mit ihrem geistigen Gehalt*. 2d ed. Leipzig: C. F. W. Siegel, 1910.

Helmholtz, Hermann von. *On the Sensations of Tone as a Physiological Basis for the Theory of Music*. Trans. Alexander J. Ellis. New York: Dover, 1954.

Hepokoski, James. "*Ottocento* Opera as Cultural Drama: Generic Mixtures in *Il trovatore*." In *Verdi's Middle Period*, ed. Martin Chusid, 147–96. Chicago: University of Chicago Press, 1997.

Heuberger, Richard. *Erinnerungen an Johannes Brahms. Tagebuchnotizen aus den Jahren 1875 bis 1897*. Ed. Kurt Hofmann. 2d ed. Tutzing: Hans Schneider, 1976.

Hilscher, Elisabeth Theresia. *Denkmalpflege und Musikwissenschaft. Einhundert Jahre Gesellschaft zur Herausgabe der Tonkunst in Österreich (1893–1993)*. Wiener Veröffentlichungen zur Musikwissenschaft, no. 33. Tutzing: Hans Schneider, 1995.

———. "Gesamtstaat versus Nationalitäten. Zur Verbindung von Politik und Musikwissenschaft bei Guido Adler." *Studien zur Musikwissenschaft* 46 (1998): 239–48.

Hinton, Stephen. "Musikwissenschaft und Musiktheorie oder Die Frage nach der phänomenologischen Jungfräulichkeit." *Musiktheorie* 3, no. 3 (1988): 195–204.

Hiroshi, Yoshida. "Zur Idee der musikalischen Öffentlichkeit: Eine erneuerte Interpretation der Musikästhetik Eduard Hanslicks." *Aesthetics* [Japan] 10 (2002): 87–94.

Hirschfeld, Robert. *Das kritische Verfahren Ed. Hanslick's*. Vienna: R. Löwit, 1885.

Horawitz, Adalbert. "Richard Wagner und die Nationale Idee." In *Erster Jahres-Bericht des Wiener akademischen Wagner-Vereines für das Jahr 1873*, 1–28. Vienna: Selbstverlag des Vereines, 1874.

Iversen, Margaret. *Alois Riegl: Art History and Theory*. Cambridge, MA: MIT Press, 1993.

Jahn, Otto. *W. A. Mozart*. 4 vols. Leipzig: Breitkopf und Härtel, 1856–59.

Janik, Allan. "Vienna 1900 Revisited: Paradigms and Problems." In *Rethinking Vienna 1900*, ed. Steven Beller, 27–56. Austrian History, Culture, and Society, no. 3. New York and Oxford: Berghan, 2001.

———. *Wittgenstein's Vienna Revisited*. New Brunswick, NJ: Transaction, 2001.

Jenner, Gustav. *Johannes Brahms als Mensch, Lehrer und Künstler. Studien und Erlebnisse*. 2d ed. Marburg an der Lahn: N. G. Engelwert'sche Verlagsbuchhandlung, 1930.

———. "Johannes Brahms as Man, Teacher, and Artist." Trans. Susan Gillespie. In *Brahms and His World*, ed. Walter Frisch, 185–204. Princeton: Princeton University Press, 1990.

Johnston, William M. *The Austrian Mind: An Intellectual and Social History, 1848–1938*. Berkeley and Los Angeles: University of California Press, 1972.

Kalbeck, Max. *Johannes Brahms*. 4 vols. Berlin: Deutsche Brahms-Gesellschaft, 1904–14.

Karnes, Kevin C. "Another Look at Critical Partisanship in the Viennese *fin de siècle*: Schenker's Reviews of Brahms's Vocal Music, 1891–92." *19th-Century Music* 26, no. 2 (2002): 74–93.

———. "Eduard Hanslick's History: A Forgotten Narrative of Brahms's Vienna." *American Brahms Society Newsletter* 22, no. 2 (2004): 1–5.

———. "Heinrich Schenker and Musical Thought in Late Nineteenth-Century Vienna." Ph.D. diss., Brandeis University, 2001.

———. "Schenker's Brahms: Composer, Critic, and the Problem of Creativity in Late Nineteenth-Century Vienna." *Journal of Musicological Research* 24, no. 2 (2005): 145–76.

Keiler, Allan. "Melody and Motive in Schenker's Earliest Writings." In *Critica Musica: Essays in Honor of Paul Brainard*, ed. John Knowles, 169–91. Amsterdam: Gordon and Breach, 1996.

———. "The Origins of Schenker's Thought: How Man Is Musical." *Journal of Music Theory* 33, no. 2 (1989): 273–98.

Kerman, Joseph. *Contemplating Music: Challenges to Musicology*. Cambridge, MA: Harvard University Press, 1985.

———. "How We Got into Analysis, and How to Get Out." *Critical Inquiry* 7, no. 2 (1980): 311–31. Repr. in *Write All These Down: Essays on Music*, 12–32. Berkeley and Los Angeles: University of California Press, 1994.

Khittl, Christoph. "Eduard Hanslicks Verhältnis zur Ästhetik." In *Biographische Beiträge zum Musikleben Wiens im 19. und frühen 20. Jahrhundert*, ed. Friedrich C. Heller, 81–109. Studien zur Musikgeschichte Österreichs, no. 1. Vienna: Verband der wissenschaftlichen Gesellschaften Österreichs, 1992.

Kienzl, Wilhelm. "Die nationale Bedeutung J. Seb. Bach's und dessen Einfluß auf das Kunstschaffen Richard Wagner's." *Neue Zeitschrift für Musik* 52, no. 27 (1885): 285–87.

Kiesewetter, Raphael Georg. *Geschichte der europäisch-abendlandischen oder unsrer heutigen Musik*. Leipzig: Breitkopf und Härtel, 1834.

Kivy, Peter. "What Was Hanslick Denying?" *Journal of Musicology* 8, no. 1 (1990): 3–18.

Knight, David. *The Age of Science: The Scientific World-View in the Nineteenth Century*. Oxford: Basil Blackwell, 1986.

Knoll, Philipp. *Beiträge zur heimischen Zeitgeschichte*. Prague: J. G. Calve, 1900.

Korsyn, Kevin. "Brahms Research and Aesthetic Ideology." *Music Analysis* 12, no. 1 (1993): 89–103.

———. *Decentering Music: A Critique of Contemporary Musical Research*. Oxford: Oxford University Press, 2003.

———. "Schenker's Organicism Reexamined." *Intégral* 7 (1993): 82–118.

Kragh, Helge. *An Introduction to the Historiography of Science*. Cambridge: Cambridge University Press, 1987.

Krieger, Leonard. *Time's Reasons: Philosophies of History Old and New*. Chicago: University of Chicago Press, 1989.

La Grange, Henry-Louis de. *Mahler*. Vol. 1. Garden City, NY: Doubleday, 1973.

Landerer, Christoph. "Ästhetik von oben? Ästhetik von unten? Objektivität und 'naturwissenschaftliche' Methode in Eduard Hanslicks Musikästhetik." *Archiv für Musikwissenschaft* 61, no. 1 (2004): 38–53.

———. "Eduard Hanslicks Ästhetikprogramm und die Österreichische Philosophie der Jahrhundertmitte." *Österreichische Musikzeitschrift* 54, no. 9 (1999): 6–20.

Langbehn, Julius. *Rembandt als Erzieher*. 31st ed. Leipzig: C. L. Hirschfeld, 1891.

Le Huray, Peter, and James Day, eds. *Music and Aesthetics in the Eighteenth and Early-Nineteenth Centuries*. Cambridge Readings in the Literature of Music. Cambridge: Cambridge University Press, 1981.

Lenoir, Timothy. *Instituting Science: The Cultural Production of Scientific Disciplines*. Writing Science. Stanford: Stanford University Press, 1997.

Lhotsky, Alphons. "Geschichtsforschung und Geschichtsschreibung in Österreich." *Historische Zeitschrift* 189 (1959): 379–448.

Lipiner, Siegfried. *Der Entfesselte Prometheus. Eine Dichtung in fünf Gesängen*. Leipzig: Breitkopf und Härtel, 1876.

———. *Über die Elemente einer Erneuerung religiöser Ideen in der Gegenwart. Vortrag gehalten im Lesevereine der Deutschen Studenten Wiens am 19. Januar 1878*. Vienna: Carl Gerold's Sohn, 1878.

Lowinsky, Edward E. "Musical Genius: Evolution and Origins of a Concept," *Musical Quarterly* 50, no. 3 (1964): 321–40. Repr. in *Music in the Culture of the Renaissance and Other Essays*, ed. Bonnie J. Blackburn, 2 vols., 1:87–105. Chicago: University of Chicago Press, 1989.

Lubben, Joseph. Review of *The Masterwork in Music: A Yearbook. Volume I (1925)* by Heinrich Schenker. *Journal of the American Musicological Society* 52, no. 1 (1999): 145–56.

Maczewski, A. "Ein deutsches Requiem. Nach Worten der heiligen Schrift für Soli, Chor und Orchester von J. Brahms." *Musikalisches Wochenblatt* 1, nos. 1–5 (1870): 5, 20–21, 35–36, 52–54, 67–69.

Magee, Bryan. *The Tristan Chord: Wagner and Philosophy*. New York: Henry Holt, 2000.

Maus, Fred Everett. "Hanslick's Animism." *Journal of Musicology* 10, no. 3 (1992): 273–92.

McClatchie, Stephen. *Analyzing Wagner's Operas: Alfred Lorenz and German Nationalist Ideology*. Eastman Studies in Music. Rochester, NY: University of Rochester Press, 1998.

McClelland, Charles E. *State, Society, and University in Germany, 1700–1914*. Cambridge: Cambridge University Press, 1980.

McColl, Sandra. *Music Criticism in Vienna, 1896–1897: Critically Moving Forms*. Oxford Monographs on Music. Oxford: Clarendon Press, 1996.

McGrath, William J. *Dionysian Art and Populist Politics in Austria*. New Haven: Yale University Press, 1974.

Mosse, George L. *The Crisis of German Ideology: Intellectual Origins of the Third Reich*. New York: Grosset and Dunlap, 1964.

Naegele, Philipp Otto. "August Wilhelm Ambros: His Historical and Critical Thought." Ph.D. diss., Princeton University, 1954.

Nettl, Bruno. "The Institutionalization of Musicology: Perspectives of a North American Ethnomusicologist." In *Rethinking Music*, ed. Nicholas Cook, 287–310. Oxford: Oxford University Press, 1999.

Nietzsche, Friedrich. *The Birth of Tragedy and the Case of Wagner*. Trans. Walter Kaufmann. New York: Vintage, 1967.

———. *Human, All Too Human: A Book for Free Spirits*. Trans. Gary Handwerk. The Complete Works of Friedrich Nietzsche, vol. 3. Stanford: Stanford University Press, 1995.

———. *Untimely Meditations*. Ed. Daniel Breazeale. Trans. R. J. Hollingdale. Cambridge Texts in the History of Philosophy. Cambridge: Cambridge University Press, 1997.

Notley, Margaret. "Brahms as Liberal: Genre, Style, and Politics in Late Nineteenth-Century Vienna." *19th-Century Music* 17, no. 2 (1993): 107–23.

———. "Bruckner and Viennese Wagnerism." In *Bruckner Studies*, ed. Timothy L. Jackson and Paul Hawkshaw, 54–71. Cambridge: Cambridge University Press, 1997.

———. "Late-Nineteenth-Century Chamber Music and the Cult of the Classical Adagio." *19th-Century Music* 23, no. 1 (1999): 33–61.

———. *Lateness and Brahms: Music and Culture in the Twilight of Viennese Liberalism*. AMS Studies in Music, no. 3. Oxford: Oxford University Press, 2007.

———. "Musical Culture in Vienna at the Turn of the Twentieth Century." In *Schoenberg, Berg, and Webern: A Companion to the Second Viennese School*, ed. Bryan R. Simms, 37–71. Westport, CT: Greenwood Press, 1999.

———. "*Volksconcerte* in Vienna and Late Nineteenth-Century Ideology of the Symphony." *Journal of the American Musicological Society* 50, nos. 2–3 (1997): 421–53.

Nottebohm, Gustav. *Beethoveniana*. Leipzig: Breitkopf und Härtel, 1872.

―――. *Ein Skizzenbuch von Beethoven*. Leipzig: Breitkopf und Härtel, 1865.

Osborne, Harold. *Aesthetics and Art Theory: An Historical Introduction*. London and Harlow: Longmans, Green, 1968.

Pastille, William. "Heinrich Schenker, Anti-Organicist." *19th-Century Music* 8, no. 1 (1984): 29–36.

―――. "Schenker's Brahms." *American Brahms Society Newsletter* 5, no. 2 (1987): 1–2.

Payzant, Geoffrey. "Hanslick on Music as Product of Feeling." *Journal of Musicological Research* 9, nos. 2–3 (1989): 133–45.

―――. *Hanslick on the Musically Beautiful: Sixteen Lectures on the Musical Aesthetics of Eduard Hanslick*. Christchurch, New Zealand: Cybereditions, 2002.

Pinkard, Terry. *German Philosophy, 1760–1860: The Legacy of Idealism*. Cambridge: Cambridge University Press, 2002.

Platt, Heather. "Hugo Wolf and the Reception of Brahms's Lieder." In *Brahms Studies* 2, ed. David Brodbeck, 91–111. Lincoln: University of Nebraska Press, 1998.

―――. "Jenner versus Wolf: The Critical Reception of Brahms's Songs." *Journal of Musicology* 13, no. 3 (1995): 377–403.

Porter, Theodore M. *The Rise of Statistical Thinking, 1820–1900*. Princeton: Princeton University Press, 1986.

Potter, Pamela M. *Most German of the Arts: Musicology and Society from the Weimar Republic to the End of Hitler's Reich*. New Haven: Yale University Press, 1998.

Rathert, Wolfgang. "Das Neue und das Alte Neue. Tradition und Fortschritt im Denken Guido Adlers." In *Alte Musik im 20. Jahrhundert. Wandlungen und Formen ihrer Rezeption*, ed. Giselher Schubert, 19–29. Mainz: Schott, 1995.

Rehding, Alexander. *Hugo Riemann and the Birth of Modern Musical Thought*. New Perspectives in Music History and Criticism. Cambridge: Cambridge University Press, 2003.

―――. "The Quest for the Origins of Music in Germany Circa 1900." *Journal of the American Musicological Society* 53, no. 2 (2000): 345–85.

Reich, Willi. *The Life and Work of Alban Berg*. Trans. Cornelius Cardew. London: Thames and Hudson, 1965.

Reilly, Edward R. *Gustav Mahler and Guido Adler: Records of a Friendship*. Cambridge: Cambridge University Press, 1982.

Repp, Kevin. *Reformers, Critics, and the Paths of German Modernity: Anti-Politics and the Search for Alternatives, 1890–1914*. Cambridge, MA: Harvard University Press, 2000.

Riemann, Hugo. *Handbuch der Musikgeschichte*. Vol. 1, part 2, *Die Musik des Mittelalters (bis 1450)*. Leipzig: Breitkopf und Härtel, 1905.

Riemenschneider, Georg. "Kritik. Alexander Glazounow. 1. Symphonie für grosses Orchester." *Musikalisches Wochenblatt* 21 (1890): 266–68.

―――. "Kritik. Andréas Hallén. Schwedische Rhapsodie No. 2, Op. 23, für grosses Orchester." *Musikalisches Wochenblatt* 21 (1890): 435–36.

―――. "Kritik. Edvard Grieg. Orchestersuite aus der Musik zu Ibsen's dramatischer Dichtung 'Peer Gynt,' Op. 16." *Musikalisches Wochenblatt* 21 (1890): 447–48.

Rimbault, Edward F. *The Rounds, Catches and Canons of England: A Collection of Specimens of the Sixteenth, Seventeenth and Eighteenth Centuries, Adapted to Modern Use*. London: Cramer, Wood, n.d.

Rothfarb, Lee A. *Ernst Kurth as Theorist and Analyst*. Studies in the Criticism and Theory of Music. Philadelphia: University of Pennsylvania Press, 1988.

―――, ed. *Ernst Kurth: Selected Writings*. Cambridge Studies in Music Theory and Analysis, no. 2. Cambridge: Cambridge University Press, 1991.

Salmi, Hannu. Imagined Germany: Richard Wagner's National Utopia. German Life and Civilization, no. 29. New York: Peter Lang, 1999.

Salzer, Felix. "Die Historische Sendung Heinrich Schenkers." Der Dreiklang 1, no. 1 (1937): 2–12.

Sandberger, Wolfgang. Das Bach-Bild Philipp Spittas. Ein Beitrag zur Geschichte der Bach-Rezeption im *19.* Jahrhundert. Beihefte zum Archiv für Musikwissenschaft, no. 39. Stuttgart: Franz Steiner Verlag, 1997.

Schäfke, Rudolf. Eduard Hanslick und die Musikästhetik. Leipzig: Breitkopf und Härtel, 1922.

Scheidt, Samuel. Tabulatura nova. Ed. Max Seiffert. Denkmäler deutscher Tonkunst, vol. 1. Leipzig: Breitkopf und Härtel, 1892.

Schenker, Heinrich. Counterpoint. Ed. John Rothgeb. Ed. and trans. John Rothgeb and Jürgen Thym. 2 vols. New York: Schirmer, 1987.

———. "Erinnerungen an Brahms." Deutsche Zeitschrift 46, no. 8 (1933): 475–82.

———. Free Composition. Ed. and trans. Ernst Oster. New York: Longman, 1979.

———. Harmony. Ed. Oswald Jonas. Trans. Elisabeth Mann Borgese. Chicago: University of Chicago Press, 1954.

———. Heinrich Schenker als Essayist und Kritiker. Gesammelte Aufsätze, Rezensionen und kleinere Berichte aus den Jahren *1891–1901.* Ed. Hellmut Federhofer. Studien und Materialien zur Musikwissenschaft, no. 5. Hildesheim: Georg Olms Verlag, 1990.

———. "The Spirit of Musical Technique." Trans. William Pastille. Theoria 3 (1988): 86–104.

———. Der Tonwille: Pamphlets in Witness of the Immutable Laws of Music, Offered to a New Generation of Youth. Ed. William Drabkin. Trans. Ian D. Bent et al. 2 vols. Oxford: Oxford University Press, 2004–5.

Schleiermacher, Friedrich. Hermeneutics and Criticism and Other Writings. Ed. and trans. Andrew Bowie. Cambridge Texts in the History of Philosophy. Cambridge: Cambridge University Press, 1998.

Schlözer, August Ludwig von. Theorie der Statistik nebst Ideen über das Studium der Politik überhaupt. Vol. 1, Einleitung. Göttingen: Vandenhoek und Ruprecht, 1804.

Schoenberg, Arnold. Style and Idea. Ed. Leonard Stein. Trans. Leo Black. Berkeley and Los Angeles: University of California Press, 1984.

———. "Vortrag, zu halten in Frankfurt am Main am 12. II. 1933." Trans. Thomas McGeary. Journal of the Arnold Schoenberg Institute 15, no. 2 (1992): 22–90.

Schopenhauer, Arthur. The World as Will and Representation. Trans. E. F. J. Payne. 2 vols. Indian Hills, CO: Falcon's Wing Press, 1958.

Schorske, Carl E. Fin-de-Siècle Vienna: Politics and Culture. New York: Alfred A. Knopf, 1980.

Seeba, Hinrich C. " 'So weit die deutsche Zunge klingt': The Role of Language in German Identity Formation." In Searching for Common Ground: Diskurse zur deutschen Identität, *1750–1871,* ed. Nicholas Vazsonyi, 45–57. Cologne: Böhlau, 2000.

Seidl, Arthur. "Zur Aesthetik der Tonkunst." Musikalisches Wochenblatt 17 (1886): 273–75, 287–88, 303–4, 318–21.

Seiler, Martin. "Empiristische Motive im Denken und Forschen der Wiener Schule der Kunstgeschichte." In Kunst, Kunsttheorie und Kunstforschung im wissenschaftlichen Diskurs. In memoriam Kurt Blaukopf *(1914–1999),* ed. Martin Seiler and Friedrich Stadler, 49–86. Wissenschaftliche Weltauffassung und Kunst, no. 5. Vienna: ÖBV/HPT, 2000.

Sheehan, James J. German History, *1770–1866.* Oxford History of Modern Europe. Oxford: Clarendon Press, 1989.

———. "Nation und Staat. Deutschland als 'imaginierte Gemeinschaft'." In Nation und Gesellschaft in Deutschland, ed. Manfred Hettling and Paul Nolte, 33–45. Munich: C. H. Beck, 1996.

Simon, W. M. *European Positivism in the Nineteenth Century: An Essay in Intellectual History.* Ithaca, NY: Cornell University Press, 1963.

Sitte, Camillo. "Richard Wagner und die deutsche Kunst." In *Zweiter Jahres-Bericht des Wiener akademischen Wagner-Vereines für das Jahr 1874*, 1–41. Vienna: Selbstverlag des Vereines, 1875.

Snarrenberg, Robert. "Competing Myths: The American Abandonment of Schenker's Organicism." In *Theory, Analysis and Meaning in Music*, ed. Anthony Pople, 30–58. Cambridge: Cambridge University Press, 1994.

Spector, Scott. *Prague Territories: National Conflict and Cultural Innovation in Franz Kafka's Fin de Siècle.* Weimar and Now: German Cultural Criticism, no. 21. Berkeley and Los Angeles: University of California Press, 2000.

Spitta, Philipp. *Johann Sebastian Bach.* Trans. Clara Bell and J. A. Fuller-Maitland. 3 vols. New York: Dover, 1951.

———. *Zur Musik. Sechzehn Aufsätze.* Berlin: Gebrüder Paetel, 1892.

Stern, Fritz. *The Politics of Cultural Despair: A Study in the Rise of the Germanic Ideology.* New York: Anchor Books, 1961.

———, ed. *The Varieties of History: From Voltaire to the Present.* New York: Meridian, 1957.

Stumpf, Carl. "Musikpsychologie in England. Betrachtungen über Herleitung der Musik aus der Sprache und aus dem thierischen Entwickelungsproceß, über Empirismus und Nativismus in der Musiktheorie." *Vierteljahrsschrift für Musikwissenschaft* 1 (1885): 261–349.

Subotnik, Rose Rosengard. *Developing Variations: Style and Ideology in Western Music.* Minneapolis: University of Minnesota Press, 1991.

Taruskin, Richard. Introduction to *repercussions* 5, nos. 1–2 (1996): 5–20.

———. *The Oxford History of Western Music.* 6 vols. Oxford: Oxford University Press, 2005.

Thausing, Moriz. *Wiener Kunstbriefe.* Leipzig: E. A. Seemann, 1884.

Treitler, Leo. *Music and the Historical Imagination.* Cambridge, MA: Harvard University Press, 1989.

Vocelka, Karl. *Geschichte Österreichs. Kultur—Gesellschaft—Politik.* Munich: Wilhelm Hayne, 2000.

Wagner, Richard. *Richard Wagner's Prose Works.* Trans. William Ashton Ellis. 8 vols. London: Kegan Paul, Trench, Trübner, 1895–99.

———. *Sämtliche Schriften und Dichtungen.* 6th ed. 16 vols. Leipzig: Breitkopf und Härtel and C. F. W. Siegel, 1911.

Weingartner, Felix. *The Symphony since Beethoven.* Trans. Arthur Bles. New York: Scribner's, n.d.

West, Shearer. *Fin de Siècle: Art and Society in an Age of Uncertainty.* Woodstock, NY: Overlook, 1994.

White, Hayden. *Metahistory: The Historical Imagination in Nineteenth-Century Europe.* Baltimore: Johns Hopkins University Press, 1973.

Williams, Alastair. *Constructing Musicology.* Aldershot: Ashgate, 2001.

Windelband, Wilhelm. *Präludien. Aufsätze und Reden zur Philosophie und ihrer Geschichte.* 6th ed. 2 vols. Tübingen: J. C. B. Mohr, 1919.

Wolzogen, Hans von. "Germanische Volksgrundgedichte als Nationalfeststoff." In *Dritter Jahres-Bericht des Wiener akademischen Wagner-Vereines für das Jahr 1875*, 3–13. Vienna: Selbstverlag des Vereines, 1876.

Zimmermann, Robert. "Ed. Hanslick: Vom Musikalisch-Schönen." *Vierteljahrsschrift für Musikwissenschaft* 1 (1885): 251–52.

Zweig, Stefan. *The World of Yesterday.* Anonymous trans. Lincoln: University of Nebraska Press, 1964.

INDEX

CPSIA information can be obtained at www.ICGtesting.com
Printed in the USA
BVOW08s2253110716

455189BV00001B/1/P